Applying Graph Theory in Ecological Research

Graph theory can be applied to ecological questions in many ways, and more insights can be gained by expanding the range of graph theoretical concepts applied to a specific system. But how do you know which methods might be used? And what do you do with the graph once it has been obtained?

This book provides a broad introduction to the application of graph theory in different ecological systems, providing practical guidance for researchers in ecology and related fields. Readers are guided through the creation of an appropriate graph for the system being studied, including the application of spatial, spatio-temporal, and more abstract structural process graphs. Simple figures accompany the explanations to add clarity, and a broad range of ecological phenomena from many ecological systems are covered. This is the ideal book for graduate students and researchers looking to apply graph theoretical methods in their work.

Mark R. T. Dale is a Professor in the Ecosystem Science and Management Program at the University of Northern British Columbia and Dean of Regional Programs. His research interests include the spatial structure of plant communities and the development and evaluation of numerical methods to answer ecological questions, including applications of graph theory. He wrote *Spatial Pattern Analysis in Plant Ecology* (Cambridge, 1999) and was co-author, with Marie-Josée Fortin, of *Spatial Analysis: A Guide for Ecologists* (Cambridge, 2014).

Applying Graph Theory in Ecological Research

MARK R. T. DALE
University of Northern British Columbia

CAMBRIDGE
UNIVERSITY PRESS

University Printing House, Cambridge CB2 8BS, United Kingdom

One Liberty Plaza, 20th Floor, New York, NY 10006, USA

477 Williamstown Road, Port Melbourne, VIC 3207, Australia

4843/24, 2nd Floor, Ansari Road, Daryaganj, Delhi - 110002, India

79 Anson Road, #06-04/06, Singapore 079906

Cambridge University Press is part of the University of Cambridge.

It furthers the University's mission by disseminating knowledge in the pursuit of education, learning and research at the highest international levels of excellence.

www.cambridge.org
Information on this title: www.cambridge.org/9781107089310
DOI: 10.1017/9781316105450

© Cambridge University Press 2017

First published 2017

Printed in the United Kingdom by TJ International Ltd. Padstow Cornwall

A catalogue record for this publication is available from the British Library

ISBN 978-1-107-08931-0 Hardback
ISBN 978-1-107-46097-3 Paperback

Cambridge University Press has no responsibility for the persistence or accuracy
of URLs for external or third-party internet websites referred to in this publication,
and does not guarantee that any content on such websites is, or will remain,
accurate or appropriate.

To my grandchildren:
Monroe and Elliot in Sydney;
Laura and Thomas in Edmonton

Contents

Preface

Applications of graph theory have been proliferating throughout ecology over the past several decades, whether explicitly realized or implicit in the approaches used, and not only in the cases which fall clearly into the popular category of networks. The reasons for this increased interest are as diverse as the areas of research. A basic impetus is that graphs and graph theory are about structure and provide the methods to analyze structure as abstracted from almost any ecological (or other) system. The second reason is the great popularity of network studies and network theory, originally applied to social relationships, communications (including the Internet as a prime example), transportation and the spread of disease. It is an obvious step to take network concepts and models from these sources and see how well they apply to ecological systems. Such network studies are obvious sources of inspiration for investigations of ecological interactions of all kinds (such as predation, competition, mutualism and facilitation) using the methods developed for those other systems. A third reinforcement for graph theory applications arises from the growing sophistication of ecologists in analyzing spatial data or time-ordered data or the complexities of spatio-temporal data; and, once again, methods based on graph theory provide the right mix of simplicity of concept but flexibility in application to provide valuable insights that would otherwise be impossible. Putting together interaction networks and spatio-temporal data brings a researcher to the challenges and rewards of studying the interplay of form and function (or "pattern and process" or "structure and dynamics") in ecological systems in which both form and function change through time by reciprocal influences and effects.

The book is organized in an order that reflects this range of sources. First is an introduction to thinking with graphs based on the theme of graphs and structure (Chapters 1 and 2). There are then several chapters on ecological interaction networks, first in general (Chapter 3), followed by more specific topics: predation (Chapter 4), social structure (Chapter 5), competition (Chapter 6) and mutualism (Chapter 7). The next three chapters are about locational graphs, in which the nodes have positions in one or more dimensions: time only (Chapter 8), space only (Chapter 9) and spatio-temporal (Chapter 10). Chapter 11 describes approaches to studying the dynamics of networks in the context of the reciprocal effects of form and function, focussing on the fascinating and promising methods based on graphlets. The last chapter (Chapter 12) attempts to draw together a number of the themes that emerged throughout the book and provide a synthesis of the common threads; it also takes on the risky task of making some predictions about future directions and developments to be expected in this field.

The working title started out as "Smart Things Ecologists Can Do with Graph Theory"; and that is a good description of the intention. The book is not primarily an introduction to graph theory developed for ecologists; it is intended to make researchers aware of the wide range of possibilities for their own research projects, even when (or especially when) they have yet to be fully tried out in ecological systems. A prime example is the many forms of analysis based on graphlets that are recently developed and applied in other biological systems (e.g. protein-protein interactions) but not yet in ecology. The goal is to provide enough background that the researcher knows how and where to start and where to find some examples that will provide inspiration and support. The treatments of the various topics are very heterogeneous; some have a good range of examples to be cited (e.g. food webs or trophic networks; mutualism), but others have virtually none.

My own interest in graph theory as a useful approach to answering ecological questions related to structure started with my MSc research many years ago, and I owe a large debt to my then-supervisor, Tony Yarranton, who suggested the area and encouraged my exploration of the field. I owe thanks to John Moon, who helped me understand some of the more formal aspects of graph theory and its application (look at his *Topics on Tournaments*, if you have not already: a great example). In acknowledging people who have helped with this book, I thank the following for reading chapters, sometimes as they developed: Alex Aravind, Tan Bao, Conan Vietch, JC Cahill and Brendan Wilson. I thank Marie-Josée Fortin, especially; she read all the chapters, and some more than once! For data used in examples, there are many to be acknowledged, including Tan Bao and JC Cahill for the *Arabadopsis* competition tournament material and Gord Thomas for the rich data set on Saskatchewan weed communities. I thank NSERC Canada and UNBC for their support over many years.

I greatly enjoyed writing this book, and discovering all the exciting material I had not known was very rewarding. It is my hope that the readers will find the work equally rewarding and that it will help create pathways to more that is useful, more that is new and more that is surprising.

1 Graphs as Structure in the Ecological Context

Introduction

Ecology is the study of organisms in the context of their environment, including both abiotic effects and interactions among organisms. Ecologists, like other scientists, are looking for patterns in these phenomena that can be used reliably to make predictions, and those predictions can extend the findings to other organisms, to ecological systems not yet studied or merely to similar groups of organisms in different places or at different times. Those predictions may also refer to how a system's form or structure determines its function and dynamics and how function and dynamics constrain or modify structure and form.

A long but not exhaustive list of the kinds of problems ecologists study might include the following:

- the fate of individuals as determined by neighbours and environmental conditions
- the interactions of individuals in a social structure and their effects on population dynamics
- the movement of individuals through their environment and their reactions to it
- the dynamics of populations and communities in fragmented habitats
- the flow of energy and the population and community effects of predation in trophic networks
- the effects of competition, both intra- and inter-specific, on survival, growth and reproduction
- the dynamics of species interactions, such as mutualism, commensalism and parasitism
- the determinants of species composition of multi-species communities in island systems

Almost all of these can be approached in a theoretical or abstracted way, or quite explicitly with locations in time or space, and almost all of these are studied in the context of a system of some sort and usually in the context of that system's structure. In fact, explicit references to "structure" arise in almost every study of ecological systems, from behaviour to trophic networks and from individuals to community interactions. The term "structure" usually refers to how systems are put together or to the relationships among units that determine how they work together. Structure, like pattern, suggests some

Figure 1.1 A graph. The basic graph consists of nodes (•) and edges (——) joining pairs of nodes. Nodes can have labels, weights or locations. Edges can have directions, signs, weights, functional equations or locations.

predictability in the way a phenomenon is organized, even if the process that gives rise to it has a random origin or stochastic component, such as the fates of individual organisms. Even structures generated by fully random processes may have predictable characteristics, as we will see in Chapter 3. Graph theory is the mathematics of the basics of structure (objects and their connections), providing a rich technical vocabulary and a formal treatment of the concepts and outcomes. Because of the importance of understanding and quantifying structure in all ecological systems, graph theory has important contributions to make to a broad range of ecological studies, including trophic networks (Kondoh et al. 2010), mutualisms (Bascompte & Jordano 2014), epidemiology (Meyers 2007) and conservation ecology (Keitt et al. 1997), where the graphs depict functional connections among organisms or physical connections among spatially structured populations (Grant et al. 2007).

The graphs that are the focus of graph theory are deceptively simple mathematical objects, each consisting of a set of points with a set of lines joining them in pairs. The points are called *nodes*, represented by dots in a diagram (Figure 1.1), and the lines are *edges*, represented by straight or curving lines in a diagram, although a range of terms can be found in the literature (see Harary 1969; West 2001).

Graphs are about connections and the pattern of connections. In a diagram of the most basic graph, the positions of the nodes on the page and the lengths and shapes of the edges joining them have no meaning; they are placed for convenience and clarity. It is the set of connections made by the edges that determines the graph's topology. The nodes usually represent components or units of organization, and the essence of the graph lies in what is connected to what: really very simple! In this way, the graph is an abstract description of *structure* or *topology* because the edges show the relationships among organizational components that the nodes represent.

Graphs and graph theory lend themselves extremely well to applications in many areas of science because there is a wealth of mathematical knowledge that has been developed over the years from studying these simple components. Graph theory investigates all aspects of combinations of nodes with edges joining them; and "all" is no exaggeration. What is continually impressive about graph theory is the way that it can go from what seems simple and intuitive to very sophisticated (and, yes, difficult) results; advances in recent decades have really changed the field, and it has important links (pun intended) to many other branches of mathematics, such as algebra, number theory and topology. An obvious example is the application of graph theory to understanding the properties and vulnerabilities of information networks like the Internet.

A second reason for the great value of graph theory for ecologists is the flexibility of the approach for meaningful applications to a range of ecological phenomena. This is accomplished by including different characteristics in the graphs beyond the simple nodes and edges. These include the following:

- node labels that identify the node as an individual and identifiable component of the system, such as a species name; labels make a difference when counting the number of different structures
- node weights that record qualitative or quantitative characteristics of the components, such as relative abundance
- node locations: the nodes may have spatial or temporal locations, such as the time and place of a single predation event; temporal location allows the possibility of nodes that come into existence or cease to exist

and

- directions for the edges so that A to B is distinct from B to A
- signs for the edges, indicating positive or negative interactions between the nodes
- weights for the edges, or equations describing flow or function
- locations for the edges, spatial or temporal, dependent on the locations of their end-nodes; temporal location allows edges to come into existence or cease to exist

For example, nodes could represent identifiable landscape patches of known locations in a particular year, with their areas as weights; the edges could be movement corridors with weights related to how frequently or how easily the routes can be used for dispersal.

This introductory chapter describes the concepts and terminology that form the foundations of a tour through graph theory and the smart ways to use it for understanding ecological phenomena. This tour illustrates the assertion that these graphs are about structure and the pattern of relationships that are the essence of structure. A subtle distinction here is that despite the fact that "graph" and "network" have come to be almost synonymous, "graph theory" is still more about structure and "network theory" is more about function and flow.

1.1   Graphs as Structure

The branch of mathematics that we know as graph theory has arisen from a number of different sources, developed to solve problems in diverse fields. The most famous of these is Euler's solution in 1736 to the "Königsberg bridge problem," which concerned walking routes around two islands in a river with seven bridges over it. By converting the question into a general problem about graphs, it could be shown that a closed route that crossed each bridge exactly once was impossible (Euler, as cited in Biggs et al. 1976). This solution is usually cited as the beginning of graph theory, although Tutte (1998) has suggested that the discipline might date back to ancient times and the study of

Platonic solids (tetrahedron, octahedron, etc.), which are essentially symmetric graphs on the sphere. Another origin is Kirchhoff's studies of 1847 (Biggs et al. 1976) on the flow of electricity through a network of circuits with different characteristics. A third beginning is Cayley's work on the combinatorics of the chemical structures of organic compounds (e.g. butane and its isomer, isobutene) and the structurally different forms any one chemical might take (Cayley 1857). Other possible sources of the discipline include studies of map colouring problems (any map can be coloured with only four colours), interactions between molecules in statistical mechanics and Markov chains in probability theory (see Harary 1969, Chapter 1). I would, however, add a different, fourth area to the list of inspirations, and that is the study of networks of positive and negative interactions between individuals in a social setting, with developments due to Harary and co-workers from the 1950s.

All these problems are clearly about structure, the structure associated with

1 spatial constraints on physical routes
2 energy flow in a system with alternate pathways and different resistance characteristics
3 physical forms from combinations of component units (atoms)
4 relationships in interaction networks

All these sources of graph theory as a branch of mathematics have close parallels in ecological research, and all require, and take advantage of, different characteristics and results developed in that discipline.

In mathematical terms, a *graph* is an object made up of two sets: *nodes* (also points or vertices) and *edges* (the lines, also called arcs or links) that join pairs of nodes (Harary 1969; West 2001; see Box 1.1). Therefore, graph G can be seen as an ordered pair of sets V and E:

$$G = (V, E) \text{ with E being pairs of the elements of V.}$$

Less formally,

graph = {nodes} and {edge joining pairs of nodes}; say n nodes and m edges.

The density of edges is measured by the *connectance*, which is the proportion of possible edge positions actually occupied; here $2m/n$ $(n - 1)$. (This is not the same as a graph being *connected*, with a path between any two nodes, nor is it the same as *connectivity*, which measures how difficult it is to separate a connected graph into pieces.)

In contemporary usage, the terms "graph" and "network" are used interchangeably as equivalents (Estrada 2012), although previous practice was to reserve "network" for graphs or digraphs which had a real number (weight) assigned to each edge (Harary 1969), such as those in trophic networks or transportation systems. Digraph networks, with directed edges, are frequently used to study the flow of material or information, one of the most important applications of graph theory, and for such applications, each edge can have several weights, including capacity, flow and cost (Bang-Jensen & Gutin 2009).

Box 1.1 Graph Theory: Checklist of Objects

Each term has a sketchy phrase to hint at its meaning, rather than a full definition, for which see the text and the Glossary. This is not all the graph theory we need but much of the important material in a concise format. Not everything required will fit into Chapter 1; more will be introduced as needed.

1.1.1 Graphs
Graph (nodes and edges)
Subgraph (subsets of graph's nodes and edges)
Induced Subgraph (subset of nodes, and all edges of the original graph joining those nodes)
Connected Graph (path exists between any two nodes)
Tree (connected with no cycles)
Dendrogram (binary tree, often from cluster analysis)
Complete Graph (all possible edges are included)
Bipartite Graph (nodes in two distinct subsets)
Digraph (directed edges)
Tournament (each pair of nodes has a one-way outcome edge)
Signed Graph and Digraph (edges are positive or negative)
Weighted Graph (nodes or edges have weights)
Weighted Digraph (ditto and edges have directions)
Line Graph (edges become nodes in the derived line graph)
Network (same as graph, or graph with directed weighted edges)
Dynamic Network (changes through time, either edges or their weights)
Spatial Graphs (nodes located in space [vs *aspatial*])
Temporal Graphs [many names] (nodes located in time [vs *atemporal*])
Spatio-temporal Graphs (nodes located in time and space)
Planar Graph (can be drawn flat without edges crossing)
Dendrogram (clustering process and levels of joins)

1.1.2 Parts of Graphs
Subgraph (subsets of nodes and edges)
Cut-point (node removal disconnects)
Cut-edge (edges removal disconnects)
Block (maximal connected subgraph with no cut-points)
Walk (sequence of nodes and their edges; may re-use)
Path (sequence of nodes and edges, no re-use)
Closed Walk (ends at its beginning node)
Cycle (path that ends at its beginning node)
Clique (complete subgraph)
Tree "Leaf Node" (degree $= 1$; "object" in classification dendrogram)
Tree "Branch Node" (degree > 1; joins objects into groups in dendrogram)
Spanning Tree (connected subgraph with all nodes, but no cycles)
Clusters or Modules (subgraphs well connected within, few connections out)
Components (maximal connected subgraphs)

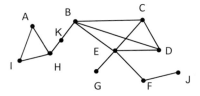

Graph is disconnected by removal of node K (cut-point)
or edge BK (cut-edge)

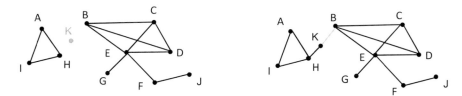

Figure 1.2 Children who play together. The graph is disconnected by removal of node K (a cut-point) or edge BK (a bridge or cut-edge).

Graph theory is usually introduced by formal development, and we cannot avoid that altogether; but we will introduce much of the basic terminology through an example, not trying to cover everything, with more to be introduced in later sections as required. The introductory narrative will be complemented by a checklist table of terms (Box 1.2) as well as the figures that go with them. This book also has a Glossary that collects almost all of the terms introduced throughout the chapters in one place.

To start with an instructive and almost-ecological example, consider children on a playground. Each child is represented by a node of a graph, G, and a simple edge is used to indicate which children are playing together during an observation period (Figure 1.2). There may be large and small groups, or individuals may play mostly alone. We can use graph-theoretical properties to evaluate this social structure for average number of playmates, maximum number of shared-play relationships between any two children and so on, and to determine the most coherent clusters. Each child has a name, and so each node has a natural label. The *degree* of a node is the number of edges attached to it, the number of nodes that are its neighbours. In the playground example, the degree is the number of shared-play interactions, ranging from 1 (nodes G or J) to 5 (node E), averaging around 2.5.

In Figure 1.2, all the children are joined together by at least one sequence of edges through the graph, so that a rumour that is passed only between these pairs of playmates will reach all children. That is, the graph is *connected*, because there is a *path* along nodes and edges between any pair of nodes. It will become disconnected, however, if child K leaves (that node is a *cut-point*) or if B and K become estranged and no longer play together (edge BK is a *cut-edge*) (see Figure 1.2, bottom). There are two obvious *clusters* or *modules*, AIH and BCDE, which are subgraphs of the whole structure. A

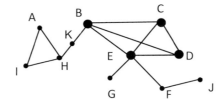

● Older

· Younger

Nodes with weights of minutes in playground

Edges with weights of shared play time (in bold)

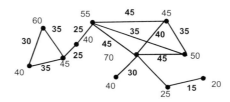

Figure 1.3 Children who play together. (top) Older children indicated by larger nodes. The subgraph of BCDE is a complete graph or clique. (bottom) Nodes with weights of minutes in playground; edges with weights of shared play time (in bold).

subgraph of G is itself a graph of which the nodes are a subset of the nodes of G and the edges are a subset of the edges of G.

Each node can also be categorized by age and gender, and so it can be determined in which categories the graph is *assortative* (most edges between nodes in the same category) or *disassortative* (most edges between nodes in different categories). In our playground example, the graph tends to be associative for age, mainly because of the *clique* (a *complete subgraph*, i.e. with all nodes joined to all nodes) of four older children (B, C, D and E), as shown in Figure 1.3 (top).

Further properties include a weight for each node, such as the total time on the playground, and weights for each edge, such as the total time or proportion of time the two children play together (Figure 1.3, bottom). The simple graph of nodes and edges in the figure is *aspatial*; space is not explicitly included, but the data on which it is based are probably truly spatial, if they were to be thus recorded. For example, some groupings may tend to spend their time by the slides and others by the swings. For some purposes, this spatial information could be included in the graph. Similarly, the graph shown is *atemporal*, but an explicitly temporal graph could be created by recording the different combinations of children at different times of day or by recording the changing links as friendships form and dissolve, evidenced by shared time on the playground. The latter approach gives a dynamic graph or network.

Of course, there are many different ways to define the edges of a graph for the same children in the playground. For example, with children, unlike some of the animals we study, we can complement the observational data by asking them their opinions of the

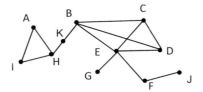

Directed Graph: Who is your best friend?

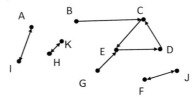

Figure 1.4 Children who play together. Nodes HKBEF with edges between form a path. Nodes AIH with three edges form a cycle. Nodes BCDE with their six edges form a subgraph, a complete graph and a module. The (undirected) graph (top) becomes a digraph (directed graph) (bottom) based on "Who is your best friend?"

others: Who do they like? Who is their best friend? and so on. This gives edges that have direction, because B may consider C to be their best friend, but the "best friend" relationship is not always reciprocated (Figure 1.4). Directional edges allow the inclusion of asymmetric relationships. They also mean that the degree of each node can be divided according to "arrow toward" edges, *in-degree*, and "arrow away" edges, *out-degree*. (In the digraph of Figure 1.4, node E has an in-degree of 2 and an out-degree of 1.)

So far only edges of shared play or liking, which are positive edges, have been included in the graph, but it might also include negative edges indicated pairs that never play together or that actively avoid each other; this gives signs to the edges creating a signed graph (Figure 1.5). By allowing asymmetric "like" and "dislike" for any pair of nodes, the graph then has edges that are signed and directed, allowing A to B to differ from B to A (see nodes K and E in Figure 1.5b). To refine further to include the intensity of "like" and "dislike," the edges may also have quantitative weights. In a real study of social structure, it would be interesting to compare the graph based on observed behaviour and the graph based on stated opinion . . .

A child shows up with a bad cold one day, and the cold spreads among the children from playmate to playmate following the edges of the shared-play graph. How far and fast the cold spreads will depend in part on the position of the initial carrier in the social network, how well connected and how central within the whole population (compare nodes B and J). The spread of the disease will follow a path in that graph consisting of a series of nodes and the edges joining them. In a path, the elements are not re-used, and in this case, the disease does not return to a child who has already had it, and so no *cycles* are formed. (A cycle is a path that ends where it began, such as A – H – I – A

(a) Mutual "like" or "dislike"
Graph: nodes (•) and signed edges: (solid = +ve; dotted = -ve).

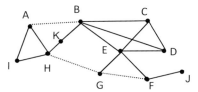

(b) Asymmetric "like" or "dislike"
Digraph of directional edges with signs.

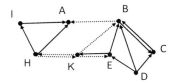

Figure 1.5 Playground children: likes and dislikes. (a) Mutual "like" or "dislike." Graph: nodes (•) and signed edges: (solid = +ve; dotted = −ve). Two complete subgraph modules: {A,H,I} & {B,C,D,E}.) (b) Asymmetric "like" or "dislike." Digraph of directional edges with signs. Some relationships are reciprocal: HK, BC. Some are not; the association of K with E is +ve, but the association of E with K is −ve.

in Figure 1.2.) A connected graph without cycles is called a *tree*. The trace of the disease through the shared-play graph is a subgraph that is a tree (Figure 1.6); the nodes are the same as in the original graph, but the edges representing the relationships are different. The edges could be labelled with directions if the actual process of disease spread was known, and they could also be labelled with dates or the order of infection if those data were available. The nodes of a tree are called "leaf" nodes if they have degree 1; "branch" nodes have degree 2 or higher; and the "root" node is a specially designated node that is functionally unique, such as the common ancestor in a phylogeny or the river mouth in a drainage basin, with its meaning depending on the application.

As another example of alternate rules for edges, consider the following. On Saturday morning, each of the four older children is assigned one, two or three of the others to

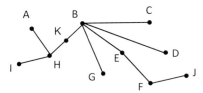

Figure 1.6 A tree made up of shared-play edges showing how a cold may spread. A tree has no cycles. A, I, G, J, D and C are leaf nodes. H, K, B, E and F are branch nodes. No node is identified as the root.

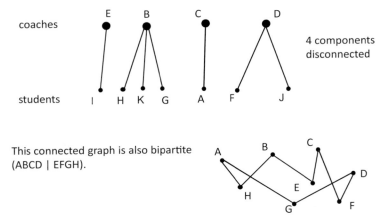

Figure 1.7 Bipartite graph of math coaching in the playground group; this one is disconnected. The lower connected graph is also bipartite (ABCD | EFGH); it is a ring graph and regular because all nodes have the same degree (2).

help coach them in their math skills. This creates a new set of edges that can replace the friendship edges of shared play; with the nodes representing the same individuals and the edges now representing that coaching relationship (Figure 1.7). Here the edges all join older to younger children, with no edges within either age cohort, giving what is called a *bipartite graph* for obvious reasons. In our example, the graph is *disconnected* (some nodes not joined by a path) and consists of four *components* (connected subgraphs).

This narrative has introduced some of the most ecologically important aspects of graphs. These are the basics only and more terms and concepts are introduced throughout the chapters that follow. All are provided in the Glossary at the end of the book.

1.2   Graphs and Ecological Relationships

The objects in ecological studies, which are to be the nodes of a graph, are often individual organisms, populations, communities, or defined spatial areas like habitat patches; and the objects are linked by physiological, behavioural, physical and dispersal processes. The edges between objects vary in weight and in vulnerability versus persistence, according to the nature and intensity of the ecological processes. Research in the related fields of evolutionary biology, population genetics and epidemiology, have as the usual objects individual organisms or other units such as taxa, traits, genes, molecular markers and so on. The edges between these nodes are the relationships of evolutionary history, functional pathways, measured similarity or ecological interactions. Graphs of these systems have the objects as nodes and their relationships as the edges (Harary 1969; West 2001; Bang-Jensen & Gutin 2009; Lesne 2006; Kolaczyk 2009). These graphs of relationships can be thought of as "abstracted" structures, because they have been derived from but taken out of the spatial and temporal contexts in which the information originated. In these studies, organisms and interactions have been modelled and analyzed for several decades using graphs and networks that are therefore *aspatial* and *atemporal* (Dale 1977a, 1977b; Proulx et al. 2005; Lesne 2006; Mason & Verwoerd 2007; Dale & Fortin 2010).

Graph theory has seen further significant applications in trophic network studies (Pascual & Dunne 2006; Kondoh et al. 2010), conservation ecology (Keitt et al. 1997; James et al. 2005), epidemiology (Shirley & Rushton 2005; Meyers 2007), and mutualisms (Bascompte & Jordano 2014). Graphs are used now in ecology for many applications depicting physical or functional connectivity among organisms (predation, pollination, competition and other forms of interactions; Bascompte 2009) or among spatially structured groupings of local populations (metapopulations [Fagan 2002; Grant et al. 2007], although the actual locations are not retained for analysis), and they can obviously be used for more. Where the locations in time or space are not explicitly maintained for analysis, many of these resulting interaction graphs or networks might be called abstracted interaction graphs.

1.3   Graphs and Locations: Spatial and Temporal

Much of the ecological data we collect originate each from a particular place at a particular time, and ecological systems usually have some spatial and temporal structure. It therefore makes sense to maintain the locations of observations for analysis, although summarizing over time and space may provide its own insights. This gives rise to graphs of the ecological systems in which the nodes (and possibly the edges) have locations in space or in time, or in both. Although many of the phenomena that inspired the development of graph theory were actually spatial (walking routes, electric circuits, maps, etc.), the graphs originally were not, but simplified the problems by removing the spatial context to become simplified combinatorial entities. In many of these applications, the locations of events in time or space are maintained explicitly for analysis, giving what might be called "locational graphs."

1.3.1   Spatial Graphs

In spatial graphs, the nodes have locations that provide an explicit spatial context and spatial meaning. The end-points of the edges obviously have locations, too, but any edge may not reflect the trajectory of any *thing* moving through space but may be an abstract indication of a relationship between the nodes. For example, an edge might be the pseudo-trajectory of a seed from its parent tree to where the seedling is eventually found; that trajectory is usually unknown. In Figure 1.8, the nodes are sites in a landscape, the edges represent the shortest set of connections between sites according to the rule of a Minimum Spanning Tree; the details of the landscape will determine whether they represent practical routes of dispersal. On the other hand, the edges between nodes may have physical locations, as well as other characteristics such as length and width,

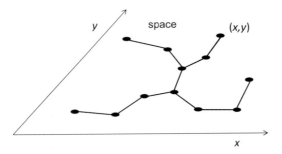

Figure 1.8 Spatial graph: nodes have spatial locations (x, y). Edges may (or may not) show trajectories or physical connections. The edges are a Minimum Spanning Tree: a tree (no cycles) that includes all nodes and minimizes the total physical length of edges (consider animals moving between landscape patches).

as in the case of hedgerows being dispersal connections for small mammals across an agrarian landscape. In this case, the level of abstraction is low and our spatial graph has become very much like a map of the system it portrays. If the corridors are actually more important than the patches, the original graph can be reformatted as its *line graph*; the original edges are now the nodes and the new edges indicate which pairs of the original edges shared nodes (Figure 1.9). In this conversion, the degree of any node created in the line graph is 2 less than the sum of the degrees of the original end-nodes; for example, the degree of node BE in the line graph in Figure 1.9 is $d(B) + d(E) - 2 = 5$. A great example of where this kind of duality might be of interest comes from studies of mycorrhizal networks: Southworth et al. (2005) found different network topologies

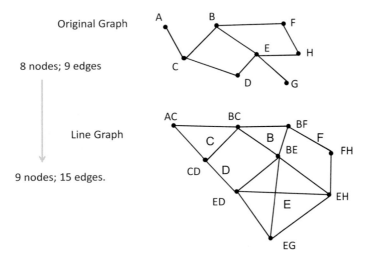

Figure 1.9 Line graph. Focus on the connections: converting a graph to its *line graph*. Edges become the new nodes; new edges determined by shared nodes in the original graph. Some are indicated by single letter labels.

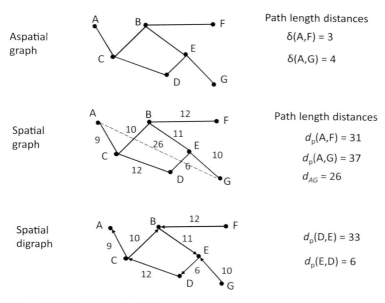

Figure 1.10 Distance and path length: an aspatial graph, a spatial graph and a spatial digraph.

when the *Quercus garryana* trees were the nodes and the fungi were the links compared to the fungi being the nodes and the trees the links. In the first case, the network appeared random with a short tail to the distribution of edges per node; in the second, the results were consistent with a "scale-free" model (more on this later) suggesting that some of the fungal species act as hubs in the network.

A key characteristic of edges in a spatial graph is the meaning of "distance." A *path* is an alternating sequence of nodes and edges joining them from u to v that uses no element more than once. The basic measure of distance between two nodes is the smallest number of edges in a path between them, called the geodesic distance. These distances are not always symmetric; in a digraph, for example, $\delta(u,v)$ and $\delta(v,u)$ may be different. If the edges have weights, the graph theory distance between two nodes $\delta(u,v)$ is the smallest total of weights in any path from node u and to node v. (A *walk* is also an alternating series of nodes and their edges that lead from node u to v; but its components may be used more than once, whereas a *path* may use an element only once [see Glossary].)

In a spatial graph, the edge e_{uv} has a weight that is the spatial distance between the nodes, call it d_{uv} or $d_s(u,v)$ for clarity. This means that there are two distances between nodes: the simple spatial distance d_{uv} between the locations of the two nodes (which is the same as $d_s(u,v)$ if there is an edge between them), and the spatial distance along the shortest path, which is the sum of the spatial lengths of the edges in that path; call it $d_p(u,v)$ with "p" for "path." Figure 1.10 illustrates these meanings of distance. Again, digraphs are different because of possible asymmetries; in fact in sparse digraphs, distance may be "infinite" because there is no path between some pairs of nodes. In the

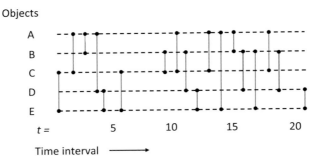

Figure 1.11 Temporal or time-ordered or time-only graph. The dashed lines serve as edges of identity, joining instances of the same node. Pairwise contacts are recorded in discrete time intervals as indicated by the temporal "locations" of the edges.

lowest panel of Figure 1.10, the distance from D to E is 33, but it is only 6 from E to D. The distance from B to A is 38, but B cannot be reached from A.

1.3.2   Temporal and Time-Only Graphs

There are many terms for graphs with nodes that have locations in time but not in space; "temporal graphs" is obviously one, and "time-varying" and "time-ordered" are other possibilities, as is "time-only graph" where it is the correct description. The nodes are located in time, and they may come into being or cease to be at particular points or in particular periods in time. Graphs in which the nodes come and go may be "time-ordered," but the same description can apply where the nodes persist but the edges appear and disappear. Figure 1.11 shows the example of a time-ordered graph of five persistent nodes observed over more than 20 time periods; the edges represent short-lived contacts between pairs of nodes, at most one per time period. Obviously the flow of information or material through the system depends on the order in which the nodes or edges form and disappear. In a system of three nodes and two time-ordered edges, A–B–C, information or disease cannot flow from A to C if the B–C edge ceases to exist before the A–B edge is formed. It is not common for a graph of an ecological study to include only temporal locations without space, but these do occur, and they have a chapter of their own (Chapter 8).

Some graphs change their structure through time, or they may document a structure that controls or influences how a system behaves through time. These are called "dynamic graphs" (Harary & Gupta 1997) or more commonly "dynamic networks" (Casteigts et al. 2011), described in Section 1.4 which follows.

1.3.3   Spatial-Temporal Graphs

In spatio-temporal graphs, the nodes have locations both in time and in space, as the term suggests. The comments about the locations of edges apply in this spatio-temporal

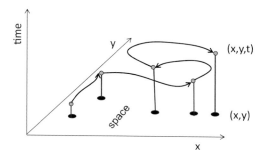

Figure 1.12 Spatio-temporal graph: nodes have temporal and spatial locations. Edges may (or may not) show trajectories.

context, too, just as in the purely spatial case. They exist in a spatial and temporal context and their end-points have locations, but they themselves may not portray actual trajectories (Figure 1.12), standing as "pseudo-trajectories" perhaps. Both time and space may each be either continuous or discrete, although most applications in ecology and related fields divide time into discrete units like days or years.

1.3.4 Aspatial and Atemporal Graphs

In aspatial graphs, space has no explicit role in the structure and presentation, so that the positions of the nodes and edges convey no meaning. The subtlety is that "aspatial" is not identical to "non-spatial"; it is a more neutral term rather than negative. The information in an aspatial graph may be derived from truly spatial data; for example, a graph of pairwise species-to-species neighbour associations is derived from the frequencies of neighbour occurrences in the spatial context of a plant community, but spatial relations are summarized, not retained, in the resulting graph. A non-spatial graph has no spatial component, neither explicitly nor implicitly. To parallel "aspatial," "atemporal graphs" are those in which the data may have a temporal component, but it is not explicit in the graphs.

1.3.5 Spatial Statistics and Local Statistics on Graphs

In the preceding sections, graphs have been discussed relative to locations in space and in time, with those dimensions being prior and external to the graph. A graph can also be seen as creating its own "space," with its own measure(s) of location, which can be very useful in studies of ecological networks that are abstracted from physical dimensions. This is not the same as embedding a graph in Euclidean n-space (see Erdös et al. 1965), but rather using the simple measure of geodesic distance (Figure 1.10) to provide the "space." Within this defined space, many methods based on standard spatial analysis or spatial statistics can be applied, even if the locations are not spatial in the traditional sense and the familiar rules of Euclidean space may be violated. This is different from the approach described by Okabe and co-authors, who apply familiar spatial analysis

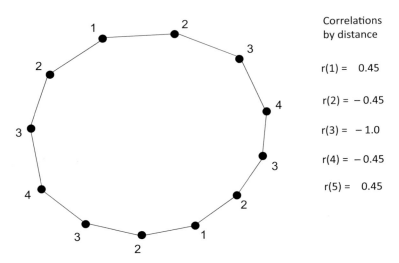

Correlations
by distance

r(1) =   0.45

r(2) = − 0.45

r(3) = − 1.0

r(4) = − 0.45

r(5) =   0.45

Figure 1.13 A ring graph with weights on the nodes, showing the correlations of node weights at various distances.

(such as Ripley's K function for point pattern analysis) to events that are constrained to occur on networks of linear structures that are embedded in "real space" (see Okabe & Sugihara 2012). The transfer of techniques from Euclidean space to "graph space" requires caution because of potential violations of the usual assumptions; however, with the correct adaptation and interpretation, almost any analysis that might be performed on grid or lattice data can be used for the irregular structure created by a non-lattice graph. For example, the observed node weights in a graph can be analyzed for autocorrelation using any appropriate statistic (e.g. Moran's I) with the distance classes defined by geodesic distance. Figure 1.13 provides the simple example of a ring graph with node weights of 1 to 4; Pearson's correlation is positive for distances of 1 and 5, and negative for distances of 2, 3 and 4. This allows an ecologist access to a rich set of familiar analytical tools to explore the structural characteristics of abstracted networks as if they were spatial data.

For spatial statistics and indices of spatial structure, measures of characteristics in "graph space" can be created both in the global form, summarizing for the entire graph, and in the local form, focussed on one particular part of the graph rather than the whole. For example, from network analysis comes the concept of assortativity: the graph is assortative if nodes with similar characteristics tend to be neighbours, joined by edges or short paths. This is positive "spatial" autocorrelation. The opposite is a graph that is disassortative (having negative autocorrelation): neighbours tend to be less similar. This property can be assigned to the whole graph as a global measure, or it may be regional within the graph, with some regions highly assortative, and others disassortative (see Piraveenan et al. 2008; Thedchanamoorthy et al. 2014). As an example, Figure 1.14 shows a graph in which the left half is assortative for the category of the nodes (many edges join nodes of the same colour), but the right half is disassortative (many edges join

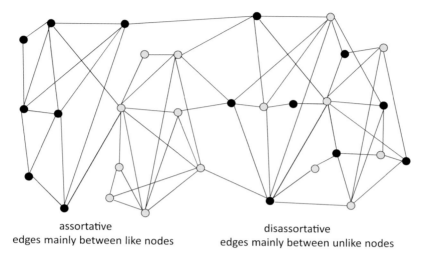

assortative
edges mainly between like nodes

disassortative
edges mainly between unlike nodes

Figure 1.14 A graph that is locally assortative or disassortative: in one part, it is assortative, with edges mainly between like nodes, and in another, it is disassortative, with edges mainly between unlike nodes.

nodes of different colours). The concept of local versus global evaluation can prove very useful in assessing the information in a graph or network that is itself heterogeneous (e.g. species interaction networks that are divided into compartments), or subject to non-stationarity (e.g. time-only graphs of interactions over a long time scale). Again, what can be done for information in graph-defined space mirrors closely the analysis options available for standard spatial data, which may prove especially useful as a route to understanding the structure of long-term or "big" data such as relating community composition and phylogeny, or modularity in microbial consortia responding to changes in hosts and environmental conditions.

1.4   Networks and Dynamics

With the growing popularity of networks for many and varied ecological applications, the term "network" has entered our ecological vocabulary from a variety of sources, so much so that it has become informally equivalent to "graph" as a general term for these abstracted structural models. Sometimes "network" is still used in a more narrow sense, referring to a graph with directed and weighted edges, used to depict or to analyze system function. These networks are often dynamic, changing in structure or with quantitative characteristics that change through time. These two cases are not identical, but obviously related. In some applications, the network is an atemporal (and frequently aspatial) summary of system function; think of a trophic network with average annual energy flows associated with each edge linking an organism of one trophic level to a consumer in the level one above it. In general, these are abstracted graphs, removed from the spatial and temporal context in which the data originally resided.

Of particular interest to ecologists are those graphs or networks in which the structure affects the dynamic function of the system it describes, as you would expect, but the processes that occur on the structure are able to change the structure itself. This is a variant on the familiar "pattern and process" or "structure and function" interaction seen in many areas of ecological study. Because these structures permit considerable complexities, they deserve a chapter all their own, and that is Chapter 11, far ahead, although the theme will recur in the intervening material.

1.5   Graphs and Data

Typically, ecological studies gather data, synthesize information from the data, analyze that information and interpret the results. To take advantage of graph theory, the data have to be converted to a graph (of course). How this is done depends on the nature of the data and the analysis method; the latter may determine the format of the graph. A graph portrayed as a diagram is good for intuitive understanding (hence so many figures in this book), and in fact one primary function of data as a graph is to facilitate the visualization and exploration of the data, including scanning for mistakes and anomalies (see Raymond & Hosie 2009). Beyond visual presentation and interpretation, most analyzes require computation and that requires a digital format for the information, and hence a good reason for the representation of graphs by matrices. Matrices for graphs can be generated in many ways, each emphasizing different features of the graph, or facilitating particular calculations.

Creating and handling these matrices becomes especially important for very large, or "massive," data sets (e.g. the Internet; see Newman 2010, Plate 1), which are just too large to be appreciated intuitively (see Hampton et al. 2013). Just displaying such large data sets as graphs requires specialized software (see Kolaczyk & Csárdi 2014). Some ecological applications may include huge numbers of nodes, especially where there are long time series and large spatio-temporal data sets (e.g. the exploratory analysis of sea surface temperature records, illustrated in Cressie & Wikle 2011, Chapter 5). Very large graphs provide great opportunities, rich with information and outcomes, but they present challenges for data conversion and processing, and visualization may require extra effort to detect the important patterns in the structure.

The descriptions of converting ecological data into graphs and of representing graphs as matrices can be presented in either order, but the data-to-graph procedure may depend on the graph format required, and so it makes sense to begin with the graph-as-matrix material. Of course, knowing the format required for the analysis should inform the development of the sampling or experimental procedure before it is carried out (the usual advice, ignored at our peril!).

1.5.1   Graphs as Matrices

This is the technical part of the discussion, but it is necessary to understand the basics of how the graphs are represented and analyzed. A matrix is an array of numbers, usually rectangular and often square, where the meaning of an entry is determined by its

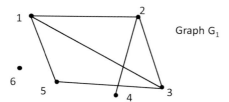

Graph G$_1$

...recast as a digraph, D$_1$

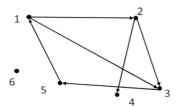

Figure 1.15 Example graph, G$_1$, with six nodes and six edges, then recast as a digraph, D$_1$, to illustrate the matrices used to represent graphs.

position in the array. It conveys numerical information in a compact format that facilitates manipulation and analysis, and matrices are fundamental to computer programs and software packages.

Most ecologists are familiar with matrices as commonly used in multivariate analysis such as principle components analysis or multivariate regression analysis. The matrices for graphs should seem less daunting because the entries in the matrices are often easy integers, and frequently just 0s and 1s (and −1s).

Given that a basic graph can be defined as the ordered pair of sets of nodes and edges, themselves ordered pairs of the nodes

$$\text{graph} = (\{\text{nodes}\}, \{\text{edges joining pairs of nodes}\}) = (\{v_i\}, \{(v_i, v_j)\}),$$

a simple data structure is a list of the pairs of nodes joined by the edges. If the n nodes are identified by integer labels, 1 to 6 in Figure 1.15, a list of the m edges can be created and the list is essentially a $2 \times m$ matrix: [(1,2), (1,3), (1,5), (2,3), (2,4), (3,5)]. An alternative is an adjacency matrix, **A**, which is a square $n \times n$ matrix with elements $a_{ij} = 1$ when nodes i and j are joined by an edge, and 0 otherwise. For the graph in 1.15, the adjacency matrix **A**$_1$ is

Matrix 1.1 Adjacency matrix **A**$_1$

$$\begin{bmatrix} \mathbf{0} & 1 & 1 & 0 & 1 & 0 \\ 1 & \mathbf{0} & 1 & 1 & 0 & 0 \\ 1 & 1 & \mathbf{0} & 0 & 1 & 0 \\ 0 & 1 & 0 & \mathbf{0} & 0 & 0 \\ 1 & 0 & 1 & 0 & \mathbf{0} & 0 \\ 0 & 0 & 0 & 0 & 0 & \mathbf{0} \end{bmatrix}$$

For a basic simple graph, a node cannot be adjacent to itself and so the entries on the main diagonal are not just zeros but structural zeros, which means that by definition they cannot be anything else but 0, and they are indicated by bold font.

One interpretation of the matrix $\mathbf{A}$ is that it shows the number of walks of length 1 between nodes i and j. What is helpful about this interpretation is that $\mathbf{A}^2$ gives the number of walks of length 2 between nodes i and j, $\mathbf{A}^3$ the walks of length 3 and so on. These counts include walks that begin and end at the same node and may re-use other elements; so these are not true "paths" in graph theory terminology. The result is that the major diagonal is no longer structural zeros, but the number of closed walks of the designated length that begin and end at node i. In $\mathbf{A}^2$ these are "cycles" of length 2, which begin and end at the same node by going out and back on the same edge, therefore also giving the node's degree, which is just the number of such edges.

$\mathbf{A}_1{}^2$ is

Matrix 1.2 Self-product of adjacency matrix $\mathbf{A}_1$

$$\begin{bmatrix} \mathbf{3} & 1 & 2 & 1 & 1 & 0 \\ 1 & \mathbf{3} & 1 & 0 & 2 & 0 \\ 2 & 1 & \mathbf{3} & 1 & 1 & 0 \\ 1 & 0 & 1 & \mathbf{1} & 0 & 0 \\ 1 & 2 & 1 & 0 & \mathbf{2} & 0 \\ 0 & 0 & 0 & 0 & 0 & \mathbf{0} \end{bmatrix}$$

The same basic information from the adjacency matrix, $\mathbf{A}$, can be contained in the $n \times m$ incidence matrix, $\mathbf{B}$, in which the rows are the nodes and the columns are the edges, with elements $b_{ik} = 1$ when node i is an end-point of edge k, and 0 otherwise. By convention, the edges are labelled in the lexicographical order of their nodes pairs (i.e. in order first by the lower label, and by the higher label if the lower labels are tied). For a digraph (a graph with directed edges), the incidence matrix has values 1, 0 and -1 as follows: $b_{ik} = 1$ when node i is the source of edge k, $b_{ik} = -1$ when node i is the sink of edge k, and 0 otherwise.

$\mathbf{B}_1$ is

Matrix 1.3 Incidence matrix $\mathbf{B}_1$

$$\begin{bmatrix} 1 & 1 & 1 & 0 & 0 & 0 \\ 1 & 0 & 0 & 1 & 1 & 0 \\ 0 & 1 & 0 & 1 & 0 & 1 \\ 0 & 0 & 0 & 0 & 1 & 0 \\ 0 & 0 & 1 & 0 & 0 & 1 \\ 0 & 0 & 0 & 0 & 0 & 0 \end{bmatrix}$$

For the digraph version (Figure 1.15), $\mathbf{B}_D$ is

Box 1.2 Graph Theory: Checklist of Properties

Node Labels (individual or class identification)
Node Weights (quantitative, possible dynamic)
Node Locations (usually as coordinates in time or space)
Node Degree (number of edges; in-degree vs out-degree for digraphs)
Node Degree distributions (for model comparison)
Node Degree joint distributions (degree autocorrelation; by neighbour category)
Edge Weights (quantitative, possibly dynamic, possibly with equation)
Path Length (geodesic or physical)
Graph Diameter (maximum shortest path)
Connectance (proportion of possible edge positions occupied)
Connectivity (how difficult to disconnect)
Clustering coefficient (frequency of third edge of a triangle)
Node Centrality [many versions] (importance in shortest paths)
Associative (positive correlation of adjacent node properties)
Disassociative (negative correlation of adjacent node properties)

Matrix 1.4 Digraph incidence matrix $\mathbf{B}_D$

$$
\begin{bmatrix}
1 & 1 & 1 & 0 & 0 & 0 \\
-1 & 0 & 0 & 1 & -1 & 0 \\
0 & 1 & 0 & -1 & 0 & 1 \\
0 & 0 & 0 & 0 & 1 & 0 \\
0 & 0 & -1 & 0 & 0 & -1 \\
0 & 0 & 0 & 0 & 0 & 0
\end{bmatrix}
$$

The adjacency matrix for the same digraph is $\mathbf{A}_D$; the entries of "1" show the direction of the edge by their position in the matrix, which is no longer symmetric about the main diagonal.

Matrix 1.5 Digraph adjacency matrix $\mathbf{A}_D$

$$
\begin{bmatrix}
\mathbf{0} & 0 & 0 & 0 & 1 & 0 \\
1 & \mathbf{0} & 0 & 0 & 0 & 0 \\
1 & 1 & \mathbf{0} & 0 & 0 & 0 \\
0 & 1 & 0 & \mathbf{0} & 0 & 0 \\
0 & 0 & 1 & 0 & \mathbf{0} & 0 \\
0 & 0 & 0 & 0 & 0 & \mathbf{0}
\end{bmatrix}
$$

Many of the matrices listed in Box 1.3 are fairly obvious in meaning based on their relation with terms in the Glossary, but the Laplacian matrix needs something more by way of explanation. The degree matrix, $\mathbf{D}$, has 0s everywhere except on the main diagonal, which contains the degree of each node in their standard order. (For a digraph we

---

Box 1.3 Graph Theory: Checklist of Matrices

This is a very small subset: there are lots and lots of matrices in graph theory, most arranged in lexicographical order, but not always square and $n \times n \ldots$

Edge list ($2 \times m$; joined node pairs, edge by edge)
Adjacency matrix ($n \times n$; symmetric, joined node pairs by row and column)
Incidence matrix ($n \times m$; nodes with incident edges)
Degree matrix ($n \times n$; nodes' edge totals on main diagonal)
Laplacian matrix ($n \times n$; symmetric, combines adjacency and degree matrices)
Digraph and network matrices ($n \times n$; asymmetric from directed edges)

---

have a choice of using the in-degree or the out-degree, which will affect the interpretation.) The Laplacian, **L**, is then $\mathbf{D} - \mathbf{A}$.

Starting with the same adjacency matrix for G_1 in Figure 1.15, the degree matrix $\mathbf{D}_1$ is

Matrix 1.6 Degree matrix $\mathbf{D}_1$

$$\begin{bmatrix} 3 & 0 & 0 & 0 & 0 & 0 \\ 0 & 3 & 0 & 0 & 0 & 0 \\ 0 & 0 & 3 & 0 & 0 & 0 \\ 0 & 0 & 0 & 1 & 0 & 0 \\ 0 & 0 & 0 & 0 & 2 & 0 \\ 0 & 0 & 0 & 0 & 0 & 0 \end{bmatrix}$$

and the Laplacian matrix $\mathbf{L}_1 = \mathbf{D}_1 - \mathbf{A}_1$ is

Matrix 1.7 Laplacian matrix $\mathbf{L}_1$

$$\begin{bmatrix} 3 & -1 & -1 & 0 & -1 & 0 \\ -1 & 3 & -1 & -1 & 0 & 0 \\ -1 & -1 & 3 & 0 & 0 & 0 \\ 0 & -1 & 0 & 1 & 0 & 0 \\ -1 & 0 & -1 & 0 & 2 & 0 \\ 0 & 0 & 0 & 0 & 0 & 0 \end{bmatrix}$$

This matrix is important in graph theory because it can be used to determine certain characteristics, such as the number of spanning trees (subgraphs with no cycles that join all nodes) or the number of connected components (see Newman 2010, Chapter 6). It is also an important approach to understanding the properties of random walks on the original graph; these are walks that develop by iteratively choosing the next node to be included at random from those available by edges from its current node (Figure 1.22; see also Section 1.7.5). The various matrices related to the adjacency matrix provide clear algorithmic alternatives for exploring a graph and determining its properties (e.g. cycles, blocks, random walk . . .), often based on the eigenvalues of a matrix. These properties will be discussed at greater length as they come up in the chapters that follow.

1.5.2   From Data to Graphs

The advice always given is to determine the analysis to be performed on the data to be collected before sampling or running experiments to obtain the data. Good advice is not always taken, but the form of the data limits the form of the graph that can be derived; for example, sampling that is itself symmetric cannot give asymmetric data or directed graphs (e.g. "A then B" is asymmetric information, but "A and B" is symmetric) whereas sampling that is asymmetric produces asymmetric data, which can be aggregated to symmetric outcomes, thus allowing either directed or non-directed graphs. The match or mismatch of spatial and temporal scales of the phenomenon being investigated and the sampling and analysis being carried out also has to be considered as an important part of the relationship between phenomenon and data, and between data and analysis (see Dale & Fortin 2014, Figure 1.8).

A few examples can illustrate the relationship between design and outcome: the data, the analyses and the graphs.

1. The first is from plant ecology, where a common approach is to investigate the community structure of positive and negative associations between pairs of species using density or presence-absence data. Plants of two species may tend to occur close together because they have similar ecological properties or because of some positive influence of one on the other. Plants of different species may tend to occur farther apart because they have divergent ecological properties or because there is some negative influence of one species on the other. Some of these causes are most likely symmetric (shared or divergent ecological properties) and others are more likely to be asymmetric (positive or negative influence), and the sampling scheme may be designed to account for that fact.

A standard approach is to record the presence and absence of all species in each of many small quadrats, randomly or systematically arranged. The data are used to create graphs of the inter-specific associations of pairs of species (also known as constellation diagrams or phytosociological structure). For each pair of species, A and B, any quadrat belongs to one of four categories: both present; A present, B absent; A absent, B present; both absent. The counts of quadrats in the four categories form a 2×2 contingency table and each pair of species can be assessed using a goodness-of-fit test with the X^2 or G statistic compared with the χ^2 distribution. There are many problems in treating this as a reliable statistical test, because of various sources of non-independence. It does, however, provide a standard by which edges between species (the nodes) can be determined for a graph of "significant" inter-specific associations; this graph has nodes representing species and signed edges joining some pairs, and so the result resembles Figure 1.5a. The edges are sometimes shown as lines of different thicknesses indicating the strength of the associations. The symmetric sampling design will not permit distinguishing between possible effects of A on B from possible effects of B on A.

To determine asymmetric associations for graphs with directed edges, the sampling must have asymmetry in its design. One such is "point-contact" sampling. Dimensionless points are set out in random or regular arrangements and at each such location the first species contacted by the point sample is recorded, together with the species

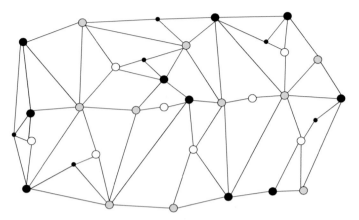

Figure 1.16 Neighbour samples for inter-specific tests: four species in a planar graph (can be drawn with no edges crossing).

closest to the initial contact that is different from the initial species. The resulting data set consists of ordered pairs of species frequencies: (initial contact, nearest neighbour to contact point). These data can be evaluated using a goodness-of-fit test, although there are technical details to consider (Dale et al. 1991). These data provide the basis for an asymmetric graph of pairwise associations for further analysis; the nodes are species with signed directed edges joining some pairs, thus resembling Figure 1.5b.

The third method for deriving association graphs requires identifiable individuals that can be mapped, like tree stems in a forest. Given the location and species of each stem, the counts of the species of neighbours, variously defined, can be determined for each species and analysis will detect unusually rare or common neighbours for each. Neighbours can be defined in a number of different ways, whether based on a quantitative distance threshold (e.g. 1.5 m), or using "topological" definitions of neighbours in spatial graphs (Figure 1.16 provides an example), such as the Minimum Spanning Tree (Figure 1.8), or other such rules for spatial graphs described below. Whatever the definition of neighbours, to produce a spatial graph of the site, an abstracted association graph for the community is based on significant deviation of neighbour frequencies from those expected based on complete spatial randomness.

2. The second example is of the interactions between two identifiable groupings of species, such as plants and their pollinators or herbivores and their predators, so that the resulting graph is bipartite, with two non-overlapping subsets of nodes, and with the graph's edges running between the subsets, not within (Figure 1.17). One intriguing question about these interactions is whether specialist species on one side tend to pair up with specialists on the other side of the interaction or whether there is a tendency for specialists to pair only with generalists (a "nested" arrangement, see Figure 1.17). The strength of any of these interactions is usually determined from some "surrogate" that is easier to observe (see Bascompte & Jordan 2014, Figure 3.7; Vázquez et al. 2005a). The data from which these graphs are produced are usually (1) counts of interaction events,

Pollinators

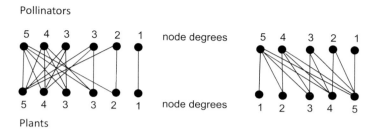

Matching: specialists with specialists
and generalists with generalists

Nested: specialists only with generalists
and generalists with any

Figure 1.17 Bipartite graphs for ecological interactions between two distinct categories of organisms, such as plants and their pollinators. On the left, there is matching of specialists with specialists and generalists with generalists. On the right, there is nesting so that specialists are only with generalists and generalists with specialists or generalists.

such as the number of visits of pollinators of species X to flowers of species Y or (2) quantitative measures, such as the amount of biomass of herbivore Y removed or consumed by predator Z. Most such data are derived from in situ field work of observation or sampling.

The count data can be converted into complete bipartite graphs, with all possible edges included, each weighted by the count of the pairwise-specific events. An alternative is to convert the count frequency data, call it f_{XY}, into proportions $p_{\bullet Y}$ or $p_{X \bullet}$ by dividing by the plant total or by the pollinator total. These values, associated with all possible edges, can then be used to determine which edges to include in the graph using a threshold value (Figure 1.17).

3. The third example concerns food webs, which are trophic interaction networks. These are generally intended to be quantitative and attempt to be complete, both in the interactions that are quantified and in the species that are included. Taxonomically difficult groups are often aggregated, giving large groupings of taxa such as "grasses" or "centric diatoms" or "parids"; an alternative to taxonomic groupings is to aggregate by function, such as "grazers" versus "browsers." The data that contribute to the construction of a trophic network graph include biomass estimates from destructive sampling, observations of encounter rates, trapping, feeding preferences, stomach content analysis, calorific measurements and so on. While demanding, the data collected produce a network graph of great richness and clear value for further study. Figure 1.18 shows a simplified trophic network for the Kluane boreal ecosystem based on a truly enormous amount of effort over decades of study and a very wide range of estimates, measures and observations (see Krebs 2010 and references therein).

To conclude this section, Table 1.1 lists some of the features of the three examples just discussed as a summary and with added notes or comments for consideration. A specific comment at the end of the table offers consoling advice on how to deal with the common problem of incomplete data, always a concern for field-based studies.

Table 1.1 Data to Graphs: Features and Considerations

Plant communities for inter-specific associations
Standard quadrat sampling
     Symmetric "constellation" graphs of association from frequency tables (many caveats!)
Point-contact sampling
     Asymmetric association digraphs from frequency tables
Stem mapping (trees)
     Many choices for neighbour definitions
     Associations from neighbour frequency
Bipartite graphs of pairwise interactions
Counts of interaction events
     Flower visits
     Foraging stops
Quantitative measures
     Pollen biomass loads
     Fruit consumed
     All edges with weights, or only strongest edges by threshold
Multi-level food webs of predation (trophic networks by taxonomic or functional group)
Biomass estimates for taxonomic or trophic groups
Encounter rates by species or group pairs
Stomach content analysis
Calorific measurements

Comment on Incomplete Data

No study is likely to be sufficiently intensive and extensive to determine all the individuals or to detect all the species that should be included, nor all the possible interactions of the species that are encountered. This means that in these studies, as in much of

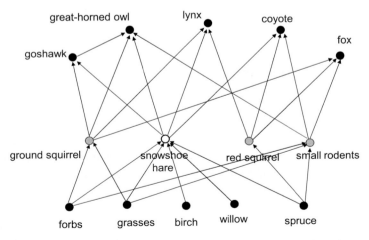

Figure 1.18 Simplified food web or trophic network: the Kluane boreal ecosystem (redrawn from Krebs 2010). Arrows are directed from prey to predator, indicating the transfer of energy and matter; some conventions use the reverse.

ecological research, we have only partial and incomplete information on which to base our conclusions. Some of these are data zeros, not structural zeros; that is, there is no observation although one is possible (structural zeros occur where no observation is possible). One approach to evaluating the importance of this incompleteness is sub-sampling known-to-be incomplete data, and by calculating the measures of interest for each sub-sample to determine the findings' robustness to missing information (Naujokaitis-Lewis et al. 2013). This is much like bootstrapping, but not intended to determine statistical significance (for more on this technique in other applications, see Efron & Tibshirani 1993; Manly 2006). This approach is not the same as sampling a graph or network, to be followed by making inferences about the whole from the sample (see Kolaczyk 2009), nor is it the same as techniques to identify missing or spurious edges and thus to reconstruct its graph and refine the determination of properties (see Giumerà & Sales-Pardo 2009).

The three chosen examples are all of abstracted graphs, rather than locational graphs for which the locations of nodes in time or space are retained explicitly. The relationship between data and graph is conceptually simple for locational cases. The nodes represent objects or events that have coordinates in time or space, and you just have to record them (sounds easy!). Of course, the practicalities of actually doing this may be daunting, expensive or overwhelmingly detailed. The maps of tree stems are locational graphs, as would be the space-time coordinates of bees' visits to orchid flowers, or of goshawk-hare encounters (labelled as to outcome). Much locational data is now collected by automatic tracking systems, such as radio-collared elk or "tagged" sharks, but the older methods of mark-recapture or trapping also provide data for location-specific graphs for further analysis. Locational data are essential for studies related to diversity and conservation, examining features such as community composition, genetic structure and patterns of dispersal through fragmented landscapes, all of which can be helped by the use of graph theory as will be detailed in Chapter 9 (see, among many others, Urban & Keitt 2001; Saura et al. 2014; Watts et al. 2015; Rayfield et al. 2011; Fall et al. 2007; James et al. 2005).

1.6   Ecological Hypotheses and Graph Theory

The relationship between hypotheses and analysis is often iterative in ecological research. The hypothesis determines the data required and the analysis that is carried out; but usually the results of the analysis generate new hypotheses which lead to further and refined studies. Graph theory lends itself well to this iterative process, particularly because it provides a natural approach to hierarchical analysis.

Hierarchical frameworks for hypothesis testing work best when each level of evaluation is independent of the previous levels, but this is not always possible and our hierarchical layers of tests may not be mutually independent. The most challenging task can be the translation of the ecological hypothesis into a well-formulated and testable formal hypothesis in the language of statistics or graph theory. The ecological hypothesis determines the formal hypothesis and the data and other information that are required to

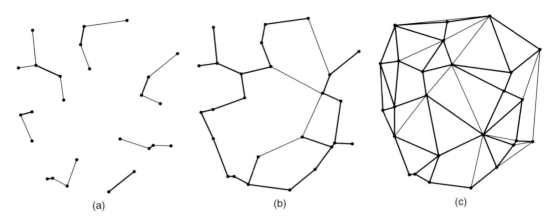

(a)   (b)   (c)

Figure 1.19 Proximity graphs or spatial neighbour networks. (a) Networks 1 and 2: First Nearest Neighbours and First Mutually Nearest Neighbours in bold. (b) Networks 3 and 4: Least Diagonal Neighbours with Minimum Spanning Tree in bold. (c) Networks 5 and 6: Delaunay triangulation with Gabriel graph in bold.

test it. These then determine the analytical approach, and the results inform the decision to reject the formal hypothesis or not. This decision is then used to evaluate the original ecological hypothesis.

In the many publications on applications of graph theory in non-mathematics (e.g. biology, technology or sociology), it is interesting how rarely the testing of hypotheses or evaluations of statistical significance are included explicitly. The many discussions of measures of graph or network properties, and many comparisons with various random "null models," are rarely formulated in these terms.

As an introductory example, consider the hierarchy of spatial neighbour networks described in Dale and Fortin (2014) and shown in Figures 1.19a, 1.19b and 1.19c. These spatial graphs form a series from mutually nearest neighbours with few edges per node (averaging 0.62), through the Minimum Spanning Tree (about 2.0) to the Delaunay triangulation with many (about 6.0); each graph in the series is a subgraph of the graph that follows (see Chapter 9). A spatio-temporal hierarchy can be more complicated, including only temporal neighbours (history explains it all), only spatial neighbours (location is everything), or some of both (Figure 1.20), with the critical question being the spatial and temporal distances at which neighbours have an influence. Similar hierarchies of inclusive subgraphs can be created in aspatial and atemporal applications, such as trophic networks, by using different threshold values for including the directed edges based on their transfer rates or feeding preferences: each change in threshold having the potential to produce a different graph that includes all the edges of the previous version. In all cases, the hierarchy allows a hierarchical series of hypothesis tests, admittedly not independent, that will permit an evaluation of ecologically interesting hypotheses.

One major goal of this book is to help ecologists understand the wide array of "smart things" that can be done with graph theory, providing some guidance on the range of

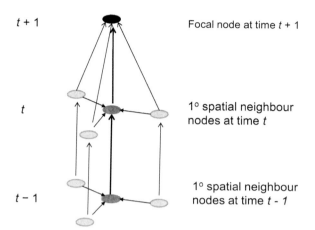

t + 1   Focal node at time t + 1

t   1° spatial neighbour nodes at time t

t − 1   1° spatial neighbour nodes at time t - 1

Figure 1.20 Ecological memory and neighbour influence: state of focal node at time $t + 1$ depends on its own history (times t and $t − 1$), or on its contemporary neighbours or on neighbours and histories.

approaches to evaluating hypotheses that graph theory affords. That range is broad and deep.

1.7   Statistical Tests and Hypothesis Evaluation

When ecological hypotheses are translated into statistical hypotheses, we need the appropriate statistics and test procedures to assess significance. The general approach is to compare a statistic calculated from the data to the appropriate reference distribution. When the reference distribution is known and tabulated, parametric tests may be used, but these significance procedures require independence of the data. When the reference distribution is not known, but the characteristics of interest can be studied by the enumeration of graph structures, enumeration can be used to provide the frequency distributions upon which tests can be based. If parametric methods are not available, and enumeration is not an option, then randomization procedures are a good alternative to generate a reference distribution from the data (Edgington 1995; Manly 2006). When inference to the population level is required, bootstrap procedures and Monte Carlo simulations can be used (Efron & Tibshirani 1993; Manly 2006). Randomization tests are an attractive approach because significance is evaluated by comparison with empirical distributions generated from the data, which is especially appealing for small data sets that do not meet the assumptions of parametric tests.

1.7.1   Parametric Tests

Parametric tests may be available only rarely for the applications described here, particularly as any source of lack of independence, and there may be several, invalidate the application of these familiar test procedures, but a common comparison for observed properties is the same characteristic in *random graphs* (Erdös & Rényi 1960). Their simple model for random graphs is to start with n nodes and to include any one of all possible edges independently and with constant probability p. Under those conditions, a number of characteristics follow binomial, Poisson or (approximately or asymptotically) Normal distributions. For example, the degree of any vertex follows a binomial distribution, and the distribution of the number of vertices of a given degree, d, is asymptotically Normal (see Barbour et al. 1989). For large graphs, this property enables parametric testing as a good approximation where appropriate. The big question, of course, is when a random graph of this type is actually a good null hypothesis for comparison.

These Erdös-Rényi random graphs have been well studied since they were introduced, and much is known about them. For example, threshold values for p and thus for the density of edges have been determined related to the appearance of certain substructures in the random graph, such as trees of a given size, cycles of a given size or complete subgraphs of a given size (Newman 2010). This knowledge can also be useful for evaluating the subgraph characteristics of an observed graph. It is because the edges in these random graphs are placed independently and with constant probability that many distributions derived from them can be assumed to converge to known parametric distributions.

1.7.2   Enumeration and Probability Calculations

Enumeration is a straightforward way to determine whether the observed structural characteristics that are related to a hypothesis of ecological interest are surprising, in the sense of being significantly different from what would be expected for "randomly chosen" graphs of the same kind. Rather than really using randomly chosen or randomly constructed graphs, it may be possible to compare an observed structure with all possible graphs in the domain of interest. For example, we might want to know how unusual it would be or it would be for a bifurcating tree, like a cladogram, to have exactly one branch node of each possible order from 1 to $n - 1$. We could generate all possible trees of that kind and determine directly how many have that property. While this approach may sound "labour-intensive," computing power now makes it easy. An alternative in some circumstances is to calculate the probability of a given characteristic, such as the cladogram example just given, from something like first principles, hoping that we have got those first principles right (!). The advantage of the "brute force" enumeration of all possible structures is that limits can be placed on the structures considered. We can therefore enumerate within subsets defined by particular characteristics, allowing us to circumvent, or at least understand, the effects of the lack of independence in how the structures are put together.

For example, consider studying competition in a community of n species by a large complete experiment that tests the competitive outcome of every pairwise combination. For each pair of species, one is determined to be the "winner," based on some criterion evaluating performance. The structure that results from all pairwise tests is called a *tournament* for obvious reasons, and can be represented by a directed graph of n nodes

Labels are node scores

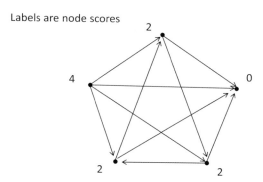

Figure 1.21 Tournament with $n = 5$: a complete graph with a directed edge from winner to loser for all pairs of nodes. Labels are node scores (wins, as here, or sometimes wins – losses). The node scores are 4, 2, 2, 2 and 0, as indicated.

and $n - 1$ directed edges pointing from "winner" to "loser." One way to examine the consistency of competitive outcomes is to evaluate the *transitivity* of the digraph. A relationship like competitive dominance is said to be *transitive* whenever, given edges A–B and B–C, we also find A–C. To evaluate the competition results, we determine the frequency of transitive triangles in the graph, compared with the frequency of "paradoxical" triangles that show cycles of competitive outcome or a kind of competitive reversal where we find A–B and B–C, but also C–A. If the tournament is almost completely transitive, we can work through enumeration and some probability calculations to determine how expected or unexpected that outcome might be, given all possible tournaments and an assumption of equal probabilities for all.

There are $n(n - 1)/2$ positions for edges among the n nodes, and each takes one of two possible directions, A–B or B–A, independently (that's important!) of the others, and so there are $2^{n(n - 1)/2}$ tournaments. If the competitive outcomes are consistently transitive throughout the tournament, then there is a strict order of all n species from the strongest competitor to the weakest. There are exactly $n!$ of these orderings, since all orders of the n species are possible, and may be considered equally probable. The best competitor outcompetes all others, and so it has an *out-degree* (or "score") of $n - 1$, the next best a score of $n - 2$, and so on, down to 0 for the weakest competitor (Figure 1.21).

For example, the tournament in Figure 1.21, $n = 5$, and the scores are 4, 2, 2, 2, 0. While not completely transitive, the competitive relationships among the species are quite consistent in their transitivity. This example will be discussed further in Chapter 6, but it shows something of the procedure to evaluate the graph-based results.

1.7.3   Other Random Graph Constructions

The Erdös-Rényi model for random graph construction is, of course, not the only model. The literature describes many others, of which the Watts-Strogatz "small world" is one of the most often cited, as is the "scale-free" network model (Newman 2010). One characteristic frequently used to differentiate among these models is the distribution of the nodes' degrees; for the small world model, this follows a delta distribution, which is bell shaped but sharply peaked; for the scale-free models, it is a power function (Albert & Barabási 2002, among many others). Several other measures are used to characterize graphs to determine the most likely descriptive model; these include average path length, *clustering coefficient*, and correlation of node degrees (Albert & Barabási 2002, among many). The clustering coefficient is essentially the probability that two neighbours of a given node (say j and k which have edges to node i) are themselves neighbours (joined by e_{jk}). One measure associated with the correlation among node degrees is the *joint degree distribution*; this edge-based statistic tabulates the bivariate distribution of the degrees of nodes joined by an edge; it can be calculated directly from the adjacency matrix (Newman 2010). It tells more about connectivity than the degree distribution because it shows whether the degrees of neighbouring nodes are positively or negatively autocorrelated. The frequency is often converted into a Pearson correlation measure that runs between -1 and $+1$, designated r, called the assortativity coefficient because it distinguishes between assortative networks with $r > 0$ in which high degree nodes tend to be first-order neighbours (path length 1) of other high degree nodes (giving positive autocorrelation) and disassortative networks with $r < 0$ in which high degree nodes tend to be first-order neighbours of low degree nodes (giving negative autocorrelation). Of course, characteristics other than node degree can be used as the basis for assortative versus disassortative designations for network graphs (Newman 2010, Section 7.13).

The many random models for graphs and networks may be tailored to the circumstances. As with randomization of existing structures, creating random models for comparison with the observed data allow us to include constraints on the random version that reflect constraints in the system being studied. For example, in a study of potential migrations between landscape patches, we might be interested in the *diameter* of the Minimum Spanning Tree as a measure of the shortest distances and fewest "steps" between patches. In that case, it would be reasonable to create a large number of realizations of randomly placed nodes of a spatial graph within an equivalent area, determine the Minimum Spanning Tree for each, and thus determine a frequency distribution for the diameter. This frequency distribution can then be used to evaluate the observed value.

1.7.4   Randomization and Restricted Randomization

Randomization tests are based on the hypothesis that all re-arrangements by re-ordering or pairwise exchanges ("shuffling") of the data are equally likely. Therefore, although randomization tests may have fewer assumptions than other forms of testing, there are still some to consider. In addition, large numbers of randomizations (e.g. 10,000) may be necessary to achieve the desired level of significance for a particular test. Randomization tests do not offer fully the familiar security of parametric statistics, but their flexibility provides the means to analyze complex ecological data using experimental or sampling designs for which classical tests have not been developed. Ecologists can also develop their own statistics, opening up the possibility of testing in novel situations.

Any lack of independence in data (due to time, space, behaviour, relatedness, phylogeny, . . .) can impair the application of either parametric or randomization tests. Parametric tests require that the errors are independent, so that each observation or data point brings a full degree of freedom. If the lack of independence is due to spatial relationships, the resulting positive spatial dependence usually makes nearby sampling units more alike and so a spatially autocorrelated sample does not bring a full degree of freedom, but rather a fraction of it, inversely proportional to the autocorrelation in the data (Legendre 1993; Dale & Fortin 2009). Several techniques in sampling design and in statistical analysis (Legendre & Legendre 2012; Dale & Fortin 2009) can correct or control for dependence in the data, so that familiar parametric tests can be used with minor modification. This issue of non-independent errors is at the core of the analysis of ecological data but it applies to the development of randomization procedures for dependent data, complete randomness is not really an appropriate comparator and so forms of randomness which incorporate some degree of structure (often spatial or temporal) should be used (Cressie 1993). These are *restricted* randomization procedures that include some of the structure of dependency already in the data (Fortin & Payette 2002; Manly 2006), or at least most of it (see Dale & Fortin 2014, Figures 8.12 and 8.13). There are several different ways to restrict the randomization on a graph depending on the system. A simple example would be a map of diseased and healthy plants, with a network of neighbours imposed upon it. A simple question is whether the diseased plants are clustered or overdispersed, and it is one that is easily answered, but a more useful question might be whether the diseased plants are clustered or overdispersed given the overall arrangement of the plants of either kind.

1.7.5 Random Walks on Graphs

A specialized form of randomization for investigating graph properties is the application of random walks on graphs, closely related to the study of Markov models. What is random here is not the graph itself or its formation, but a walk, a sequence of alternating nodes and edges, on the existing graph. The basic random walk begins with a single randomly chosen node (step 0), and then moves with equal probability to any of the adjacent nodes by the edge that joins them (step 1). The number of possible next steps is the degree of the current node, d_i, and the probability for any one of them being next is d_i^{-1}. The process is then iterated many times, as illustrated in Figure 1.22, and in general, the relative frequencies of the nodes in a long random walk approaches a stable distribution determined by the graph's structure. Many properties of these walks have been investigated and they provide important insights into how graphs work. More specifics on random walks on graphs will be discussed in Chapter 9, related to spatial graphs and the implications for conservation ecology in fragmented landscapes.

1.7.6 Models

An obvious extension for understanding ecological systems using graphs is the development and evaluation of models. It is an easy step to go from restricted randomizations

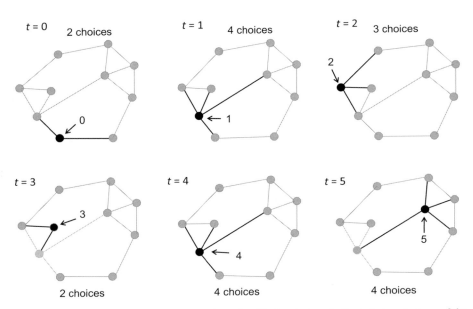

Figure 1.22 Random walk on an undirected graph with the choices indicated at each stage of the iterative process.

for generating the distributions of variables, to Monte Carlo models where new "data sets" are generated with known characteristics and built-in forms of dependence. This is closely related to the approach that provided an understanding of random graphs versus small world graphs versus scale-free graphs; but there, the graphs themselves were generated by random processes, rather than the "data" on which graphs are subsequently based. The latter version can be useful for much more highly specified circumstances. For example, in models of spatio-temporal bipartite graphs studying plant-pollinator relationships, the creation of "random" edges needs to be limited by the phenologies of both plant flowering and pollinator activity; and to avoid adding in "forbidden links" (Olesen et al. 2008; Jordano 1987), pollination interactions that cannot occur, such as the combination of a long-tubed flower and a pollinator with short mouthparts. Models can also help in dealing with the complexity of large-scale many-factor systems by integrating pattern and process (e.g. Peterson et al. 2013) or by modelling spatial decisions for resource exploitation by simulation and evaluation (Walker et al. 2013). More examples of the use of a range of model types will arise in the following chapters, but this is another area of applying graph theory in ecological studies that deserves more emphasis and exploration.

1.7.7   Sampling and Inference

Many of the ecological systems of great interest involve very large numbers of individuals or of taxa or of observations, producing graphs of networks that have many nodes and many edges. Very large graphs present serious challenges for data collection, data analysis, and inference (see e.g. Ahmed et al. 2014). One obvious solution is to choose a sample of the entire graph or network and use the information from the sample to make inferences about the whole, whether the questions of interest are about the system's topology and structure or about its function and dynamics (Leskovec & Faloutsos 2006; Maiya 2011). There are many different ways of selecting the sample, but a simple approach is to take a random subset of the nodes of the graph and to include all edges between pairs of those nodes, giving an "induced subgraph sample" (Kolaczyk 2009). Samples can be based on nodes, as in this case, or on randomly chosen edges, or on a node's edges or its neighbour clusters ("star" and "snowball" sampling) with many variations (Lee et al. 2006). Such a sample can be the basis for estimates of several characteristics of the whole graph: average node degree, betweenness centrality, the clustering coefficient or graph transitivity, and so on (for details, see Lee et al. 2006; Kolaczyk 2009, Chapter 5; Ahmed et al. 2014). Most ecologists are familiar with the effect of spatial autocorrelation on the analysis of locational data (see Legendre 1993; Dale & Fortin 2009); similar effects are to be expected within the "graph space" of network graphs, due to the positive autocorrelation called "homophily" or "assortativeness" or the negative form called "heterophily" or "disassortativeness," but much of the emphasis in network graph sampling is on estimation rather than on significance levels.

1.8 Concluding Comments

The purpose of this chapter was to introduce the most important concepts of graph theory as they can be applied in ecological studies, without duplicating the formality of standard graph theory texts. A second criterion was not to include everything that would be needed throughout the book. That would seem overwhelming. More objects and properties will be introduced throughout the chapters that follow as they are required. Some themes and concepts are included more than once throughout the book; the repetition is intentional because the reader is not expected to work through the material cover to cover and in the order imposed by the chapters.

The basic message for the reader from the material of Chapter 1 on applying graph theory to their own ecological research is "You can do this . . . " The chapters that follow provide the next important level, showing some of the details of " . . . and here's how." Many of the investigations that we may wish to pursue can be improved or facilitated by the application of graph theory, and there are many which would be impossible without graph theory to develop and test the hypotheses of interest.

I do not apologize for the lack of "real" examples for some of the suggested applications. The whole point is that these are things that can be done, but many have not. We should not wait for others to complete their studies and present us with their mature and considered results before following up on these promising approaches. In some cases, there have been applications in other fields of endeavour that are sufficiently similar to act as models for ecological applications to follow. There is a long and varied (and enticing) list of ideas for us to explore!

That's it for the introduction! There is lots to learn, but worth the effort. The long list of the subjects of ecological studies is matched by a long list of the ways in which graph theory can be employed to support and facilitate, or even to direct those studies, and that is the focus of the rest of this volume. The next chapter is designed to complement this chapter's introductory material by reviewing the range that graph theory covers from a different angle: the shapes of graphs, from trees to triangles.

2   Shapes of Graphs: Trees to Triangles

Introduction

This chapter is designed to help "unpack" many of the concepts introduced in Chapter 1, with a more in-depth treatment and some pre-figuring of material that will be covered in more detail by later chapters. Complementary presentations should ease the intense list of concepts and details, and help with getting into the mode of "thinking with graphs." The main topic is a quick tour through a range of different shapes or topologies for graphs and some of the variations on these basic forms that are helpful in ecological applications.

One theme is how seemingly small changes in the rules that control how graphs are created have large effects on the graph that results. For example, what happens if graphs are not allowed to have cycles in their structure? What is the effect of having directions to the edges? If the edges occur at random positions, how many triangles should the graph have? There are good reasons for starting with the first question and considering the consequences of "acyclic" graphs.

2.1   Acyclic Graphs

A graph with undirected edges and no cycles (i.e. no paths that form closed loops) is a "tree" when it is connected, and (of course) "a forest" when it is not (Figure 2.1). Trees are common structural forms in almost all branches of science (pun intended), from hydrocarbon molecules and river basin drainage networks to evolutionary diversification, to data storage and retrieval and to modelling clonal growth (see Box 2.1). Compared with graphs of interaction networks, these are simple structures with simple rules for associated functions, but they are both useful and powerful for applications in the ecological context.

Considering trees as spatial structures, one feature is that while there is always a path through the tree between any two nodes, there is only one path, with no detours or alternative routes between nodes. This fact has implications for tree-shaped structures in a natural setting based on their vulnerability to disconnection or disruption.

In ecology, as in other fields, classification is one way of organizing multivariate data sets; for example, using species abundance data to group quadrats into a hierarchy of clusters based on similarity. When the objects or clusters are joined two at a time, the

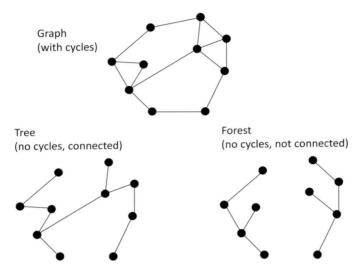

Figure 2.1 Graphs and cycles: a graph may have cycles (or not) and may be connected (or not); here connected with cycles. A tree is connected and has no cycles. A forest has no cycles and is not connected.

clustering process can be depicted as a dendrogram, which is a binary tree (Figure 2.2). It is often of interest to ecologists (1) to evaluate the shape of the dendrograms and (2) to determine the similarity of two dendrograms. Graph theory can be helpful in providing guidance to both these evaluations.

Dendrograms are rooted trees (see Box 2.2), with the "root" node representing the grouping of all objects (a node of degree one), "leaf" nodes that represent the original n objects (nodes of degree one), and $n - 1$ "branch" nodes of degree three, that represent where the groups are joined (Figure 2.3).

2.1.1   Shape

The "shape" of a dendrogram can be defined in different ways, but one difficulty is the fact that, for a single data set, the dendrograms that result from clustering can be very

---

Box 2.1 Trees

A tree is a connected undirected graph with no cycles. Trees can be used in ecology to provide a spatial framework for locations (e.g. Minimum Spanning Tree or radial spanning tree), to model the growth of branching organisms (e.g. trees [of course!], corals or clonal herbs and grasses) and to describe the evolutionary history of related organisms (a phylogenetic tree). Trees are also fundamental as data and computational structures, important to ecologists as well through the analyses they do! In some cases, one node is designated as the "root" of the tree; this gives an implicit directionality to the structure.

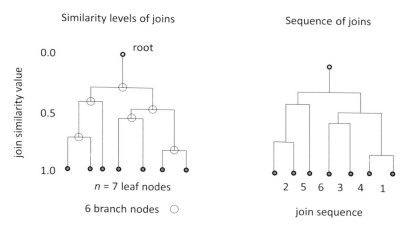

Figure 2.2 A dendrogram (a binary tree) is a graph that shows the process of a cluster analysis. Usually it records more than shape, often values at which joins occur or their order.

different, depending on the similarity measure and clustering algorithm on which the dendrogram is based. This fact needs to be considered in interpreting the results. One description of shape is the frequency distribution of the sizes of the subtrees (the number of leaf nodes) at each branch node: m_k is the number of branch nodes with $k + 1$ leaf nodes (Dale & Moon 1988). In the example in Figure 2.3, there are three groups of two objects, one of three and one of four. The subtree shape is $M = (m_1, m_2, \ldots, m_{n-1})$; in Figure 2.3, $M = (3, 1, 1, 0, 0, 1)$.

Another shape characteristic is the number of "terminal singles," single objects that are joined to the all-inclusive group only at the very end of the clustering process (Dale & Moon 1988). In Figure 2.3, the dendrogram has no terminal singles; in Figure 2.4, there are four in the first example, and two in the second. Terminal singles are interesting

---

Box 2.2 Dendrograms

Dendrograms are trees. They are binary rooted trees, used to depict and analyze the results of classification procedures or cluster analysis; n objects classified produce a dendrogram of n leaf nodes and $n - 1$ branch nodes. The branch nodes may be located in the diagram at the similarity level of the join represented, or may be ordered by the size of the subtree. The shape of dendrograms can be characterized by the frequency distribution of the numbers of subtrees of a given size (m_k subtrees with k leaf nodes) and by the number of "terminal singles" which are leaf nodes that are joined as singletons at the end of the process. Of course, by some measures, all dendrograms are the same "shape" for any given n, with the same number of leaf nodes, branch nodes and edges. Dendrograms' shapes can be compared to determine similarity based on probability calculations or on more recently developed approaches that use graph kernels.

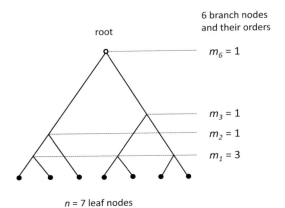

Figure 2.3 Dendrogram shape: one evaluation of shape is the numbers of subtrees of any given size (the number of leaf nodes included), often recorded as the orders of the branch nodes. Here the tree is drawn with equal heights for same-size groupings in triangular form.

because they represent species or sites that are not closely related to any group and should be more common in data that are not strongly structured into sub-groupings of the objects. Calculating the frequency distribution of the number of terminal singles, S, provides the expected values, and S is significantly larger than expected if $S > 1$ for $n > 10$, and (surprisingly) if $S > 0$ once n is greater than 40. That means that, for larger values of n, terminal singles should be very rare.

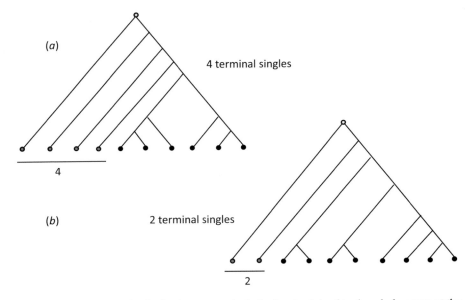

Figure 2.4 Terminal singles in dendrograms: single leaf nodes joined to the whole group at the end of the clustering process. Here the dendrograms are presented in their triangular versions.

2.1.2   Comparison

To compare two dendrograms of the same objects based on similar or different data, there are several methods, but the general approach was developed in the early 1960s (Sokal & Rohlf 1962), which uses the correlation of the values of the joins of the same pair of objects in the two classifications. One variant of this method is to use the correlation of the subtree sizes in which the pair of objects first occur together. The significance of the outcome can be determined by a simple randomization procedure that maintains the overall structures but re-labels the leaf nodes at random.

A more recent approach is to compare two dendrograms by a technique based on "kernels" or kernel functions, which was developed for trees in general. Kernels are mathematical functions used extensively in pattern analysis and machine learning (Shawe-Taylor & Cristianini 2004). A kernel is a function of two mathematical objects (like two graphs) that measures their similarity, based on an inner product or on a direct product of the two objects to map them into a more usable space (Shervashidze et al. 2011). Chapter 9 of this book describes one such kernel method for determining similarity that is based on random walks on the graphs. Imagine comparing a set of random walks (as described in Chapter 1) on dendrogram 1 with a set of random walks on dendrogram 2, more similar graphs will have more similar sets of walks. Interestingly, Oh et al. (2006) used the kernel approach in determining phylogenetic trees based on metabolic networks to quantify similarity from the original data and based their classification on those values. This approach has also been used in the analysis of natural languages (Moschitti 2006; Sun et al. 2011) and to compare characteristics of phylogenies of RNA viruses (Poon et al. 2013). In those phylogenetic trees, the patterns discerned in the analysis seemed to reflect modes of transmission and pathogenesis, and the authors concluded that the kernel approach represents an important new tool for characterizing evolution and epidemiology of viruses (Poon et al. 2013). That paper provides the information needed to apply this technique to comparing trees from ecological data, for example in studies related to functional diversity (see Petchey & Gaston 2002; Poos et al. 2009) and it seems like a smart thing to try!

2.2   Digraphs and Directed Acyclic Graphs

The next change in the rules of graph construction to be considered is allowing the edges to have directions, giving digraphs (Box 2.3) and other directed structures.

With digraphs, some of the familiar concepts needed adjusting. For example, a non-directed graph is connected when there is a path between any two nodes. In a digraph, if there is a (directed) path between any two nodes, it is *strongly connected*; if there are only semi-paths between some nodes with paths between all others, it is *weakly connected*. (The tree in Figure 2.5 is weakly connected because there are only semi-paths to the root node.) The other adjustment is in the possible existence of an edge in each direction between a pair of nodes, which is easy to see for symmetric interactions like associations, but it can apply to asymmetric interactions too. There can be edges

---

Box 2.3 Digraphs

Digraphs have edges that have direction, and any pair of nodes can have two edges between them: A to B as well as B to A. Properly, a cycle in a digraph is a directed cycle: that is a directed path from a node back to itself following the directions of the arrows on the edges. Not following the edge directions yields a semi-path and thus a semi-cycle. Digraphs have obvious applications for asymmetric relationships, such as the influence of one organism on another (whether positive or negative), but they can also be used to signal reciprocal relationships explicitly in contrast to unidirectional affects. Predation, competition, facilitation and other asymmetric interactions are portrayed by digraphs, but so are systems with physical routes for movement, flow or transportation; in those digraphs the edges often have weights to indicate capacity, rates or distances.

---

representing predation between the nodes representing species; consider the situation in which large fish of species A eat small fish of species B and large fish of species B eat small fish of species A. Schematically:

$$A \leftrightarrow B \text{ because } A \leftarrow B \text{ and } A \rightarrow B.$$

A system that has directionality and directed edges and no cycles combines some of the features of trees with those of digraphs. A directed acyclic graph (DAG, see Box 2.4) is a digraph that contains no directed cycles but may have semi-cycles (Harary 1969) (i.e. which would be cycles if the direction did not count); this is, its underlying graph may not be a tree and may have non-directed cycles (cf. Newman 2010, Section 6.4.2). Figure 2.5 shows a directed rooted tree, sometimes called an arborescence, and a directional acyclic graph. In the directed tree, there is exactly one directed path from the root to any other node, and at most one directed path between any two nodes; in the acyclic digraph, there can be several. Every arborescence is a directed acyclic graph but

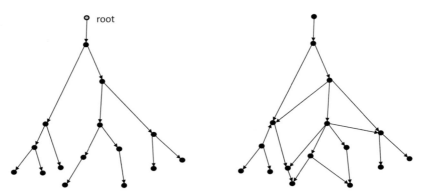

Figure 2.5 Directed and directional graphs. (left) A directed rooted tree is an arborescence and its underlying graph (undirected version) has no cycles. (right) A directed acyclic graph (DAG) is similar, but its underlying graph has cycles. Both are partial orders.

Box 2.4 Directed Acyclic Graphs

These DAGs are digraphs that have no directed cycles, and so are acyclic like trees. Unlike trees, however, they can have more than one path between any two nodes, but not all pairs of nodes will have a path between them. Their chief applications are in causal and data structures, but their ecological application can include the spatial context for physical paths like braided streams, anastomosing hyphal systems, or the trails or movements of animals (like transportation systems).

---

not every acyclic graph is an arborescence. Any directed acyclic graph has at least one source node of in-degree 0, and at least one sink node of out-degree 0.

Obvious examples of directed acyclic graphs are deltas and braided streams in hydrological systems, or the anastomosing networks of fungal colonies. These may have multiple paths between nodes, not just one as in a tree, but they can also have more than one source and more than one sink. Figure 2.6 shows a system of braided trails that form a graph with cycles (top), but the migration of a herd along those trails form an acyclic digraph (Figure 2.6a, bottom). The acyclic digraph does not need to be a connected graph (Figure 2.6b). Directed trees and acyclic digraphs arise naturally in many applications, including causal structures in epidemiology (Greenland et al. 1999); genealogical, phylogenetic, and recombinant networks (e.g. Strimmer & Moulton 2000); and search and topological ordering algorithms in computer science (Cormen et al. 2009). They are also key structures in the study of correlation, causality and the development of structural models (Mitchell 1992; Shipley 2000, 2009; Pearl 2009). In a rooted tree, the structure creates a "partial ordering" (see Box 2.5) of the nodes determined by (path) distance from the root (see Figure 2.7); similarly, DAGs give partial order to the nodes (Figure 2.6b).

As remarked, trees are also a standard format for data storage and retrieval, with a number of different techniques for organizing and finding information. A distinguishing feature for examining any of these trees is whether the nodes represent the same or different things. In a Minimum Spanning Tree, which provides a skeleton that joins spatially located nodes, the nodes are all the same (e.g. locations of individual organisms); but in a dendrogram, the leaf nodes and the branch nodes represent different things (e.g. individual units vs joins forming groupings of such units), and thus have different roles. The difference between the roles is reflected in their graph theory properties; for example, leaf nodes have degree 1 and branch nodes have degree 3 (or more). In digraphs, generally, and in DAGs, each node has both an in-degree (upstream neighbours) and out-degree (downstream neighbours). Some nodes will have only outgoing edges (sources) and some will have only incoming edges (sinks). In the functioning of the ecological system depicted by a digraph, sources and sinks obviously have different roles, and for intermediate nodes, the ratio or difference between in-degree and out-degree is expected to indicate role differentiation. Further on in the discussion of graph properties and system function, the topic of what can be understood about function

Braided trails

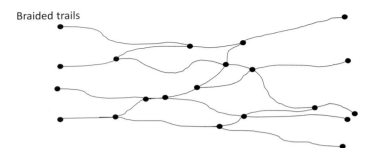

Acyclic digraph of migration routes followed

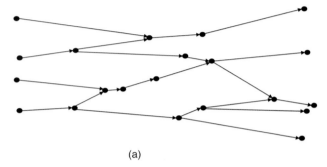

(a)

Acyclic digraph of migration routes followed
not be connected

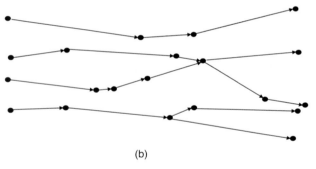

(b)

Figure 2.6 Braided trails created by wildlife movement can give rise to DAGs (acyclic digraphs) when herd movement or migration is recorded; these can be connected, as in (a), or not, as in (b).

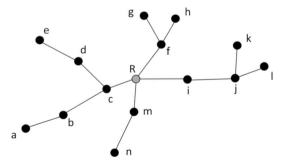

Figure 2.7 A rooted tree (no cycles, connected, one node identified as root) creates a partial order of nodes by distance from root: R < {c, f, i, m} < {b, d, g, h, j, n} < {a, e, k, l}.

Box 2.5 Partial order

A partial ordered set is one in which there is a pairwise relationship of some kind, say precedence, where the relationship is indicated for some pairs of elements in the set but not all. A familiar example would be the subsets of a given set with the relationship of inclusion: {a,b,c} includes both {a,b} and {b,c}, but there is no inclusion relationship between {a,b} and {b,c} because {a,b} does not contain {b,c} and {b,c} does not contain and {a,b}. Hence the relationship gives only a partial order. For a DAG, the relationship indicated by the directed edge gives a partial order, which is the relationship of a node to its downstream neighbours. A directed cycle for that upstream-to-downstream relationship would seem paradoxical; it would indicate A → B and B → C, but C → A, which seems to reverse the direction of the first two.

from network structure, as well as predicting structure from function, will be developed in greater generality and in more detail.

2.3   Weighted Directed Trees

Graphs can have weights associated either with the nodes or with the edges (or both). The analysis of data from streams and rivers, referred to as "dendritic" spatial networks, gives good examples of weighted directed trees and their usefulness in ecological studies (Figure 2.8).

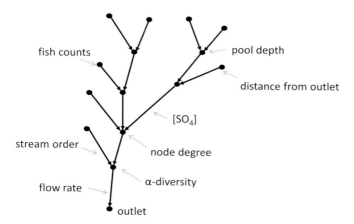

Figure 2.8 Dendritic aquatic system: stream variables that could be used as weights for nodes or edges of a directed tree representing a dendritic aquatic system include physical, chemical, biological and structural characteristics, such as pool depth, sulphate concentration, fish counts and stream order or node degree.

In a comparison of the determinants of juvenile Coho salmon densities, Flitcroft et al. (2012) used individual pools in a stream network as the nodes, with weights being the counts of the fish in them. Position in the network was determined by variables such as stream "order" (first-order streams have no tributaries, second order have only first-order tributaries and so on). The pools were characterized both by habitat variables, such as depth and boulders, and by "connectivity" measures of proximity to spawning habitat, winter rearing habitat and summer habitat. Their finding was that the network variables were better predictors of juvenile Coho numbers than the traditional habitat measures. In a more methodological work, Ganio et al. (2005) used counts of cutthroat trout as the nodes of trees representing stream networks to illustrate calculating variograms (Dale & Fortin 2014) in dendritic systems, as an approach to spatial pattern analysis.

The directionality in drainage networks is not only in the physical flow of the water, but also in the fact that downstream water bodies tend to have greater volume, potentially confounding position in the network with habitat "patch size" as factors determining species diversity. Carrara et al. (2014) used an experimental system of aquatic microcosms linked in different landscape structures ("riverine," "random" and "homogeneous") populated by protist species to separate these two effects on diversity. The tree nodes were the microcosms and their weights were their volume and their diversity. Graph characteristics of the nodes were their degree and their distance from the outlet (much like stream order or distance from the root). Patch size, node degree and distance to outlet were all found to affect α-diversity, but there was considerable dependence on the spatial covariance of the three in the riverine structures that most closely mimic natural stream networks.

The last example is also from a dendritic system, with data from the Maryland Biological Stream Survey (Ver Hoef et al. 2006) and with the nodes being stream junctions or delimiters of stream segments and the edges are the segments themselves. Here the weights, which are sulphate concentration, are known only for some of the edges, and the challenge was to model the variable for the entire system. This was achieved using spatial covariance models incorporating both flow and stream distance, leading to an ability to adapt many of the usual models for Euclidean distance for the tree structures.

2.4   Lattice Graphs

Some graphs can be drawn as regular geometric structures in two dimensions and are referred to as lattice graphs (Box 2.6). As one example, given a spatial grid of community composition data, cluster analysis can be used to create groupings of similar locations, which can then be mapped onto the grid. Often, constrained clustering will be used, so that only adjacent sites or groups of sites are joined at each stage of the process. Because this creates a lattice graph embedded in space, it is the same as spatially constrained cluster analysis.

As a specific application, consider a square lattice of nodes in a plane with edges joining only adjacent row and column neighbours (the "rook's move" definition). The edges

---

> **Box 2.6** Lattice Graphs
>
> These are graphs that can be drawn as a lattice in two dimensions: usually square, but possibly triangular or hexagonal. The edges then form a tiling of the plane, with all the tiles being the same shape, and all the nodes (except those on the boundary) having the same degree. Another view is that a lattice graph is made up of regular repetitions of the same small cycle. The lattice is most often regular but variations of irregular "lattices" are certainly possible, for example when based on geographic regions or political boundaries (see Box 2.7). In ecology, the main application of lattice graphs is for raster or grid data, such as surveys on square grid; each node that is not on a boundary of the lattice has degree 4, being contiguous with four other grid cells as neighbours. In a regular triangular lattice, each node has six neighbours. (In a hexagonal lattice, each has degree 3.)

are of two kinds: open edges allow transmission between the nodes, and closed edges do not. The question of interest is that of "percolation": if any given edge is open with probability q (and closed with probability $1 - q$), what values of q guarantee that there is (or is not) an open path from one side of the lattice to the other (Figure 2.9). The analogy in ecological applications would be the spread of disease through a population, such as a large plantation of trees (the nodes), based on the probability or rate of transmission between immediate neighbours. The phenomenon of percolation and its mathematics have been well studied and there are many known results available to ecologists who might apply this model to the spread of fire through a forested landscape or disease through a plantation. For example, the behaviour of transmission changes rapidly from very restricted to very prevalent near a critical threshold probability, q_c. For a square lattice, that value is 0.50. For natural populations, the square lattice may not be a good

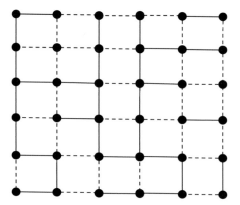

Figure 2.9 Percolation in a lattice graph with open and closed edges. Percolation through open (solid) edges is bond percolation. Are there paths from top to bottom or left to right on open edges?

Percolation through a square lattice graph. The nodes are open or closed
and are adjacent to their contiguous (rook's move) neighbours.
This is *site percolation*.

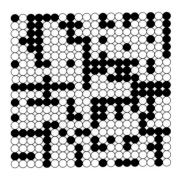

Figure 2.10 Percolation in a lattice graph with open and closed nodes. Percolation through a
regular square lattice graph of open or closed nodes by universally open edges between
contiguous (rook's move) nodes. This is site percolation.

model, and the value may be lower, such as 0.37 for a triangular lattice, which might be
a better approximation for defining spatial neighbours (Figure 1.20c). Just as a review
of percolation can be based on the ability of edges to allow passage, called bond percolation, it can also be approached with nodes that are either open or closed, called
"site percolation" (Figure 2.10). Despite all that has been discovered about percolation
on regular lattices, simulations with random graphs based on different neighbour rules
may provide the best comparisons for percolation results in ecological applications, for
which the underlying structure is often irregular.

In three dimensions, a rectangular lattice graph is essentially cubic, and each node
has six neighbours. Such a lattice graph fits with the use of voxels (3D volume cells,
cf. "pixel") for the analysis of remote sensing data (e.g. Wang et al. 2008; Bienert et al.
2010), and there are useful examples for comparison from medical fields from which we
ecologists might learn, for example brain structure and connectivity (see Loewe et al.
2014 for an application in neuroscience that combines voxels with a graph-theoretical
analysis of connectivity).

Box 2.7 Triangulation

A triangulation is a planar graph in which the edges create a tiling of the plane
made up of contiguous triangles. This creates a graph very similar to a lattice graph,
but not a regular lattice, that is useful for spatial analysis (e.g. epidemiological data
are often tabulated by township or county, producing irregular structures). A graph
such as that in Figure 1.20c is essentially an irregular version of a triangular lattice
graph and one way in which it is irregular is that not all the nodes have the same
degree.

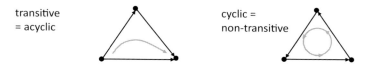

transitive
= acyclic

cyclic =
non-transitive

2 other possible shapes if reciprocal edges are allowed

Compare w_{AC} with $E(w_{AC})$...

Figure 2.11 Digraphs with three nodes and three edges. These include two triangles as digraphs, one transitive (acyclic) and one cyclic. There are two other possible shapes if reciprocal edges are allowed.

2.5   Triangles

Triangles are critical components of graphs, and have many uses and interpretations, mainly as subgraphs (it's all about subgraphs!). For example, they are the smallest cyclic structures in most graphs (although some digraphs may allow reciprocal edges on two nodes), they are used in measures of local edge density, and they are the basic unit of space-filling spatial "tilings," which are mosaics of contiguous polygons that cover the whole plane.

As with the regular lattice graph, triangulations can be used as the basis for a spatially constrained cluster analysis of compositional or other spatially referenced data. Some authors include them in discussions of lattice processes, even when they are irregular (Cressie & Wikle 2011, Figure 4.9). As mentioned above, they also provide the underlying structure on which to study percolation phenomena in natural systems.

One way to study the properties of graphs is to consider a null model of how a graph might form if the edges are placed between randomly chosen pairs of nodes (the Erdös-Rényi null model). For triangles, consider the question of how many there may be in one of these random graphs, which have undirected edges that occur independently between any pair of nodes with a constant probability, p. Connectance refers to the proportion of possible edge positions that are actually filled, and that should be close to the value of p in the Erdös-Rényi model. Triangles are fundamental to the measure called the clustering coefficient; it is the rate of "triad completion," the proportion of triplets of node with two edges that have the third edge as well. In a random graph based on the E-R model, what is the probability that three nodes have all three edges? It's p^3. What is the probability that three nodes have only two edges? It's $3p^2(1-p)$.

For digraphs, triplets of nodes with three directed edges can have cyclic or noncyclic (transitive) structure as already mentioned. In some cases, it is possible for two of the three edges to join the same pair of nodes with reciprocal directions (Figure 2.11).

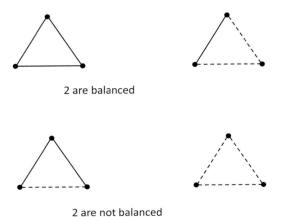

2 are balanced

2 are not balanced

Figure 2.12 Triangles with signed edges: two are balanced (even number of negative edges, here 0 and 2) and two are not (odd number of negative edges, here 1 and 3).

For graphs with signed edges (+ and −), a triangle can be "balanced" with none or two negative edges, or unbalanced, with one or three negative edges (Figure 2.12).

Lastly on triangles: looking at the interactions of three things in a graph (e.g. three species) as three nodes is the first step toward understanding the interactions of more than three. The third actor added to an interacting pair makes things complicated. Think of the "three-body problem" from physics (!), in which the addition of a third object renders the system more sensitive to small differences and less easy to make long-term predictions of the dynamics (Gleick 1987). In ecology, three-species interactions often result in unexpected or indirect effects such as apparent competition between prey connected by a shared predator (more on this in Chapter 4).

2.6   Smaller Than Triangles: Singletons, Isolated Pairs and Whiskers

In the discussion of triangles, it was mentioned that in a graph with edges occurring at random with probability p, the probability that three nodes have all three edges that form a triangle is p^3 in the random edge placement model. The probability that three nodes have only two edges is $3p^2(1-p)$, and $3p(1-p)^2$ for exactly one edge; for no edges at all it is $(1-p)^3$. Moving down from triplets of nodes to singles and pairs, consider the probability of an isolated node, a singleton, which has no edges at all; from standard probability calculations, that must be $(1-p)^{(n-1)}$, so the expected number of singletons is $n(1-p)^{(n-1)}$.

The probability of two chosen nodes forming an isolated pair (an unattached "toothpick"), following the same reasoning is $p[(1-p)^{(n-2)}]^2$; the expected number is then that probability times the number of such pairs, $n(n-1)/2$. Based on the interest in the numbers of terminal singles in dendrograms, calculate the probability that any node in a random graph has degree 1 (a leaf node or a whisker); that is $(n-1)p(1-p)^{(n-2)}$

Graph with crossing edges: not planar?

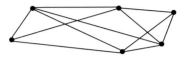

Redrawn as obviously planar

Figure 2.13 Planar graph: no edges cross, but the edges do not need to be straight lines. Using curved edges allows the graph to be drawn as obviously planar.

for an arbitrary random graph and so the expected number is $n(n - 1)p(1 - p)^{(n-2)}$. Results are also available for a tree or for a connected graph (Palka 1981). For a random tree, the expected number of these "pendant vertices" (leaf nodes) is $n(1 - 1/n)^{(n-2)}$. Remember that a tree of n nodes always has $n - 1$ edges, and so p is no longer a factor in the calculations and a randomly chosen tree is just one of the $n^{(n-2)}$ that are possible (Palka 1981).

These probabilities can be used for comparison in examining the graphs that result from ecological studies, although the random edge model is not often expected to be the most realistic comparator for ecological interpretations. There will be more to say about small subgraphs in the following chapters, the usefulness of which may not require the appropriateness of an underlying model.

2.7   How It Looks

The appeal and usefulness of graphs for ecological data are enhanced by the fact that graphs can be presented visually, which can greatly facilitate our understanding of the structure and our determination of how to proceed with analysis. What a graph looks like, however, depends in part on how it is drawn as well as on its actual underlying structure. The drawing of any graph should show its structure as clearly as possible.

Graphs are typically displayed on a two-dimensional surface, a screen or a piece of paper, even when they are created as multi-dimensional or projected to give the impression of a 3D structure. A planar graph is a graph that can be drawn in the plane without any edges crossing (remember, the edges do not have to be straight; Figure 2.13). With the exception of some spatial graphs, most graphs in ecological applications are not planar, but the visual confusion can be reduced by keeping the number of edge crossings to a minimum. There are no set rules for drawing graphs, but the main goal is clarity and effective use of the elements drawn, focussing on the "data-ink" that conveys the information. The criteria and principles for graphical excellence in graphs are the same as those for any other format for conveying quantitative information, and these have been clearly presented in *The Visual Display of Quantitative Information* (Tufte 1983). Elegance and effectiveness should be high priorities in how graphs are drawn. The ratio of data-ink to non-data-ink should be maximized "within reason," partly by the erasure of non-data-ink, again within reason (i.e. without sacrificing clarity) (see Tufte 1983, Chapter 4). Respecting that principle should include positioning the nodes so that more of the edges can be shorter, especially where the relationship between the nodes is strongest.

While there are no rules for drawing graphs, there are a number of metrics that can formalize the criteria introduced above (see Purchase 2002, and references therein). These are included to various degrees by the many algorithms available to draw graphs from their matrices (see Di Battista et al. 1994). In addition, there is a range of software packages that implement those algorithms for graph analysis and display (names that might be familiar include PAJEK, FoodWeb3D, igraph and Graphviz; see Juenger & Mutzel 2003; Newton 2010, Table 9.1). A search of the Web will provide up-to-date choices.

The drawing of a graph should portray its structure as clearly as possible because a drawing is the only way to present that information; other information can be provided by other means. For some interaction networks, for example each node and each edge may have a large amount of quantitative data associated with it. The temptation is to include much of it in the diagram, to provide as much information as possible all in one place. That may be a bad idea; too much data, coded or not, can make the drawing cluttered and detract from the primary purpose of depicting the structure that the graph represents. Aim for clarity.

2.8   Concluding Comments

To ease into thinking with graphs, it makes sense to start with the simpler forms, from trees and related structures that have no cycles, to triangles that are the smallest cycles and lattice graphs that consist of many copies of the same small cycle. These can be considered in the context of the shapes that graphs can take, but also in the context of the implications of simple rules governing the nodes and edges. Not only do the simpler graph forms introduce much of how graphs can be used, but they are also fundamental structures in the development of graph theory and in its application in the ecological context. The discussion has also allowed the introduction of some of the themes to be developed for more complex graphs, such as the importance of directionality and flow, the information contained in subgraphs, and comparisons of structural details with the null models of random graphs with simple rules.

Moving onward from the relatively simple topologies of trees and triangles, the next chapter introduces the potentially very complex graphs of species interaction networks.

The simple forms and concepts re-appear in the networks of greater complexity, as do digraphs and the results of independent edge placement in random graphs. The species interaction networks are complex in structure and complex in their function and dynamics, but graph theory provides the appropriate (and the only) approach to understanding both.

3 Species Interaction Networks

Introduction

Individual organisms interact with many other organisms, both of their own species and of others, and those interactions are of many different kinds. Textbooks often classify interactions based on their effects on individual fitness or on population numerical responses: competition is a $(-, -)$ relationship, predation is $(+, -)$, mutualism is $(+, +)$ and so on. This classification suggests that the interactions are pairwise (although they are probably more complex) and so graph theory, which is based on pairwise relationships, is an obvious approach to study these interactions. As ecologists, we can begin by studying one kind of relationship at a time: the trophic networks that result from predation, the positive and negative affinity associations among species within a community or individuals in a population, competition between functionally similar organisms, or the nested hierarchies of mutualisms like pollination or of antagonistic relationships like endoparasitism. It is possible to integrate different interactions "all at once," but the increasing complexities suggest that treating the categories separately, at least at first, makes sense. The "sum-of-all-interactions" concept will be discussed in more detail in Chapter 11, examining the interplay of network topology (the graph properties) and network dynamics (function and change). Whatever individual interaction is investigated, there are some features that are common to those interaction networks that graphs can portray, but we can also ask questions about their differences, such as whether there are network characteristics that are sufficiently distinct among interaction networks that they can be used to tell one kind of network from another.

The first and most fundamental assumption is that the structure of the pairwise connections portrayed by a graph can be analyzed and interpreted, with the findings applying back to the system itself in a number of ways, including through the dynamics of interacting populations (May 2006), as studied in network theory. Originally, networks were considered to be a subset of graphs distinguished by real weights or functions associated with the edges (see Chapter 1), but currently, the terms are used as equivalents; although graph theory might still be considered to be more general than network analysis and perhaps more formal. Network analysis is based on graph theory, but also includes elements of applied probability, statistics and modelling; network theory can be considered as a specialized branch of more general graph theory.

The second assumption is that the network's pattern of connections, the topology, affects the network's functions ("If you want to understand function, study structure";

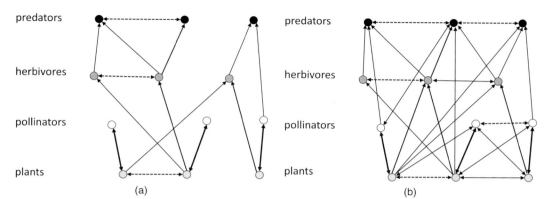

Figure 3.1 Network structure of species interactions. (a) Pairwise interactions and measured outcomes. Dashed horizontal edges are competition; upward edges are feeding links; bidirectional edges are mutualism. (b) Do more edges give more stability? Do stronger edges? Solid horizontal bidirectional edges are positive association.

F. H. C. Crick, quoted in Estrada 2012), and how they may change through time (Newman 2010). Obviously, the network's structure and function can influence the evolution (and coevolution) of the organisms in it (Pascual & Dunne 2006; Bascompte & Jordano 2014), but the structure and function of the network itself can be said to "co-evolve" (although the use of the same term can be confusing) by reciprocally affected changes. At any level, whether molecular, cellular or organismal, a system's form (or structure or topology) will be affected by the system's function, just as function is constrained by form (see Guimerà & Sales-Pardo 2006), as will be discussed further in Chapter 11. It is the reciprocal interplay of structure and function that makes the understanding of the structure so important for ecological applications. The third assumption is that some basic graph-theoretical characteristics (probably few in number) will identify key features of these interaction networks. There is virtue in summarizing these networks by a graph for clarity and visualization, but the important step is to use graph theory for better understanding. The fourth and last assumption in this list is that structural analysis and key network features can lead researchers to consider appropriate conceptual models and algorithms of graph formation (or "evolution"), and "signatures" that can be seen in those key features. Comparison of graphs observed from inter-specific interactions with those models will allow researchers to create and test hypotheses about features of these interactions.

The "interaction network" displays the outcome for a group of species, often with measures determined by the kind of interaction and the data used to evaluate it (Figure 3.1). In many ecological contexts, motivation includes the decades-long debate on the relationship between complexity and stability (see Thébault & Fontaine 2010); comparing Figure 3.1b with Figure 3.1a, a question is whether more edges or "stronger" edges somehow increase the stability of the system. The motivation for ecologists also includes our intense interest in biological diversity and the effects of evolution and

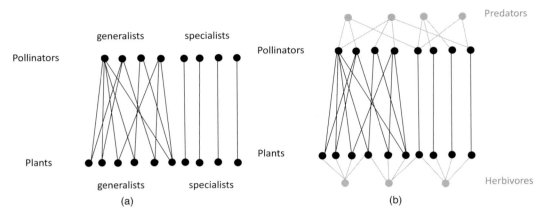

Figure 3.2 Bipartite graph of pollination network. (a) In considering only plants and pollinators, the specialist pairs seem not be connected. (b) The specialists among plants and pollinators would be seen to be connected if the plants' herbivores or the predators of the pollinators are included.

coevolution on that diversity, especially when driven by predation and parasitism, or pollination and dispersal mutualisms.

For both antagonistic and mutualistic interactions, an important feature is the prevalence of reciprocal specialization: for example, how rare is it for a pollinator to specialize on a single plant species, which has only the one pollinator. There are well-known instances, such as Darwin's prediction of a moth-orchid pairing (Darwin 1862), but is this a common phenomenon? Joppa et al. (2009) suggested that reciprocal specializations are not more common than expected from reasonable null models, but actually rare in a large sample of both antagonistic and mutualistic interaction networks. We can speculate about the implications of this finding both for the stability in these networks and for the coevolution of such species pairs. One graph theory approach to this question is to determine the correlation of the degrees of nodes joined by an edge; reciprocal specialization should give a positive correlation of degrees, produced by low values for the specialists on either side of the interaction and larger values for the remaining generalists (Figure 3.2). Nestedness produces the opposite condition with low degree nodes joined only to high degree nodes, causing low or negative correlation.

Not all the smart things ecologists can do with the data gathered over the years are based on graph theory, but it has an important contribution to make. The resurgence in studying ecological networks through graph theory, and the rich data now available permit a synthesis to be developed based on shared approaches to analysis. There is growing evidence that it is the distribution of interaction strengths and the configuration of complexity (that's the graph theory part) that determine network stability or resilience, rather than just the number or strength of the interactions (Ings et al. 2008). The interactions affect evolution and coevolution, and the whole network moderates or informs those effects (think of the community effects of the "arms race" between keystone predators and prey). Of course, many of the interactions are not truly pairwise and so studies of "two at a time" can be limited in insight. It may be necessary to study separately the whole expanded network that includes several kinds of relationships, identifiable node-neighbourhoods smaller than the whole graph, or well-defined clusters in the network, always considering that there may be reciprocal changes between the structure of the interaction network and the organisms in it, or between the network's structure and the dynamics it includes. Similar studies and advances in the application of graph theory are proceeding in other fields, parallel to those in ecology, including social networks, information networks, and brain networks (Estrada 2012).

3.1   Objects

Given a set of nodes that represent the species, there are many ways of determining which pairs are to be joined by edges depicting the interactions. As discussed in Chapter 1, many species interaction studies are based on counts, whether counts of organisms in sample units, counts of behavioural elements such as flower visitations, or counts of prey items consumed. This is not universally true, however, and competition outcomes may be evaluated by measures of such characteristics as individual height, weight, growth rates, reproductive output and so on. All possible edges could be included together with a weight for each one reflecting the measure of interest, or only a subset of edges, selected for inclusion based on a quantitative threshold.

3.1.1   Graphs

The basic structure of graphs is determined by the relationships being studied. Some interactions produce strictly bipartite graphs: pollination and seed dispersal mutualisms, for example provide a clear division into the plants, which produce the pollen or seeds, and the animal agents, including insects, bats, birds and so on. This requires nodes to be in two parts of the graph and the edges run only between and not within (Figure 3.2). Often, the organisms fall similarly into three clear-cut categories, giving a tri-partite graph, such as plant–herbivore–carnivore in a simple trophic network, although the trophic levels in real trophic networks tend to blur somewhat, with omnivores feeding at more than one level or intra-guild predation occurring within a single level (cf. McCann 2009; Holt 2009). An obvious advantage of graph theory is its ability to deal clearly with levels thus blurred. The basic structure of single-level communities have different complications: there inter-specific interactions may range from clearly negative like competition $(-, -)$; to clearly positive, mutualism $(+, +)$; with many variants between: commensalism $(+, 0)$, amensalism $(-, 0)$, facilitation $(+, 0?)$, inhibition $(-, 0?)$ and so on. There are also different forms of intra-specific interactions, such as inter-cohort competition or juvenile cannibalism. In addition, some critical inter-specific interactions are indirect, involving a third species beyond the focal pair and possibly from a different trophic level; for example, a plant may defend against herbivory by attracting and supporting its herbivores' predators. Even if the final resulting graph ends up as unipartite, different kinds of edges may be needed to portray accurately the range of interactions.

A bipartite graph has implicit directionality in the edges and the two-part structure means that some of the usual measures for ordinary graphs, such as average path length or a measure of node centrality, have less meaning or interest for researchers. Other characteristics such as compartments and nestedness are important in these bipartite graphs, but possibly less interesting or not applicable to the situations of many social networks. A third set of characteristics, such as the distribution of degree nodes or the bivariate distribution of neighbouring node degrees, are important in most interaction network graphs whether they are one, two or many layers. The graph characteristics most of interest will be determined by the ecological questions that motivate the study. One key characteristic is simply "connectance," the proportion of possible edge positions that are occupied, and so an important step in creating the graph of an ecological system is determining what counts as an interaction in the system, and thus how many edges there are (see Poisot & Gravel 2014). That determination will, in turn, constrain the nature of the graph itself, and of the substructures within it.

3.1.2   Subgraphs

One could say "It's all about subgraphs," but that would be an exaggeration. Let's say "A lot of it is about subgraphs." The search for clusters in graphs is essentially defining the best subgraphs according to specific criteria. Many of the graphs used in ecological applications are connected, almost by definition because all organisms have some interaction with *many* other organisms, but not all interactions may appear in a graph of the system being studied. A graph that is not connected consists of two or more *components*, which are defined as maximally connected subgraphs. The identification and characterization of giant or small components in random graphs identifies subgraphs (similarly for blocks, cut-points and units of compartmentalization). Figure 3.2a shows only plant-pollinator interactions, and consists of five connected subgraphs, which are not connected to each other. If the plants' herbivores are included, or the pollinators' predators, the graph would be connected (Figure 3.2b). Modules and motifs are specially defined subgraphs, as will be shown, as are the triplets used in determining transitivity or balance. These are all subgraphs defined by the structure itself.

Other kinds of subgraphs are defined in studying localized properties associated with neighbourhoods of individual nodes; each node and its first-order neighbours define the subgraph of interest. Some of the analyses that use graph theory are much like some forms of spatial analysis, but with space defined in more abstract manner, and studying the properties of neighbourhoods of individual nodes is exactly parallel to the use of local, as opposed to global, measures in spatial statistics (Dale & Fortin 2014, Chapter 6).

3.1.3   Modules, Clusters, Motifs, Triplets, Hubs . . .

For current purposes, "modules" and "clusters" are very similar in concept, being more or less well defined subgraphs, often with more edges within than between. Sociologists also use the term "community" for this kind of internal structure, which can be

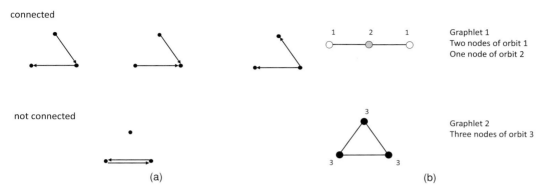

Figure 3.3 Motifs and graphlets. (a) Motifs for $n = 3$ and 2 directed edges; three are connected and one is not. (b) Beyond motifs: graphlets for $n = 3$. Graphlet 1 has two nodes of orbit 1 and one node of orbit 2. Graphlet 2 has three nodes of orbit 3.

very confusing for ecologists who use the same term in a different way. These modules may be of a range of sizes, but their existence gives rise to the concept of "modularity": a measure of how well the whole graph can be divided into identifiable modules and of how distinct those subgraphs actually are. This is an important feature of food webs: whether the whole trophic network is one web or whether it can be divided into functional sub-groupings of more tightly interacting species.

"Motifs" are even more specifically defined than modules, because a motif is a distinct arrangement of edges on a small subset of nodes. The usual approach is to use "triplets" of nodes and to enumerate the observed frequencies of all possible distinct combinations of directed edges on three nodes. There are 13 such triplets that are connected and those are the ones used, omitting the 3 that are not connected (Milo et al. 2002; Sporns & Kötter 2004; see Figure 3.3a). Examining a graph's structure by concentrating on the relationships among all triplets is another version of the "local statistics" approach. By evaluating and tabulating the structure of these triplet motifs, some of the larger-scale characteristics of the graph can be formulated, and different graphs can be structurally compared (e.g. Sporns & Kötter 2004). For example, Paulau et al. (2015) compared the observed and expected frequency of three-node motifs in node-ordered digraphs for food webs (the nodes have a strict ordering based on body size), and showed that including body size to distinguish among non-ordered motif frequencies provides better understanding of the food web structure and function. The appeal of studying motifs in networks of interactions is that the frequency and nature of these small subgraphs can provide insights into the dynamics of the functioning network (see Deshpande et al. 2005; Gollo & Breakspear 2014).

Another network structural feature often cited are "hubs." A hub is one of very few nodes with very high degree; such nodes are highly improbable in a purely random graph, but are to be expected in other models of network formation with preferential attachment of new edges to high degree nodes. These high degree nodes are common in some well-studied networks such as the Internet or airline routes (think of a highly connected airport). Hubs are often also cut-points, nodes whose removal disconnects big portions of the whole structure, as we well know from experience when an airport hub is closed by weather. There is clearly a close connection between the positions of hubs in the structure (and their degree) and the dynamics of the network in which they function (see Sporns et al. 2007 on hubs in brain networks). For example, Rozenfeld et al. (2008) used network analysis to identify hubs in the metapopulation structure of a seagrass, *Posidonia oceanica*, because these hubs are important features for gene flow and for sustaining the dynamics of the system.

3.1.4   Graphlets

The idea of using the occurrence and frequencies of small subgraphs throughout the structure of larger graphs began with motifs of 3 or 4 nodes (see Figure 3.3a for motifs of three nodes and two edges in directed graphs). Important structural properties of a graph or network can be determined by the frequencies of distinctive motifs in a range of applications from engineering and biochemistry to ecology (Milo et al. 2002). The concept has been extended to include *graphlets* of up to five nodes (Pržulj 2005, and thereafter) as an approach to comparing biological networks. It is not the frequency of the graphlets themselves that is important; it is the frequency of the occurrence of nodes in particular locations on the graphlets, called "orbits" that counts (Figure 3.3b). These have yet to be applied much in ecology (at time of writing), but more will be said on the topic in Chapter 11.

3.2   Properties

Graph theory, and the network analysis that is based on it, has defined and developed a broad range of properties and measures to help understand and quantify the structural features of the systems represented. Frequently, these have been produced specifically to investigate or reflect properties that are closely related to the function or dynamics of the systems being studied. This section will review many (but certainly not all) of these that seem to be most important in the ecological context, but the list is notably similar to those for other applications such as connectivity in the brain (see Rubinov & Sporns 2010), or for temporal networks in which the nodes have locations only in time (see Nicosia et al. 2013).

3.2.1   Asymmetry

This term appears often, in part because it is a fundamental property, but also because it is applied in many different contexts. Here are five to start (more will be discussed in Chapter 7):

1 Asymmetric relationships that are different in sign in their effect, such as parasitism being positive for one organism, but negative for the other, are suitably portrayed in a digraph, with edges of different signs running in different directions.

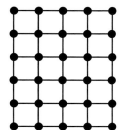 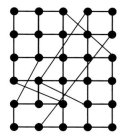

Figure 3.4 Lattice graph as a grid with $n = 30$ and $m = 49$. Right panel derived from the strict lattice by some re-wiring.

2 Even if the signs are the same, as in the (+, +) of mutualism, the effects on the two participants may be of different strength, giving another kind of asymmetry. Bascompte and Jordano (2014) suggested a measure for this property in plant-animal interactions, based on the difference between the proportions of interaction events accounted for ("mutual dependence asymmetry," their Appendix A).

3 In a bipartite graph of a particular interaction, asymmetry may just refer to the difference in the numbers of participants in the two strata: n_1 (the plants) and n_2 (the animals). A simple measure is then $W = (n_1 - n_2) / (n_1 + n_2)$. If the two strata have equal numbers, the asymmetry is zero. Bascompte and Jordano (2014) called this one "web asymmetry" (their Appendix A). In Figure 3.2a, this value is $W = 2/18 = +0.11$, which is very low asymmetry for such systems that typically are less balanced. For example, Bascompte and Jordano (2007) cited Eberling and Olesen's arctic tundra data with 30 plants and 76 pollinator species: $W = -46/106 = -0.43$. On the other hand, they (Bascompte & Jordano 2014) also cited an example of frugivorous birds and the fruit they eat in a Brazilian Atlantic rainforest with about 90 birds and 140 plants: $W = +0.27$.

4 In a bipartite graph of species interactions, only high degree nodes in one part (a host with many parasites, or a plant with many pollinators) may be adjacent to a low degree node in the other stratum (a highly specialized parasite or pollinator). Each such pair of nodes contributes to the negative correlation of adjacent nodes' degrees. This version of asymmetry is closely related to the familiar concept of nestedness and some authors refer to it as "dependence asymmetry" (see Dormann et al. 2009).

5 The "re-wiring" of a lattice graph, which starts with a regular structure of "short" edges by adding occasional "long" edges creates an asymmetry among the nodes, most of which have edges only to near neighbours, but others have long-distance shortcut edges to otherwise more distant nodes. See Figure 3.4. This could be called "node shortcut asymmetry," and it is one feature of the Watts-Strogatz "small world" model described in Section 3.3.3.

This does not exhaust the list of the types of asymmetry in graphs and networks as applied in ecological contexts, but it gives a start (more in subsequent chapters!).

A shared characteristic of most inter-specific interactions is that they are indeed asymmetric, even where the short-form summary has the signs the same, such as (−, −) or (+, +), quantitatively if not qualitatively. There may be legitimate concern, however,

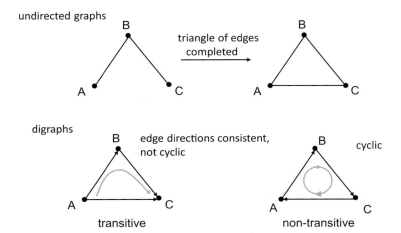

Figure 3.5 Transitivity. In undirected graphs, transitivity can refer to the completion of a triangle of edges on three nodes. In directed graphs, it refers to the consistency of flow direction in a triangle of nodes and edges; the directed edges do not form a cycle.

that perceived asymmetry can result from few observations of rare species versus many observations of common ones, creating an inbuilt bias in the data (Blüthgen et al. 2008). The two directions are often unequal in effect for the species involved, or of different importance for their success, such as obligate for one participant versus facultative for the other. This asymmetry is not usually so great that the interaction is reduced to a one-way outcome for the graph and a single directed edge between nodes, although that may be how it is portrayed for predation and in some cases for competition (a tournament with a single designated "winner" from each pair; Chapter 6). In looking at asymmetry of species specialization, the amount of specialization for each species is often evaluated simply by the number of edges for each node in an interaction graph, but this simple measure may be affected by interaction frequencies or network size (numbers of species; see Blüthgen et al. 2006).

3.2.2   Transitivity

The property of "transitivity" is based on triplets of nodes, and its meaning depends on context, depending on whether the edges are directed, and whether the relationships are symmetric.

Symmetric and Undirected Edges

For undirected edges depicting symmetric relationships, transitivity occurs whenever edges A – B and B – C also have the edge A – C (Figure 3.5). Used in this sense, it is closely related to the concept of a clustering coefficient, which is the proportion of two-edge triangles of nodes that are completed by the third edge.

Asymmetric and Directed Edges

For directed edges, "transitivity" refers to the property that when edges A → B and B → C occur, so does the edge A → C (Figure 3.5). The edge C → A is not the same and does not imply transitivity. This property is further discussed in the context of competitive outcomes: are there hierarchies of predictable competition results, with identifiable superior competitors that always out-compete the weaker one? Or, is competition not transitive so that A beats B, B beats C, but C beats A, as in the game "rock-paper-scissors"? Is it possible for a species that on average does poorly in competition to out-compete one that on average does well (a competitive reversal)? As an example, in a study of competition among four grassland species, Silvertown and Wilson (2000) found that competition among the four grasses was transitive with a pecking order of invasion rates, but that the actual order depended on the grazing regime. More will be said about competitive hierarchies and competitive reversals (see Grace et al. 1993; Shipley & Keddy 1994) in Chapter 6.

3.2.3 Nestedness

One type of asymmetry is the association of high degree nodes in one stratum of a bipartite graph with low degree nodes in the other stratum; for example, very specialized parasites are found on hosts of high parasite richness but only generalist parasites on hosts with low parasite richness (Vázquez et al. 2005a). This is the concept of nestedness familiar from studies of island communities: rare species tend to be found only at speciose sites and only common species occur at species-poor sites. A parallel finding from the studies of Vázquez et al. (2005b) is that abundant host species tend to have richer parasite fauna and have a higher representation of rare specialist parasites. Nestedness is a well-defined form of degree asymmetry, and it will be discussed in greater detail in Chapter 7.

3.2.4 Degree Distribution

The degree of a node is the number of edges that join it to others. For digraphs, in-degree and out-degree are distinguished. For signed graphs or signed digraphs, the degree can also be divided between positive and negative. The degree of a node tells something about its role in the structure, and the frequency distribution of the degrees for all nodes summarizes something about the graph itself; for example, a narrow range of node degrees, indicating a somewhat homogeneous structure, versus many singletons and very few nodes of very high degree (the hubs). The distribution of degrees can give clues as to the processes that gave rise to the network in the first place, but also provide information on how the network may be expected to perform. As a next step, it is often useful to examine the relationship between the degrees of nodes that are neighbours, looking at the correlation, positive or negative, among node degrees (see Figure 3.6). This property is often included within the context of the assortative or disassortative distribution of quantitative properties among neighbour nodes (Newman 2010), but one might also consider the bivariate distribution of the degrees of nodes that are separated

Degree distribution uniform
A regular graph

Degree distribution not uniform and disassortative:
three hubs, negative degree correlation

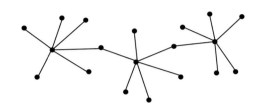

Degree distribution not uniform but assortative:
positive degree correlation

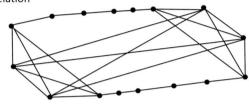

Figure 3.6 Degree distribution: if the degree distribution is uniform, all nodes have the same degree and it is a regular graph. If it is not uniform (here there are three hubs) and disassortative, the result is negative degree correlation of adjacent nodes. If it is not uniform but assortative, there is positive correlation of the degrees of adjacent nodes.

by paths of length greater than 1: 2, 3, 4 and so on. This approach is seldom pursued in ecological applications, but perhaps it should be.

3.2.5   Assortative Coefficient

Where nodes of similar degrees tend to be adjacent, low degree to low degree and high degree to high degree, the graph is said to be "assortative" for degree (Figure 3.6, bottom). The opposite, with a strong tendency of adjacency between nodes of low degree and nodes of high degree, is called disassortative (Figure 3.6, top right). This property for node degree, or for any other characteristic of the nodes, is measured by an assortative coefficient. This is obviously analogous to a measure of spatial autocorrelation in the space defined by the graph's own adjacency structure. It is also a measure of the relationship between the degrees of only first-order neighbour nodes (joined by an edge, which is a path of length 1), but it may be useful to look at the correlation of neighbours of second order, third order and so on.

3.2.6   Path Length

A path is an alternating sequence of nodes and the edges between them, with no repetition. A special case is a cycle, a path that begins and ends at the same node. For a simple

(a)

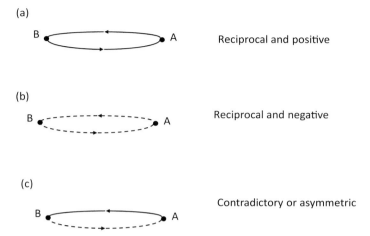

Reciprocal and positive

(b)

Reciprocal and negative

(c)

Contradictory or asymmetric

Figure 3.7 Reciprocity: two nodes can have reciprocal adjacency with (a) both edges positive, (b) both edges negative or (c) opposite signs being thus contradictory or asymmetric.

graph, path length is just the number of edges in the path. The graph distance between any two nodes is the length of the shortest path between them, and the diameter of the graph is the greatest graph distance between any two nodes within it. The concepts of length and diameter, and so on, become more complicated when the edges have associated weights that are actual physical (or other) distances. Then there is a distinction to be made between graph distance and physical or weight distance (as discussed in Chapter 1).

3.2.7 Reciprocity

In some digraphs, mutual outcomes are possible, allowing both A → B and B → A. In that circumstance, "reciprocity" is a measure of how frequently the relationship actually is bidirectional, usually as the proportion of edges that occur in a pair of edges between the same two nodes (Figure 3.7). This property does not arise in all applications, but when does arise in trophic networks, for example where it means A consumes B and B consumes A (perhaps at different life stages), there are interesting implications for feedback loops, the flow of energy and the cycling of elements. In competition, the expectation is that the relationship is mutually negative in its effect.

3.2.8 Centrality

"Centrality" is one measure of the "importance" of a node in the graph, related to how well connected the node is, or how well positioned it is in many of the shortest paths between other nodes. There are many "flavours" of this concept and many measures of it, as described in Table 3.1. Kolaczyk (2009) suggested some useful diagrams to illustrate

Table 3.1 Centrality Measures for Graphs (Figure 3.8)

Degree Centrality: In some treatments, a node's degree is used as a measure of its importance in the structure and is called "degree centrality." The basic concept of a node's degree is the number of edges attached to the node. This is the corresponding entry in the major diagonal of the degree matrix, $\mathbf{D}(v, v)$. In digraphs, the edges have direction, and so there is a distinction between in-degree and out-degree (the number of edges where v is the receiver or sink; the number of edges where v is the broadcast node or source).

Betweenness Centrality: The betweenness centrality of node v is the proportion of the shortest paths (measured by path length) between any pair of nodes in G that pass through node v. For applications related to information flow, the shortness of the path may be combined with the shortest of retention times at the node before the information is relayed to the next node in the path. In general, betweenness centrality is based on a comparison of the number of shortest paths between nodes u and w that include node v, call it $\sigma(u,w|v)$, and the total number of such paths $\sigma(u,w)$. It is usually scaled to run between 0 and 1:

$$C_b(v) = \sum_{u \neq v} \sum_{w \neq u \neq v} \frac{2\sigma(u, w|v)}{(N - 1)(N - 2)\sigma(u, w)}.$$

See Figure 3.8b.

Closeness Centrality: The basic closeness centrality measures the average path length distance, $\delta(u,v)$ from node v to all other nodes, u. Nodes with shorter distance to other nodes on average have a greater centrality. In general, for N nodes, closeness centrality, scaled to run from 0 to 1, is:

$$C_c(v) = \frac{N - 1}{\sum\limits_{u \neq v}^{N-1} \delta(u, v)}.$$

See Figure 3.8c.

Eigenvector (Spectral) Centrality: Includes all possible paths in its measure, not just the shortest paths, accounting for the greater importance of shorter paths by weighting each path by a factor based on its length, λ, α^λ for some constant α. The actual calculation by which this concept is realized can be based on the adjacency matrix $\mathbf{A}$ and its eigenvalues and eigenvectors: α^{-1} is the largest eigenvalue and $\mathbf{c}_e$ is the corresponding eigenvector. There are several versions of the measure possible, but the usual form is due to Katz (1953) and Bonacich (1972). This measure is:

$$C_e(v) = \alpha \sum_{(u,v)\in E}^{\mathbf{D}(v,v)} \mathbf{c}_e(u).$$

See Figure 3.8d.

Spatial Centrality: For a spatial graph, the betweenness and closeness centralities can be modified to use actual physical or geographic distance in place of the path length or geodesic distance of the original formulation: $d(u,v)$ instead of $\delta(u,v)$. A simple weighting of a node's geographic centrality in a spatial graph is its distance from location of the centre of gravity of all N nodes, γ, giving an index constrained to run between 0 and 1:

$$c_g(v) = \frac{d(v, \gamma)}{\max_u[d(u, \gamma)]}.$$

This weighting can then be used to modify existing measures of centrality into a spatially responsive form. It can also be the basis for weighting measures of edge centrality, as opposed to the measures of node centrality discussed so far. This is illustrated in Figure 3.8e.

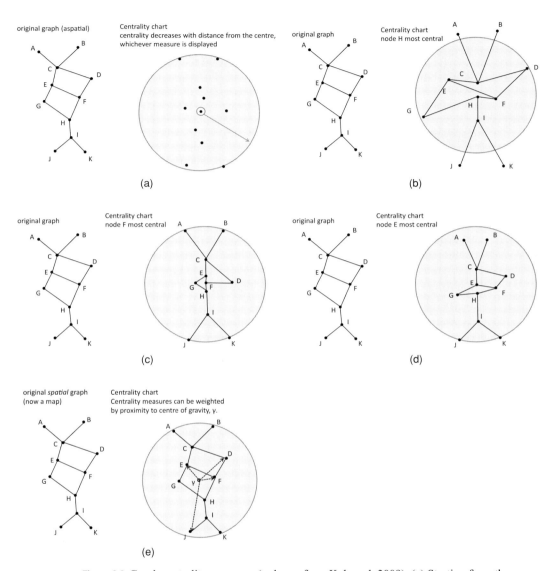

Figure 3.8 Graph centrality measures (redrawn from Kolaczyk 2009). (a) Starting from the same aspatial graph, each diagram shows a centrality chart in which centrality decreases with distance from the centre, whichever measure is being illustrated: (b) betweenness centrality, (c) closeness centrality, (d) eigenvector centrality and (e) now with a graph that is spatial: spatial distance centrality, which is proximity to the graph's centre of gravity.

the properties of centrality, which show the centrality of each node in a centripetal chart: centrality decreases with distance from the chart's centre (Figure 3.8a).

Centrality measures have many applications in ecology, and one obvious use is the evaluation of the importance of individual landscape patches to overall connectivity and the local migration and dispersal of organisms in the landscape (see Estrada & Bodin 2008). They have also been used in evaluating how social or trophic network structure affects individual parasite loads or diversity (Chen et al. 2008; Anderson & Sukhdeo 2011; Duboscq et al. 2015) and the transmission of disease through time (Kim & Anderson 2012).

3.3   Generative Models

One approach to understanding graphs and the properties they display is to create models of how graphs are formed, and with different assumptions, algorithms or parameter values, to determine the factors that could or might lead to the properties we observe. We can compare the observed with the results of the models based on different characteristics, although a few such as node degree distribution, path length and clustering coefficients are the most popular. Just as there are many characteristics to consider, there are also many different models that can generate graphs with different combinations of properties. The ones presented here are probably the three most commonly used for comparison and understanding. Part of the inspiration for investigating these models was to mimic or explain characteristics of large real networks, such as the Internet. These tend to exhibit (a) degree distributions with a small modal value, but a very long tail, related to very few nodes with very many connections (hubs); (b) "small world" characteristic of surprisingly short average path lengths between nodes; (c) clustering coefficient (proportion of completed triangles of edges) that is high for the edge density; and (d) assortativeness coefficient that is positive if not large, indicating some autocorrelation of characteristics among near neighbours.

The small world characteristic gets its name from the concept that the global social network ensures that no one in the world is more than six "degrees of separation" or six phone links away from anyone, Prime Ministers and Presidents included. This idea has a long history, but it is often credited to Karinthy (1929 as cited in Watts 2003) although best explicated in its modern form by Watts (2003). The culture of graph theory itself has its own version of this; each author has an "Erdös number," which is the number of co-author links that must be traversed to get back to Erdös himself as a co-author. My own is low (2), because I published with John Moon (see Chapter 2 of this book; and then Erdös & Moon 1964). (Remember that there may be 5000 researchers around the world with an Erdös number of 2.) A good topic for discussion with our ecology graduate students (over beer, perhaps) would be to determine the ecologist who would be the best choice as the "Erdös" of publications in ecology. (What's your MacArthur number?) Watts (1999) pointed out that the secret of small world social networks is that almost anyone can be considered central to the structure, with almost everyone just a few steps away. While the "six degrees of separation" idea is almost an urban myth, short inter-node path length is an important feature to characterize graphs of model networks.

The small world characteristic also takes the form of mutual adjacency, in which "my friends are your friends," giving a high clustering coefficient, and many triangular motifs in the network graph. In a slightly more diffuse form ("my friends are friends of your friends"), the graph is highly modularized, even if triangles are not surprisingly common, with a high degree of modularity (highly connected subgraphs) evident.

I cite Newman's (2010) book frequently in what follows, not that it is the only source, but it provides an authoritative and comprehensive review of this material, conveniently in a single work that is up-to-date and easily available. Kolaczyk (2009) has provided a very useful account of statistics for these structures and properties, which we ecologists may tend to neglect as being too technical; but certainly worth the effort.

3.3.1   Random Graphs (Erdös-Rényi or Poisson Random Graph)

The inquiry into the development and characterization of random graphs as null models for comparisons was begun by Erdös and Rényi in the late 1950s and early 1960s (starting with Erdös & Rényi 1960), building graphs in an unconstrained manner by sequentially adding edges to a set of nodes into random positions not already occupied. Edges can be added with a given and constant probability, or they can be added up to a predefined density, K edges for N nodes. The properties of such graphs are well known and understood; for example, the node degrees follow a Poisson distribution. Their properties, however, are not usually a good match for the graphs encountered in real networks, whether from sociology, molecular biology or ecology, or from transportation or communication network studies. Because they are purely random in their construction, they tend not to have much internal structure: no clustering, for example, and no correlation between the degrees of neighbouring nodes (see Newman 2010, Chapter 12). This is not surprising. In addition, if the edge density is low, the path length between randomly chosen pairs of nodes tends to be large or effectively infinite in that the graph may have disconnected components. Typically, there is one large connected component, the "giant component," and a few or many small ones. With increasing edge density, the average path length declines markedly, so that even very large random graphs can have short path lengths, as in the small world phenomenon. Even so, the clustering coefficient (the frequency of completed triangles of edges) remains low. All these characteristics, and many more besides, have well-studied properties and distributions in random graphs (see Newman 2010), which can then provide useful comparisons.

3.3.2   Scale Free (Barabási-Albert)

Unlike the random graph model, which adds edges but not nodes as the graph develops, the Barabási-Albert approach pictures a growing network to which nodes are added sequentially. Edges are added, too, as the network grows, but not in an unconstrained random way. Each new node has a set number of edges to add, c, but they connect preferentially, with the probability that a potential recipient node receives the new edge is proportional to the number of edges it already has. It's a case of "The rich get richer." to quote Watts (1999). Because each node has at least c edges, c of its own to start plus any number it acquires from subsequent node additions, the node degree distribution has a well-defined minimum at c (Newman 2010, Chapter 14). As a result of the preferential attachment algorithm, the degree distribution follows a power law: most nodes have a

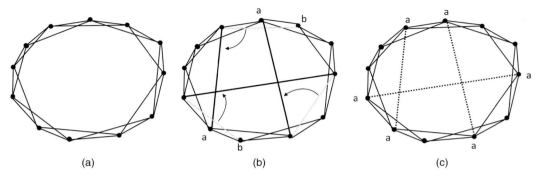

(a)   (b)   (c)

Figure 3.9 Re-wiring a ring graph. (a) Double ring graph of 12 nodes and 24 edges; each node has degree 4. The maximum distance between nodes is 3. (b) Rewired with three edges moved as indicated to create shortcuts. This creates nodes with degree 5 "a" due to gain and 3 "b" due to loss. The maximum distance between nodes is 2. (c) Rewired with three added "shortcut" edges as indicated. Six nodes now have degree 5, labelled "a." The maximum distance between nodes is 2.

small degree, with a small-valued mode, but there is a very long tail, with very few nodes have very large degrees (hubs), just as observed in well-studied networks like the Internet or airline routes (see Newman 2010, Chapter 8). The term "scale free" comes from the lack of definite end to or marked drop-off in the tail of the distribution (because it is governed by a power law); if present, that drop-off would indicate the inherent scale of the first-order neighbourhoods (Watts 1999; Newman 2010). The straight-line decay of the degree distribution, without a clear point of sharper decline, gives no indication of a limit to the maximum degree.

3.3.3   Small World (Watts-Strogatz)

This model is based on random "re-wiring" of an initial graph to create shortcuts between nodes that are initially distant from each other. The starting structure is typically a homogeneous "ring graph" of N nodes, each initially joined to its $2m$ nearest neighbours (most easily visualized as a spatial graph in the plane Figure 3.9a), giving $K = mN$ edges. The randomness and "long-distance connections" are added by moving one edge from each node to a randomly (and uniformly) chosen node with probability p, leaving the edge in its original position with probability $(1 - p)$ (Figure 3.9b). A variant is to leave the original ring graph intact and merely add random edges as shortcuts between distant nodes (Figure 3.9c; Newman 2010, Chapter 15). The result in either case is a graph with the small world property that the greatest distance between any two nodes is typically very short (remember "six degrees of separation") even for nodes that were very far apart in the original. This model resembles many real network graphs in its clustering and short path lengths, but the distribution of node degrees is tight and unimodal with a non-zero lower bound and a short but heavy upper tail, quite unlike the very long-tailed distributions often observed.

Table 3.2 Summary of Three Generative Models

Context: Large-scale real networks tend to exhibit (a) degree distributions with a small modal value, but a very long tail; (b) small world characteristics of short inter-nodal paths; (c) a clustering coefficient that is high for edge density; and (d) an assortative coefficient that is positive if not large.

Erdös-Rényi (E-R) (Random)

Process:	start with N nodes; sequential addition of edges 1 to K in random positions
Characteristics:	degree distribution is binomial to Poisson (bell shaped)
	path lengths surprisingly short for higher densities of edges (paths long for very low density)
	clustering coefficient low
	no clusters, no autocorrelation (node characteristics not assortative)
Note:	Some results apply to bipartite graphs, as well as to unipartite, but not all. The clustering coefficient in the unipartite projection of a bipartite graph can remain high as N becomes large.

Barabási-Albert (Scale free)

Process:	sequential node addition, each with c edges, but positively preferential edge insertion
Characteristics:	degree distribution: low mode, long tail governed by power law
	path lengths increase logarithmically with N, but are shorter than E-R
	clustering coefficient low, but higher than E-R
	no clusters, but assortative by node degree

Watts-Strogatz (Small world)

Process:	start with homogeneous regular graph, random re-wiring or edge addition
Characteristics:	degree distribution is compact, unimodal, with no long tail but not symmetric (more weight in the tail above the mode)
	path lengths short
	clustering coefficient high
	clusters of nodes, no autocorrelation (not assortative by node degree)

These are only three of many possible approaches to modelling the development of graphs. The fully random model sets a good benchmark for comparison, as a very simple null model, but ecologists should remember that the other two were developed specifically to mimic small world and scale-free properties observed in some social and anthropogenic networks (see Table 3.2). These are null models developed for a specific set of characteristics. They may not be the best descriptions or even good comparators for network graphs arising from natural species interactions, especially in the bipartite format appropriate for mutualisms and antagonistic relationships among species.

Some guidance for applying findings from unipartite networks to bipartite cases is provided by Newman et al. (2002) (see also Watts 2003; Newman 2010). The bipartite structure they considered began with (1) groups of people, and (2) the individuals that belong to the groups; edges run only between the two groups not within. These particular bipartite graphs represent what are called "affiliation networks" for obvious reasons; the individuals are related through their common membership in groups and groups are related through having individual members in common. Associated with the bipartite structure are two unipartite graphs: (a) a cluster diagram (undirected graph) of the groups with edges between the groups that are similar based on the individuals that are their members, and (b) a cluster diagram (undirected graph) of the individuals with edges between those that are similar based on the groups of which they are members (Watts 2003, Figure 4.6). The comforting result is that most of the properties discovered for random unipartite graphs (E-R model) extend naturally to random bipartite graphs or to their unipartite projections. What emerges, however, is that there are some important differences. In a random unipartite graph, the clustering coefficient declines as the number of nodes increases, but a fully random bipartite network will continue to exhibit a high degree of clustering as N increases, despite the fact that there is no extra structure built into it, just because of the way the graph is constructed (Newman et al. 2002). This insight is very helpful in interpreting structural features of the bipartite graphs we use in studying mutualistic or antagonistic species interactions. These ecological bipartite graphs do not arise in exactly the same way as the original affiliation graphs, but the properties should be the same. For example, a pollination network is the equivalent of an affiliation network because plant A belongs to groups defined by its pollinators, one group per pollinator, and the pollinators can be grouped according the plants they pollinate, A, B, C, D and so on, thus creating an affiliation network in either direction, as in the social grouping case that gave rise to the concept. This comment applies equally well to other ecological interactions that give rise to bipartite graphs.

3.4   Comparisons

3.4.1   Comparing Observed Network Graphs with Models

For comparing observed graphs to models, Table 3.2 gives an obvious place to start: a beginning can be made by comparing the shape of the degree distribution, the characteristic path length or average inter-node distance, the clustering coefficient and clustering and assortativity measures with those typical of the various models available with the same number of nodes and same density of edges. Watts (1999) provided a good example of this comparative approach. He tabulated the number of nodes, average degree (equivalent to edge density), characteristic path length, clustering coefficient, a model-independent shortcut index, φ, and a contraction index, ψ, for a number of real network graphs to illustrate the characterization of network graphs by their properties.

The last two measures may be unfamiliar. The first is related to the concept of a "shortcut," defined as an edge between nodes i and j which if removed results in the shortest path remaining between edges being of length greater than 2 (consider Figure 3.9b). That means that there is no triangle of edges on edge i to j; neither is it a bridge whose removal disconnects the graph. The index, φ, is the proportion of edges that are shortcuts thus defined. The second index, ψ, is the fraction of all the pairs of nodes that have no edge between them and that share one and only one neighbour. Obviously both these indices are based on the existence (or not, in this case) of triangles of edges in the network graph.

In the comparison that Watts (1999) compiled, three network graphs were used for illustration. The first is the "Kevin Bacon Graph," documenting the association structure of actors in films based on joint appearance with and separation from joint appearance with Kevin Bacon. This is the film equivalent of the graph theorists' Erdös number, well almost… The second example is the Western States Power Graph which details the structure of the electricity transmission grid in the western USA. The third example is the neural network of the nematode *Caenorhabditis elegans*, one of the most completely "decoded" organisms in the scientific world.

To compare these real graphs with models, the main focus of Watts's (1999) investigation was on the characteristic path length (one aspect of the small world property, the title of the work after all!) and the clustering coefficient (a small world property related to the presence of internal structure). Where a model is well defined and its properties are known, as for the Erdös-Rényi model, the observed value of a measure can be compared with its expected value, given N nodes and K edges. In comparison with the fully random (E-R) graph, all three real graphs had high values of the clustering coefficient, indicating significant amounts of small world internal structure; the social network and neural network had small values for the characteristic path length, comparable to the random graph, but the transmission network had longer paths between nodes than expected. The conclusion from these comparisons was that all three networks had graph-theoretical properties associated with the small world phenomenon (Watts 1999). The use of path length and the clustering coefficient continues to be an appealing approach to the evaluation and comparison of networks for different sizes and edge densities in a number of applications (see e.g. van Wijk et al. 2010).

3.4.2   Monte Carlo Graph Generation

In theory, the advantage of comparing real network graphs to theory-based graph models is that the models can be engineered to resemble the characteristics of the networks being studied. For example, it is often desirable to make comparisons with random structures that have been created with the same distribution of node degrees as the original network of interest (Newman 2010, Chapter 10). Clearly this is a kind of restricted randomization and its possibilities are limited only by programming and the potential lack of independence among the network properties constrained to give the best comparability with the observed structure. There are also practical limitations depending on the size of the network to be imitated (very large networks can present computational challenges even today), but in theory, again, large numbers of random-but-constrained networks can be generated in a "Monte Carlo" approach, thus producing distributions of the measures of interest.

The other form of constrained randomization that can work well in this context is the repeated permutation of observed structures to generate distributions for evaluating observed parameter values. Straying a bit from ecological applications, in a study of the modular dynamics of human brains, Bassett et al. (2011) randomized the edges from an observed network structure to show that its modularity was very significantly high. This approach is certainly within the range of methods ecologists can and should take advantage of in their own research.

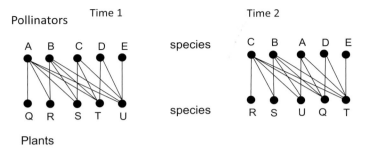

Figure 3.10 Bipartite graphs for ecological interaction intensities change with season or year. All network properties of connectance, nestedness, degree distribution, assortativeness and so on are unchanged.

3.4.3   Comparing Two or More Observed Network Graphs

Comparing two observed network graphs is not necessarily the same as determining how similar they are, as discussed in Chapter 1. Consider two graphs on the same set of labelled nodes and with the same number of edges. A high proportion of the edges may occupy the same positions in the two graphs, giving a high similarity between them, but with important differences in such characteristics as degree distributions or assortativity. For example, comparing the graphs in Figures 3.9a and 3.9b, the graphs share 21 of 24 edges, but have different degree distributions and different graph diameters. On the other hand, it is possible under the same conditions to have two graphs that are very similar in their properties, but differ markedly in the positions occupied by the edges (just consider relabelling the nodes!), as shown in Figure 3.10. As one of many examples, in a study of plant-pollinator networks in the sub-alpine over several years, Burkle and Irwin (2009) found that although joint flower-insect interaction frequencies changed from year to year, properties like connectance and nestedness did not; nor were these properties affected by nitrogen addition.

The Monte Carlo approach described in Section 4.3.2 has potential, but each observed network is like a single realization of some underlying model (unknown) with many possible (unknown) parameters, and we researchers do not have the opportunity to observe many realizations to evaluate the range of variability, nor do we have the opportunity to "tune" the results by examining a range of values for the parameters. (We don't even know what the parameters ought to be!) The outcome is that while we can compare many runs of two models, one for each network to be compared, and we can then examine similarities and differences between the distributions, we will not know how well the models actually represent the structure and processes that underlie the two networks of interest.

That may leave only comparing individual values of measures thought to be important indicators of relevant characteristics for the two network graphs. The comfort is that interpreting these results can be informed by "playing with" "reasonable" models of the two networks so that we understand better the performance of the measures we have chosen and their response to changes in the parameters that govern the structure. Again, there are theoretical and practical limits on what can be accomplished, but it should be an improvement over simple naïve comparisons of a large number of characteristics.

3.4.4   Randomization by Edge Permutation

Most of these comments apply not only to network graphs in general, but also to bipartite graphs, with modifications to distributions generated for null hypotheses. For example, in a fully random graph for a bipartite structure, there are limitations on the positions for edges, allowing only $n_1 \times n_2$ possible positions. This is fewer than the $\frac{1}{2}(n_1 + n_2)(n_1 + n_2 - 1)$ available in a unipartite graph with the same number of nodes; for example, for a total of ten nodes with five in each part, the number of edge positions is only 25 in the bipartite version, not 45. With these or similar modifications to account for the structure, most of the results from the general case can apply.

3.4.5   Graph Kernels

Recent and current developments for the comparison of graphs and for measuring their similarity have been based on "graph kernels" (Gärtner 2003, 2008; Vishwanathan et al. 2010; Shervashidze et al. 2011), related to the general use of kernel functions for pattern analysis and machine learning (Shawe-Taylor & Cristianini 2004; Gärtner 2008; Hofmann et al. 2008). A kernel is a function of two mathematical objects (such as two graphs) that measures their similarity, and it is commonly used in applications such as pattern analysis to compare structures in mathematical space (e.g. two sets of multivariate data in s – dimensions; think of principle components analysis data). The kernel function is often based on inner products in the mathematical space in which the objects (e.g. the graphs) exist, or on a direct product of the two objects (Shervashidze et al. 2011). This approach is popular in machine learning where the graph kernels can be based on (random) walks, shortest paths, small subgraphs of limited size (like motifs or graphlets), or subtree patterns (Gärtner 2003; Bunescu & Mooney 2005; Shervashidze et al. 2011). Figure 3.11 gives two graphs to be compared; short independent random walks beginning at nodes 4 and 4′ (or nodes 1 and 1′) will often be the same similarities based on the structures of the graphs; the graph kernel captures those similarities in a computationally efficient way.

The basic advantage of the kernel approach comes from the concept of mapping a mathematical object, x, from its own data space into a "feature space" in which analysis is simplified, by some mapping function $\varphi(x)$. In order to compare two objects of interest, x and x', mapping them both explicitly with function φ may pose computational complexity for more detailed objects; but the explicit mapping may not be necessary because a kernel function, $k\,(x, x')$, can be based on their cross product from which $k\,(x, x') = <\varphi(x), \varphi(x')>$. The stratagem that avoids the explicit mapping is sometimes called the "kernel trick" (Hofmann et al. 2008), but the usefulness is that the kernel function itself measures the similarity of x and x', because it takes higher values with more features they share (Gärtner 2003, 2008).

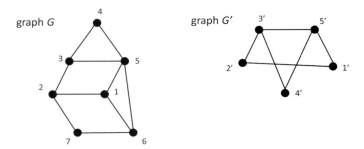

Figure 3.11 Two undirected graphs to be compared by graph kernels based on random walks (based on Vishwanathan et al. 2010). Independent random walks beginning at nodes 4 and 4′ (or 1 and 1′) will often be similar based on the graphs' structures.

This is an interesting and directly useful approach to comparing graphs, but as far as I know, it has yet to be used in ecological applications, although closely related techniques based on motifs to compare internal substructures of graphs have been used to good effect (e.g. Stouffer et al. 2007). One aspect of this technique that is not clear is whether it can be refined to identify parts of the graphs that are most or least similar, to determine what characteristics are most or least similar, or how similarity changes with scale, such as the size of the subgraphs used in the kernel. More details about this approach and its properties will be provided in Chapter 12.

As described in Chapter 2, tree-based kernels are an obvious approach to comparing the dendrograms or classification structures and have been used in the analysis of natural languages (Moschitti 2006; Sun et al. 2011) and in phylogeny (Poon et al. 2013). I have not seen this approach used in ecological studies, but the models are there to follow and Poon et al. (2013) have provided a good example of its use in a biological application.

3.4.6   Special Case of Graph Comparison: Distances

If the two graphs to be compared are on the same nodes and the nodes can be located within some kind of space, most easily a spatial context but not necessarily, and **if** the two graphs are based on independent sets of data, their similarity can be tested using an eigenfunction decomposition. For graphs with undirected edges (symmetric relationships) Moran's eigenvector maps ("MEM" eigenfunctions; Dray et al. 2006) can be used, and for digraphs, the parallel method is the use of asymmetric eigenvector maps ("AEM" eigenfunctions; Blanchet et al. 2008). The method begins with the graphs represented as standard adjacency matrices in binary form, or with non-zero weights for adjacent nodes, which is then converted to a distance matrix. Without giving the details here (see Borcard et al. 2004; Dray et al. 2006, 2012; Blanchet et al. 2008, 2011), the graphs are converted to eigenvectors and then a generalized Pearson correlation coefficient, called *RV* (for vector correlation; Escoufier 1973; Abdi 2007), is calculated to evaluate their similarity. (This measure is available in R, as ***coeffRV*** in FACTOMINER.)

of changing spatial aggregation on the results of analysis is called the "modifiable area unit problem" (Openshaw 1984; see Dale & Fortin 2014, Section 6.3).

An additional complication is that, if the relationship between predators and prey depends on their phylogenetic histories (see Ives & Godfray 2006), the aggregation of taxa may blur what might otherwise be clear results. Lastly, when considering the dynamics of and changes to trophic networks, aggregation of possibly sporadic species may give an exaggerated impression of persistence and stability where it is actually absent (cf. Olesen et al. 2011a; Petanidou et al. 2008).

This all sounds bad, doesn't it? But ... aggregation may be unavoidable, and it does have some benefits. While taxonomic aggregation can have a big effect on perceived structure, it is often not the result of error or lack of effort; it may be unavoidable based on the limitations of the study, its methodology or its data requirements. Sometimes we cannot know the taxonomic details. Aggregation may be preferable if it allows a quantitative evaluation of the aggregated taxon where that would be impossible with non-aggregated information. In his discussion of ecological food webs as networks, Newman (2010) suggested that this aggregation of many similar taxa into "trophic species" has the benefit of simplification, which may be worth the small loss of information. In addition, in some cases, separate species of forbs, as food plants, may be more similar for the herbivore in all the functionally important ways than different chemical races of the same species, especially those based on anti-feedant chemicals (e.g. cyanogenic vs acyanogenic genotypes; see Jones 1966). An additional factor in the Kluane example, as in many others, is that anti-feedant chemicals in plants can change through time and may be induced by herbivory, although their role in driving herbivore (snowshoe hare) demography in the Kluane system seems to be minor (Hodges et al. as cited in Krebs et al. 2001).

4.2.3   Trophic Hierarchy

One clear theme in the use of graph-theoretic measures is the evaluation of a general property of "orderliness" in ecological systems. In the case of trophic networks, one particular form of orderliness is the degree to which the network has consistent and clearly defined trophic levels, with each species being unambiguously in one of the well-defined levels. In the ideal, primary producers (usually plants) occupy trophic level 0, herbivores (grazers) feed on the plants and thus occupy level 1, those that feed on the herbivores occupy level 2, and so on (Figure 4.7a), giving exclusive membership in each level. In real trophic networks, omnivory and other variants of mixed diets that upset the simple scheme are common (see Figure 4.1), and a number of proposals have been provided for the calculation of (non-integer) trophic levels for species under such circumstances (see, among many others, Williams & Martinez 2004; Thompson et al. 2007), whether based on proportion of prey items or on biomass consumption ratios. Even the bottom level of the hierarchy can add confusion with many bacteria and algae being mixotrophic, with the ability to use different sources for energy, such as either light or chemical, photosynthesis or phagotrophy (see Hammer & Pitchford 2005; Eiler 2006). Even among terrestrial plants, there is the ambiguity caused by plants that are

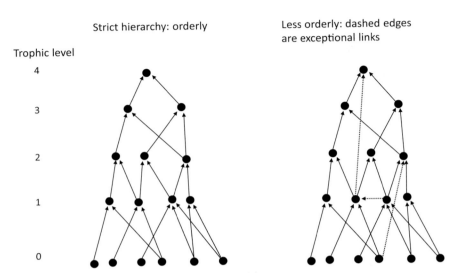

Figure 4.7 Trophic hierarchies: strict with well-defined levels or less orderly with exceptional links blurring the levels.

both autotrophic and parasitic: "hemi-parasites" (Smith 2000). Having determined a hierarchy of trophic levels, even if neither strict nor with consistent integer values, it may be useful to determine how some of the basic graph statistics vary with level, for example average degree (in- vs out-degree) or the distribution of node degrees by level. In a study of the trophic networks of fish in tropical streams and swamps, Winemiller (1990) found that the distribution of trophic levels calculated in a trophic continuum were very similar among systems despite large variation in species compositions; fish that fed at more than one trophic interval were "extremely common" in all the networks. In addition to the question of how to assign appropriate trophic level values in non-strict trophic networks, another challenge is to provide an appropriate graph-theoretic measure of how close or how far any trophic network is from the ideal strict hierarchy (Figure 4.7). That is a question about the orderliness of trophic networks, and there are more: what are the correlates of greater or less order? Is there predictable variation with system or geography?

Any questions about the trophic hierarchy of a food web are going to be related to the food chains in the network, which are the paths of directed edges from the bottom of the network to the top, and lengths of those chains (and the variance of chain length). Digraphs of ecological trophic networks are "acyclic," with no cycles of the directed edges (see Newman 2010), and some characterization of the nature of the structure would be useful. In addition to obvious statistics for comparing trophic networks such as number of species, number of edges and number or proportion of predators, measures of average chain length, trophic levels and connectance are commonly used (see e.g. Kitching 2000); but measures of hierarchical orderliness seem to be lacking.

A simple measure is the number of edges that have to be deleted or moved to make the observed network strictly hierarchical. A second measure would be to use every food

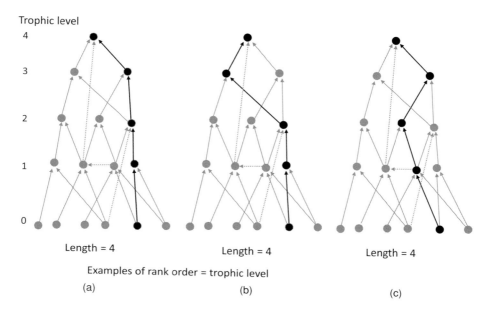

Examples of rank order = trophic level

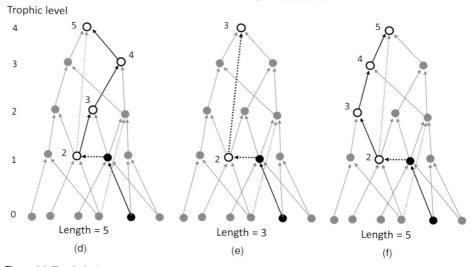

Examples where rank order and trophic level differ

Figure 4.8 Food chains in a trophic hierarchy. The length of the chain depends on the links included and the use of the exceptional links. (a–c) Chains of length 4. (d–f) Chains of length 3 to 5. Range of chain lengths = (3, 5); $R/L_{max} = 2/5 = 0.4$; variance/mean = 2.83/4.17 = 0.68.

chain in the network and record for each node its rank order in every chain of which it is part. Then, each node has range score of the range of ranks it takes in all the chains relative to the maximum rank it could achieve, and the whole network gets the average of all those scores. Figure 4.8 shows the same approach based on the lengths of all possible food chains between one node at the base of the trophic network and the one at the

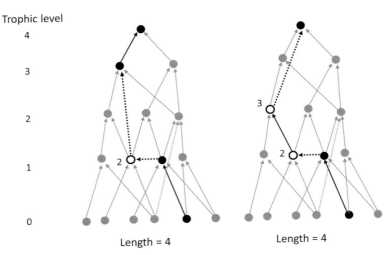

Figure 4.9 Food chains in a trophic hierarchy: alternative examples in which the rank order is not equal to trophic level where indicated, but the chain length is unchanged.

top. The range of lengths relative to the maximum length or the variance/mean ratio for chain lengths would be a suitable statistic. Chain length however, is not the best indicator; Figure 4.9 gives examples of chains in which rank order and trophic levels do not match, but the chain length is unchanged. Therefore, the suggestion is to use the chain order rank for each node over all possible food chains to give a variance/mean score, which can then be averaged over all nodes (Figure 4.10). Obviously, a strict hierarchy will produce an average of 0, because all nodes in all chains will have a rank equal to their average trophic level, thus having individual scores of 0. This seems to be an important measure for trophic network studies because both chain length and omnivory

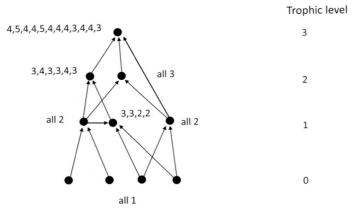

Figure 4.10 Ranks in food chains in a trophic hierarchy: the non-zero rank variances are 0.364, 0.267 and 0.333; the variance/mean ratios are 0.091, 0.08 and 0.13. The average for the six non-basal nodes is 0.05.

Separable into
compartments   Less separable

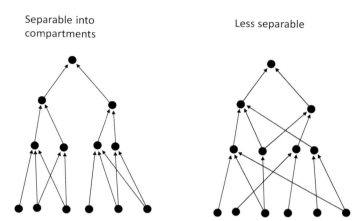

Figure 4.11 Compartments in artificial strict trophic hierarchy networks: clearly separable into compartments versus not easily separated.

(or other departures from the textbook model of strict hierarchies) are expected to affect population and community dynamics (see, among many others, Morin & Lawler 1996), with omnivory now recognized as common, and weak omnivory recognized as a stabilizing influence (see Thompson et al. 2007; McCann 2012).

4.2.4   Compartments and Sub-webs

The term "compartments" refers to the separation of a food web into "sub-webs," within which many strong interactions take place and between which there are few (Krause et al. 2003). Compartments in food webs or trophic networks are the equivalent of "modules" or "clusters" in other applications of graph theory. It is easy to imagine a food web consisting of two recognizable sub-webs or compartments united by the top level, or two, of a textbook trophic structure hierarchy. Perhaps the sub-webs are determined by the phases of a landscape mosaic of forest and grassland, with different plants and herbivores in the two parts; or perhaps benthic versus planktonic parts of a shallow marine system (Krause et al. 2003), or lentic versus lotic components of a watershed. Whatever the basis for the sub-web separation, here the trophic network can be divided fairly cleanly into two compartments (Figure 4.11, left), unlike those where there is no clear compartmentalization (Figure 4.11, right). Real trophic networks are not likely to be cleanly or clearly separable in this way, but this gives rise to the questions of how separable or how close to being separable into compartments any particular trophic network actually is (Krause et al. 2003) and how best to measure that property (see Table 4.1 for one approach). Again, this is the trophic network equivalent of asking how modular or clustered a given graph of social interactions is. For the function of ecological systems, however, the most important point is that compartmentalization seems to enhance the stability and persistence of trophic networks (Teng & McCann 2004; Stouffer & Bascompte 2011; see also Thébault & Fontaine 2010; Rozdilsky et al. 2004).

Table 4.1 Using an Odds Ratio Approach Based on the Frequency Table for Potential Predator-Prey Pairs to Determine the Compartmentalization of Trophic Networks

	No Predation	Predation
Different compartments	A	B
Same compartment	C	D

Note: See Krause et al. (2003).

The procedure is to assign the taxa to non-overlapping compartments, but the prior specification of the number of compartments is not required. The odds ratio is AD / BC and increases in this ratio signal more effective compartments; significance is determined by a Monte Carlo procedure. They used weights for the predation interactions: interaction frequency, measures of carbon flow (gC m^{-2} y^{-1}), or interaction strength (see Neutel et al. 2002), and the software "KliqueFinder" (Frank 1995) to find compartments in several versions of each of five well-documented food webs (Ythan Estuary, Little Rock Lake, Saint Martin Island, Chesapeake Bay and a cypress wetland; see their Appendix A for details). The method identified significant compartments in three of the five food webs, and the ability to detect compartments was influenced by food web resolution, such as using interactions with weights, and by taxonomic aggregation. By combining methods from physics for network analysis with phylogenetic statistics, Rezende et al. (2009) showed that compartments identified in large marine trophic networks were associated with body size, phylogenetic relationship and spatial structure.

A closely related concept and approach to characterizing the structure of trophic networks, and the flow of energy through and within them, is the search for strongly connected components (Allesina et al. 2005); these are the largest sets of nodes that are mutually reachable by directed paths in the digraph (Figure 4.12). This is called

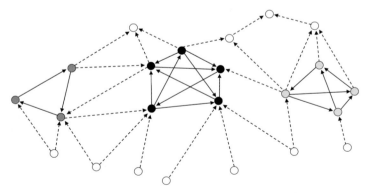

Figure 4.12 Strongly connected components: three multi-node components are identified by shading. Edges of solid lines are within components; dashed lines are between. Most components consist of only one node.

strongly connected because the directions of the edges are taken into account in identifying a path from node i to node j. This definition ensures that these components are node-disjoint, and thus each one is a compartment as well. These components must have cycles to permit mutual reachability, and so the network is bound to look very different from the textbook hierarchy like the one in Figure 4.1, in which most strongly connected components will be individual nodes because cycles of edges are unexpected. Strongly connected components are an extreme version of the basic concept of the "separability" of a food web into compartments. Just as food chains and food chain lengths are important manifestations of the flow of energy through a food web, strongly connected components are important structural features related to cycling dynamics in these systems (Allesina et al. 2005).

An obvious simplification of the original network is to replace each strongly connected component by a node in a derived graph with edges showing the flow of energy between these component nodes. The derived graph is a digraph, but because the components are mutually reachable subsets, there can be no directed cycles (making it a directed acyclic graph). This second level is a graph-of-graphs because its every node has associated with it a set of nodes and edges from the original. Allesina et al. (2005) investigated 17 ecosystem food webs and found that each consisted of at least four strongly connected components. In the four aquatic food webs they investigated in detail, there was a division between benthic and pelagic sub-communities (see their Table 1), consistent with the findings of Krause et al. (2003) for the same or similar ecosystems.

What has not been addressed is a quantitative measure of the separability of a given trophic network: the extent to which the food chains can be placed into separate compartments or the extent of changes that would make the structure truly separable, whether by edge deletions or re-assignments, and the number of such changes that are required.

An approach to this question has, however, been taken using the concept of the k-sub-web, introduced by Melián and Bascompte (2004). A k-sub-web is a subset of species each of which is connected to at least k species in the subset, whether predators or prey (Figure 4.13). That is, extracting the subgraph of those species only, each node has a total degree (in-degree + out-degree of k or greater, no matter the number of nodes in the subgraph. The subgraphs are not required to be strongly connected, nor do all its nodes have to have the same degree total. The authors compiled the frequency distributions for the k-sub-webs for 12 trophic networks and found that these tend to be highly skewed, with frequency decaying with k following a power law. They also focussed on the most dense sub-web in five of these data sets, and compared its structure with a number of null models. The structures showed a cohesive organization, with many small sub-webs highly connected with each other, but through the most dense sub-web. That study provides a model of the approach that other researchers can follow in their own investigations.

Not only do trophic networks commonly consist of compartments, it seems that they also can be built up of highly nested sub-webs rather like those in mutualistic networks. Kondoh et al. (2010) studied 31 published food webs looking for common bipartite

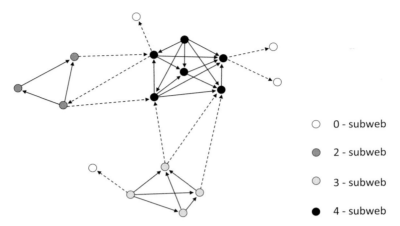

Figure 4.13 Illustration of k-sub-web (modified from Melián & Bascompte 2004). Value of k coded by shading as indicated. Edges of solid lines are within k-subsets; dashed lines are between.

sub-webs. This suggests that generalist predators' prey species include some with very few predators and that specialist predators' prey species tend to be those with many different predators, running counter to the maintenance of compartments by creating overlap of prey species' predator lists or of predator species' prey lists. The relationship between these two tendencies needs to be worked out. (You can do this!)

4.2.5   Keystone Species

A keystone species is one that has a disproportionately large effect on the trophic network or ecosystem in which it occurs, given the species' density or biomass. Frequently quoted examples include predators (e.g. sea otters or wolves); herbivores (snowshoe hare, beaver, elephants); and some plants (fig trees, nitrogen fixing cyanobacteria). From the graph theory point of view, the important question is whether keystone species can be detected from their topological position in the trophic network and other graph-theoretical characteristics. The quick-and-dirty answer is that topology is important, but other factors must be included to determine the "keystoneness" (Libralato et al. 2006) of any species. A number of studies have focussed on centrality measures as useful indices of topological importance of any node in a trophic network (Jordán 2009; Estrada 2007; Jiang & Zhang 2015), although Libralato et al. (2006) used interaction strength and biomass in a "sum-of-all-paths" approach ("mixed trophic impact") to evaluate key-stoneness in models by including both direct and indirect interactions throughout the trophic network. This is similar to the centrality measures based on current flow investigated by Freeman et al. (1991), Borgatti (2005) and Brandes and Fleischer (2005). Fedor and Vasas (2009) investigated the robustness of 13 different keystone indices to the addition or deletion of edges in a trophic network. They found that the most robust were betweenness centrality, already described (Table 3.1); an index of topological importance, which looks at indirect effects a number of steps away (Jordán et al. 2006); a keystoneness index that emphasizes vertical, rather than horizontal, interactions; and "mixed trophic impact," which distinguishes the negative effects of predators from the positive effects of prey (Jordán et al. 2006).

Although not exactly a graph-theoretic concept, the measurement of mixed trophic impact seems to be a good complement to measures of topological position (such as centrality) for identifying keystone species in trophic networks, and it seems to have achieved some currency in the literature (e.g. Angelini et al. 2010; Gasalla et al. 2010; Pinkerton & Bradford-Grieve 2014), particularly for marine systems. For such systems, and particularly for planktonic trophic networks, structure is determined by particle size, and the individuals of species A can be the prey of species B when they are small and then a key predator of the same species when they are larger. This greatly increases the likelihood of cyclic and strongly connected components in the graphs (already discussed) and it greatly increases the number and complexity of indirect effects for evaluating mixed trophic impact in determining keystone species.

This approach begins with estimates of the positive and negative effects between species or trophic species i and j: g_{ij} is the proportion of the diet of j contributed by i and f_{ij} is the proportion of the net production by i that is consumed by j. The net impact of i on j is then the difference

$$q_{ij} = g_{ij} - f_{ij}. \tag{4.1}$$

These differences are the elements of a $n \times n$ matrix $\mathbf{Q}$ of the single-step trophic impacts. Then, the mixed trophic impact matrix $\mathbf{M}$ estimates the effects of a small increase in any node of the trophic network on all the other nodes through all pathways, both direct and indirect. For example, an increase in the first level of carnivores can have an indirect positive effect on plant biomass by causing a slight decrease in herbivore density; this is the phenomenon known as a "trophic cascade" (cf. Paine 1980), closely related to the concept of a keystone species, which may be the initiator of the trophic cascade. The matrix $\mathbf{M}$ is derived from the matrix $\mathbf{Q}$ as

$$\mathbf{M^T} = \left(\mathbf{I} - \mathbf{Q^T}\right)^{-1} - \mathbf{I}. \tag{4.2}$$

($\mathbf{I}$ is the identity matrix and T is the matrix transpose.) Positive values of its elements, m_{ij}, indicate an increase of biomass of j in response to small increase in biomass of i; and negative values indicate a decrease. These $n \times n$ values can be used to give a good visual summary of the net pairwise effects within the trophic network, either with a grid of single entry bar-charts of positive and negative values (e.g. Angelini et al. 2010) or a bubble plot with magnitude indicated by circle size and sign indicated by filled (black = negative) or empty (white = positive) circles (e.g. Pinkerton & Bradford-Grieve 2014). A small artificial example of the latter format is given in Figure 4.14. The overall importance of any species can be calculated from the elements of $\mathbf{M}$, for

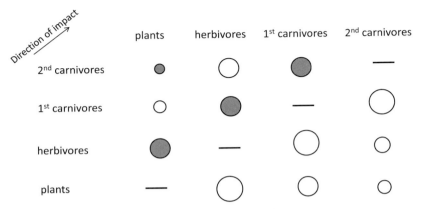

Figure 4.14 Mixed trophic impact: summary in the form of a bubble plot in which radius indicates magnitude; light fill for positive; dark fill for negative. Direction of impact as indicated.

example, as the sum of their absolute values (Ulanowicz & Puccia 1990; see Fedor & Vasas 2009):

$$T_i = \Sigma_j \left| m_{ij} \right|. \qquad (4.3)$$

Valls et al. (2015) suggested combining this kind of measure with simple rank by biomass to emphasize those species with the biggest impact but the smallest biomass. This is easy to do and their recommended best index is a multiplicative combination of Libralato's impact measure with biomass descending rank order.

Figure 4.15 shows the bubble plot of mixed trophic impact for a subset of the functional groups for Prince William Sound (redrawn from Valls et al. 2015). The full 53 × 53 matrix includes the expected organisms like Orcas and squid, but also less usual functional groups like commercial and recreational fishing fleets. (As an aside, the matrix seems to have no evidence of a trophic cascade providing positive effects on phytoplankton by consumers of herbivorous zooplankton.) When trophic impact was combined with low biomass to give a keystoneness measure, the top two keystone species were "transient Orcas" and "avian predators" (bald eagle); porpoise and seabirds were both close to these two in the same quadrant of high trophic impact and lower biomass.

4.2.6   Further Complications: More on Indirect Effects

Predation is obviously the fundamental interaction that determines the structure of trophic networks, but it also is a key component of a number of interesting and important multi-species interactions referred to as "indirect effects," described in a systematic format for rocky intertidal communities by Menge (1995). One of these is, of course, "keystone predation" in which a predator has a positive effect on the competitors of its preferred prey by reducing the density of that prey species (Figure 4.16a). To describe these indirect or induced interactions by simple one-way edges depicting flow from prey

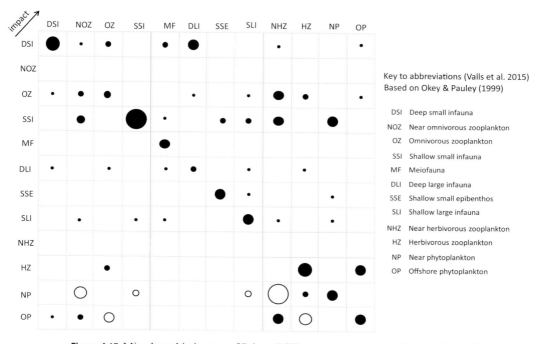

Figure 4.15 Mixed trophic impact of Prince William Sound (based on Okey & Pauly 1999): a subset of functional groups with abbreviations given in the accompanying table (see Valls et al. 2015).

to predator is not enough; the two effects, negative on the prey and positive on the predator need to be made explicit where appropriate (Figure 4.16). A variant of the keystone predation effect is the "trophic cascade" of a predator allowing higher plant densities by controlling a herbivore by predation (Figure 4.16b). Two predators that use the same prey create an induced negative effect on each other by the consumption of that prey; this is called "exploitation competition" (Figure 4.16c). "Apparent competition" (Figure 4.16d) occurs when one prey species declines in response to increases in another prey species due to its ability to enhance predators and predation on the first species. "Habitat facilitation" is the positive effect of one predator on another through the reduction of a prey species which thus inhibits feeding by the second predator (Figure 4.16e); "indirect inhibition" (or "second level inhibition" or "reversed trophic cascade") is also based on feeding inhibition by a plant, which reduces herbivore density thus having a negative effect on the predator by reducing its prey base (Figure 4.16f); this is a reversed version of the trophic cascade. Another variation, "apparent predation," is the indirect defence that occurs when the plant attracts or supports a predator by chemicals or resources, thus reducing the effectiveness of herbivores and herbivory on the plant itself (Figure 4.16g). Two more indirect interactions are illustrated in Figure 4.16h and 4.16i: "indirect mutualism" and "indirect commensalism." The mutualistic version occurs when two predators' densities are positively correlated because they each reduce their own prey species,

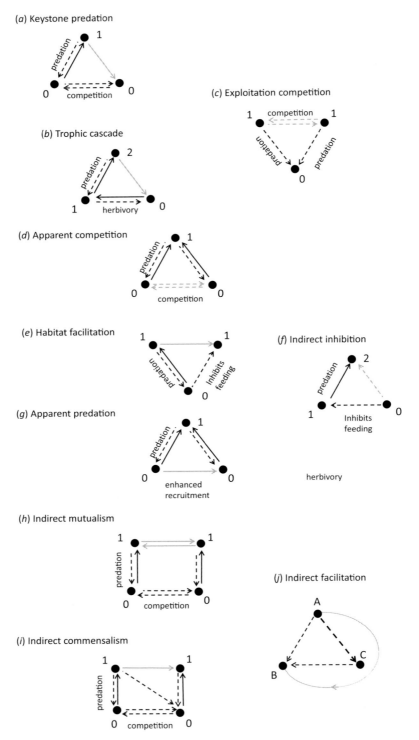

Figure 4.16 Indirect effects in trophic networks (redrawn from Menge 1995). Nodes are species. Arrows toward affected species. Solid edge: positive effect. Dashed edge: negative effect. Grey edge: indirect effect. Numerals 0, 1 and 2 are nominal trophic levels: (a) keystone predation, (b) trophic cascade, (c) exploitation competition, (d) apparent competition, (e) habitat facilitation, (f) indirect inhibition, (g) apparent predation, (h) indirect mutualism, (i) indirect commensalism and (j) indirect facilitation

releasing the other predator's prey from competition (Figure 4.16h). Indirect commensalism is just an asymmetric version of this same phenomenon (Figure 4.16i), although the biology of hemiparasitic terrestrial plants allows a range of indirect positive interactions between these plants and their hosts (Smith 2000). The last example does not involve predation, and that is "indirect facilitation" among three competitors in a single trophic level: this is the indirect positive effect of a species on another when the suppression of a shared competitor outweighs the direct competitive effect (Levine 1999). For example, species C would normally out-compete B, driving it to local extinction, but strong competition from A reduces C, allowing B to persist (Figure 4.16j).

Given the possible importance of these indirect interactions, there are questions arising. What do you see in your study? Are indirect effects discernible? Most of the methods for deriving the graph for trophic networks or other interaction networks are based on observations such as counts, as already described, and so the indirect effects are not observed. Trophic network positive edges from prey to predator can be seen as representing food, matter and energy flow; but negative edges from predator to prey represent population effects: limitation, suppression or control of densities. In general, these cannot be observed or measured without experimental manipulation of populations (Menge 1995), or the occurrence of "natural experiments" of large fluctuations or removals by catastrophe or disease, which have problems of interpretation all their own, and field experiments often are focussed on the effects on a single species. Sotomayor and Lortie (2015) have recently identified a number of gaps in the research on indirect interactions in terrestrial plant communities, including studies on interactions that do not involve feeding and the use of more realistic and complex designs involving several trophic levels. It may seem that graph theory itself may not help so much because the edges may persist with different weights, and the weights of the nodes (species densities) are key features and will fluctuate through time. What is important is the dynamics of the systems portrayed. Treating the subgraphs of Figure 4.16 as motifs to be detected and catalogued may not help because they will be intertwined with other subgraphs, with their own dynamics. Network theory and the study of dynamic networks and of the dynamics on networks may help, but this is a complex area of ecological structural studies. This topic will return in Chapter 11.

Another aspect of trying to include these indirect interactions is that their motifs rely on the quantitative balance of the weights of the individual edges to determine the outcome, and the diameters of the motifs considered will also have a profound influence. As a simple example, start with the familiar three species, three level trophic cascade as in Figure 4.16b. Now add a second herbivore ... what is the effect? It may change nothing, but it could also cause the indirect positive effect to disappear: with two prey species, the predator can control neither sufficiently, and the plants suffer. From the same three-species structure, add another plant species; the outcome may depend on herbivore preferences. If a second predator is included, it may merely reinforce the trophic cascade effect, or it may dilute it. Adding species to simple diagrams immediately complicates the dynamics on the subgraphs, and predicting outcomes is very difficult. In addition, these effects may depend at least in part on the phylogenies of the organisms involved (see Ives & Godfray 2006).

Where's the graph theory? The graph theory contribution to understanding the importance of these indirect interactions comes into play with the sum-of-all-paths concept as well as in the basic understanding of dynamics in trophic network structures. All possible "flows" of effects through the edges identified in the system must be considered. It is difficult to call on graph theory for assistance if the edges of interest are not detected because the detection methods are based on direct effects. Knowing the structure of indirect interaction motifs, with and without the edges of the indirect effects, can point to sections of the system being studied where indirect interactions are likely and should be looked for.

Graph theory does have a lot to tell us about the complications of indirect effects when the system is moderately well resolved and with quantitative estimates. Abrams et al. (1996) describe an example from the Benguela marine ecosystem (South Africa) focussed on the predatory fur seal and a commercially important fish, the hake. What would happen to the hake population density if the fur seals were greatly reduced by a culling program? It's not obvious. The seals eat hake and some of their prey, but the seals also eat some of their competitors and predators. Yodzis used an energy-based dynamic model of this system (unpublished, cited by Abrams et al. 1996) and enumerated all trophic network paths of lengths up to seven (equivalent to finding the inverse of the Jacobian matrix of the network) for 20 versions of models of this system (20 sets of parameter values), ten with a positive hake response to seal culling and ten with a negative response. There were many paths to be considered, over a million of length seven, and the results showed that the effect of seal on hake can be very diffuse. The main message from this approach is that we cannot expect to understand the net effect by using a small subset of the paths, especially only short ones, but that the network model provides some guidance as to what can be expected based on a fairly well resolved system. The graph theory approach of examining all paths will include the indirect interactions, even if it is not done explicitly. The real conclusion for understanding indirect interactions in trophic networks and in natural communities is that it requires much more information than we currently have for most trophic networks. This is true even for those that are well studied, and particularly true for the functional relationships within them (Abrams et al. 1996). Only with better information will the more powerful applications of graph theory be able to help fully in evaluating the nature and importance of the role of indirect interactions in these systems.

4.3   Concluding Comments

Trophic networks are hierarchical, but realistically include non-integer trophic levels to account for omnivory, cannibalism and mixotrophy (and how to fit in resource theft by hemi-parasites?), and so measures of rank and of rank variance in the food chains are appropriate for evaluating one kind of layer consistency. These partially ordered networks are the graph theory approach to studying the flow of energy through the nodes of a directed graph and are obviously related to the pyramids of numbers and biomass of the food web diagrams familiar from text books. Remember "Big Fierce Animals are

Rare"! (Colinvaux 1979; i.e. large carnivores require extensive areas to support them because of the inefficiency of energy transfer through several trophic levels). One obvious advantage of the use of graphs and graph theory in the analysis of trophic networks is in the ability to quantify and analyze the hierarchical characteristics of the network.

Characteristics like compartments in the network or separability, if they are found, allow the examination of some of the detail of the whole network and its composition from smaller sub-webs, each with a certain amount of autonomy within the hierarchical context. On the other hand, strongly connected components indicate something about cycling within the network of consumers. Keystone species have a disproportionate effect on function, and may be determined from a combination of their topological position within the network and other features such as flow centrality and measures of mixed trophic impacts.

Trophic networks, like other systems of ecological interest, occur in space and time, and their structure and dynamics are affected by both. Trophic network studies or their summaries often recognize the importance of changes in time (e.g. Schoenly & Cohen 1991), but less frequently acknowledge place-to-place differences (although see Careddu et al. 2015) and the critical role played by the spatial structure of the environment or of the populations involved (Holyoak 2000; Holt 2002; Pillai et al. 2009). In particular, the interactions in trophic networks are constrained by local extinctions and recolonization events, and obviously have their own effects on those processes (Huffaker 1958). Trophic network dynamics cannot be fully separated from trophic network structure, nor from the spatial structuring of their environment, and so an understanding of those processes requires an integration of metacommunity research and trophic network knowledge at both the detailed and theoretical levels (see Holt & Hoopes 2005). Graphs and graph theory provide the means by which to analyze and quantify these details, whether by measures like modularity and centrality, through modelling dynamic digraphs with elements of self-organization, or in the use of graphs-of-graphs and the comparison of their subgraphs. There are many possibilities to be explored.

The "to do" list for applying graph theory to trophic network ecology therefore involves determining such features of the trophic network structure: How compartmentalized? How truly hierarchical? How critical are keystone species? What characteristics enhance or diminish stability? What kind of node or edge centrality is most predictive? What structural features determine the dynamics on the trophic network? How does the spatial structure of the environment and of the community affect trophic network dynamics? What characteristics most affect the dynamics of the trophic network, as it changes with season, succession or external forces?

Looking at examples, and comparing terrestrial and marine ecosystems, it seems that planktonic and open water trophic networks may differ from others, and mostly in the fact that their structure is determined by particle and body size, rather than by anything else. As the individuals of one species, call it A, grow in size, they can switch from being the prey of another species, call it B, to functioning as an important predator. For example, copepods may be the key prey of larger fish, but predators of the larvae of the same species. In addition, mixotrophy may be much more common as a mode of nutrition in aquatic systems, with many organisms that are facultatively autotrophic and heterotrophic (see e.g. Eiler 2006). This fact has two important implications for the trophic networks as studied with graph theory. The first is that this greatly increases the likelihood of cyclic and strongly connected components in the graphs. The second is that it greatly increases the number and complexity of indirect effects for mixed trophic impacts and thus the importance of indirect effects in determining the keystoneness of species.

Studies of trophic networks, perhaps more than any other ecological endeavours, illustrate the inter-gradation of observational and experimental studies and modelling. This is especially true of attempts to understand the relationship between graph-theoretical characteristics, such as the general topology of connections, and the dynamic responses of the networks, such as robustness or stability. For example, McCann (2012) described a model trophic network that consists of two compartments of five nodes each, and what happened when the maximal set of 25 edges between the compartments were varied from strong to weak, or were removed one by one. The two manipulations did not produce the same result: starting with all edges, removal led to a decline in stability with an eventual return to the initial value when no edges were left, but the progressive decline in interaction strength produced a series of peaks and valleys in stability that had no immediate intuitive interpretation (see his Figures 10.4 and 10.5). The complex but fascinating topic of the relationship between network topology and network dynamics will be taken up again in greater detail in Chapter 11, but in trophic networks it has critical implications for our understanding of stability and resilience. It is not to be expected that the same structural characteristics of networks that provide or enhance stability for one interaction (e.g. mutualistic networks) will do the same in others (e.g. trophic networks), as shown by Thébault and Fontaine (2010), and it is not clear what the implications would be for networks that include more than one kind of interaction.

A further critical advantage, however, of using graph theory in trophic network studies is related to the need to go beyond looking at trophic networks in isolation from other inter-specific interactions, if only to understand the trophic networks! This point needs repeated emphasis, I think, but it is clearly expressed in several reviews (Abrams et al. 1996; Bukovinszky et al. 2008; Ings et al. 2008; Ohgushi 2008; Sotomayor & Lortie 2015; Kéfi et al. 2015). The shared prey and shared predator graphs (Figure 4.2) derived from the original trophic network indicate good places to start to identify the existence and strengths of indirect interactions; but the other "direct" ecological interactions, of competition, facilitation, mutualism and parasitism may need to be included also to varying degrees depending on the system. From the graph theory point of view, the inclusion of a range of different ecological interactions will necessitate a revised system for identifying which edges depict which kinds; in turn, different classes of edges will require some modifications of the usual measures and tests of graph structure. This complex and engaging topic deserves further attention, with graph theory as an essential analytical approach.

5 Species Associations, Communities and Graphs of Social Structure

Introduction

When you look up "social networks" on the Web, you find many references to human social networks that use basic graphs to depict the structure of relationships, with nodes being individuals and undirected unweighted edges between them representing contact or positive affiliation, such as trust or friendship (Figure 5.1). In fact, however, social relationships between individuals are usually asymmetric in two important ways, as illustrated in Chapter 1 with comments about children in a playground. First, while the quality of the relationship may be similar for both, they may be unequal: individuals A and B like each other, but B considers A to be their very best friend, and A feels less strongly and does not consider B to be theirs (Figure 5.2a). Second, the interactions can be positive or negative, as when A likes and trusts B, but dislikes and distrusts C (Figure 5.2b). I have used the relationship of "trust" here in a naïve way, but the concept has taken on a technical meaning and a more technical treatment in the network literature related to security of communications particularly for e-commerce (see Beth et al. 1994; Guha et al. 2004, and references therein; Leskovec et al. 2010; Agresti et al. 2015). Having signs allows the relationship between individuals of a pair to be contradictory or conflicted with opposite signs for two relationships, and social instability often arises in that situation (Figure 5.2c). The graphs for these social relationships, therefore, need to incorporate asymmetries both of sign and of quantity, and so it is not surprising that graphs for relationships among species in a community have the same requirement, as do any of the other "social" relationships that occur in ecological studies.

From simple undirected unweighted graphs, including these asymmetries lead us to modify the graphs for depicting and studying social structure to signed digraphs with the following characteristics:

Starting with

- nodes have labels indicating the individual identity or category; their positions in a drawing of the graph have no meaning but are chosen for convenience and clarity;
- simple edges that join nodes in pairs without direction, sign or weight, but they allow the detection of clusters of highly connected nodes;

Then

- edges have directions distinguish A to B from B to A, allowing the properties of reciprocity and transitivity;

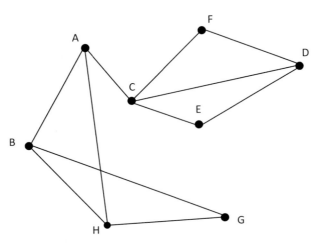

Figure 5.1 Graph of basic social network: individuals (nodes) joined by undirected edges, with no weights, showing contact or positive affiliation.

- edges that have signs, plus and minus, usually indicated by solid and broken lines, and possibly quantitative weights, such as +0.5 or −0.9, often indicated by line width (Figure 5.3a), allowing the property of structural balance;
- edges that have directions and weights allow other properties such as quantitative transitivity.

But

- not all ordered pairs of nodes need to have edges, because there is no opportunity for interaction, or because the interaction is too weak to be included.

(*a*)

(*b*)

(*c*)

Figure 5.2 Qualitative and quantitative differences. (a) Mutual "friendship," but unequal strength indicated by different line thickness: quantitative asymmetry. (b) A does not like or trust C (dashed line), but A likes and trusts B: interaction qualitative difference. (c) A likes B but B dislikes A: qualitative asymmetry.

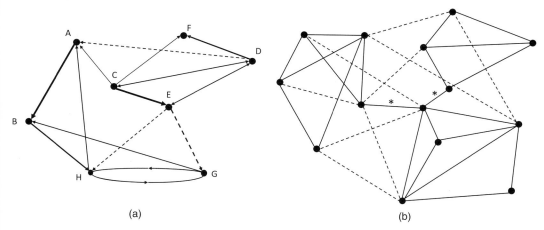

Figure 5.3 (a) Graph of a social network: individuals (nodes) joined by directed edges with signs (solid line + or dashed line −) and weights (line width). (b) Graph of inter-specific associations in a plant community. Nodes are species; edges have signs but not directions or quantitative weights. The species occur in clusters, but there are some positive edges between clusters, marked by asterisks.

This chapter describes some of the smart things that graph theory can help with in ecological studies of "social interactions" such as the phytosociological structure of plant communities or the social dynamics of animal groups. These are often based on concepts from human sociology and, more recently, from technologically enhanced social networks ("social media"), Internet commerce and other networks of information technology.

5.1   Graphs of Social Structure

5.1.1   Communities

One source of confusion for this chapter is the inconsistent use of the term "community." Ecologists use the term to refer to all individuals and all species (of interest) found at a particular location at a particular time. Therefore the digraph of a plant community includes all the plant species and all interactions detected. Unfortunately, in the language of general network analysis, a "community" is a subgraph of the graph of the whole system, in which the nodes are more highly connected or more positively connected than the graph as a whole, or in which the nodes are perceived to interact as functional subunits. A serious confusion indeed! Since this is a book for ecologists, it is probably best to stick with the ecological usage for "community," and to find another term for the highly interacting subgraphs. They can be called "clusters" although the term is not perfect, but it does fit also with usage in some network literature. For example, Newman (2010) refers to the detection of clusters, which are highly connected subgraphs, in "social" networks such as graphs of co-authorships in an academic department. The only weakness of this choice is that "cluster analysis" is an analytical procedure by which dendrograms ("cluster diagrams") are derived from multivariate data. However, the concepts are similar, and so the parallel may be acceptable, if "cluster detection" is carefully specified. The matching dual of cluster detection in graphs is partitioning, which has parallels with cluster analysis because partitioning usually has the goal of dividing a graph into groups of nodes with the fewest (positive) connections between groups and the most within. For example, the graph in Figure 5.1 (with only positive edges) can be divided into two clusters with many connections within and only one between: {A, B, H, G} and {C, D, E, F}. This criterion is very similar to that used for the detection of clusters in multivariate data by divisive techniques, that start with the whole collection of objects and divide it recursively with "minimum similarity between; maximum similarity within." When the edges have signs associated with them, the definitions need to be modified for clarity: the partitioning of the graph into clusters is to maximize the positive edges within clusters and maximize the negative edges between them or minimize the positive edges between. A graph that is perfectly balanced can always be partitioned into such clusters (Harary 1953; see Newman 2010, Section 7.11).

(As an aside, when dealing with spatial graphs, the clusters detected by "within versus between" algorithms lead to the identification of a nested hierarchy of spatial clusters. These can be used, in turn, as spatial patches, the spatial extents of which can then be used as the basis for determining spatial scale of the spatial structure [the patches and the inter-patch gaps]. This approach is very similar to a number of methods for the detection of spatial scale in patterns of point events [see Dale & Fortin 2014, Chapter 3].)

The conclusion is that the term "community" will follow the ecological definition, and the structure of graphs of these systems will be investigated by detecting "clusters" as subgraphs but also by studying other characteristics of the graphs based on the signs and quantities associated with the edges. Properties of these structures that will be of interest include the transitivity of the relationships portrayed by the edges and the sociological balance of the smaller subgraphs (the consistency of relationships among positive and negative associations).

5.1.2   Plants and Animals

It would be easy to start with the generalization that, in graphs of the social networks of plants, the nodes are usually species, whereas in graphs of the social networks of animals, the nodes are usually individuals. There are obvious exceptions, for example, the spatial graphs of tree stems study plants at the level of the individual, and studies of coral reef dynamics may focus on the turnover of species through time, not individuals, but for the purposes of this chapter let us at least start with this generalization. In defence of this starting point, plants are usually fixed and so interactions between them depend on their relative locations and may be mediated by their effects on light, moisture, nutrients, chemicals and so on. The positive interactions between plants may always need to be balanced by their shared need for the same resources, so that there is a tension between any "facilitation" (mutual or one-way benefits through effects on moisture, nutrient release, protection from herbivory) and the background of competition for shared resources. That facilitation and its balance with competition may be both fluid, in that it changes through time or with circumstances such as moisture or nutrient regime, and diffuse, in that it may affect a number of species with various degrees of effectiveness and not obviously a one-on-one focussed pairwise interaction. The changing nature of an inter-specific relationship in plant communities can provide different interpretations of common motifs in such networks. For example, the apparently contradictory structure of "A likes B; B dislikes A" in the social context (Figure 5.2c), may be an indication that species A is a positive influence on species B because it acts as a "nurse plant" when the plants of B are small, but when they grow up, they then tend to shade out the species A plants, creating the negative edge in Figure 5.2c. In addition, while many discussions of indirect interactions between species focus on those related to trophic networks, there are some that affect the relationships between plants (see Figure 4.16d apparent competition and 4.16j indirect facilitation).

Because most animals can move, while the same kinds of facilitative and more diffuse interactions may occur (shared vigilance against predators, physical sheltering, environmental engineering by beavers or elephants), the more obvious interactions are more direct. These may involve movement and contact (habitual physical proximity, joint foraging, grooming, aggression, mating, disease transmission and so on), or communication by visual or audible signals. Social network analysis for animals is therefore most usually individual-based, and often focussed on social behaviour (Krause et al. 2007; Wey et al. 2008; Farine & Whitehead 2015). As another version of the same overgeneralization, one could suggest that terrestrial plants explore and sample their environment by having many individuals (think of all those seedlings and Harper's "environmental sieve"; Harper 1977) whereas animals like birds and mammals explore and sample their environment with fewer individuals that move. This difference is a partial explanation of the greater emphasis on species-level interactions in plant ecology and individual-level studies for animals, but of course there are exceptions. Plant population ecology is well known for its emphasis on studying the fates of individuals (Harper 1977) and trophic network studies (Chapter 4) look more at species and guilds, although species-level inclusive studies of non-trophic interactions are becoming more prevalent (see Kéfi et al. 2015).

In Newman's (2010) book on networks, social networks are introduced with an example from the 1930s depicting friendships in a class of schoolchildren originally drawn by Jacob Moreno. It is clearly a graph, then called a "sociogram," with triangles as nodes for boys and circles as nodes for girls, with edges indicating friendships, almost all between two boys or two girls. In fact, many of the edges have direction indicated, because the question on which the graph was based was one of preferences of association, friendships that were not necessarily fully reciprocal or even partially so. The structure reveals a social hierarchy, with some individuals preferred by many, and others sought by none. The structure is based on positive preferences, but ecological studies often need to include the "negative preferences" as well, the equivalent of the factor of social avoidance.

Table 5.1 The 2 × 2 Contingency Table to Evaluate
Pairwise Species Associations

	Species A		
Species B	Present	Absent	Total
Present	a	b	$a + b$
Absent	c	d	$c + d$
Total	$a + c$	$b + d$	n

As discussed in Chapter 1, the data on which these ecological community graphs are usually based on counts of some kind: counts of plant individuals in quadrats, counts of contact neighbours, counts of pollinator visits or counts of communication events. Because basic graphs depict pairwise relationships between nodes, it makes sense to start with examining pairwise associations of species for whatever interactions are of interest. In plant community ecology, we often look at the spatial association of pairs of species based on co-occurrence in sample units (quadrats) or based on physical contact. With simple count data of s species in n quadrats, for any pair of species, A and B, the numbers of quadrats which contain each of the four possible combinations of presence and absence are enumerated in a 2 × 2 contingency table (Table 5.1).

The data are evaluated with the X^2 or G statistic and the χ^2 distribution comparing observed and expected frequencies. A significant result is interpreted as positive association between the species if $ad > bc$ and a negative association if $ad < bc$. Usually all $s(s - 1)/2$ pairs of species are tested, although there are problems with lack of independence among the tests (Dale et al. 1991). Admitting the lack of independence, the useful product of the analysis is a graph of s nodes with solid line edges joining pairs that are significantly positively associated and broken or dotted line edges joining pairs that are significantly negatively associated (such as Figure 5.3b). These edges are symmetric for simple quadrat count data, but different sampling schemes such as "point-contact" sampling, or sampling between defined vegetation layers, can produce asymmetric data, and thus edges with directions as well as signs. Different sampling designs may require a different approach to the analysis; for example "point-contact sampling" (see de Jong et al. 1983), and the basic approach of the many 2 × 2 tables has been extended to an evaluation of $k \times k$ frequency tables of the k most frequent species (or broader categories) or even multi-way 2^k tables. For analysis using graph-theoretical properties, the aim is usually to evaluate the relationship between each pair of species, often requiring the use of the Freeman-Tukey standardized residual to identify the most aberrant cells of a contingency table, and to indicate the outcome in an association graph (or "constellation diagram") of s (or k) nodes, with edges indicating the most "significant" positive and negative pairwise associations (Figure 5.3b). The positions of the nodes in the diagram have no meaning, but are chosen for clarity and convenience. In some applications, the nodes' positions can be determined by the species coordinates resulting from a complementary ordination, but personal experience suggests that this does not guarantee either clarity or convenience. For example, if the identification of clusters of species is an important feature, it is best to arrange the nodes so that the clusters are obvious (Figure 5.3b shows three almost exclusive clusters although there are two positive edges between the clusters, as indicated). The obvious next step is to look at the characteristics of this species association graph, however derived and whether with symmetric or directed edges. The following list suggests of some of the smart things we can do with such graphs.

The (Smart) Things to Do

- Find clusters:
  - Using the positive edges, this is the "standard" approach, with many methods.
  - Using both positive and negative edges, some adaptation of techniques is required.
- Find key nodes (often functionally key species or socially key individuals) in structure:
  - With basic edges, indicated by high positive degree.
  - With signed directed edges, indicated by high positive and high negative out-degree.
- Identify and characterize individual nodes with unusual properties, such as characteristics of the sizes of reachable sets as a function of path length.
- Measure reciprocity in a digraph or a signed digraph, where it is appropriate: given a significant association of A with B, is the association of B with A the same sign and same strength?
- Measure triad completion in a digraph or a signed digraph (and in subgraphs): given significant associations of A with B and B with C, is A also associated with C or C with A? The proportion of completed triads is also termed the "cluster coefficient," easily confused with other terms containing "cluster," alas.
- Measure transitivity in a digraph or a signed digraph (and in subgraphs): given significant associations of A with B and B with C, is A also associated with C? This is different from the association of C with A, which creates an intransitive triangle. Lack of transitivity may be related to the difference often observed between pattern and process.
- Measure balance in a signed graph (and in its subgraphs): the proportion of cycles with an even number of negative edges, reflecting the extent to which "friends' enemies are enemies" and "friends' friends are friends" … This will have different interpretations in different kinds of graphs, and depending on whether the nodes represent species or individuals.
- Determine the effects of environmental conditions on these interaction graphs. For example, how does the structure of an association network change along an environmental gradient or when moisture or fertilizer is added?

- How extensive are the changes to the network when a species is lost or a new
  species is introduced? Determine which characteristics change and how "far" or
  how extensively in the network changes are felt.

One motivation for some of the "to do" list is the attempt to distinguish causes of
inter-specific association as determined from the relative positions of plants of different species. There is a distinction between (a) "ecological coincidence" (positive
or negative) where the plants of different species are found together or apart because
of shared or divergent ecological requirements and capabilities, and (b) "ecological
influence" (positive or negative) where the plants of one species have a sufficiently
strong effect on local environmental conditions that they change the probability that
plants of the other species will be found in proximity (Dale 1977a). Within the limitations of detection, coincidence should result in graph structures that are reciprocal
(symmetric) and weakly transitive (decaying with the path length) where edges are
of the same sign. On the other hand, influence is asymmetric and not reciprocal,
and unlikely to be transitive except in special circumstances. Dale (1977a) provided
guidance to interpreting association graphs from plant communities based on such
principles, illustrated in Dale (1977b), but I will not repeat that material here. In
some sampling schemes, associations at very short distances where the plants are
touching may be interpreted as confounding influence and coincidence, with slightly
greater spatial lags and no touching being mainly coincidence (see Dale 1982). That,
however, is not a general solution to distinguishing the two and depends on special circumstances in the physical structure of the plants as well as the sampling
regime.

This list is phrased in terms suitable for plant communities, but it can also be
interpreted more generally for other examples of "social" association structure. The
items in this "to do" list are not all independent. In fact, Newman and Park (2003)
suggest that some of the common features of social networks, positive node degree
correlation (often negative in other network graphs), and a greater than expected
cluster coefficient (triad completion) can be attributed to the prevalence of internal
group structure (clusters). That makes the detection of these internal groupings a
high priority, and, having detected groupings with a range of sizes and exclusiv-
ity, to determine which of them have characteristics that seem "significant" or most
extreme in the distribution of the values expected. Remember that there is a long history of work on evaluating the significance of species clusters in association analysis,
which have implications for our understanding clusters in graphs (e.g. Strauss 1982).
To determine "greater than expected" for most of these characteristics of social network graphs, hypothesis testing or evaluation is best carried out by randomization
procedures, whether node label permutation, edge position rearrangement, or (where
applicable) shuffling group membership designations (see Chapter 1; cf. Croft et al.
2011).

5.2 Cluster Detection in Graphs and Networks

5.2.1 Why?

Cluster detection has the obvious goal of identifying meaningful subgraphs within a graph of social structure, and often the delineation of hierarchical structure within the larger graph. In a useful general review of cluster detection ("community detection"), Fortunato (2010) has provided some examples of the importance of this kind of analysis. For example, in appropriate business network applications, clusters of Web clients or of commercial customers may reflect similar interests, which can than allow improved or more focussed service to those customers. In the phytosociological graphs of plant communities, clusters may reflect ecological groupings such as shade-tolerant versus shade-intolerant forbs in a savanna, or zonal associations of species on an environmental gradient, such as the marine algae on rocky intertidal shores (see Dale 1984, 1986). The zonation example provides a clear illustration of the trade-off between facilitation (mutual benefit of reduced desiccation of species growing close together) and competition (access to light reduced by neighbours' shade). In general, the structural relationships among clusters detected within the network graph provides information on the functional relationships among the species represented by the nodes, and the positions of nodes within or between clusters and the topological relationships can indicate the key species in the community dynamics (keystone species; Paine 1969). Knowing that plant communities change through time means that it may be worthwhile to look in the social interaction graph for indications of what changes are most likely to occur (as will be discussed below.)

In animal social networks, defining social groups is often a key step in studying sociality, identifying important individuals and their structural roles, determining the characteristics of stable groups, quantifying some anthropogenic effects on animals, and understanding disease transmission in natural populations (Wey et al. 2008). As one example, a clear relationship between social network structure and parasite load and associated diseases has been found for a territorial reptile by Godfrey et al. (2010) and I'm sure that this kind of relationship between social network position and aspects of fitness are very common. In fact, the identification of clusters of nodes in a network also allows the classification of those nodes according to their positions in the clusters, which may determine or reflect their functional role in the cluster and the effect on control and stability; an important part of network analysis is the relationship between a nodes' functional role and its position in structural subgraphs, which will be investigated more in Chapter 11. It is usual to think that most disease transmission is a consequence of social interactions, but there are also the positive effects of information transmission on potential fitness, such as the culturally derived benefits of learned tool use in chimpanzees (Hobaiter et al. 2014). Whether positive or negative, the social structure and its clusters are key to understanding the functional role for these effects.

In rare cases, animal social structure turns out to be hierarchical and well defined as multi-level. One example is the population of sperm whales in the Eastern Pacific, which is organized into a higher level of clans unified by similar patterns of clicks used

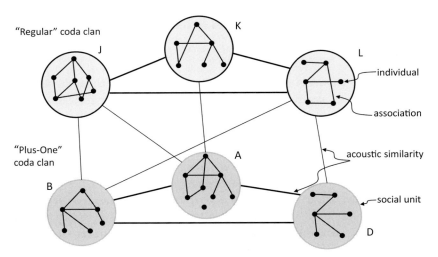

Figure 5.4 Three levels of sperm whale society: individuals (small nodes) within units with edges based on social relationships; units (large nodes) with edges between based on acoustic behaviour similarity, divided into two vocal clans indicated by black versus grey outline on large nodes. Based very loosely on Cantor et al. (2015, Figure 1).

for communication (the "coda"); each clan consists of a number of social units to which individual animals belong (see Cantor et al. 2015) (Figure 5.4). In such a case, the original network can be reworked as a graph-of-graphs with each cluster reduced to a single node; the edges between these cluster nodes can be based on rules of combining the information used for the original edges, and then used to study the relationships among the structures. In some cases, as in the sperm whale example from Cantor et al. (2015) sketched in Figure 5.4, the edges between the cluster nodes are actually based on different information, but that opportunity will be rare. In addition, a hierarchical approach to cluster identification allows us to study the hierarchical structure of the original graph, examining the contributions of smaller clusters to larger clusters, as they are formed. In particular, harking back to a discussion in Chapter 2, it can be determined whether larger groups are formed by the aggregation of subgroups of similar sizes, or whether larger groups are formed by the accretion of very small subgroups or of single nodes one by one.

5.2.2   How?

To detect and then to evaluate clusters in graphs, there are many, many methods available. It is not appropriate to describe them all nor to dwell on the algorithmic details, but a short summary of a few may be helpful. More specialized references (e.g. Newman 2010, Chapter 11; Fortunato 2010; see also Malliaros & Vazirgiannis 2013) give more detailed advice and include more methods.

5.2.3   Basic Graphs: Edges without Sign or Direction

Cluster Detection

Most ecologists are familiar with a range of methods generally called "cluster analysis" or "numerical classification" that are part of the toolbox of multivariate analysis, particularly as applied to ecological communities. All are based on a measure of similarity or dissimilarity between the objects or groupings of the objects under study. In most applications to graph-theoretical analysis, the nodes are the primary objects that are the subject of any clustering approach. The methods themselves, and their algorithms, can be classified by several criteria, such as sequential versus simultaneous, agglomerative versus divisive, monothetic versus polythetic, and so on (see Legendre & Legendre 2012, Chapter 8; Kent & Coker 1992, Chapter 8). Sequential approaches apply a repeated series of operations to the data, and may be agglomerative, starting with the objects being treated as separate entities which are then combined into larger and larger groupings, or divisive, starting with all objects in one big group which then gets divided into smaller and smaller sub-groupings. Hierarchical methods are those that provide sequences of smaller-within-larger groupings, which are often depicted by dendrograms (see Chapter 2); these usually produce non-overlapping groupings at each level of the hierarchy. Non-hierarchical methods produce a single partition of the whole set of objects into groupings, again usually non-overlapping, but possibly with overlap, allowing a single object to belong to more than one cluster. I suggest that the cluster analysis methods with which most ecologists are most familiar are ones that are sequential, agglomerative and hierarchical, such as unweighted arithmetic average clustering, also known as UPGMA for "unweighted paired group method with arithmetic averaging" (again see Legendre & Legendre 2012, Chapter 8).

Minimum Cut Size

This method begins by dividing the whole network into the desired number of sub-groupings, say two, of the required sizes, say approximately equal. The cut size is the number of edges between the clusters. Pairs of nodes in different clusters are chosen and exchanged between clusters if the exchange reduces the cut size. This process is iterated according to one of a number of different specific rules until a final configuration is reached. The basic version of this approach is the Kernighan-Lin algorithm (Kernighan & Lin 1970). As an example, the graph in Figure 5.1 can be divided into two "good" clusters by cutting edge AC.

Betweenness Centrality

This method resembles minimum cut size in some ways. Rather than cut size as the criterion, it uses the measure of betweenness, which is a value associated with each edge based on the number or proportion of geodesic paths that go through it (paths with the fewest edges), as described in Chapter 3. The method proceeds by removing the edges with the highest betweenness values one at a time, with recalculations after each removal, until the graph is divided into two groups, then into three and so on. One particular version of this approach is the Girvan-Newman algorithm (Girvan & Newman 2002), which is not as fast as some other algorithms, but which gives a full hierarchical decomposition of the network, as in a dendrogram (Newman 2010, Section 11.11.1).

Modularity

As with minimum cut size and betweenness centrality, this one uses a single metric which is then maximized in the final cluster configuration. Modularity is essentially the proportion of edges that are within identified clusters, rather than between. With Figure 5.1 as the example, 10 of the 11 edges occur within clusters, and only 1 between. Again, this kind of measure will be familiar to ecologists from the context of multivariate cluster analysis. The strength of the clustering is determined by comparing the proportion of edges within identified clusters with the proportion expected in randomly constructed graphs with the same numbers of nodes and edges (Newman & Girvan 2004).

Spectral Methods

Different authorities use different classifications for the methods for cluster detection, and the list so far is certainly not exhaustive. There is a set of methods referred to as "spectral" (e.g. spectral clustering or spectral optimization), which use the Laplacian matrix of the graph (the degree matrix minus the adjacency matrix). Chapter 1 briefly introduced the concept of spectral graph theory, which is based on the eigenvectors and the related "spectrum" of eigenvalues of the adjacency matrix, the Laplacian or another matrix to represent a graph. In particular, the adjacency matrix $\mathbf{A}$ for a simple graph has one wherever there is an edge between nodes i and j and 0s elsewhere. The degree matrix, $\mathbf{D}$, has 0s everywhere but on the main diagonal, which contains the degree of node i as element d_{ii}. The Laplacian, $\mathbf{L}$, is then $\mathbf{D} - \mathbf{A}$. Some derivations are based on the normalized Laplacian $\mathcal{L} = \mathbf{D}^{-1/2} \, \mathbf{A} \, \mathbf{D}^{-1/2}$ but the general approach of using the eigenvalues and associated eigenvectors of the Laplacian matrix of either form, is the same.

Spectral partitioning is a process to divide a graph into two subsets of n_1 and n_2 nodes, with the cut size being the number of edges between the two partitioned subsets of nodes. Newman (2010) describes the process of spectral partitioning as follows:

1 Based on the spectrum of eigenvalues of $\mathbf{L}$, calculate the eigenvector corresponding to the second smallest eigenvalue (called the "algebraic connectivity").
2 Order the elements of that eigenvector from largest to smallest.
3 The nodes of the graph corresponding to the n_1 largest elements are put in partition group 1, and the rest in group 2; calculate the cut size.
4 Then, the nodes corresponding to the n_1 smallest elements are put in group 1, and the rest in group 2; recalculate the cut size.
5 Of steps (3) and (4), choose the partition that gives the smaller cut size.

Although this algorithm does not guarantee the best partition (however defined), it has the advantages of being fast and practicable for very large graphs of hundreds of thousands of nodes (Newman 2010). For our purposes, the important feature may be that an analogous method detects clusters in graphs, using modularity as the criterion rather than cut size.

Other Methods

There are also methods based on possibly overlapping "cliques" of nodes (subgraphs of all mutually adjacent nodes), which may have less application in ecology than in computer science or information network analysis. For the ecologist, while theoretical or technical advantages and disadvantages will always be important considerations in choosing an approach, the availability of software that is not too difficult to implement will also be a consideration. This is an area of active investigation in studies of networks and algorithms for analysis, but this short outline should help point researchers in the right direction for their purposes, however much "the devil is in the details."

5.2.4   Signed Graphs

In a signed graph, an edge is not just an edge. (!) A cut-set or the set of edges between two identified clusters means something very different depending on whether the edge is positive or negative. It may be very satisfactory to have two clusters in a graph with only positive edges within clusters and only negative edges between them. In graphs of real networks, that ideal is unlikely, but an achievable goal is to consider algorithms that minimize positive edges between and negative edges within the clusters created. It is easy to imagine changes to methods developed for positive edges that take advantage having both negative and positive edges. The graph in Figure 5.3b has only two edges (marked by ∗) between what would otherwise be perfect clusters with only positive edges within and only negative edges between. Only two edges therefore, or only one node, need to be cut to achieve a complete partition. At a more technical level, Kunegis et al. (2010) provided details on how a somewhat modified version of graph spectral analysis can be used for clustering procedures in signed graphs; see also Kunegis (2014) on applications of structural balance algorithms for social networks: triangles versus global measures (more will be said about balance in Section 5.4).

5.2.5   Digraphs

In a digraph, an edge has direction, and so, as for signed graphs, edges are not all the same, and a cluster detection algorithm would do well to include that information in its process, as appropriate. To treat these edges as if they were symmetric and to proceed with the basic methods would throw away potentially important information and the simplistic approach and the results could be misleading or unsatisfactory; for example, spectral clustering methods based on the Laplacian matrix (see Chapter 1) cannot be easily applied to the directed case because the matrices are asymmetric (Malliaros & Vazirgiannis 2013). Malliaros and Vazirgiannis (2013) provide a very useful classification scheme of cluster detection methods for digraphs, and again, there are more than need to be described here. The principal approaches are the following (see their Figure 4):

1 Naïve graph transformation (i.e. ignore directions).
2 Transformations maintaining directionality (to unipartite weighted graph or to bipartite graph).
3 Extending objective functions and methods to digraphs (includes modularity and cut-based measures).
4 Alternative approaches (includes information theory and probabilistic models).

Of these, purely for comparison with undirected graphs, consider the changes required for the spectral approach based on the second eigenvalue of the Laplacian matrix. For directed graphs, the Laplacian matrix that is suitable for this purpose must be modified from that for undirected graphs to be called $\mathbf{L_d}$ (for details, see also Malliaros & Vazirgiannis 2013). As for non-directed graphs, it is the second smallest non-zero eigenvalue that is used, and its eigenvector is used to create a good (but not necessarily the best) partition of the graph into two parts. Several variants of this algorithm are available, with different modifications of the matrices and their spectra used, but the technical details of the differences are not appropriate here. Cluster detection is complicated from a computational point of view, but it is clearly and obviously a smart thing for ecologists to do with digraphs of social structure of almost any kind, and worth pursuing for this kind of data, even when very large. Our example, in Figure 5.3a, which mimics the naïve graph of Figure 5.1, is overly simple, requiring the removal of only one weakly positive directed edge (C to A) to produce two separate clusters.

5.2.6 Clusters of Edges not Nodes

The preceding discussion has dealt with the detection of clusters of nodes under a variety of circumstances, especially under the conditions of different kinds of edges (signed or not, directed or not, weighted or not). It is also possible, and sometimes advisable, to study the graphs or networks by looking for clusters based on the edges, rather than on the nodes (Ahn et al. 2010), producing what they refer to as "link communities." The reason offered is that nodes usually represent entities such as individuals or classification units (like species) and therefore tend to form different kinds of relationships with other entities, based on what they have in common (or not). For example, the same plant species will have different relationships with the other species of its regional flora depending on the criteria or sampling method used, and will therefore be a member of a number of overlapping clusters of species, possibly based on phylogeny, functional group, habitat preference, growth form, herbivore resistance and so on. The approach is based on the creation of a line graph of the original network of interest, and that concept has been described elsewhere (Chapter 1).

The method begins with a measure of similarity between any pair of edges that share a node, call them e_{ik} and e_{jk}, based on the set of first-order neighbour nodes of node i, designated $n_+(i)$ and the equivalent set for node j, $n_+(j)$ (both sets include the shared

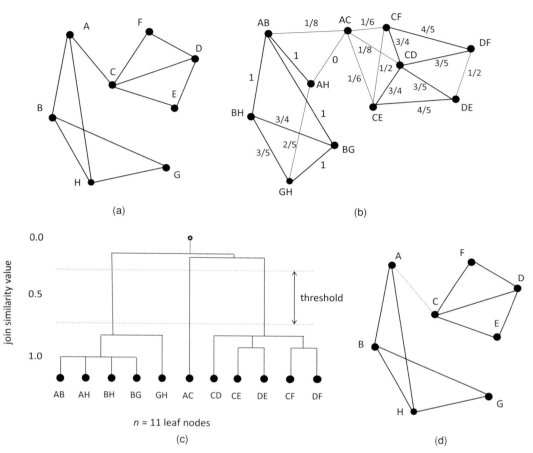

Figure 5.5 Link communities. (a) "Link communities" = edge-based clusters. Similarity of pairs of edges that share a node = number in intersection of first neighbour sets/number in their union, illustrated in the figure, the same graph as in Figure 5.1.$S[e_{AC},e_{CE}] = |\{ABCH\} \cap CDE\}|/|\{ABCH\} \cup \{CDE\}| = |\{C\}|/|\{ABCDEH\}| = 1/6.S[e_{BG},e_{GH}] = |\{ABGH\} \cap \{ABGH\}|/|\{ABGH\} \cup \{ABGH\}| = |\{ABGH\}|/|\{ABGH\}| = 1$. (b) Link communities for the line graph of Figure 5.1; the values on the edges are the similarities, calculated as in the examples in Figure 5.5a. (c) Single-linkage hierarchical clustering dendrogram for edge clusters: for network Figure 5.5a and its line graph Figure 5.5b. A broad range of threshold values gives the same pattern of clusters. (d) Clusters identified in the graph. Cluster 1 is $\{AB, AH, BH, BG, GH\}$. Cluster 2 is $\{CD, CE, DE, CF, DF\}$. Edge AC belongs to neither.

node k). The similarity is the number of nodes in the intersection of those two sets over the number in their union:

$$S(e_{ik}, e_{jk}) = \frac{|n_+(i) \cap n_+(j)|}{|n_+(i) \cup n_+(j)|}$$

(see Figure 5.5a). This similarity measure can be used as weights for the edges of what is called the "line graph" of the original network, in which the edges become the new nodes, and the new edges reflect shared nodes in the original (see Chapter 1). An example is given in Figure 5.5b, being the line graph of Figure 5.5a. Based on this similarity measure, single-linkage hierarchical cluster analysis creates a dendrogram of the edges (Figure 5.5c) and a threshold value delimits the edge clusters. In this simple example, the identified clusters of edges (Figure 5.5d) mirror the obvious node clusters, and the structure is so clear that the results are robust for a range of threshold values. In the context of metabolic reaction networks, the technique of transforming the original network to its line graph has been used to investigate the scaling laws of these hierarchical networks (Nacher et al. 2004); a similar approach may prove useful in the more complex ecological networks.

Using the edges as the unit for cluster definition allows the identification of more appropriate clusters accounting for this kind of overlap and without "penalizing" nodes for belonging to more than one cluster (Ahn et al. 2010). The suggestion is that the link community approach can incorporate overlaps while revealing hierarchical organization in a way that is superior to node-focussed methods. It will take more research and more examples to reveal to what extent this claim is true, but it is certainly a good idea to try this approach and to compare the results with the more usual cluster detection methods.

5.2.7 Clustering More Generally Considered: Assortative and Disassortative Structuring

Ecologists who are familiar with multivariate analysis are used to cluster analysis techniques of various kinds: hierarchical groupings of the primary objects are produced based on one or more characteristics on which some measure of similarity or dissimilarity can be based. The objects are joined into ever-larger groupings based on greatest and then decreasing similarity, with the most similar being joined first. A parallel concept comes from the study of social networks: *homophily* is the tendency of edges to be found between nodes that are similar in qualitative or quantitative characteristics. For example, people might tend to associate with others of similar educational background, or similar economic status, and this will be evident in a graph of inter-individual associations based on surveyed opinion or observations of behaviour. This concept can be generalized by determining whether any given graph is **assortative** for a particular character, meaning that there tend to be edges between nodes that are similar in that regard. The alternative is for a graph or network to be **disassortative**, meaning that the edges tend to be found between dissimilar nodes. For a quantitative characteristic, this is the equivalent of positive autocorrelation between first-order or near neighbours in the graph. Chapter 1 of this book referred to an assortativity index for graphs as might be applied to the degree of nodes, to characterize the neighbour structure of node degrees. A similar index could be produced for other properties of interest. As a simple example, Figure 5.6 shows two colourings of a graph with 10 nodes and 16 edges. In the assortative version, there are seven black-to-black edges and seven light-to-light; in the disassortative version, there are 11 of the 16 edges that join black-to-light, both far from the approximately 50:50 ratio that might be expected. Clearly, this is the same approach as the join-count statistics familiar to most ecologists (see Dale & Fortin 2014, Section 6.1). As with many spatial statistics and related measures, while a global statistic can

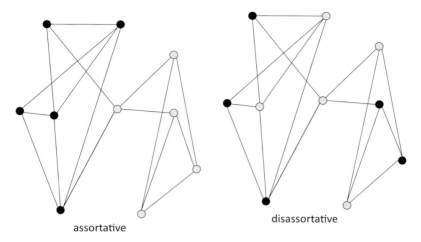

Figure 5.6 Assortative versus disassortative node label structures.

summarize the assortativity of the whole graph, a local statistic can also be calculated for regions of the graph, in case there is heterogeneity across the graph. An alternative is to focus on individual nodes and their immediate neighbourhood to determine exceptional nodes in the overall network structure (see Piraveenan et al. 2008, 2012).

5.2.8   The Smallest of Clusters: Clustering Coefficient

The term "clustering coefficient" can be a bit confusing, because it may sound like a measure of the proportion of nodes in a network that are members of well-defined clusters. In fact, as introduced in Chapter 1 (and see Glossary), it is the proportion of completed edge triangles: given edges A — B and A — C, the frequency with which B — C is also an edge ... This property is sometimes referred to as "triadic closure": a question of whether a triad of nodes has edges on two sides of the triangle, "open," or all three sides, "closed" (Newman 2010, Section 8.6). It is, however, clearly related to the concept of clusters, as well as to the overall consistency of the relationship portrayed by the graph and the "local" concentration of edges, depending on the overall ratio of edges to nodes or of actual edges to potential positions for edges to occur ("connectance"). The clustering coefficient is a useful measure to characterize and compare various kinds of graph-theoretical structure; for example, Fuller et al. (2008) studied the spatial structure of a tropical dry forest and found that this measure indicated non-random species associations for one size class of trees (stem diameter 30–35 cm).

5.3   Transitivity and Reciprocity

As for balance, transitivity is a characteristic related to the imprecise concept of the consistency of the relationships among nodes depicted in a graph. For transitivity, the

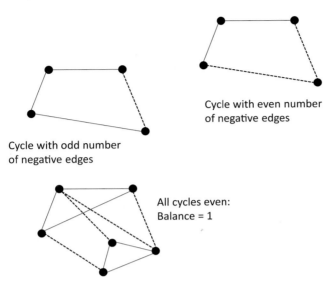

Figure 5.7 Balance: proportion of cycles with an even number of negative edges. In the spirit of "My friends' enemies are my enemies; my friends' friends are my friends."

focus is on directed graphs, initially without signs, where the edge from node A to node B signifies an asymmetric relationship. In ecological applications, the relationship of "A outcompetes B" can be used as a working example, which will appear again in Chapter 6, although transitivity is relevant to a number of less obvious relationships, too. A relationship like inter-specific competitive success is **transitive** whenever edges A → B and B → C guarantee A → C. To evaluate the overall transitivity of a graph's structure, determine the frequency of transitive triangles in the graph, compared with the frequency of intransitive triangles which have the equivalent of A → B, B → C, and then C → A.

For some digraphs, depending on the application (and competitive outcome is not one), it is possible to have both A → B and B → A. Think of social interactions: if A likes B, it may or may not be the case that B also likes A (see Figure 5.2a and 5.2c). Where mutual positive outcomes are possible, **reciprocity** is a measure of how frequently the relationship is bidirectional.

5.4   Balance

The concept of balance for signed graphs, whether directed or undirected, comes originally from studies of human sociology or social psychology (Harary 1953; Cartwright & Harary 1956). In those terms, the basic questions are related to the consistency of the relationships among interpersonal relationships: Are my friends' friends also my friends? Are my enemies' friends my enemies? Are my enemies' enemies therefore my friends (Figure 5.7)? In graph-theoretic terms, for undirected signed graphs, the question for triplets of nodes is whether there are an odd or an even number of pairwise negative relationships; none or two create a balanced pattern. For more than three nodes, balance is achieved if all edges are positive, or when the nodes can be partitioned into clusters (two or more) with only positive edges within clusters and only negative edges between them. Usually, the pattern of associations is not so clear-cut, and the interest of the researcher is in a measure of the graph's balance. A cycle is said to be positive when it has an even number of negative edges, and a graph is fully in balance if all its cycles are positive. Otherwise, a general measure of balance for a signed graph is the proportion of all cycles that are positive, having an even number of negative edges (Harary 1959). A graph that is balanced can be divided into two clusters of nodes with only positive edges within clusters and negative edges between them (Harary 1953; Davis 1967). Other potential measures of balance are the number or proportion of edges that must (a) be removed or (b) have their sign changed in order to achieve perfect balance (see Wasserman & Faust 1994).

For ecologists, the important question about the networks we study is not just whether the graph as determined is balanced, but whether there are social, ecological or evolutionary forces that will cause the network to become more balanced through time, whether balance is evaluated at the local level of triads or motifs or at the global network-wide level. The answer seems to be often "yes"; Ilany et al. (2013), for example, provide a good illustration of the tendency to greater balance in the social organization of wild rock hyrax (*Procavia capensis*) populations. More generally, very large human social networks tend to be extremely well balanced, in part because the distributions of the edge signs are highly skewed to more positive than negative, and because negative edges cluster at a small number of nodes, rather than being broadly distributed (Facchetti et al. 2011). These nodes are "unpopular individuals" which tend not to have a large effect on the whole network broadly considered. With further studies of ecological associations, it will be interesting to see how commonly this kind of structural feature appears in non-human networks.

Integrative Example: Mixed Forest

As an example that integrates some of the concepts already discussed, consider the graph theory-based study of the phytosociological structure of a mixed forest in southern Ontario, Canada. The sampling was carried out using three sizes of cylindrical sample volumes, one for each of three forest layers (tree canopy, shrub and ground) of different sizes appropriate to the plants in the layer. This design enabled the production of a digraph with directed edges, both positive and negative, within layers and between layers from upper to lower (Dale 1977a).

Various graph-theoretical properties were investigated to evaluate the hypothesis that the community consists of a group of species that co-occur by ecological coincidence, together with a group of "hangers-on" with presence determined by the positive influence of species in the first group (Goodall 1966). The first group of nodes should have high out-degree, high positive in-degree and large reachable sets, with few negative edges and much reciprocity within the set. (The reachable set of node u is all the nodes, *v*, for which there is a path from *u* to *v*; in a digraph, the strong form of reachability requires that the directions of the edges in that path are consistent in leading from *u* to *v*.) The second group of nodes should have low out-degrees, more negative edges within the group and small reachable sets. The whole digraph should consist of a single cluster, with small diameter and no cut-points.

The results included some unexpected details, such as a certain polarity in the tree layer with the two oak species forming a small subgroup of their own, and the large negative in-degree of sugar maple in the shrub and ground layer, because it is extremely common. In this example, sugar maple seedlings and sapling were so prevalent that positive associations could not be detected by the sample size available; whereas, for very rare species, only positive associations could be found to be significant. The basic graph theory properties, however, were consistent with the structure described. One detail that was expected was a significant tendency to disassociative node degrees, whether using positive or negative edges, and in- or out-degrees (the "adjacent sums" test; Dale 1977a). As determined by the goodness of fit and variance/mean tests, the out-degrees' distribution was not significantly different from random expectation, but the in-degrees were, both overall and for the three layers considered separately. Despite the unexpected details, the plants of all layers form a single natural grouping of small diameter (3 for all reachable nodes) but with differences among species as predicted for the Goodall hypothesis.

The details of the example aside, the most important point is the following:

- Only with graph theory can this hypothesis be expressed in a testable form and only with graph theory can it be tested!

The second lesson from this example is that (obviously) the edges found for a graph depend not only on the biology and ecological circumstances (think of "forbidden" edges in mutualisms), but also on the practicalities and mathematics of the sampling design and the analysis it supports. For very common species, only their negative associations can be detected without very large sample sizes; and for very rare species, only positive associations are likely to be found to be significant.

5.5   Change

Sometimes, or perhaps only rarely, our studies of social networks allow us to evaluate or even to predict change. Change may be the result of conditions external to the network itself, for example in response to gradual continuous temporal (or even spatial) differences in environmental conditions or in response to sudden changes, perhaps experimentally applied, as when moisture or fertilizer is added. Equally important are questions about how a network may change when a node is removed or a new node is introduced. In those circumstances, it will be useful to determine which characteristics change and how "far" in the network the changes are felt.

The second kind of change through time that can be observed in social networks are changes that result from the interactions within the network itself. For example, social

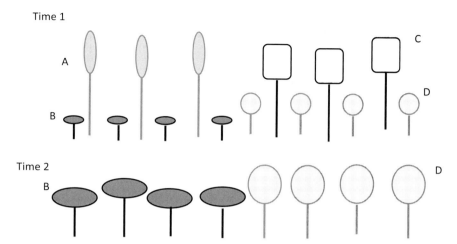

Figure 5.8 Replacement networks in a plant community. Species B and D grow under individuals of A and C and then replace them when they die.

networks with unbalanced subgraphs may tend to change through time to resolve that tension or instability within the structure, and thus the local elements that contribute to balance and imbalance (triads or motifs) are important as the basis on which to predict changes to the network (Ilany et al. 2013). Here, the structure of the graph is affected by the dynamics within in, just as the dynamics within any network graph is determined or strongly influence by its structure. The complex and reciprocal relationship between the structure and dynamics of network graphs will be discussed at greater length in Chapter 11 of this book.

One of the examples of "social" networks already mentioned is the concept of the "phytosociological structure" of a plant community, that being the network of positive and negative associations between the plant species as determined from their positive or negative tendency to be found in each other's spatial neighbourhoods. Those neighbourhoods may be tricky to define, particularly in dealing with vegetation in which the plants exhibit a broad range of sizes, either height or volume (biomass). In some vegetation, especially forests, it is possible to consider the asymmetric association of smaller plants with different tree species in the canopy (cf. Dale 1977b), whether the plants in the lower layer are bryophytes, grasses, forbs or the seedlings of the trees themselves. Where they are tree or shrub species growing beneath the canopy, an obvious suggestion is that these will replace the canopy species above them at that location when the canopy tree dies. If there is a tendency for plants of tree species A to be found under canopy trees of species B, the replacement of A by B can be predicted (Figure 5.8). There are similarities between this approach and other examples of species replacement in plant ecology, for example, the pairwise mutual invasion rates by tillers of four grasses (*Lolium perenne, Festuca arundinaceae, Festuca rubra, Poa pratensis*) under different grazing regimes (Silvertown & Wilson 2000); tiller invasion rates allow predictions of species replacement. This is also directly comparable to Horn's Markov models of succession which

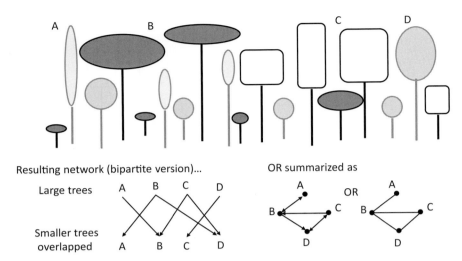

Figure 5.9 Vertical forest structure for network analysis (Fuller et al. 2008). Species A and D have smaller individuals below large trees of species B, B and D with C, only B with A, and only C with D.

include probabilities of stand type replacement (Horn 1975). This concept has been revived in the interaction network context, as replacement networks that predict change based on the dynamics of the system based on data more localized than stand-level, and using individual species (Alcántara et al. 2015).

With different motivation, Fuller et al. (2008) also looked at the relative locations of understory trees with canopy trees, but in a tropical dry forest and to evaluate how well network analysis could detect spatial patterns of association. For each of 106 species, they identified each large tree (diameter at least 40 cm) and created a link from it to any species with trees with crown overlap of 50 percent or greater (Figure 5.9). They examined the influence of sub-canopy tree size (seven stem diameter classes) on that association, based on the network characteristics of node degree distribution, characteristic path length and clustering coefficient. Assessing the results using randomized data, they found no significant departures in the degree distributions, three of seven diameters were apparently significant for path length, and only one of seven for the clustering coefficient. The path lengths were shorter for the three significant size classes, despite an overall increase when all seven were combined, showing less mixing of species as neighbours than in the randomized versions. What is not clear from their analysis is what predictions can be made from the understanding thus generated, although they conclude by recommending the network approach to other researchers.

5.6   Key Nodes; Key Edges

In any graph of social structure, an obvious place to begin identifying those nodes that play important roles in the structure is with those that have an influence on a large number of nodes, as indicated by the node degree. That's a place to start, but there are a number of caveats. In a situation where the relationship being studied may be asymmetric but the portrayal is symmetric or ambiguous, it will not be known whether a high degree is the result of being an influence on many or of being influenced by many (it could be both …). In a digraph, the answer may be to look first to nodes that have high out-degrees, and high out-degrees whether positive or negative, although the edge directions may not always be fully reliable indicators of the true directions of effects, depending on how they are derived.

Another important way in which a node may be singled out as important to the overall structure or function can be measured by **local assortativity**, that is, the node may be a hot spot (or cold spot) of positive autocorrelation (or negative autocorrelation) of qualitative or quantitative characteristics of nodes, especially of interest when the characteristic is the node degree, which again can be divided for many biological applications into in-degrees and out-degrees in a directed graph (Piraveenan et al. 2012).

5.7 Concluding Comments

The "social structure" of ecological systems and the methods of analysis to be applied to them clearly have much in common with studies of other societies, whether human, animal or electronic. The "to do" list for these ecological applications are therefore also similar, and suggestions of what should be included are given earlier in the chapter: identify clusters and key nodes; measure reciprocity, triad completion, transitivity and balance; determine the effects of the environment on social structure and the causes and impacts of change. That all sounds easy, but as usual, getting the right graph for the intended purposes can be an imposing difficulty, and interpreting the results of the graph theory analysis can also be challenging. The real challenge for ecologists is to integrate the elements of social structure and the graphs and graph properties that go with it into a larger understanding of the structure of ecological interactions and their dynamics in a changing environment.

6 Competition: Hierarchies and Reversals

Introduction

In the preceding chapter, competition was cited as a key interaction contributing to social structure for almost any organism; in addition, competition between individuals and between species is one of the strongest and most important interactions for both the ecological function of natural systems and the evolution of organisms (Chave 2009). Graphs in several formats can be helpful in studies of competition, depending on the system and the data. For example, in a graph of plant community social structure as described in Chapter 5, a negative directed edge from species A to species B may result from competitive exclusion or suppression of B by A, whether through interference caused by allelopathic chemicals or through light preemption by overgrowth. In this case, the edges detected in a social structure graph can be combined with graph theory to help develop and evaluate ecological hypotheses (see Dale 1977a).

Graphs can also be used to summarize and to analyze the encounters of competitors, whether only in time, as with records of periods of close proximity allowing opportunities for competitive interaction between animals; only in space, such as the regions of contact between the margins of colonies of crustose lichens; or in space and time, such as data from GPS collars on mobile animals.

A third application of graphs in competition studies is the depiction of hierarchies of competitive success. In animal behaviour, this is often considered as a dominance relationship, individual A dominates individual B, and B dominates C, producing a hierarchy or "pecking order" (see Schjelderup-Ebbe 1975). This kind of hierarchy can be a complete ordering with a clear dominance relationship between any pair, or there can be ties or ambiguities between some pairs with others well defined, thus giving a "partial order" (Brüggemann & Carlsen 2006). Hierarchies can also be found among species, for example among plants where competitive success can be correlated with growth rates and leaf area (see Grime 1979),producing a partial order of competitors; but also among boreal ants (Savolainen & Vepsäläinen 1988) and frugivorous birds in tropical forests (Thornton et al. 2015), where the ordering is complete. It is this third application that will be the focus of this chapter, describing these hierarchies and exceptions within them. For ecologists, graph theory can help in generating explicit hypotheses about the structural characteristics of ecological systems, often using hierarchical series for sets of similar relationships among individuals or among classes of organisms. This chapter focusses on applying graph theory to the quantifiable outcome of competition among

Output reduced to 90%   Output reduced to 70%

Summarized as:

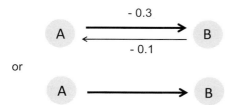

or

Figure 6.1 Competition reduces performance. Asymmetric competition: A affects B more than B affects A.

several competitors and its translation into hierarchies of competitive success, whether among ecotypes, genotypes, species or genera. As a general term, competition among several taxa ("competitors") can be referred to as "multi-species" competition and here are a few concepts and assumptions to be considered:

- Competition is an interaction between organisms with the potential to share resources; for each individual, it leads to a reduction in resources captured, growth, reproductive output, overall fitness and so on. It is often measured by the reduction in output attributable to the interaction; for example, plants producing fewer seeds when in competition compared to having no competitors at all or competitors only of its own species (Figure 6.1). This can apply to individuals or to species.
- Competition is usually asymmetrical; the effects of the interaction are greater, or proportionally greater, for one of the competitors, even in a simple pairwise situation. Again, this is true whether it is individuals or species competing.
- Competition occurs between individuals of the same species (i.e. "intra-specific"), as well as between individuals from different taxa of whatever level of classification ("inter-specific"). The effects of intra-specific competition can be evaluated by comparison with performance in the absence of competition; the effects of inter-specific competition are usually evaluated by comparison with intra-specific performance.
- Plant competition studies are often based on trials of pairs of competitors and extrapolation to larger sets may be difficult, even from two at a time to three at a time. For three competitors, it is conceivable that the combined competition of competitor A and competitor C on competitor B may be stronger than the simple addition of their separate effects ("competitive amplification"; Weigelt et al. 2007); the stronger combined effect could drive B to local extinction, where competition from A alone (suppose that effect is chiefly above-ground) and from C alone (suppose that is chiefly below-ground) is less severe and allows coexistence (Figure 6.2, top). On the other hand, it is also possible that where strong competitive effects from competitor C might

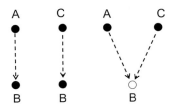

Negative effects of competition shown by dashed edges.

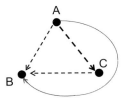

Figure 6.2 (top) Combined competition. From two to three species: B persists in competition with either A or C alone but is eliminated in competition with both, which may show "competitive amplification." (bottom) Indirect facilitation (apparent facilitation). Both A and C have negative effects on B by competition. Strong competition from A suppresses C (thicker dashed edge), preventing it from outcompeting B to local extinction. The presence of competitor A has a positive effect on B as shown by solid edge: "indirect facilitation" or "competitive release."

drive B to local extinction, competition from A reduces the effect from C ("competitive release"; Weigelt et al. 2007); allowing B to persist despite competition from both. This was referred to as "indirect facilitation" in Chapter 4 (Figure 4.16j; see Figure 6.2, bottom).

Although competition is a key interaction that structures the spatial arrangement of plants and their mutual dynamics in natural communities, it is difficult to assess in the multi-species context. As suggested above, a common approach is to break down the competitive interactions among *n* competitors into pairwise trials and the challenge is then to evaluate those results to make sense of the whole multi-species set. Fortunately, graph theory provides the right "machinery" for approaching and solving this difficulty. An initial step is to abstract the essentials of the study in a graph, with nodes representing the competitors and their interactions portrayed by edges. The edges will usually have directions, and signs (+ or −) or quantitative labels. The use of graphs to depict multi-species competition is especially appropriate when the tests have been pairwise because the edges are also pairwise.

6.1   Concepts for Competition Interaction Graphs

The concept of "competitive structure" is the set of outcomes of competition for a group of competitors, tested in pairs, and portrayed by a digraph with nodes representing the

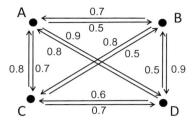

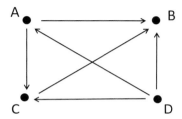

Figure 6.3 The complete digraph with all edges having weights that show the quantitative effects of competition for all pairings can be simplified to a tournament that shows only the winner and loser of each pair tested. The arrow is directed from winner to loser.

species or ecotypes and directed edges indicating the pairwise outcomes. Not all possible edges need to be included and these will depend on the format of the experimental results and on criteria for inclusion. One choice is to retain all edges (two per pair, one in each direction) with a quantitative weight related to competitive performance for each edge; this is a "weighted complete digraph" (Figure 6.3, top). This produces many edges, which may be reduced by retaining some and discarding others based on a threshold value for the weights. An alternative starting point is a digraph with one edge for every pair of nodes, directed from the better competitor to the less successful, usually without a weight. This digraph is called a "tournament" for obvious reasons (Figure 6.3, bottom; see Moon 1968). Even starting with the lower connectance (half that of the complete graph), it may still be useful to reduce the number of edges by retaining only those that exceed some threshold that distinguishes strong or clear competitive dominance from less convincing outcomes. Whichever the starting point for developing the digraph of competitive outcomes, one important purpose is to examine the full set of outcomes for the consistency of competitive performance in a range of combinations or conditions. Key concepts for that investigation are the "transitivity" of the competitive relationship and the strictness of the resulting competitive hierarchy.

The concept of transitivity is first a qualitative property of the interactions among three competitors: if A → B and B → C, then A → C, so that the competitive dominance represented by the arrow is a transitive relationship. The triangle of edges in a transitive structure is directional overall (for example, A to C); the alternative is a triangle of edges that give a functional cycle (functionally cyclic), as in A → B, B → C and C → A (Figure 6.4). The relationship in such a cyclic triangle is not transitive. Transitivity

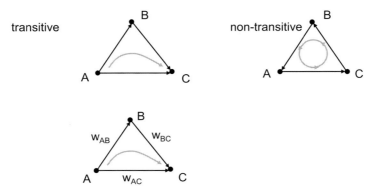

Figure 6.4 Qualitative transitivity refers to the fact that if A → B and B → C, then A → C. Quantitative transitivity is the relationship among competitive effects. Predict the effect of A on C w_{AC} from other values, e.g. $E(w_{AC}) = w_{AB} \times w_{BC}$, and then compare w_{AC} with $E(w_{AC})$.

is the key characteristic of multi-participant competitive structures, such as hierarchies, because it is the basis for measures and understanding of consistency among competitive outcomes or the extent of and reasons for departures from that consistency. Given a transitive triangle of nodes and one-way competitive outcomes, a quantitative version of transitivity can be investigated: given quantitative assessments of the effects of each of the competitive interactions on the participants, how well can the value of the third edge, say A → C, be predicted from the values of A → B and B → C? Determining an appropriate measure in order to calculate an expected value with the observed is a complicated issue (Figure 6.4) and will be treated in more detail below.

The concept of a "competitive hierarchy" for a set of competitors is that the outcomes of competition, even if not perfectly consistent and as represented by the directional arrows of the edges, form a complete or partial ordering. Even in a partial order that allows ties, the result is a hierarchical structure from strongest to weakest competitors.

If, on the other hand, the competitive relationship is completely transitive throughout the entire set of competitor interactions, the results should give a complete and unambiguous hierarchy in which all the competitors can be assigned a rank from best (outcompetes all others) to worst (outcompeted by all others). Unambiguous hierarchies can be the result of experiments even when not every pairing gives a clear winner, as long as the order based on "wins" and "losses" has no ties (see Roxburgh & Wilson 2000). Such strict hierarchies are likely to be rare, even without an appeal to allow some apparent inconsistency based on merely probable outcomes or habitat dependence (see Petraitis 1979). If the competitive relationship is not completely transitive, a simple measure of how intransitive it is can be constructed from the number of edges which would have to be reversed to make the structure completely transitive (Petraitis 1979). This measure can be adapted to deal with other cases, such as where the edges have weights quantifying relative performance (Petraitis 1979).

In plant ecology, we speak of a "competitive reversal," referring to a competitive outcome of a pairwise test that is in contradiction to the overall ranking of a hierarchy

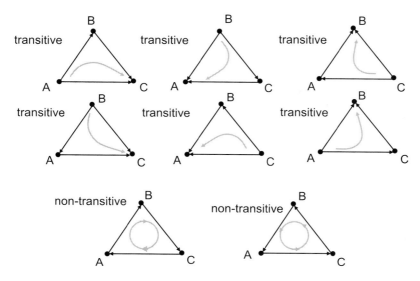

Figure 6.5 There are eight tournaments of three nodes: six of the eight are transitive.

(the sense to be used here) or that is unexpected based on past outcomes under other growing conditions (not to be the sense here). The competitive structure may not be a true hierarchy nor a partial ordering, because it contains triangles of edges that are not transitive (functionally cyclic) or because it includes some sort of structural competitive reversal. These can be viewed in two ways. First they may be seen as edges that are somehow wrong and these are the ones to be flipped to revert to a perfect outcome, as just described. The second interpretation is that these are edges that can tell us much more about the process of competition and the natures of the competitors because they produce outcomes at odds with the expected. These reversals encourage us to examine more closely the pattern and process of competition, and will be discussed further in reference to a specific example below.

6.1.1   More on Transitivity in Tournaments

In a full tournament, all pairs of nodes are joined by exactly one edge that goes in one direction or another, and so for any three labelled nodes and those three edges, there are 2^3 possible graphs, and thus 2^3 triplet subgraphs (or sub-tournaments). Of those eight triangles, six are transitive in which there is one overall winner and one overall loser, and the in-degrees for the sequence 0, 1, 2, and the out-degrees form the sequence 2, 1, 0. The other two triangle digraphs ($n = 3$ tournaments) are "functional cycles" or cyclic, with all out-degrees and all in-degrees being 1 (Figure 6.5). In simple terms, this means that A outcompetes B, B outcompetes C, but C outcompetes A. This is the children's game of "paper-rock-scissors" in which each element in the cycle defeats one and loses to one (see Maynard-Smith 1982). While the transitive triangles have the potential to fit in theories of competitive hierarchies, the cyclic triangles are essentially

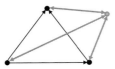
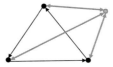

transitive triplet   non-transitive triplet

Figure 6.6 Adding a fourth node to each of the two triplets (one transitive, one not) adds three edges, each of which has two possible directions.

anti-hierarchical. In most ecological theories, competitive cycles should not exist, based on the concept of consistent unidirectional competitive superiority. On the other hand, the long-term outcome of competitive hierarchies should be the exclusion or extinction of the weakest competitors, and intransitivity can be appealed to as a mechanism for enhanced coexistence and species richness (Ulrich et al. 2014; Soliveres et al. 2015; Permogorskiy 2015).

In graph theory, any tournament that is not strictly transitive (all triplets have the transitivity property), is referred to as "paradoxical"; in fact a tournament is k-paradoxical if for every subset with k nodes there is a node external to the subset that dominates all its members (Erdös 1963). The non-transitive triangles are 1-paradoxical because every node has an "external" node that defeats it.

Of the triplet competition digraphs (the $n = 3$ tournaments), two are cyclic, six transitive. What happens when a fourth competitor is added? The addition of a fourth labelled node to a digraph of three labelled nodes creates eight new graphs (or subgraphs of a larger tournament). There are now six positions for edges, and so $2^6 = 64$ digraphs in total (see Figure 6.6). If the initial graph is already cyclic, of the eight new graphs, two have an extra 3-cycle created by the addition of the new node, and four have both an extra 3-cycle and a 4-cycle created; only two have no new cycles additional to the original. If the initial triplet graph is transitive, not cyclic, of the eight new graphs, two have a 3-cycle created, and two have both a 3-cycle and a 4-cycle created by the additional node. Starting with a transitive digraph of the three nodes, given random directions of the new edges, half the resulting digraphs now contain at least one cycle, and therefore are not completely transitive. For three nodes, 2 of 8 graphs are cyclic; for four nodes, it is 36 out of 64, if the edge directions are randomly assigned. With a leap of logic, rather than analysis, one might guess that, with randomly directed edges, large single-edge digraphs very probably have some subgraphs that are cyclic not transitive, representing competitive reversals. This conjecture was proved by Erdös (1963): for any fixed value of k, large numbers of nodes (something like $k^2 2^k$ nodes) almost guarantee that the tournament is k-paradoxical. This suggests that transitivity is not expected **if** the edges are random in a tournament structure; **but** in an ecological setting, truly independent randomness of direction is not expected. It is important, however, to be able to compare the results with those that are expected from randomness! One might propose that non-transitive subgraphs will be much more rare in real data than in random tournaments, because the directions are neither random nor independent. However, this aspect of potential competitive hierarchies is definitely worth pursuing, along with the transitivity of relationships in directional triplets, and the relationship of transitivity to position in a competitive hierarchy.

This discussion only begins to describe the wide range of possible analytic opportunities there are to enhance our understanding of competitive networks among species, genotypes or ecotypes using weighted directed graphs that depict the outcomes of pairwise competition tests. There is much yet to be discovered!

6.1.2   Quantitative Transitivity

For a complete digraph of competitive structure, because it has all possible directed edges, qualitative transitivity is everywhere because for any three nodes, the directed triangle of edges is always present: $A \rightarrow B$, $B \rightarrow C$ and $A \rightarrow C$. Only when the outcome weights are taken into account is there much to learn from or about transitivity: it must be a quantitative concept and have a quantitative measure. Even in a tournament structure, there is more to be learned about these interactions from a quantitative approach than from simple qualitative transitivity.

The qualitative definition of transitivity is simply that if $A \rightarrow B$ and $B \rightarrow C$, then $A \rightarrow C$ (Figure 6.4), without any implications about the strength of the unidirectional relationship depicted by the arrow. A complete digraph, which has all edges and a weight on each edge, should allow a test of the transitivity of quantitative competition relationships. For any triplet of competitors, A, B and C, the observed value of some measure of the competitive effect of C on A, call it the weight $w(AC)$, should be able to be compared with its expected value $E(w(AC))$, based on $w(AB)$ and $w(BC)$ if the quantitative relationship of competitive effect is perfectly transitive. This requires the right measure of competitive effect. Dormann (2006) and Freckleton and Watkinson (2001) have provided what seems to be an appropriate measure that will allow this quantitative comparison. Dormann (2006) explained it this way: if ε_{AB} is to represent the competitive effect of B on A, for example measured by reduced biomass, but somehow expressed in equivalents of A, then what is needed is a measure properly designed so that if one unit of competitor A reduces the growth of A by 0.5 g and one unit of competitor B reduces it by 2 g, $\varepsilon_{AB} = 2/0.5 = 4$. Then, given this approach, and with ε_{BC} representing the competitive effect of C on B expressed in equivalents of B, and so on, perfect quantitative transitivity leads to $\varepsilon_{AC} = \varepsilon_{AB} \times \varepsilon_{BC}$. For this to work with the kind of data most likely to be available, the suggested measure is $w_{AB} = ([A]_0 - [A]_B) \div ([A]_0 - [A]_A)$ where $[A]_0$ is the output of A when grown without competitors; $[A]_A$ is the output of A in competition with A, and $[A]_B$ is the same but in competition with B. With transitivity, $E(w(AB)) = w(AC) \times w(CB)$, $E(w(BA)) = w(BC) \times w(CA)$, and so on, for the general comparison of observed and expected values.

6.2   Measuring Competitive Outcomes

The "strength" of the inter-specific competition is often assessed by comparison with the results of competition within the same type ("intra-specific"). Because competition is often, or almost always, asymmetric, we tend to speak loosely about one type out-competing another, at least under the conditions currently tested: "A outcompetes B" or summarized as "A → B." The strength of this effect can be quantified in many ways, but start with $[X]_Y$, meaning "the output of type X in competition with type Y," whether the output is biomass, seed heads or a count of seeds produced. In many cases, the information available will be output observations of the form $[A]_B$ and $[A]_A$. On that basis, the inter-specific to intra-specific ratios $R(A|B) = [A]_B / [A]_A$ and $R(B|A) = [B]_A / [B]_B$, can be proposed as measures of inter-specific competitive success; suppose the values are 0.9 and 0.7 (see Figure 6.1, top). Even if $[B]_A > [A]_B$, one might conclude that the competition between A and B has a more negative effect on B than on A, based on the values of $R(A|B)$ and $R(B|A)$. In creating a digraph for the results of a competition study, edges can be placed between the nodes for A and B in both directions, each with a weight based on the competitive success index, $R(A|B) - 1$. For example, the weight is -0.3 for "A → B" and -0.1 for "B → A" in Figure 6.1 (middle). An alternative is to use a threshold to eliminate some edges, allowing only the "stronger" results as edges (Figure 6.1, bottom). For example, inclusion could be determined by the ratio of the weights:

$$[A]_B/[A]_A \div [B]_A/[B]_B = R\,(A|B) \div R\,(B|A) = 1.29\,(\text{vs } 0.7 \div 0.9 = 0.78). \quad (6.1)$$

The difference between these weights can also be considered as a reasonable measure for determining edge inclusion:

$$[A]_B/[A]_A - [B]_A/[B]_B;\ 0.9 - 0.7 = 0.2. \quad (6.2)$$

In cases where the output values for the "no competitor" situation are available, the index already introduced is a good choice:

$$w_{AB} = ([A]_0 - [A]_B) \div ([A]_0 - [A]_A). \quad (6.3)$$

Consider the directed pair transitivity measure, $T_{AB} = w_{AB} \div [w_{AC} \times w_{CB}]$. For any triplet of nodes with all six directed edges, there are six measures of transitivity (see Figure 6.5, top two rows). Another complication is the fact that for n competitors, any one of the $n(n - 1)$ directional edges of a complete weighted digraph is one side of $(n - 2)$ triangles, and therefore has the same number of possible evaluations of its contribution to the overall transitivity of the whole structure. For example, in Figure 6.7, n is 5; node triplet ABC has the six measures of transitivity illustrated at the top of Figure 6.5, but the directed edge A →B itself has three measures of transitivity, one for each triangle created by nodes C, D or E. It may be easier to aggregate the results for each edge rather than for each triplet. One appealing way of using these edges is to designate some as "hot," for large values of T_{AC}, and others as "cold," for small values; these could be colour coded for clarity in the competitive outcomes graph (not illustrated, but worth trying).

The discussion of which measures have the best and most preferred properties may suggest that the measures should be the focus; but, in fact, the focus should be how the results are used. The outcome of pairwise competition changes with growing conditions,

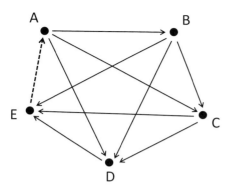

Figure 6.7 A competitive reversal occurs when a seemingly superior competitor is outcompeted by one that is usually less successful. Here competitor A seems to be at the top of the hierarchy but is outcompeted by E, which seems to be at the bottom.

such as high versus low nutrient or high versus low light. Therefore all discussions about outcomes are in the context of those particular conditions.

6.3 Choosing Edges and Finding Hierarchies

Given a set of nodes that represent the competitors, whether they are species, genotypes or ecotypes, there are many ways of determining the pairs to be joined by edges to create a graph of the competitive outcomes. The number and density of edges is maximal at two edges per pair of nodes, giving $n(n - 1)$ edges, which is useful only if they have weights (as in Figure 6.3, top). Low connectance, such as a spanning tree, may be too sparse to be useful. Intermediate connectance may work best, say 2 or 3 edges per node. If priority is given to the edges with the largest weights, this may create a graph that is not fully connected, but the number of edges could be adjusted to ensure full connectivity. Two approaches worth discussing are the use of threshold values applied to all possible edges and the identification of the stronger competitor of each pair in the tournament.

6.3.1 All Edges with Weights and Asymmetry Thresholds

Assuming there is a measure of competitive success for both A → B and B → A, there are $n(n - 1)$ positions for possible edges. Any reasonable single threshold value for that index can be chosen, say 0.8 indicating that all edges show combinations where the target competitor was able to achieve 80 percent of its intra-typic output. Any threshold produces a digraph, but some pairs of nodes may have edges in both directions and some pairs may have no edges between them; in fact, some nodes may have no edges. Rather than choosing a single threshold value, edges can be added one at a time, starting with the largest weights, and decreasing the threshold value until a desired density of edges,

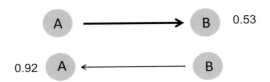

Figure 6.8 Tournaments: selecting edges for inclusion in analysis. All pairs are assessed with asymmetric outcomes [A with B] and [B with A], as well as [A with A] and [B with B]. Include the stronger edge unless (a) the asymmetry index is below a certain threshold, or (b) the difference between the values too small, as determined by another threshold value, or (c) larger weight is below a chosen threshold. Any of these threshold values can be adjusted to determine the number of edges that are included.

or a desired level of connectedness, is achieved. For example, using the edge density of the Gabriel graph as a somewhat arbitrary comparator but intermediate in the range of connectance, the threshold could be adjusted to give $2n$ edges. The sliding threshold provides the opportunity to monitor the "evolution" of the graph: how its characteristics (such as number of connected components, number of singletons, average non-zero degrees, etc.) change with the density of edges.

6.3.2   Tournament Edge Selection by Dominance

The second general approach begins with a tournament, a digraph that designates a "winner" of competition from each pair of competitors, which can to enhance our understanding of competitive hierarchies. This is a complete simple digraph, in which every node has $(n - 1)$ edges, one to or from each other node, representing the asymmetric competitive relationship. In the vocabulary of tournament graph theory, if A → B, A "dominates" B, which is similar to the ecological description of the relationship between A and B. With an index of competitive success for each directional pair, A → B and B → A, a variation is to include only the edge of any pair that has the larger competitive index and exceeds the lesser weight by some "reasonable" difference (e.g. 20 percent) or ratio (see Figure 6.8). Again, the difference or ratio could be adjusted to produce a chosen density of edges (e.g. 2 per node), or a sliding cut-off could be used in order to follow the evolution of the digraph and its characteristics.

In summary, four choices available for digraphs of competitive structures are as follows:

- **Full complete graph**: Edges for all $n(n - 1)$ directional relationships, each edge weighted by quantitative outcome(s), for which there are several choices.

1 Ratio of final outputs: $R_{AB} = R(A|B) = [A]_B \div [A]_A =$ (e.g. biomass of A at three weeks when grown in competition with B)/(biomass of A at three weeks when grown in competition with itself).

2 Ratio of output reductions: $w_{AB} = ([A]_0 - [A]_B) \div ([A]_0 - [A]_A)$ where $[A]_0$ is the output of competitor A when grown without any competition; subscripts A and B representing intra-typic and inter-typic competition.

The complete digraph preserves almost all the information, or can, but it may be insufficiently abstracted to be very useful.

- **Reduced complete graph with inclusion based on weights**: Select relationships depending on the largest outcome weights using a threshold value; for example, include all edges A → B for which A|B > 0.8. Obviously, the choice of threshold value is going to have a big effect on the graph produced from a given data set.
- **Full tournament** ("Dominance"): One directional relationship per pair, being the one with the larger weight, that is A →B if A|B > B|A or B →A if A|B < B|A, giving $n(n - 1)/2$ directional edges. This approach captures the notion of "winner" versus "loser" in competition, and may omit weight values by using only the sign of the difference.
- **Reduced tournament** ("Greatest Dominance"): At most one directional relationship per pair, being the one with the larger weight, and
  1 ("Value Limit") only if that weight exceeds a certain threshold OR,
  2 ("Difference limit") only if the difference or ratio between higher and lower index exceeds a certain threshold.

Obviously there are other choices possible, but these four provide a good range of possibilities, especially with the flexibility afforded by adjusting the threshold value used to select or remove edges. This description of methodological choices is more detailed than in some other discussions, but this is an area that has been well worked out with specific examples as illustration.

6.3.3 Creating a Competitive Hierarchy from the Results

Including only selected edges to study the structure of competitive relationships enables the creation of a partially ordered set to approximate a competitive hierarchy through ranking competitors by the out-degrees and in-degrees of their nodes in the digraph based on the measure of the asymmetry of the outcome of pairwise competition interaction. The simplest approach is to assign each node a score corresponding to its level in the hierarchy calculated as the out-degree minus the in-degree (Figure 6.9). This approach allows taking a digraph of the outcomes (Figure 6.10), and converting it to a hierarchical structure (Figure 6.11), although more than one node can occur in a particular level, because of potential ties (nodes A, E and K all have a score of +1). Those with high out-degrees and low in-degrees will tend to be at the top of the competitive hierarchy, even if it is not perfectly ordered; those with low out-degrees and high in-degrees will be near the bottom. Of course, the literature shows that competitive reversals do

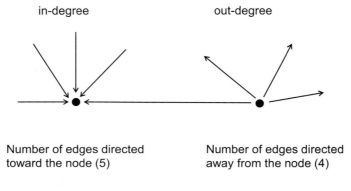

Number of edges directed   Number of edges directed
toward the node (5)   away from the node (4)

Index = 0 − 5 = -5 (low)   Index = 4 − 0 = +4 (high)

Figure 6.9 The difference between a node's in-degree and out-degree is an index of its position in competitive hierarchy. For example, for the node on the left, that index is −5, which is low; for the node on the right, it is +4, which is high.

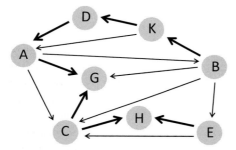

Figure 6.10 Hierarchy of competitive success: is there a clear hierarchy, with obvious strong and weak competitors? Thicker arrows indicate a stronger competitive effect.

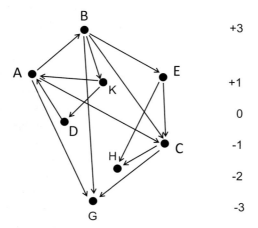

Figure 6.11 Figure 6.10 redrawn as a hierarchy. Marginal numbers are the nodes' scores = (out-degree − in-degree).

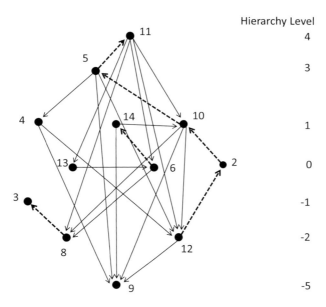

Hierarchy Level

Figure 6.12 Arabidopsis low nutrient treatment competitive hierarchy. The tournament outcomes with edges selected by value limit threshold. The dashed edges are competitive reversals.

occur, in which a competitor with low out-degree may nevertheless "out-compete" one with high out-degree in a pairwise test. What is potentially of interest is to colour the edges here by the "hot" versus "cold" scheme described above to determine whether the observed/expected ratios tend to be surprisingly large or surprisingly small higher or lower in the hierarchy or evenly mixed throughout.

6.4   Example: *Arabidopsis thaliana* Ecotypes

An example is always helpful in explaining concepts and principles, and this one examines competition among ecotypes of *Arabidopsis thaliana*, a small winter annual known as Rock Cress that is famous as the subject of genetic studies. The same concepts and principles, here within a species, apply equally to competition among less closely related plants (such as the many species in a natural plant community) as well as to relationships other than plant competition which may be conceptually less straightforward. The experiment started with 13 ecotypes of *Arabidopsis thaliana* and an out-group for comparison, which was left out of this analysis, grown in both high and low nutrient conditions. The data for the ecotype called 7 are incomplete, and so it also was omitted, leaving 12 ecotypes for analysis. We looked at both the "value limit" and the "difference limit" rules for creating edges among the 12 nodes representing the ecotypes. For both rules, we adjusted a threshold value to produce about $2n = 24$ edges, which is a moderate level of connectance (comparable to the Gabriel graph, which is intermediate in the well-known hierarchy of "topological" rules for neighbour networks; see Dale & Fortin 2014, Section 3.1.1). For the "value limit" rule, the low nutrient data gave 24 edges with a threshold of 0.68 (Figure 6.12) and the high nutrient data gave 28 edges

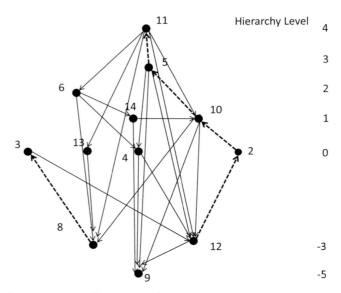

Dashed edges are competitive reversals

Figure 6.13 *Arabidopsis* low nutrient treatment competitive hierarchy. The tournament outcomes with edges selected by difference threshold. The dashed edges are competitive reversals.

with a threshold of 0.5. For the difference rule, the outcomes were 24 edges for low nutrient with a threshold of 0.3, and 30 edges for high nutrient with a threshold of 0.2 (not shown). For each of the four digraphs, a partial hierarchy was derived based on the difference between the nodes' out- and in-degrees. Larger out-degree and smaller in-degree place the node further up in the hierarchy. Nodes that are tied for the difference between out-degree and in-degree are at the same level in the hierarchy. A "reversal" is counted whenever there is a dominance edge from a node lower in the hierarchy to one that is higher. The positions of the reversals in the hierarchies were tabulated, to determine whether they were highly localized among the weakest competitors, or among the strongest, or whether they appeared throughout the hierarchy. This also allowed an examination of whether the reversals tended to be short, between closely ranked competitors, or long, between more distant ranks.

6.4.1   Results for Arabidopsis Competition

Figure 6.12 *Arabidopsis* ecotype competition outcomes, evaluated by the asymmetry index with a limit to its value for inclusion (0.68), at low nutrient. The threshold value was adjusted to give approximately $2n$ edges. The hierarchy levels were determined by the difference between out-degree and in-degree. The dashed edges are reversals: all short but at all levels of the hierarchy.

Figure 6.13 *Arabidopsis* ecotype competition outcomes as a partial tournament digraph, evaluated as pairwise dominance with a limit to the difference for inclusion (0.3), at low nutrient. The

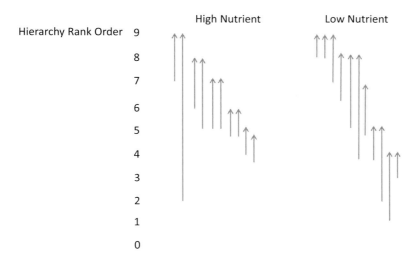

Figure 6.14 Arabidopsis competition: summary of competitive reversals for both low and high nutrient and based on both value and difference thresholds. The positions of reversals in the tournament hierarchies.

threshold value was adjusted to give approximately $2n$ edges. The hierarchy levels were determined by the difference between out-degree and in-degree. The dashed edges are reversals: one long (5 rank levels), others mainly short.

Figure 6.14 Reversals in the competitive hierarchies in all four digraphs were not restricted to the strongest or the weakest competitors, but tended to be short, usually spanning only 1 or 2 ranks. None involved the very weakest competitor.

Notes: The same ecotypes, 5, 6 and 11, were involved in reversals in all four of the competition digraphs. The very weakest competitor was never in a reversal, but in three of the four examples, the best competitor in the hierarchy was outcompeted by one other less successful ecotype.

Different measures and different thresholds or rules for edge inclusion will give hierarchy graphs that differ in their details, but given the overall characteristics of the interaction among the competitors, the general features of the hierarchies and reversals are expected to be similar but not the same.

The (Smart) Things to Do

For the results of a complete tournament of pairwise competition tests:

1. Create a digraph of the outcomes with an intermediate edge density (e.g. $2n$ edges).
2. Determine a partial order of the competitors based on the nodes' in-degrees and out-degrees.
3. Measure the overall degree of transitivity in this structure and determine local hot- or cold spots of high or low transitivity.

4 Find any edges of competitive reversal and characterize their positions in the digraph:
  a Are they random in placement or are they throughout the hierarchy?
  b Are they concentrated near the top of the hierarchy indicating that the better competitors are less predictable?
  c Are they concentrated near the bottom of the hierarchy, indicating that the weaker competitors are less predictable?
  d Are the reversal edges comparatively short or tall, indicating competitors of similar overall ability or ones that differ greatly?

6.5   Concluding Comments

6.5.1   Experiments with Phytometers

The reversals and other complexities revealed by the tournament approach to evaluating competition highlight some of the difficulties inherent in other approaches. The phytometer method for evaluating comparative competitive ability among a group of several plants uses performance with a single reference competitor to evaluate the success of many without the large number of pairwise tests. Usually only one competitor, the phytometer, is chosen and all other competitors are tested against it to assess relative competitive abilities. Suppose that by some unlucky chance, ecotype 5 in the *Arabidopsis* trials had been chosen as the phytometer. Based on the hierarchy graph of Figure 6.12, one might conclude that 10 was the strongest competitor with 4, 9 (the weakest in our hierarchy), 11 (the strongest), and 12 being similar in competitive ability, and all inferior to 5.

This approach also leads to more questions, such as:

Do the competitive reversals enhance coexistence in the absence of spatial effects?
How does spatial structure alter the effects of competitive reversals on coexistence?

Many questions such as these have been investigated using a variety of modelling approaches (e.g. Laird & Schamp 2006, 2008), and spatial heterogeneity clearly plays a role in allowing or promoting coexistence (Schreiber & Killingback 2013), as do interactions with organisms such as the soil biota (Lankau et al. 2010).

6.5.2   Animals and Competitive Hierarchies

The same basic structure of competitive hierarchy or competitive ranking, as described in detail for plants and in the *Arabidopsis* example, is commonly observed in animals, too, usually at the level of inter-individual interactions in a "social" context, often easily observed based on behaviour and often described in terms of "dominance" relationships. The familiar term "pecking order," was originally used to describe a behavioural dominance ranking in domestic fowl (Schjelderup-Ebbe 1975). In many animals, the dominance hierarchies are based on and reinforced by a broad range of behaviours, including pecking (among birds), mock or real fights, physical displays of aggression, dominant versus submissive postures and so on. There are cases of animal communities being structured by competition resulting in hierarchies, with good examples among ant communities, for instance (Savolainen & Vepsäläinen 1988), and possibly other social insects. There is a large body of literature on dominance hierarchies, how to measure them, and their effects on social structure and evolution (Landau 1951; de Vries et al. 2006; Vehrencamp 1983). It is not clear whether these hierarchies often allow the sorts of reversals that seem to be prevalent in the plant competition examples, but there are similar inconsistencies in competition among corals (Buss & Jackson 1979), and there is a well-documented example of a reversal among boreal ants, with a submissive species excluding a dominant (Vepsäläinen & Czechowski 2014).

6.5.3   Network Context

Competition is not the only interaction for which transitivity is an interesting and potentially highly important property. For example, the transitivity of "trust" in social networks can have both social and economic implications (see Richters & Peixoto 2011). Transitivity, as well as triad closure, turns out to be an important property of protein-protein interaction (PPI) networks, whether the network edges have weights (e.g. affinities; Yugandhar & Gromiha 2016), signs (e.g. activated or repressed; Vinayagam et al. 2014), or implicit directions (e.g. preference relations or signal flow; Liu et al. 2009). There are many interesting parallels between ecological interaction networks and those at the cellular and molecular level as exemplified by these protein-protein interaction networks (Ding et al. 2006; Itzhaki et al. 2010; Peterson et al 2012; see also the reviews by Pržulj 2010 and Raman 2010). For example, one motivation is the belief that by combining knowledge of the shape of an individual protein with knowledge its position in the interaction network and the topology of that network itself, will allow good predictions of the protein's function and its role in the network (see Pržulj et al. 2004; Borgwardt et al. 2005; Pržulj 2010; Winterbach et al. 2013; Peterson et al. 2012). This motivation is similar to the search in ecological studies to understand the relationship between the pair of concepts variously labelled as form and function, structure and dynamics or pattern and process, as will be pursued in Chapter 11.

   Competition in natural communities is very different from the relatively clear results of pairwise competition tournaments. Not only will there be the complicating effects of multi-species competition from individuals with a range of physical sizes and at a range of physical distances from the focal plant, there is also a range of possible mechanisms of competition (Weigelt et al. 2007). There are also indirect effects such as apparent competition (see Figure 4.16d) or apparent facilitation (Figure 6.2, bottom) that come into play where the interactions with herbivores, pathogens and mutualists have their own impact on what is observed (or not!) (see Clay 1990). In addition, it is well known that the outcome of competition depends upon environmental conditions in a very sensitive way (e.g. Lankau et al. 2010) and natural environments tend to be heterogeneous both spatially and temporally, all contributing to the natural disorderliness of plant communities (see Fowler 1990). Just determining the basic graph of competitive outcomes in a natural community is an enormous challenge. Even if the discussion of hierarchies and reversals in pairwise competition trials seems removed from what happens in multi-species communities and multi-level ecosystems, the results and understanding derived from them have important implications, both for ecological theory and for practical application. The contribution of intransitivity in competition to species coexistence is a critical component for community ecology, despite the multiplicity of underlying causes and any lack of clarity of under what circumstances it most strongly applies. Graph theory and its application to these ecological systems are essential for understanding how competition in these systems really works.

7   Mutualism, Parasitism and Bipartite Graphs

Introduction

In some kinds of inter-specific interactions, the interacting species belong to two distinct functional classes; for example, in mutualisms these classes may be flowering plants and their pollinators, plants and mycorrhizal fungi, etc. and in antagonistic interactions these classes may be mammals and their ectoparasites, insects and endo-parasites, etc. Such two-class inter-specific interactions can be positive, negative or neutral, and they are key factors in the functioning of communities and ecosystems, as well as strong driving forces, through the coevolution of the interacting species, in evolutionary change, speciation and community diversity.

Studies of these interactions are portrayed by bipartite graphs, which have two subsets of nodes representing the species in the two functional classes, and edges that run between nodes in different subsets but not within subsets. Although there are interactions between species within a subset, especially direct or indirect competition, they are not usually included in this interaction graph, because the focus of analysis is the interaction between the two functional classes.

The basic structure of the bipartite graph means that some of the measures used to characterize other types of graphs (e.g. average path length or node centrality) are less appropriate for the purpose, while other characteristics (e.g. modularity [compartments], nestedness and symmetry vs asymmetry) are more informative. A third set of characteristics, such as the distribution of the nodes' degrees and the distribution of neighbouring node degrees, are of special importance here.

This chapter describes how mutualistic interactions between plants and animals, including pollination, seed dispersal, and herbivory, and antagonistic interactions, in the various forms of parasitism, can be studied using bipartite and other kinds of graphs, and how graph-theoretical characteristics provide insights into these ecological systems.

7.1   Internal Structure of Bipartite Graphs

7.1.1   Nestedness and Modularity

One important feature of these bipartite interaction graphs is their internal organization, perhaps most clearly expressed in the contrast between nestedness and separation

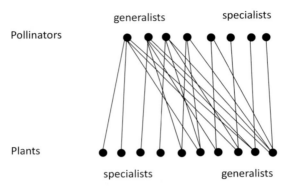

Figure 7.1 Bipartite graph showing nestedness, no specialist-specialist interactions and negative correlation of adjacent nodes' degrees. It is one large component.

compartments. For plants and pollinators, *nestedness* means that highly specialized pollinators are associated only with plants that have many pollinators and that plants with very few pollinators are served by generalists (Figure 7.1). This structure increases negative autocorrelation among the degrees of adjacent nodes. A modular bipartite relationship has subsets of the plants that are pollinated by well-defined subsets of the pollinators, with reciprocal specialization for both classes (giving small subsets) as well as reciprocal generalists in both parts of the graph (Figure 7.2). This produces strong positive autocorrelation of the degrees of nodes linked by interaction edges (low with low for specialists and high with high for generalists); or fairly uniform subsets of both partners forming modules, which need not be fully isolated from each other. The same data, in the form of a plant × pollinator combination table, can be arranged to emphasize its nestedness or re-arranged to emphasize compartments, and while neither will be a perfect fit, one will be better than the other (for an example, see Bascompte & Jordano 2014, Figure 3.6). Fortunately, these possibilities can be evaluated easily by comparison with null models (see Dormann et al. 2009; Dorman 2011) or by means of restricted randomizations. (The R package "bipartite" does the former.) Most of the general principles for network evaluation apply to distributions generated for null hypotheses

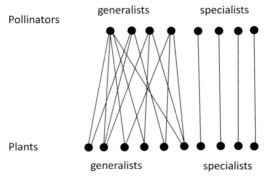

Figure 7.2 Bipartite graph showing modularity and reciprocal specialization, with positive correlation of joined nodes' degrees. It consists of five components: one large and four small.

in bipartite graphs, with the obvious limitations on the possible positions for edges, of which there are only $n_1 \times n_2$.

While most of the properties of interest in these graphs are accessible when the data are in the "binary" form (interaction: yes or no), some studies have or require quantitative data on the strength or intensity of the interaction. For example, researchers may want to assess how important a particular interaction is to each of the partners, because that may be quite asymmetric: critical to one and negligible to the other. Importance may be harder to measure, but frequencies of interactions may be good indicators to be used as weights in these interaction networks (Thompson 2006).

For host-parasite systems, nestedness may take the form of finding only very specialized parasites on hosts of high parasite richness, and only generalist parasites on hosts with low parasite richness (Vázquez et al. 2005b). A parallel finding, based on host abundance rather than on parasite richness, is that the more abundant host species tend to have richer parasite fauna and to have a higher representation of rare specialist parasites (Vázquez et al. 2005b). The same kind of structuring with a mismatch of generalists versus specialists is found in plant-pollinator systems and other similar species interactions (Dormann et al. 2009).

In both mutualistic networks and antagonistic networks reciprocal specialization involving single species or small groups of species is unexpectedly rare (Joppa et al. 2009). Bascompte and Jordano (2014) make the point that the observed infrequency of specialist-specialist interactions in pollination networks is both unexpected from randomness alone and contrary to earlier assumptions about the prevalence of specialist-specialist mutualisms based on natural history observations without statistical confirmation. It is not clear what mechanisms give rise to the commonly observed nestedness in mutualistic networks, but it may be related to selection pressures that tend to increase species abundances with which nestedness in the interaction matrix is correlated (Suweis et al. 2013). Using spectral graph theory (Chung 1997), it can be shown that highly nested graphs are those with the largest dominant eigenvalues, for both binary interaction graphs (just 1s and 0s) and for graphs with quantitative measures of interaction strength for each edge (Staniczenko et al. 2012). Those researchers found that while most binary mutualism graphs were significantly nested, the quantitative versions were not, suggesting reduced consumer overlap that would reduce competition (Staniczenko et al. 2012). Medan et al. (2007) showed a close relationship between nestedness and the truncated power law for node degree distributions, and that nestedness arises spontaneously in a self-organizing network model with the equivalent of preferential attachment. It is not clear, however, how well these factors apply in the relatively small sizes of the mutualistic networks observed in nature. Relative species abundance seems to be an important factor, based on studies of neutral mutualist communities which develop neither random nor compartmentalized structures (Krishna et al. 2008). The presence of forbidden or impossible linkages, as described in 7.1.4, can also be an important factor in these structures. The interest in nestedness in mutualistic systems is based at least in part on the possible relationship between structural properties of ecological systems and their functional dynamics. In particular, an important question is whether nestedness contributes to stability and the sustainability of diversity (Pascual & Dunne 2006, among many others). Although there is some evidence that nestedness

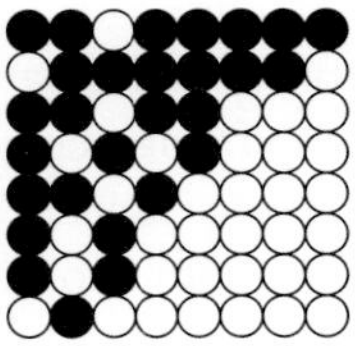

plants

Figure 7.3 Nestedness measure example. Filled circles represent observed interactions. Nestedness is measured by the "node overlap, decrease filling" (NODF) index, $N = 0.65$.

contributes to the stability of mutualistic systems (Bastolla et al. 2009; Bascompte et al. 2003), it seems that the real effect is not from nestedness itself, but from an increase in the mean number of mutualistic associations per species, thus making each species less vulnerable (James et al. 2012). Staniczenko et al. (2012) reach the same conclusion that connectance, not nestedness itself, is important for persistence (their supplement, p. 25). This is essentially the "spreading of risk" as a stabilizing mechanism, like the greater food security of polyphagy versus monophagy, avoiding dependence on very few species in any mutualism (den Boer 1968). (Remember the story about a tree that required the Dodo as a seed disperser and risked its own extinction following the loss of the Dodo; whether the story is true or not.) If the populations of the generalists on either side of the relationship are stabilized in this way, the antisymmetry of specialists interacting mainly with generalist counterparts may help stabilize those populations too, if only indirectly (Bascompte & Jordano 2014, Chapter 3).

Even if the spreading of risk is part of the explanation for nestedness in mutualist interactions, the same logic would not apply to antagonistic relationships such as parasitism, where an excess of such interactions could lead to extinction, rather than to stability. This thinking might lead to a prediction that negative interactions are less likely to exhibit nestedness, and there seems to be some evidence that this is true, although many host-parasite networks show nested structure and uneven edge distributions (Graham et al. 2009; Poulin 2010). It seems, however, that host-parasite networks more frequently exhibit "anti-nested" patterns than mutualistic networks (e.g. McQuaid & Britton 2013; see Poulin & Guégan 2000), although the concept of anti-nestedness can itself be controversial or unclear (Almeida-Neto et al. 2007). In general, however, "anti-nestedness" refers to a structure which is less nested than a random set of associations, often due to compartmentalization in the data or matching modularity (see Figure 7.2).

Several different measures of nestedness have been proposed and periodically evaluated. Bascompte and Jordano (2014) have provided a useful and brief summary of the choices available (their Appendix C; see also Ulrich et al. 2009). One of the most popular is the *nestedness temperature calculator* (Atmar & Patterson 1993), which draws on an analogy between the disorder of an observed binary interaction matrix, compared to an isocline in its reordered form, and the temperature related to physical disorder. (Figures 7.3 to 7.5 give the binary interaction matrix in pictorial form, with filled circles representing observed interactions and empty circles representing those absent from the data.) This temperature measure has been criticized for its dependence on the black box

plants

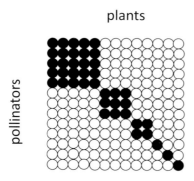

Figure 7.4 Modularity or anti-nestedness example. Specialist pollinators are found only on specialist plants. Generalist plants have only generalist pollinators. The nestedness (NODF) index is $N = 0$.

of its software (Almeida-Neto et al. 2007), although it has been improved by comparison to reference values from a population of randomizations (Bascompte et al. 2003). An attractive alternative is the *node overlap, decrease filling* (NODF; Almeida-Neto et al. 2008), which is more directly defined as

$$N = \frac{\sum\limits_{i<j}^{n_1} M_{ij} + \sum\limits_{i<j}^{n_2} M_{ij}}{\binom{n_1}{2} + \binom{n_2}{2}}, \tag{7.1}$$

where $M_{ij} = 0$ if $d_i = d_j$, and $M_{ij} = c_{ij} / \min(d_i, d_j)$ otherwise, with the d's being the nodes' degrees and c_{ij} is the number of interactions shared by the two nodes. This NODF measure is essentially the all-pairs average of the pairwise relative nestedness described in Box 10.2 of Dale and Fortin (2014). Rigidly nested data produce NODF $= 1.0$. A moderately nested structure will give values in the middle of the range from 0 to 1 (e.g. 0.65 in Figure 7.3), and complete exclusively modularity gives the value 0 (Figure 7.4). It is possible to have nested interaction structures within separate modules, which will

plants

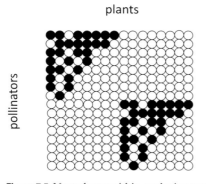

Figure 7.5 Nestedness within exclusive modules; the nestedness (NODF) index is $N = 0.325$.

give low but non-zero values (see Figure 7.5; two modules of Figure 7.3, NODF = 0.325).

Other measures are available, but the main advice is to be consistent in application and to understand the features to which the index may respond as well as the well-discussed strengths and weaknesses.

7.1.2   Modularity and Compartments

Modularity is often used as a measure of the extent to which the nodes of the graph can be divided into subsets such that the proportion of edges within subsets, compared to edges between subsets can be maximized (see Chapter 1); the identified subsets or modules do not need to be totally separate. In general, it is the sum over modules of the difference between the observed fraction of edges within modules and the expected value of that fraction. Because we are dealing with bipartite structures, the expected value requires evaluating the two parts (call them A and P, for animal vs plant) separately, using their within-module degree totals, $D_{A,m}$ and $D_{P,m}$:

$$M = \sum_{m}^{m-\max} \left(\frac{e_m}{E} - \frac{D_{A,m}}{E} \frac{D_{P,m}}{E} \right). \tag{7.2}$$

The sum is over all modules, indexed by m, with e_m edges out of the total E in the whole graph.

In addition to the index of modularity as a general measure, there are many techniques available to detect and characterize the modules or compartments themselves that can be found in networks, including the bipartite networks of interest here. For example, in a study of the fruit flies associated with the flowerheads of one tribe of the Asteraceae (the Vernonieae, the Ironweed tribe) in mountains of Brazil, Prado and Lewinsohn (2004) used Correspondence Analysis (CA) to detect compartments and a multi-response permutation procedure to confirm their distinctness. In the data of 35 insect and 81 plant species, they found six well-delimited compartments that were shown to be related to single sub-tribes or genera of the plants. They did not proceed to determine the degree of nestedness of the data, either for the full network or within the network compartments, but the results presented in their Table 1 suggest significant nestedness at least within compartments. For example, there are several insects that are themselves generalists but that are found on plants that only host a single insect species. An obvious suggestion when modularity is encountered in either mutualistic or antagonistic interactions is to determine whether the modularity can be related to the phylogeny of one or both of the interacting groups (see Bellay et al. 2011).

Nestedness may be seen as an alternative to modularity or compartmentalization, where there are identifiable subsets of species in both strata of the bipartite graph, with edges occurring mainly between matching subsets. The two are not completely exclusive because either they coexist, provided one or other characteristic is not extremely strong; or nestedness can exist within the compartments of a modular structure (see Figure 7.5).

7.1.3   Asymmetry

This term has many different meanings in the application of graph theory to bipartite graphs, but it is an important feature of mutualistic and antagonistic interaction networks in its variety of forms (Thompson 2006):

1 **Interaction strength asymmetry.** The effects on the two participants may be very different in strength, resulting in a kind of asymmetry, even if qualitatively the effects are of the same sign, such as the $(+, +)$ of mutualism. Bascompte and Jordano (2014) suggested a measure for this property in plant-animal interactions, based on the difference between the proportions of interaction events accounted for (their Appendix A). Where $b_{ij} = a_{ij}/A_i$ and $b_{ji} = a_{ij}/A_j$ are the proportions of interactions for species i and for species j accounted for by the a_{ij} interactions between the two, this asymmetry is $S_{ij} = |(b_{ij} - b_{ji})|/\max(b_{ij}, b_{ji})$. Some authors refer to this as *dependence asymmetry*. The overall asymmetry measure for all species is then the mean of all these pairwise values (see Dormann et al. 2009).

2 **Web asymmetry**. In a bipartite interaction graph, asymmetry may be in the difference in the numbers of participants in the two parts of the graph, call them n_1 and n_2. A simple measure of that asymmetry is $(n_1 - n_2)/(n_1 + n_2)$. If the two sides are equal, the asymmetry is zero. Bascompte and Jordano (2014) have called this one *web asymmetry* (their Appendix A).

3 **Degree symmetry and asymmetry**. In a bipartite graph of a relationship like parasitism, there may be a range of node degree values in both parts of the graph, and one arrangement of links is to have generalist parasites associated with many-parasite hosts and greater degrees of specialization creating links between nodes each with small degree values (Figure 7.6a). This is a kind of degree-based symmetry where the degrees match. A second possibility is that only high degree nodes in one part (a host with many parasites) may be adjacent to a low degree node in the other part (a highly specialized parasite); this is a kind of negative symmetry of node degrees, or anti-matching (Figure 7.6b). Bascompte and Jordano (2014) referred to the absence of interactions between specialists in the two parts of the structure as a kind of "asymmetry"; it is better described as an *antisymmetry* being more extreme than just the lack of symmetry (e.g. specialist with specialist, generalist with generalist). A third possibility is that the distributions of node degrees are qualitatively different in the two parts of the graph, so that neither matching nor anti-matching are possible (Figure 7.6c). When all the nodes in each part of the graph have the same degree (uniform distribution) and thus no true specialists or generalists (the interactions are "average-with-average"), there is a certain symmetry to the structure, but it is not clear that the term can be meaningfully applied in that circumstance, because the alternative of asymmetry is not really possible (Figure 7.6d). This version of symmetry and asymmetry is closely related to nestedness and to the assortative or disassortative relationship of neighbouring nodes' degrees (see Johnson et al. 2013). There are many different measures related to nestedness, but this particular kind of asymmetry may be quantified as $\frac{1}{2}(1 - \text{cor}(d_j, d_i) \mid a_{ij} > 0)$.

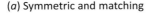

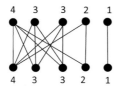

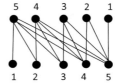

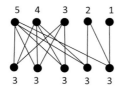

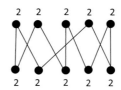

Figure 7.6 Degree-based symmetries and asymmetries for bipartite graphs. (a) Symmetric and matching, (b) antisymmetric or anti-matching, (c) asymmetric and (d) uniform (and thus symmetric?).

7.1.4   Forbidden Links

Another factor to be considered in the interpretation of these bipartite networks is the phenomenon of *forbidden links*. The term refers to the fact that many of the interactions that are not observed are essentially structural zeros (i.e. some combination that cannot occur), rather than data zeros (i.e. could occur but did not), because the interaction is ruled out by physical or ecological effects (Olesen et al. 2011b). In pollination biology, large differences in size or large phenological separation may cause such zeros to occur (Jordano et al. 2003, 2006; see Bascompte & Jordano 2014). In fact, the phenological cycles of the plants and the animals play a key role in the structure and function of these mutualism networks and it is conceivable that the amount of nestedness or assortativity can change over time of year within a single network (see Bascompte & Jordano 2014, Figures 5.3 and 5.5). Under those circumstances, a particular link may be possible in some weeks of the year when the plant and the animal overlap in suitable phase, but may be of the "forbidden" variety at other times (Figure 7.7). Forbidden links are not unique to these bipartite graphs but can be a factor in almost any ecological application.

7.1.5   Partner Overlap and Derived Graphs

In trophic networks, we can evaluate the relationship between organisms in the same trophic layer by looking at the number or proportion of predator species that they share or at the number and proportion of shared prey species (Chapter 4). In a similar approach to mutualistic networks, we can evaluate the overlap of the pollinators of any pair of

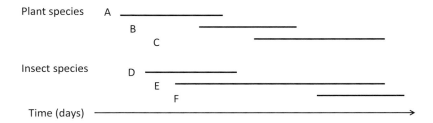

Links made impossible by phenology (no temporal overlap):   A – F, B – F, C – D

Bipartite graph of pollination

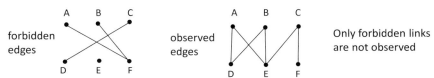

Figure 7.7 Forbidden links. Line segments depicting phenology: flowering of plants and potential pollination activity by the insects. Some links made impossible by species phenology when there is no temporal overlap. The bipartite graph of pollination can then illustrate the forbidden links or the observed link; in this example, all possible links are observed.

plants or the overlap of the lists of plants pollinated by any pair of pollinators. To formalize this concept, any bipartite graph can be converted to two single-stratum graphs, one for each part, containing the same nodes, but with no edges between strata; instead, the edges join nodes in the same stratum where they are adjacent to at least one node in the original graph (which must be in the other stratum). An example is given in Figure 7.8 (see also Bascompte & Jordano 2014, Figure 3.4). Not only can the edges of the single-stratum graphs be determined by sharing at least one partner species, the edges can be given a weight equal to the number that are shared, as shown in Figure 7.8. These weights, the numbers of shared partner species, can be provide a comparison ratio with the number of possible partners, to create a measure of the mutualist overlap. For example, in the upper stratum of Figure 7.8, A and C share two of the four species (U and W of U, V, W, Y) to which either are adjacent in the original graph, giving an overlap measure of 0.5. In the lower stratum, species U and X share one species (D) of their combined list of four (A, B, D, E), giving 0.25.

By transforming the bipartite network of plants and pollinators into two corresponding single-stratum graphs (two nodes in the same stratum joined by an edge where they share a plant or pollinator in the other stratum; see Chapter 3 of this volume), the bipartite graphs can be shown to have a small world property of short average path lengths (less than 2; see Bascompte & Jordano 2014), suggesting that perturbations of individual nodes can spread quickly and easily throughout the entire system.

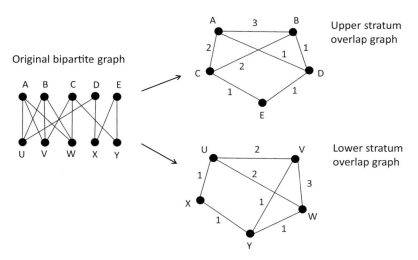

Figure 7.8 Two derived graphs with partner overlap measures (number of shared partners): one for the upper stratum and one for the lower.

7.1.6   Degree Distributions (First and Second Order) and Assortative Coefficients

The degree of a node is the number of edges that join it to others. The degree of a node may indicate its importance in the overall structure, and the frequency distribution of the degrees for the whole set of nodes summarizes a property of the graph itself; for example, a narrow range of node degrees, indicating a homogeneous structure, contrasts with having many singletons and very few very highly connected nodes as high degree hubs. The distribution of degrees can give clues as to the processes that gave rise to the network, but can also provide information on how the network may perform. It may also be useful to examine the relationships among the degrees of nodes that are neighbours. If nodes of similar degrees tend to be adjacent, low with low and high with high, the graph is assortative for degree. The opposite situation, with a tendency to have low adjacent to high and vice versa, is disassortative. This property for node degree, or any other characteristic, is measured by an assortative coefficient.

There are two kinds of analysis that make sense as a consequence of this discussion. The first is to plot and then analyze the distribution of node degrees to determine whether any model provides a good fit. As with other networks, this distribution can be compared with the reference models of Poisson, exponential, power law, or truncated power law distributions (others are possible). Bascompte and Jordano (2014) have given detailed guidance to this process (their Appendix B). For bipartite graphs, it is probably a good idea to treat the degrees of the two strata separately before combining them.

The second simple analysis is to plot the bivariate distribution of the degrees of adjacent nodes. Figure 7.9 shows the bivariate degree distribution plots for the artificial examples of structures given in preceding figures (e.g. Figures 7.1, 7.2, and 7.6). If there are matching specialists and matching generalists, the degrees of partners will be highly and positively correlated (first panel). If the graph consists of modules or compartments

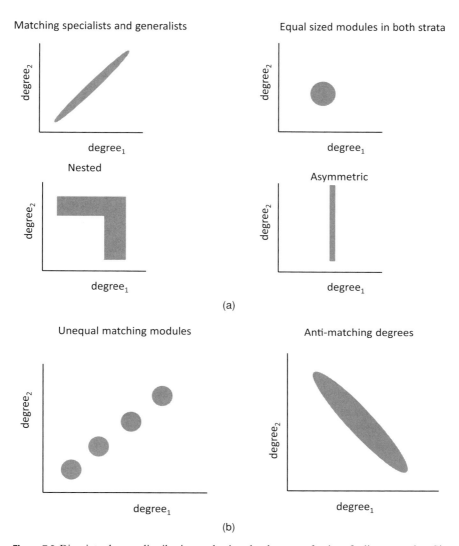

Figure 7.9 Bivariate degree distributions: plotting the degrees of pairs of adjacent nodes. Six examples as noted in captions.

of approximately equal sizes, the node degrees will both be limited to a small range of moderate values. Nestedness or antisymmetry for a broad range of degree values gives a bivariate distribution with no small-valued pairs (third panel). The "asymmetric" case with uniform distribution paired with a gradation of values produces a rectangular distribution parallel to one of the axes (fourth panel). Figure 7.9 gives two other cases: modules of unequal sizes and anti-matching degrees. Obviously, there is more to be gained from this analysis than just an assessment of positive or negative correlation between the degrees of adjacent nodes. Newman (2010) discussed these neighbouring node relationships under the heading of "assortative mixing by degree" (his Section

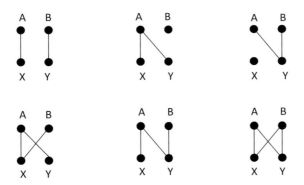

Figure 7.10 Motifs for bipartite graphs: six motifs of two partner pairs (from Jordano 2010).

7.13.3) because the degree of a node can be treated as any other quantitative label. For large networks and network degree distributions with "heavy tails" (many large values), the statistical association of neighbour node degrees is better evaluated using Kendall's τ rather than the more usual Pearson correlation coefficient (Raschke et al. 2010). There seems to be the opportunity for more research on this aspect of the structures of these bipartite graphs.

7.1.7   Motifs

In bipartite graphs of interactions, recall that motifs are not based on triplets of nodes as they are in standard graphs, but on double pairs of nodes, two nodes from each part. There are six such motifs possible, as enumerated by Jordano (2010, Figure 3.5). As for a standard unipartite graph, the fine-scale structure of the bipartite graphs can be characterized by the frequency distribution of these double-pair motifs. Figure 7.10 illustrates the possibilities. The enumeration of motif frequencies as they occur in a mutualistic or antagonistic network obviously is one way of quantifying some of the structural properties of the network, but their occurrence may also have dynamic network implications (Stouffer & Bascompte 2010), as there should be consistent relationships between network topology and network functioning, at least among networks of the same interactions (see Gómez et al. 2011). This provides another example of the important interplay of structure and dynamics in ecological networks (topology affects function and function affects topology) that will be developed further in Chapter 11.

7.2   Applications of Bipartite Graphs

7.2.1   Interpretation of Graph Properties with Examples

Just like the desire among ecologists to deduce ecological processes from observed spatial patterns, there is the hope that some aspects of these bipartite graphs are sufficiently distinctive that we can use them to distinguish positive from negative interactions or facultative from obligate relationships. For example, Poisot et al. (2013) showed that, in systems of mammalian hosts with gamasid mite ectoparasites, obligate relationships tended to produce networks that were modular, whereas facultative relationships were more nested.

Many of the graph-theoretical properties that are of interest for these bipartite graphs may be informative only for comparisons, not as absolute measures of particular characteristics in a single example.

An interesting hypothesis is that nestedness should have specialist pollinators being associated only with common species (it's too risky to specialize on rare plants) but generalist pollinators can include rare plants. There are two versions to be considered: (1) rare partners are found mainly associated with speciose hosts (those with many such partner species) and (2) rare partners can be supported best by abundant hosts (those with the highest densities). In the literature on mutualism, the former is usually assumed: specialists interact with species that are subsets of the interaction set of generalists; but it may be that generalist species are themselves more abundant and more stable because they can rely on many interactions (Bascompte & Jordano 2014, Chapter 3).

Bascompte et al. (2003) studied 25 plant-pollinator and 27 plant-frugivore mutualism networks and found that they were highly nested, as measured by the nestedness temperature calculator (Atmar & Patterson 1993), adjusted by expected values from randomizations. The significant nestedness means that both the set of animals and the set of plants each have a core of generalists. Specialists of either layer do not interact with corresponding specialists in the other layer, but rather with generalists of that other group. This means that the network is non-assortative for nodes of low degree (specialists) because their interactions are with generalists, but assortative for high degree nodes (generalists) because most of their interactions are with other generalists.

Dormann et al. (2009) studied 19 plant-pollinator networks and came up with similar findings:

- The degrees tended to follow a truncated power law.
- There was dependence asymmetry (generalists with specialists and vice versa) and nestedness.
- Pollinators tended to be complementary.
- The networks studied seemed to be more robust to extinctions than random graphs would predict.

Vázquez et al. (2009) provided a review of plant-animal mutualisms more generally (pollination, seed dispersal, plant-ant protection mutualisms) hoping to elucidate the relationships between pattern and process in these networks. Their observational findings can be summarized as:

- The animal species tended to outnumber the plants.
- The degrees tended to follow a truncated power law.
- The connectance was generally low.
- There was dependence asymmetry (generalists with specialists and vice versa) and nestedness.

- As well as nestedness, there was also evidence of modularity.
- The networks exhibited both degree asymmetry and interaction strength asymmetry.

Turning from general reviews to a specific example, Petanidou et al. (2008) examined the year-to-year fluctuations of a plant-pollinator network in Mediterranean scrub vegetation near Athens. Most striking in the four years' data is the high turnover in the interactions observed, both due to species turnover (70 percent) and interactions with new partners (30 percent), with only 53 percent of plant species common to all four years, 21 percent of the pollinators and 5 percent of the interactions. But the structural characteristics of the network itself were remarkably consistent despite the large changes in the list of actors.

- The insect species outnumbered the plants (about 200 vs about 90).
- The degree centralization, which is the variance of the nodes' degree centrality scores, ranged from 0.10 to 0.15.
- The connectance was generally low (around 3 percent).
- There was dependence asymmetry (generalists with specialists and vice versa) and high nestedness values of 0.97 to 0.98 (based on a "temperature" calculation). The identity of individual species as generalist or specialist (only one partner) changed from year to year.
- As well as nestedness, there was also some modularity, with two to six components in four of the five years.
- The network diameter remained constant near 8, ranging from 7 to 9, and the average distance between nodes was constant near 4 (3.49 to 4.04).

With less emphasis on network structural measures, Olesen et al. (2011a) came to similar general conclusions from a 12-year study of nectar-feeding butterflies and their nectar-providing plants. Broad characteristics such as species numbers and connectance stayed fairly constant despite rapid turnover both of linkages among generalist species and of species themselves. The difference is that there seemed to be a clear difference between stable generalist species and sporadic specialists (Olesen et al. 2011a).

Fodor (2013) provided some interesting comparisons from the networks of woody plants with ectomycorrhizal fungi in temperate forests. This was a single site, but the characteristics observed were:

- The symbiont species outnumbered the host plants (87 vs 7).
- Connectance was high (246 out of 609 = 0.41).
- There was nestedness in both groups with "super-generalists" as hubs in both parts; overall nestedness was significantly high based on "temperature" calculation, at N = 0.83).
- Modularity was weak compared to other bipartite networks, but a useful indicator of species roles.

In contrast, Toju et al. (2015) found that networks of below-ground plant-fungus associations differed from the generally nested topology of above-ground plant-animal networks, being anti-nested due to weak modularity. This study included DNA sequence data on the fungi at three sites along a latitudinal gradient in Japan, with more than

30 plant species at each site and hundreds of phylogenetically diverse mycorrhizal and endophytic fungi.

A last example, again for comparison, is the host-endoparasite networks of Neotropical marine fish described by Bellay et al. (2011). They found the following characteristics:

- The parasite taxa outnumbered the host species (170 vs 39).
- Connectance was low (0.048).
- Nestedness was significantly high, with NODF $= 5.5$.
- Modularity was clearly defined, $M = 0.68$, with 12 modules identified, containing between 5 and 31 species. Here is an example with both significant nestedness and well-defined modules.

The search for generalities for all interaction networks, or even for interaction networks of the same category, is not always rewarded. It is worth the effort, however, and the richness is in the comparisons made, even if no unambiguous generality results. For our own studies, we can calculate "the usual suspects" and interpret the values of the indices with those in the review summaries (see above), or with those in particular examples which have biological or environmental similarities to the context of our own. A main worry for such comparisons is the comparability of the data, not just the taxonomic level and reliability of identifications, but also the ratio of detection to presence, the effects of sampling intensity, as well as the inherent variability in the study system; there is reason to expect that ecological variability will usually be accompanied by network structure continuity as it was for Petanidou et al. (2008). Carstensen et al. (2014) examined the beta diversity of plants, pollinators and their interactions and found that while the pairwise interactions were highly variable across space, some pairs had interactions that were "locally frequent and spatially consistent," possibly representing "cornerstone" interactions that deserve intense investigation.

7.2.2 Incomplete Data

No study is likely to be sufficiently intensive and extensive to detect all the species that would be of interest, nor all the possible interactions of the species that are encountered. This means that for these studies, as in much of ecological research, we have only partial and incomplete information on which to base our conclusions. Some of the absent data points are just missing although possible (data zeros), not forbidden links that are impossible (structural zeros) (see Olesen et al. 2011b), but often it will not be known which are which. In Chapter 1, the concept of sub-sampling the known-to-be incomplete data was introduced, as a way to determine the findings' robustness to missing information; that suggestion is repeated here, although it cannot distinguish the impossible from the just missing.

7.2.3 Beyond Mutualism: Parasitism and Other Potentially Antagonistic Relationships

There are obvious similarities between the specificity or generality of species interactions between hosts and parasites and the characteristics of the various mutualisms discussed here. We must be cautious, however, about the apparent parallels of pollination and other mutualistic systems with parasitism and other exploitative relationships. The advantages of being generalist and speciose as a pollinator host may not obtain with parasites; more parasites or more types of parasites may create non-linearly disadvantageous effects.

In teaching Introductory Ecology, we try to emphasize that inter-specific interactions represent a continuum from almost completely positive effects to almost completely negative. For example, when one plant species grows on another, the relationship may be almost fully mutualistic (+, +), as with a cynobacterium or other nitrogen fixer growing on the bark of a tree; one of commensalism (+, 0) for small epiphytes (if they do not create too much load stress on the branches); to parasitic (+, –) for lianas, mistletoe and strangler figs. Blick and Burns (2009) produced an interesting study that investigated the network properties for a range of arboreal plants in New Zealand: epiphytes, mistletoes and lianas. They are different. Mistletoe and liana networks have fewer edges, indicating stronger host preferences; and they have less nestedness with mutually exclusive host preferences (negative association between the two). Epiphytes show stronger nestedness and positive co-occurrence. (Very cool!)

Studies of parasitism networks and the bipartite graphs they produce use many of the graph-theoretic measures we have discussed for other such networks, including connectance, nestedness, and modularity (e.g. Bellay et al. 2011). In addition, they often include *generality*, which is the mean number of interactions per parasite species (mean degree of nodes in the parasite stratum), and *vulnerability*, which is the mean number of interactions per host species (mean degree of nodes in the host stratum), as well as different measures of interaction strength, such as counts of parasites per host individual (see Poisot et al. 2013; Canard et al. 2014). As a comment on preference: it seems to be somewhat misleading to give a graph-theoretical property (mean degree in the host stratum) a name that is really a biological interpretation ("vulnerability"); the identification of the two as if they were actually the same may not always be appropriate.

As well as parasites and parasitoids, antagonistic interactions can be interpreted as including the relationships between plants and their herbivores. As with studies of hosts and parasites, this kind of interaction is a bridge from bipartite graphs to graphs of full trophic networks, raising the problems and promises of how these two kinds of study fit together (see Poulin 2010).

The (Smart) Things to Do

- Find distinguishing characteristics of the network structure (e.g. nestedness or compartments).
  - Measures of different kinds of symmetry and asymmetry.
  - How do these characteristics vary in time and space?
- Determine the first-order distribution of the nodes' degrees.
- Determine common repeated structural elements of the graph, such as motifs' frequencies.
  - Interpret these distributions.

- Find key species or species groups in the structure; this can be indicated by high node degree.
- Quantify patterns of neighbouring node degrees (positive and negative autocorrelation).
- Determine the effects of conditions on these bipartite graphs. For example, how does the structure of a plant-insect pollinator network change along an environmental gradient or when moisture or fertilizer is added?
- Compare structural characteristics with those of other interaction systems.
  - Can they be used to distinguish mutualisms from antagonisms?
  - Can they be used to distinguish facultative from obligate relationships?
- How extensive are the changes to the network when a species is lost or a new species is introduced? Determine which characteristics change and how "far" in the network the changes are felt.

7.3   Concluding Comments

This is all "good stuff" and clearly well defined as helpful applications of graph-theoretical principles to ecological studies. The main weakness, if it is really a weakness, is that by concentrating on the interactions between the strata of a bipartite graph, we are omitting all the other interactions: competition between the pollinators, competition between the plants, the predators and parasites of both, and so on. Some studies that have begun with mycorrhizal associations have been heading in the direction of considering the broader context within which mutualistic interactions occur (see Southworth et al. 2005; Gehring et al. 2014), even to the extent of including external environmental factors (drought). Including more categories of interaction in a single analysis is a tall order but in this era of big data, it is something that needs to be considered as a way to understanding the functions and dynamics of complete ecological communities (see van Veen et al. 2006 on the range of interactions in insect communities). Already cited is the work of Kéfi et al. (2015) in describing the known trophic network and non-trophic interaction network of more than 100 species in a rocky intertidal community; the non-trophic interactions were highly non-random both when considered alone and when combined with the trophic network edges, suggesting a promising approach to developing a comprehensive network approach in ecology. Chapter 11 will discuss combining the concepts from the several species interaction chapters (Chapters 3–7) and the "location" chapters (Chapters 8–10), by examining the relationship between structure and dynamics in these systems and their extended networks.

8 Temporal and Time-Only Graphs

Introduction

Ecological phenomena and processes occur in both space and time, whether or not the spatial or temporal locations are acknowledged explicitly in the methods used to study them. Where the previous five chapters (Chapters 3–7) were concerned with the aspatial and atemporal graphs of species interaction networks, this is the first of three chapters about *locational graphs*, graphs in which the nodes at least have locations in time or in space, or both.

Some ecological phenomena are essentially or exclusively temporal, without explicit spatial locations, and are best portrayed by temporal graphs. Such time-only graphs and temporal (aspatial) networks emphasize the order and timing (relative or absolute) of the functioning of graph or network components, and thus are the right format for formalizing schemes of possibility, causation and combinations of events that are impossible due to temporal order. Important to applications of these graphs is the *orderliness* of the ecological phenomenon through time and thus the choice of graph-theoretical measures that best reflect this property. More complex phenomena require that both space and time be included, giving the spatio-temporal graphs to be covered in Chapter 10.

For many ecological systems, it is necessary to include the dimension of time in their graphs to help understand the relationships among objects and processes (think of causal relationships), and also because ecological systems are dynamic with processes that can change through time. This dimension is usually included by giving the nodes locations in time, creating temporal graphs, and there are several approaches to working with the temporal dimension. For example, the set of nodes or the set of edges may change through time, with the loss or gain of either kind of element, although there are limitations because the deletion of a node necessarily removes all the edges attached to it.

Temporal graphs have been introduced in the literature as *dynamic graphs* (see Harary & Gupta 1997). The graphs of standard graph theory are *static*, because they do not portray changes with time, or because they aggregate events of that occur for short durations in a summary graph that includes the entire time span (Kostakos 2009; Tang et al. 2009). These aggregated graphs are really atemporal, because time is not explicit in their development or interpretation, although they include temporal events. Dynamic graphs, on the other hand, change in at least some of their characteristics with time. Dynamic graphs are typically aspatial, but they have a temporal setting for both nodes

Objects

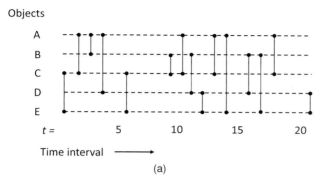

(a)

Objects

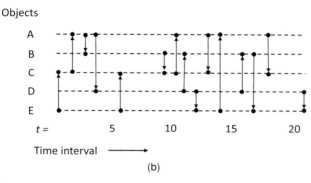

(b)

Figure 8.1 Temporal or time-ordered graphs: basic structure. (a) Pairwise contacts recorded in discrete time intervals. (b) Directional contacts recorded in discrete time intervals.

and edges. In addition to the usual two sets, V (the nodes) and E (the edges), there can be functions that assign weights to nodes and edges, call them f and g, increasing the flexibility of applications for these graphs. A classification of dynamic graphs can be based on the nature of changes in nodes or edges (cf. Harary & Gupta 1997):

- *Node dynamic*: the set V changes with time, with nodes being gained or lost.
- *Node-weight dynamic*: node weights change with time as their weight function f varies.
- *Edge dynamic*: the set E changes, in that edges can be gained or lost.
- *Edge-weight dynamic*: edge weights change with time as their weight function g varies.
- *Fully weight dynamic graph*: both f and g weight functions can vary with time.

Much of the recent development in temporal graphs, however, has been for sets of nodes that can be treated as constant, with the edges being pairwise contacts such as phone calls or e-mails between individuals, recorded for discrete time periods (summarized in Holme & Saramäki 2013). Rather than treating the nodes as persistent, the same structure can be described as persistent objects with associated nodes that have temporal locations; the nodes then appear and disappear during the recorded activity, such as the phone calls mentioned above. Figure 8.1 illustrates this description with five persistent objects, connected from time to time by time-located interactions, each with two nodes and a single edge. Here, either there is no directional implication (Figure 8.1a) or a direction can be made explicit (A to B distinct from B to A; Figure 8.1b). This chapter will focus on these edge-dynamic graphs, with time treated mainly as discrete intervals.

Further augmentations of the basic concept of temporal and dynamic graphs have been proposed, such as dynamic digraphs (the edges have directions) and dynamic signed graphs (the edges are positive or negative) in the same basic classes listed, and thus providing many structural types in this scheme. In fact, the most familiar ecological example of a dynamic graph is probably the trophic network (see Chapter 4), which is a dynamic aspatial network with varying weights on the nodes representing species biomass and varying weights on the edges representing rates of consumption which fluctuate with prey availability and predator switching behaviour. In this example, however, the temporal locations of the nodes may be aggregated or inexplicit, and these are the edge-dynamic graphs of the previous classification (Harary & Gupta 1997). The terminology for these graphs is diverse. Kostakos (2009) referred to *temporal graphs* and Casteigts et al. (2011) preferred *time-varying graphs*, but also used the term of *dynamic networks* (Casteigts et al. 2011) where Kempe et al. (2002) preferred *temporal networks*. They can also be called *time-only graphs* to emphasize the lack of a spatial dimension or *time-ordered networks* (Blonder & Dornhaus 2011) emphasizing the fact that the order of the contacts, which the edges represent, has important effects on the outcomes (Nicosia et al. 2013). Because of the emphasis on the order of edges, these may be called *time-ordered graphs*. Whatever the terminology, these graphs enable researchers to study changes and continuity through time, and in an ecological context, they can provide the means to examine the dynamics, persistence or recovery of ecological features.

Order and Orderliness

One of the potentially key features of temporal or time-ordered graphs is the property of orderliness. As the word itself suggests, orderliness is related to order in the sense of sequence, the ordering of nodes and of edges, and also to the consistency of sequences and thus to the predictability of those orders. The absence of orderliness can take different forms, as we can illustrate.

Phone calls, as contacts between individuals and as the mode for information flow, provide a good starting example: the order of the contacts is known (e.g. A to B, then B to C, then C to D, then D to E), but not what items of information were transferred or in which direction. Given the A to E order of contacts just listed, the most orderly structure would seem to be the transfer of the one item of information, x_1, from A to B to C to D to E (Figure 8.2a). Alternatives to this orderly chain would be changes in the item transferred somewhere in the chain, for example, x_2 instead of x_1, delivered from C to D, and then on to E (Figure 8.2b); or a change in the direction of information flow, for example, x_3 from C to B, when the second contact occurs, thus breaking the chain of information flow (Figure 8.2c). Disorder in the sequence of contacts disrupts the potential flow of information; the orderliness here is the sequence of contacts in a time-dependent path.

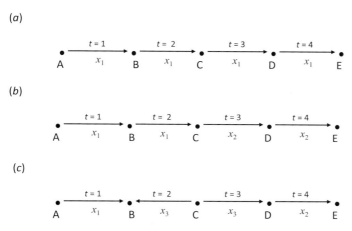

Figure 8.2 Time-ordered graph with information flow. Contacts in discrete time. (a) Temporal path for information from A to E. (b) Information changes within temporal path. (c) No temporal path for information flow from A to E.

Ecological Examples

In this chapter, I describe some smart things that can be done with graph theory, playing in only the temporal dimension, before proceeding to space and then to both space and time in the following chapters. There are some notable examples of ecological systems and phenomena in which the temporal graph approach is most useful.

The first is well documented in the literature: the spread of disease through the same structure of contacts depicted in the basic temporal graph, as originating from the study of social networks (Klovdahl 1985; Keeling 2005; Krause et al. 2007; Newman 2010, Chapter 17). In these graphs, contacts occur between pairs of individuals in discrete time, with any contact having the potential to change the state of the individuals involved, for example, from susceptible to infected. These studies have been greatly facilitated by developing technologies such as proximity loggers that can quantify the interactions between individual animals and the inferred contacts (Drewe et al. 2012; Ryder et al. 2012). Temporal networks provide exactly the right approach to conceptualize and understand these proximity and contact time data. The second fascinating application of this approach is to the study of the behaviour of social insects, both individual and collective (Blonder & Dornhaus 2011; Charbonneau et al. 2013). The applications from social network studies can be adapted for repeated asymmetric animal behavioural interactions such as grooming, which can be counted as a third application (Wey et al. 2008; Krause et al. 2007).

The fourth is time-ordered graphs of bipartite systems, such as plants and pollinators (Figure 8.3, shown in a different form in Figure 8.4), with changes in network structure throughout the flowering season, or from year to year (Olesen et al. 2008; Petanidou et al. 2008). For example, it is easy to imagine the plants and the pollinators each forming a temporal series from early season to late, with the edges between them (pollination events) also forming a consistent early to late sequence as in Figure 8.3. This is "orderly" in every way. This also illustrates a kind of homophily or positive assortativeness (like

Objects

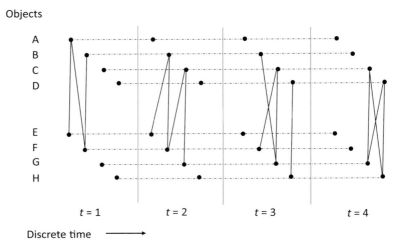

Discrete time ⟶

Figure 8.3 Time-ordered bipartite graph. Both parts with consistent orders of early to late season. Contact edges in time slices, with identity edges (dotted) which can be omitted.

positive autocorrelation), with nodes most commonly joined to nodes with similar characteristics (e.g. early vs late). Real examples may not be so neat, but the matching of orders in both sets of nodes and in the edges of the graph can be evaluated for any such example. For plants and pollinators, the standard "phone call" model needs to be modified to take account of the restrictions on where (or when) the contact edges can appear in the temporal structure. These changes will also affect the randomization procedures that can be meaningfully applied.

The fifth application is also from behavioural ecology, and looks at the "broadcast contact" structures, such as alarm calls among animals within groups (and perhaps chemical alarms as plant communication). In the electronic communication literature, this is parallel to multi-recipient e-mails. Again the basic model needs to be somewhat

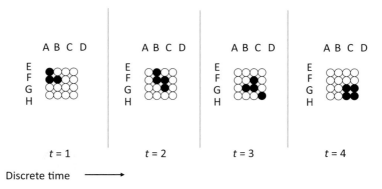

Discrete time ⟶

Figure 8.4 Inter-part contacts in time slices from Figure 8.3. Filled circles indicate edges between node pairs for observed contacts.

Objects

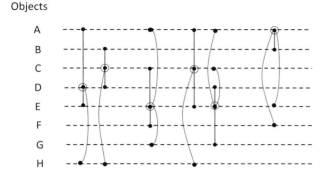

Discrete time ⟶

Figure 8.5 Time-ordered graphs: multi-contact structure. Broadcast contacts: two kinds of nodes, source circled, receiver plain.

modified to allow a single source of information (the source node) to have simultaneous contacts with several other (receiver) nodes, as in Figure 8.5, providing two different kinds of nodes for any broadcast contact event. The phenomenon of alarm signals, including various kinds of audible calls, is common in birds and mammals, and the response of the receivers, upon hearing an alarm call, varies with the "reputation" or status of the sender of the alarm, the signal in the alarm and the kind of danger it indicates, and the maturity or sophistication of the receiver (Hollén & Radford 2009). A further slight modification of the broadcast communication structure can be one that distinguishes between instances of "call and answer" versus "call with no reply," as in Figure 8.6 (think of flocks of geese: "Here am I; where are you?"; see Lorenz 1991). In addition to two kinds of nodes (source and receiver), there are now two kinds of edges (answered and not answered). An interesting question to pursue in such a system is the

Objects

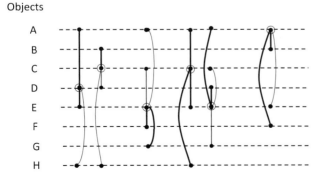

Discrete time ⟶

Figure 8.6 Time-ordered graphs: multi-contact structure with two kinds of node and two kinds of edge. Broadcast contacts (source node circled; receiver node plain). Call-and-answer (thick edges) versus unanswered calls (thin edges).

extent to which the social hierarchy observed in physical behaviour is reflected in the temporal structural hierarchy of calling.

The (Smart) Things to Do

- Find distinguishing characteristics of the network and its temporal structure (partial list below).
- Determine key features of the graph for the dynamics of interest.
- Determine the "busiest" nodes, or the nodes that are in the positions of most control.
- Identify and characterize individual nodes or common forms of interlinked sets of nodes (temporal motifs) with unusual properties or mere prevalence.
- Use randomizations (more than one) to determine the "significance" of the observed properties.
- Compare temporal characteristics of one system with those of other ecological systems. Can we use the comparisons to determine causality?

8.1   Properties of Temporal Graphs

A list of the characteristics of these temporal graphs that will be of interest for ecological applications will look very familiar. Many are properties or measures already encountered in earlier chapters in an atemporal form. For example, the list of graph metrics for temporal networks provided by Nicosia et al. (2013) includes temporal path length, temporal distance, temporal connectedness, graph components, motifs, temporal clustering, centrality measures, betweenness and so on. There is, however, a smaller subset of these that exist only for the temporal context, such as *burstiness*, *persistence*, and *topological overlap* and related measures of temporal autocorrelation of the network edges (Nicosia et al. 2013). As with the names of the kinds of graphs under discussion, there is much variability in the terms that are used, probably because the area is developing so rapidly; but here we will follow what seems to be currently most orthodox.

As with any graph, there are nodes, N of them, and edges between pairs of nodes, potentially $N(N − 1)/2$ of them. The full length of time under consideration starts at 0 and ends at T, and for current purposes, time is in discrete intervals. Each pair of objects represented by nodes may interact (appropriately defined for the study under way) in any time interval, called a contact, and each time interval has its own graph, or time slice of the whole, with edges corresponding to contacts within it. Of course the "contact" of record may be more than just touching, for example, the transfer of certain information or material; or it may be less, for example, mere proximity (see the San Francisco taxi example in Tang et al. 2013). A static aggregated graph can be derived to summarize the entire time, in which the edge for each pair of nodes has a list of contact times associated with it, as in Figure 8.7 which summarizes the contacts in Figure 8.1;

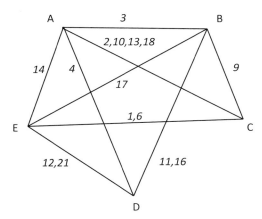

Figure 8.7 Aggregated graph based on Figure 8.1, with contact times noted.

the list can also be converted to a simple weight of the total length of contact time. An edge with no contacts throughout the whole time period is essentially a null edge in the aggregated graph. Time-aggregated graphs summarize the overall structure, but only somewhat; these summary graphs can provide misleading results for predicted system dynamics because the real dynamics on temporal graphs depends on the topology of the individual time slices (see Holme & Saramäki 2011).

Because time is often measured in discrete intervals, a different set of edges may be used to join instances of the same object at different times or in different time "slices" (see dotted lines in Figure 8.3). These are "edges of identity," called "identity arcs" by Moody (2008) and "interslice connections" by Mucha et al. (2010), but they are not usually necessary in time-only graphs and are seldom made explicit. They are much more important in spatio-temporal graphs in which identifiable individuals move through space as well as forward in time, and identity edges help keep track (literally) of where individuals are or of "which are which."

The most important concept for these time-ordered graphs is that of the temporal path, which must take into account the order in which links or contacts between nodes appear, these are also called time-respecting paths. These paths are a sequence of nodes and the pairwise contacts between nodes (along edges) such that the times of the contacts (in their path order) are non-decreasing. Obviously, if the contacts are not all contemporaneous in the path, it becomes asymmetric and the reachability of node A from node B does not imply the reachability of node B from node A. Similarly, transitivity is not guaranteed: temporal paths from A to node B and from B to C do not imply a path from A to C if the A to B path occurs after B to C. Figure 8.8 illustrates this property for simple temporal paths.

The sensitivity of paths to temporal order requires a modification of measures of centrality, too. Based on Kim and Anderson (2012) and Tang et al. (2009), and the usual model for temporal graphs of persistent nodes and contact edges in discrete time, different measures of centrality can be defined.

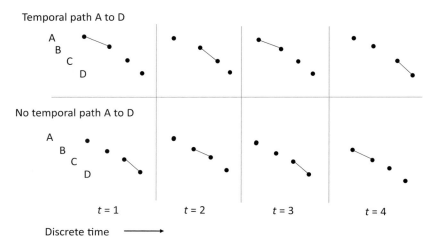

Figure 8.8 Time-ordered graphs arranged in discrete time slices. Top series: there is a path from A to D. Bottom series: no such path exists.

8.1.1   Centrality Measures for Temporal Graphs

These are the same as described in Chapter 3, Table 3.1, but distance is now interpreted as temporal distance:

> *Betweenness Centrality*: The temporal betweenness centrality of node v is the proportion of the shortest temporal paths between any pair of nodes in G that pass through node v.
>
> For applications related to information flow, the shortness of the path should be combined with the shortest of retention times at the node before the information is relayed to the next node in the path.
>
> *Closeness Centrality*: The temporal closeness centrality measures the average temporal distance from node v to all other nodes. Nodes with shorter temporal distance on average have a greater centrality in the temporal graph.
>
> *Eigenvector (Spectral) Centrality*: Includes all possible paths in its measure, not just the shortest paths, accounting for the greater importance of shorter paths by (down-) weighting each path by a factor based on its length, λ: α^λ for some constant α.
>
> *Broadcast (Source) Centrality* and *Receive (Sink) Communicability*
>
> Broadcast Centrality is a measure of how well node i can communicate to all others, based on communicability. The count of all temporal paths of any length is expressed by the communicability matrix, $\mathbf{Q}$ (Grindrod et al. 2011; Nicosia et al. 2013):

$$\mathbf{Q} \equiv [\mathbf{I} - \alpha \mathbf{A}\,(\mathbf{t}_0)]^{-1} [\mathbf{I} - \alpha \mathbf{A}\,(\mathbf{t}_1)]^{-1} \ldots [\mathbf{I} - \alpha \mathbf{A}\,(\mathbf{t}_m)]^{-1}. \tag{8.1}$$

Broadcast centrality is then

$$C_i(B) = \sum_{j=1}^{N} Q_{ij}$$ (8.2)

(Grindrod et al. 2011; Nicosia et al. 2013). Receive (Sink) Communicability is a measure of how well node i can be reached from all others:

$$C_i(R) = \sum_{j=1}^{N} Q_{ji}$$ (8.3)

(Grindrod et al. 2011; Nicosia et al. 2013). As for paths in a digraph consisting of directed edges, in a temporal graph, there are several kinds of connected components for any node I: the out-component of I is the set of all nodes, J, for which there is a temporal path from I to J; the in-component of I is the set of all nodes, J, for which there is a temporal path from J to I (Nicosia et al. 2012). A strongly connected component has temporal paths in both directions between any pair of nodes within it. These components represent the most highly connected subgraphs, and are related to the internal "community structure" of temporal graphs representing social interactions (Nicosia et al. 2012), and those authors describe a method to find these components in temporal graphs and provide some examples of the application and outcomes.

Another consequence is that any path has two kinds of length: (1) topological length, which is the number of edges traversed, and (2) temporal length, which is the time taken to traverse it. For example, in Figure 8.9, the path A – B – E has topological length 2, but temporal length 5. As a result, there are two measures of distance between two nodes: the topological distance is the length of the topologically shortest path between them, and the temporal distance is the length of their temporally shortest path. For example, in Figure 8.9, the topological distance between A and E is 1 (by the path A – E, with temporal length 7) and the temporal distance between A and E is 4 (by path A – B – C – D – E, with topological length 4). Different definitions of short temporal paths are possible and some refer to the *fastest path* (Wu et al. 2014). Figure 8.9, with accompanying tables, illustrates some of these concepts. The term *latency* refers to the shortest time required to go from A to B by a time-respecting path. There may be challenges in computing shortest temporal paths, but comparing them with the distances in the associated static summary can be very revealing (Wu et al. 2014), with the characteristics of the aggregated graph being possibly very different from the characteristics of the temporal graphs it summarizes. This result echoes the important understanding that the dynamics on temporal graphs depend on the topology in the time slices, so that time-aggregated graphs can provide misleading results (Holme & Saramäki 2011). In ordinary static graphs, a useful measure of graph "size" is the characteristic path length, which is just the average distance between all possible pairs of nodes. In temporal graphs, many pairs may have no temporal path between them, giving a distance of ∞ (for example nodes C and G in Figure 8.9 are mutually unreachable), and so the average may not be helpful, although we might use the average of those that are finite. Nicosia et al. (2013),

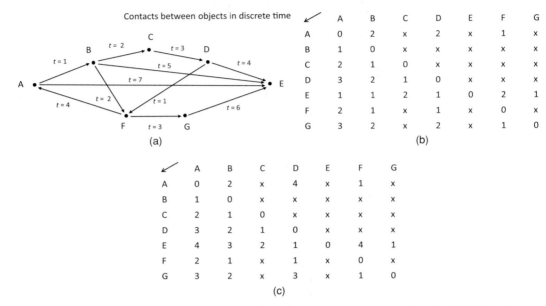

Figure 8.9 (a) Time-ordered graph path lengths and distances. The path A, B, C, D, E has four edges and uses $t = 1,2,3,4$. It is longest but arrives first. The path (A,B); (B,E) has two edges and uses $t = 1, 5$. The path of edge (A,E) has only one edge and uses $t = 7$. It is shortest but arrives last. (b) Shortest paths in edge counts. (c) Shortest paths in time units.

suggested using the average of the distances' inverses, d_{ij}^{-1}, then called the temporal efficiency. Pairs of nodes with no path between them now contribute zero to the average.

8.1.2   Burstiness and Persistence

Measures related to temporal distances between pairs of nodes are important evaluations of the structure of the graph, but there are also properties based on the distribution of the actual contacts between pairs of nodes. The first is the comment that contacts in many time-ordered systems tend to be "bursty": the distribution tends to have a "heavy tail" with more contact events far apart in time (Nicosia et al. 2013). (I think the implication is also that there are temporal clusters of contacts that are closer together than expected from randomness; think of the "broken stick" statistics for one dimension; Dale & Fortin 2014, Section 4.4.1.) A measure of this characteristic can be based on the distribution of the waiting time between consecutive contact events of any pairs, τ, call it $P(\tau)$. For a Poisson process, the waiting time follows an exponential distribution, and of course, for a Poisson distribution the variance and the mean are the same. The logical approach is to then base a burstiness measure on the coefficient of variation of the waiting times (Min & Goh 2013), which is the ratio of the standard deviation, s_τ, and the mean m_τ, giving

$$B = (s_\tau/m_\tau - 1) \div (s_\tau/m_\tau + 1). \tag{8.4}$$

Pairwise contacts in time units

Objects

A

B

C

D

E

Discrete time ⟶

Figure 8.10 Time-ordered graphs: bursts of contacts and persistence through discrete time. The contacts occur in bursts, and some contacts (e.g. B − C) are persistent, appearing in adjacent time units.

This parameter runs from −1 when the events are perfectly regular, through 0 when they are independent, to +1 for maximum burstiness (Min & Goh 2013).

The second property is the feature that contacts tend to be "persistent," with higher frequencies of contacts between I and J at time $t + \tau$ when there is already contact between them at time t. Figure 8.10 gives an example in which the inter-pair contacts occur in bursts and in which some contacts are more persistent than others (e.g. B to C and D to E). This characteristic of persistence is essentially temporal autocorrelation among the times of contact for the same pair of nodes, and Nicosia et al. (2013) introduced a temporal autocorrelation measure, $C_i(t_m, t_m + \Delta t)$, which they refer to as "topological overlap" for node I at time t. This measure becomes a "temporal [auto-] correlation coefficient" when averaged over all times at node I to give C_i for node I, and then averaged over all nodes, to give C as a measure for the whole graph. The concept of homophily or positive assortativeness of neighbour nodes for temporal graphs can include the proximity in time of the nodes' edges, as well as other characteristics such as aggregate degree.

In addition to the autocorrelation of the contacts themselves, Min and Goh (2013) suggested examining the autocorrelation of the waiting times, τ, as a complement to the measure of burstiness. The measure they propose is just the correlation coefficient of successive waiting times, τ_k and τ_{k+1}, and they refer to it as a memory coefficient, M, which can be positive or negative, reflecting the short-term autocorrelation. They suggested comparing temporal sequences in a bivariate plot of burstiness, B, and memory, M, since the two are more or less independent. They provide examples of different phenomena plotted in a "burstiness map space" (M vs B) in two dimensions, which does prove informative and seems worth pursuing for ecological data.

Temporal autocorrelation is a key feature of these time-ordered networks, noting that it can be positive, indicating persistence, or negative, indicating rapid change. For example, a temporal graph of a community trophic network with several panels representing different time periods makes it possible to evaluate, for each "location" in the network, the degree and specificity of the greatest change in and the greatest persistence of characteristics. The continuity represented by persistence can be thought of as the system's "memory" more generally than just waiting times: the extent to which past behaviour of the system affects current and future processes, thus persisting through a number of realizations or observations of the processes.

If temporal autocorrelation is very strong, the result may be contact edges that persist more or less continuously through a number of time slices. Just as the phenology of individual plant or insect species of a pollination network can be portrayed as parallel line segments running through time (Figure 8.11a) (see also Olesen et al. 2008, Figures 3b and 3c), the observed pairwise pollination interactions can be portrayed in the same way. In the case of discontinuities in actual observations, it may be reasonable to assume continuity that is just not observed. The result for either the species or their pairwise interactions is a sheaf of parallel line segments depicting the phenomenon's duration, as well as start and stop time. In some applications, the temporal overlap of strings of contact edges can be an important characteristic of the overall structure. Then, there may be good reason to extend the concept of "overlap" as it applies in these graphs, beyond its introduction by Nicosia et al. (2013) in the context of autocorrelation. Earlier in this book (somewhere!), the concept of an "interval graph" was described. This graph is based on a set of N intervals on the real line, like a set of finite line segments. The nodes of the interval graph are these intervals or line segments and an edge joins any pair of nodes for which the line segments overlap (see Figure 8.11b). This approach does not usually distinguish between cases of partial overlap, like segments A and B, and cases of complete overlap, like segment E which is completely within the range of segment D; but it easily could by using different edge designations. There are a number of statistics already available to summarize the characteristics of possibly overlapping line segments (see Dale & Fortin 2014, Section 9.2.3.2), and the analogy with possibly overlapping time periods (of contact) in a temporal graph is obvious, but the relationship will need further clarification if only because the time segments in a temporal graph can be intermittent.

8.1.3   Motifs

Previously, the concept of a "motif" in a graph was described as a subgraph of consistent structure that was repeated as many instances in a single graph or in a family of graphs based on similar applications. In time-ordered graphs, a "temporal motif" is a class of isomorphic subgraphs that are topologically similar and have the same order of corresponding contacts (Nicosia et al. 2013; Kovanen et al. 2011). For ecological applications, such as studies of the spread of disease, temporal networks with "coloured" (labelled) nodes are of particular interest (see Kovanen et al. 2013a), such as individuals with the three labels of disease progression: S = susceptible, I = infected, or R = removed (recovered or deceased). In such a case, there can be different motifs with the same topological and temporal structure distinguished by the labels on the nodes (e.g. Figure 8.12). Then, we can find the answers to interesting questions such as whether the presence of the disease affects behaviour or system dynamics as shown by changing frequencies of the temporal motif frequencies.

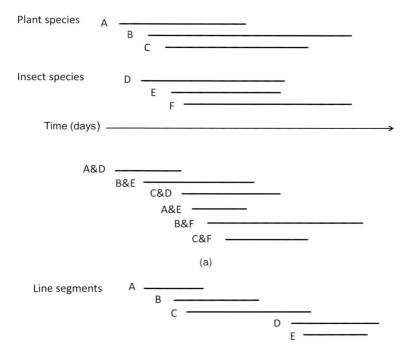

(a)

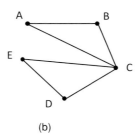

(b)

Figure 8.11 (a) (top) Line segments depicting species phenology, flowering of plants and pollination activity by insects. (bottom) Line segments depicting pollination contact phenology. (b) Interval graph: derived from parallel line segments with edges between nodes representing the line segments when they overlap.

Example of a temporal motif with "coloured" (i.e. labelled) nodes: I = infected; S = susceptible; R = removed (dead or recovered and no longer susceptible). There are two nodes, and one edge possible, indicating contact in only one time interval (Figure 8.12):

$$t = 0 \quad \text{I} \ldots \text{S},$$

$$t = 1 \quad \text{I} \rightarrow \text{S} \ \text{(contact, allowing infection)},$$

$$t = 2 \quad \text{R} \ldots \text{I} \ \text{(second node now infected)},$$

$$t = 3 \quad \text{R} \ldots \text{R}.$$

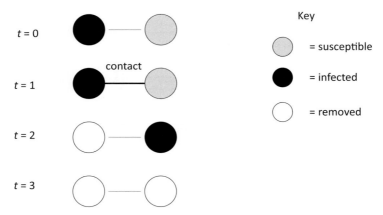

Figure 8.12 A temporal motif in a time-ordered graph, based on contact and infection.

Obviously, the motifs that are of interest will be different for different applications. For example, the temporal motifs for broadcast alarm signals will have many more edges than the common motifs in bipartite graph applications. The simplest motifs for two time units are shown in Figure 8.13; if the node labels are ignored, there are six with the six descriptions given there. If node labels are considered, or if the nodes have distinct "colours," there are more than six. In studying human social networks as revealed by mobile phone contacts, Kovanen et al. (2013b) found that temporal motif frequencies revealed both homophily (greater than expected similarity of node characteristics when joined by a contact event), and gender-specific patterns. For example, an analysis of the two-edge motifs (those in Figure 8.13) with 24 node types (classified by gender, age group and payment type) found an over-representation of both chain and star formats

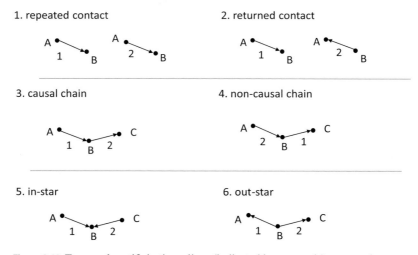

Figure 8.13 Temporal motifs in time slices (indicated by numerals): repeated contact; returned contact; causal chain; non-causal chain; in-star; out-star.

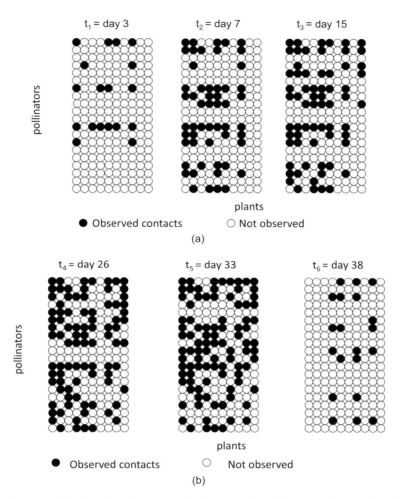

$t_1 = $ day 3 $t_2 = $ day 7 $t_3 = $ day 15

pollinators

plants

● Observed contacts   ○ Not observed

(a)

$t_4 = $ day 26 $t_5 = $ day 33 $t_6 = $ day 38

pollinators

plants

● Observed contacts   ○ Not observed

(b)

Figure 8.14 Arctic pollination network at different time slices, from Olesen et al. (2008). Filled circles indicate edges between pairs of nodes.

(bottom four in Figure 8.13) for all nodes being female. Although this is obviously not an ecological example, the approach and application can obviously be transferred to many ecological phenomena with behavioural or social structural components.

With labels included, so that repeated contact is distinguishable (if necessary) from contact returned, the repeated contact motif in the basic time-ordered graph is a building block of what was termed "persistence," which is temporal autocorrelation of edges across time slices. In the bipartite temporal graph of predation, parasitism or mutualism such as pollination, the directionality of any edge is implicit, and the repeated directional contact remains the structural basis of longer-term persistence. Figure 8.14 introduces an example (which will return later) of plant-pollinator interactions in arctic tundra (from Olesen et al. 2008) observed over several dates through the short summer.

Persistence between time units is an obvious feature of the data, but limited by the strong effect of the seasonal progression.

8.2   Techniques for Temporal Graphs: Testing Significance

The simplest version of testing significance in temporal graphs is the use of restricted randomizations for the characteristics of interest. These may be characteristics of the whole graph such as path length, the burstiness of events, or the frequencies of classes of motifs; or characteristics associated with individual nodes, or edges or time slices. These include centrality measures for nodes or edges, local indices of persistence and autocorrelation (local by node, edge or time slice), and topological properties such as connectivity or connectedness within a time slice. The combination of frequency enumeration and the comparison of observed and expected values can also be used, but the restricted randomization approach is more general and has much to recommend it.

8.2.1   Random Assignment and Restricted Randomizations

As already hinted, one of the key methods for the analysis of these graphs, and one of the strengths of this general approach, is the application of more than one randomization procedure (Holme & Saramäki 2011). Having a choice of procedures allows a choice of which characteristics are to be preserved by the algorithm used, and makes a hierarchical analysis possible. It is worth describing several of these algorithms in detail and for comparison. The following material is based on Holme and Saramäki (2011) with some modification for conventions, and some additional comments.

"Randomized Edges" (RE) is the first method in their list, and it is based on swapping the end-nodes of pairs of contact edges. It can be thought of as a "re-wiring" approach, since the contact edges are the focus, not the nodes themselves. Proceeding sequentially through all possible contact edges (I, J), for each, a second edge (K, L) is chosen at random. The edges (I, J) at time T and (K, L) at time Y are then replaced with probability 0.5 by (I, L) and (K, J) or by (I, K) and (J, L) at the original times, T and Y. If a self-edge or multiple edge results from this replacement, a new (K, L) is chosen and the process repeated. Figure 8.15a provides an illustration of this randomization.

For contact edges that are not directed, this algorithm preserves the degree of each node as well as the number of contact edges in each time unit, but not the number of times each pair of nodes are in contact. For directed edges, depicting the follow of information, for example, the node degrees are not necessarily conserved. For example, if edges (I, J) and (K, L) are replaced by (I, K) and (J, L), node K becomes a sink node where it was a source, so its in-degree decreases by one and its out-degree increases by one. Node J becomes a source node where it was a sink, so its in-degree increases by one and its out-degree decreases by one. A solution is to offer two choices, each with probability 0.5: (I, L) and (K, J), as above, or (I, J) and (K, L), the original configuration. Figure 8.15b illustrates the basic algorithm, and also an alternative to consider. The alternative is to preserve the in-degrees and out-degrees by offering three choices for

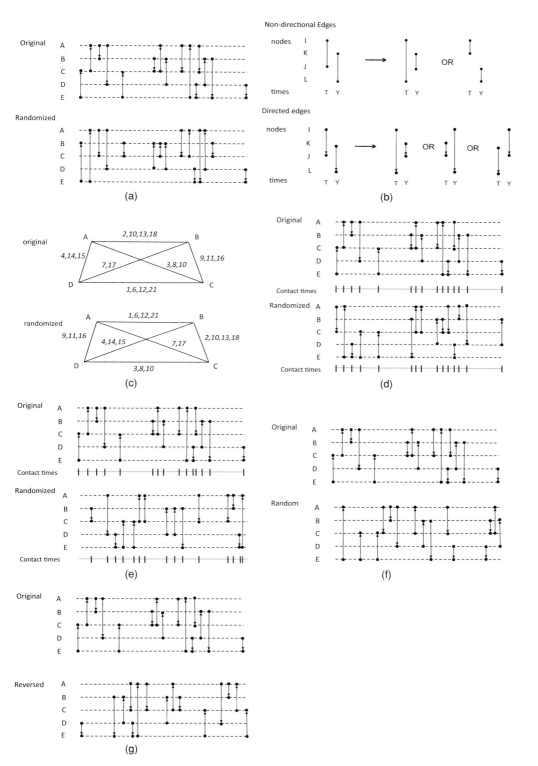

Figure 8.15 Temporal graph randomizations: contact node swaps (RE*). (a) Original and randomized. (b) Details for non-directed and for directed edges. (c) Link sequence shuffle: complete contact time sequences are exchanged. (d) Permuted contact times (RP). (e) Random contact times (RT). (f) Random contact edges at random times (RC). (g) Reversed contact times (TR). *Abbreviated designations are from Holme and Saramäki (2011). T and Y are time periods.

the two contact edges: swap the sinks of the two directed edges; swap their sources; swap both sources and sinks. The last choice is the same as switching the two edges from times T and Y to times Y and T.

Karsai et al. (2011) described a similar method, which they refer to as "link-sequence shuffled" or "DCB": entire contact time sequences are exchanged between randomly chosen pairs of edges. For example, if A and B were originally joined at times 1, 3 and 7, and C and D were joined at times 2, 4 and 8; the randomized version might have A and B joined at 2, 4 and 8, and C and D at 1, 3 and 7. No novel contact time sequences are produced, and the figure for RE in Holme and Saramäki (2011) showed a similar preservation of the edge contact time sequences (my interpretation of their algorithm seems to make that possible). On the other hand, the contact sequences associated with particular nodes can be reorganized in either process; for example, in Figure 8.15c, any randomization of the node labels in the original configuration would preserve the common node for edges with link sequences (4, 14, 15), (2, 10,13, 18) and (3, 8, 10).

"Randomly Permuted Times" (RP) is the second method in the Holme and Saramäki list of randomizations. Here, the times of the observed contact edges are randomly shuffled, preserving the distribution of edge numbers in each time unit, the degrees of each node, and the number of contacts between each pair of nodes, but breaking up the details of which pairs of nodes are in contact at which times. It also preserves the burstiness of the distribution of the contacts through time. This technique is referred to as "time-shuffled" or "DCW" by Karsai et al. (2011). Figure 8.15d illustrates this randomization and shows how the distribution of positions of contact events remains unchanged along the time axis.

A third choice of randomization is to combine the first two: RE + RP, with contact edge randomization preceding the permutation of the contact times (not illustrated). I think this is the same as the "configuration model" of randomization, also called "D" by Karsai et al. (2011).

The "Random Times" (RT) technique uses the observed set of contact edges but repositions them at randomly chosen positions on the time line, thus disrupting any autocorrelation and any clustering or burstiness of these events through time. Figure 8.15e gives an example of the outcome of this technique and makes it obvious that the distribution of event timing is not preserved.

The "Random Contacts" (RC) approach is really a modelling technique, rather than a randomization method, since it essentially creates a new "data set" for comparison, rather than rearranging observed data. Here, the equivalent number of edges are created between randomly chosen pairs at randomly chosen times. Restricted versions of this algorithm are also possible, for example, by having the numbers of random edges per given time period constrained to be the same as in the observed data (Figure 8.15f).

The list provided by Holme and Saramäki (2011) includes three more randomizations. Two require very large data sets and may be less of interest for ecological analysis (see comments in 8.3), but the third is intriguing. Again, it is not really a randomization; it is "Time Reversal" (TR), running the observed sequence backward (Figure 8.15g). This can provide the opportunity to determine causal sequences. As a simple example, if contact (A, B) is frequently followed by contact (B, C) in the observed sequence, but never in the reverse, this may provide evidence of a causal connection rather than mere association of the two edge types. This approach looks beyond temporal autocorrelation to examine the temporal asymmetry of the sequences. It essentially looks at pairs of temporal motifs that can indicate causal relationships, as in the chains shown in Figure 8.13. It may be especially useful in cases where the edges have direction, with (A, B) distinct from (B, A), but that is not essential.

Clearly these various randomization procedures can be applied to data that take the form of time-ordered bipartite graphs, such as plant-pollinator networks (Figure 8.14), with some modification of their restrictions. In adapting these randomization tests for bipartite graphs, little change of procedure may be required, but an understanding of the ecology should be included in making any modifications. Taking the arctic plant-pollinator data as an example, while a full randomization for the random times (RT) approach could be used (Figure 8.15e), it would be more appropriate to constrain the time of edges by the phenology of the plant and of the insect, so that edges only appear when the plant is flowering and the insect is active. Similarly, the creation of random edges in any model needs to be limited by avoiding "forbidden links" (Olesen et al. 2008; Jordano 1987), here including pollination interactions that just cannot happen, such as a long-tubed flower and a pollinator with short mouth-parts.

It is an easy step, in concept, to go from restricted randomization to a modelling procedure that includes the same restrictions in the generation of artificial "data" for comparison with the observed results.

8.3   Applications of Techniques

Applications of these techniques to ecological data provide some challenges and advantages that may not arise in other data sets. Studies of social networks such as those reviewed by Holme and Saramäki (2011) or Kovanen et al. (2013b) frequently involve huge data sets, with possibly billions of contacts (the edges) between millions of phone users (the nodes). This scale has the disadvantages associated with analyzing huge data sets, although many of the problems have been solved, but the scale also makes it possible that very small effects are highly significant if they are consistent. Data sets such as the network of phone calls of millions of users have the additional advantage that with many nodes, the study duration can be short and still provide large numbers. This reduces the potential for temporal non-stationarity. Ecological data sets, on the other hand, will tend to have relatively small numbers of observations, both nodes and edges, and larger numbers may require longer duration, increasing the risk of non-stationarity. Our data will also lack the temporal fine-scale precision and accuracy of the electronic examples, with even hourly observations being rare. As elsewhere in data analysis, temporal networks can have an important but difficult relationship between the scale of the process being studied, the scale of the data recorded, and the scale at which the analysis is performed (Caceres & Berger-Wolf 2013; see also Dale & Fortin 2014, Figure 1.8).

Figure 8.14 gives a sample of the results of a study by Olesen et al. (2008) of how an arctic plant-pollinator network changes through the growing season. The study site was of mixed vegetation in northeastern Greenland and the observation period was determined by the end of snow-melt and the first snowfall. There were 31 species of flowering plants and 76 pollinating insect species, and a daily census was taken of insect pollinator visits to all plants in flower. The networks of such contacts in six time slices are provided in Figure 8.14 for a subset of 10 plants and 20 insects. Sophisticated randomization tests are not required to detect the basic characteristics of short-term persistence and longer-term turnover, with a slow build-up of edges being added to the network followed by a rapid decline. The authors studied the same system in two consecutive summers and found remarkable structural similarities between the two instances, despite strong year-to-year differences in the identities of the pollinators and in the plant-pollinator links. The degree distributions were best fit by a power law or a truncated power law model, consistent with the attachment of new pollinators to old plants being intermediate between fully preferential and fully independent of node degree. The message to other ecologists is that this is an approach you might try; you can do this too.

In a different vein, Nicosia et al. (2012) discussed the concepts, methods and some applications of finding the various kinds of connected components in time-varying graphs. Of greatest ecological relevance is their study of components of graphs of the co-location of individuals through time, humans in this case, but the extension to other organized and mobile social populations is obvious. The study was of about 100 individuals at MIT during 6 months, with their locations sampled every 5 minutes. Of particular interest were the sizes of the in- and out-components in the social structure, and how they change from the work-week (Monday to Thursday) to the weekend (Friday to Sunday). In the work-week, almost all the nodes have in- and out-components of size about 72, but around the weekend, the components vary greatly among the different nodes (Nicosia et al. 2012, Figure 4), and are usually smaller than 72 (approximately 30 to 50 for in-components; 40–60 for out-components). In contrast, the static time-aggregated graphs usually have a single large component of 70+ in the work-week and around 65 on the weekend. Once again, the static time-aggregated summary can be misleading when compared to the true dynamics of the system.

Networks, social and otherwise, are important as models for studying and predicting the behaviour of epidemics in populations, and as frameworks for analyzing observed patterns of disease spread. Despite the fact that many of the underlying networks of inter-individual contacts, which are the mechanism of contagion, are actually dynamic and ephemeral, aggregated static summary graphs of these interactions have been shown to be very useful in this context (e.g. Craft & Caillaud 2011; Newman 2010, Chapter 17). Disease dynamics, however, may be uneven in both space and time. These networks can include the spatial components of structure (see the following Chapters 9 and 10), but the unevenness in time suggests a need to separate the time slices of the phenomenon. A number of authors have argued that summary networks are a poor substitute for the changing temporal graphs that provide much better insight into the temporal structure of inter-individual contacts, and thus into the transmission of disease (e.g. Karsai et al. 2011; Horváth & Kertész 2014). For example, it has been demonstrated that "burstiness," the clustering of events in time, has an effect on the dynamics of disease spread, in part through the "small world" characteristics, such as short paths, that can result. The temporal structure of contact events can slow or speed up the spread of disease (Horváth & Kertész 2014). Depending on the topology, the burstiness tends to slow the spread of disease and can lead to longer-term persistence (Karsai et al. 2011; Vázquez 2013); and dynamic centrality measures are good predictors of the ability of infected nodes to spread the disease through the network, whether based on the proportion of the network infected in a fixed period or the time to infect half the network (Mantzaris & Higham 2013).

In applied ecology, the studies of proximity and contact networks as temporal structures have been especially useful in understanding the dynamics of the spread of diseases of economic or conservation importance, and temporal network analysis is ideal for this purpose, particularly when it can go beyond the time-aggregated summary graph. The data can be derived from mark-recapture methods, radio-collar tracking (Perkins et al. 2009), or (more recently and potentially much better) proximity data loggers. Network analysis has been used to understand the influence of proximity or contact on the spread of facial tumour disease in wild Tasmanian devil (*Sarcophilus harrisii*) (Hamede et al. 2009), bovine TB in brushtail possum (*Mycobacterium bovis* in *Trichosurus vulpecula*) (Porphyre et al. 2008), and the potential effects of social association strengths in populations wild rabbit (*Oryctolagus cuniculus*) (Marsh et al. 2011). Similar approaches have been used for the study of parasites and the factors affecting their transmission through natural populations, reviewed by Godfrey (2013). In many such applications, whether for disease or macroparasites, the aggregated network is used, although the importance of non-stationarity, especially in the form of seasonality, is well understood (Perkins et al. 2009; Hamede et al. 2009). Technological advances like the automated proximity logger provide data that can be more easily resolved in to true temporal networks, such as those described here, and will provide an improved understanding of these highly dynamic systems (see Danon et al. 2011). The required analysis methods already exist and have been used to analyze human social network data of various kinds, including physical proximity, for which the data sets can be very large (see Panisson et al. 2012). Applying these methods to ecological studies should prove highly informative.

8.4   Conclusions and Advice

When the outline of this book was originally sketched, this chapter did not exist. However, in beginning to put together and to revise the material for the chapter on spatio-temporal graphs, and in the context of the work on spatial graphs, it became clear that a chapter on time-only graphs was needed. As often in book writing, research revealed a very rich, if yet very incomplete, body of work on this topic, which now seems an essential aspect of applying graph theory in ecological research.

There are other kinds of graphs for ecological applications that include the dimension of time but not space, including models or field-based examples of state transitions. Here, the nodes of the graph represent some kind of object or unit, which is identified as being in one of several possible states. Directional edges indicate the possible or

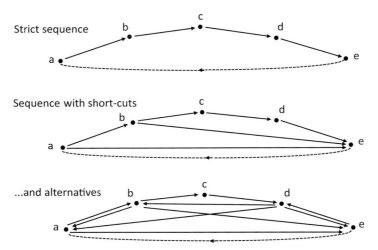

Figure 8.16 State and transition: the labelled nodes represent the states of a single object. Strict sequence; sequence with shortcuts; sequence with alternatives. The solid edges are spontaneous transitions; the dashed edge may depend on external forces to intervene.

observed transitions between states for a single object. For example, the top face of a die can be in one of six possible states; starting with state A (1, 2, 3, 4, 5 or 6), when the die is rolled, the transitions to all six states (including A itself) should be equally probable. The transition graph is then a complete digraph with edges in both directions between every pair of states (30 edges). On the other hand, if the object of interest is a forest tree which can be in one of three states (healthy, diseased and dead), the transition graph is not a complete digraph because the third (and final) state must have out-degree zero.

In applied ecology, such as rangeland management, the vegetation of sites is placed in one of several categories (e.g. shortgrass prairie, tallgrass savanna, oak woodland, etc.), with the challenge being the quantification and prediction of transitions in time between the identified states (Phillips 2011). With the states as nodes, and possible transitions being the edges between nodes, each set of transitions forms a network, and the structural characteristics of that network can be subjected to analysis using graph theory measures, such as spectral radius and algebraic connectivity (Phillips 2011). Figure 8.16 shows some basic possibilities: (1) a strict sequence where state **a** can transition only to **b**, **b** to **c** and so on, with a return to the starting condition possibly requiring external intervention; (2) a similar sequence, but with shortcuts (e.g. state **b** to state **e**) possible; and (3) a less orderly system in which the original strict sequence is easily lost. Of course, this model of vegetation dynamics is much less "crisp" than the original time-only phone call model; the state transitions may be very indistinct, as may the point in time at which the transition in fact occurs.

One elaboration of the state transition model is to have the probabilities of different possible transitions depend on the history of the object represented: the sequence of states in which it existed previously and the times of the transitions between states. This is very similar to the familiar higher order Markov model of temporal sequences.

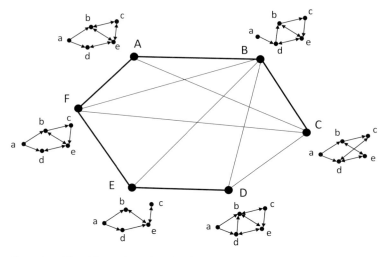

Figure 8.17 Six objects, A to F, each with a transition sequence among five states, a to e. Edges are interactions between objects. There are two versions: thick edges and thick + thin. Edge thickness indicates proportion of time of occurrence.

A second elaboration is to consider more than one object, each with its own sequence of transitions between states, but those transitions are affected by the interactions between the objects. Figure 8.17 illustrates the idea with a graph in continuous time six objects, each with five possible states and sequences of transitions among them. Suppose a transition at one object tends to trigger transitions in its network neighbours or that it tends to "pull" neighbours toward the same state or "push" them toward something quite different. Then the dynamics of transitions will differ between the sparse graph with few edges (only the thicker lines) and the more highly connected graph (all lines). Under these circumstances, the network topology (the positions of edges) will affect the state transitions at individual nodes and thus the dynamics of the whole network. If the edges are transient in time, and appear and disappear, we can imagine a situation in which the states of the nodes can affect the topology. For example, if edges are more likely to form between nodes in similar states, the nodes' dynamic sequences will affect topology, with topology having its own effect on the dynamics. The reciprocal effects of structure and function can be thought of as their "coevolution" in these dynamic networks, sometimes called "adaptive networks." The concept of adaptive networks is important in ecology and will be returned to in a later chapter (Chapter 11).

To complement Figure 8.17, Figure 8.18 gives a discrete time example of six objects with four states. The time unit edges join objects that interact in the time period indicated. The "arm-chair" version of what the figure represents is a small herd of grazing animals that are monitored both for individual behaviour (the node states) and pair proximities (the time-located edges), like the proximity logger data described for white-tailed deer by Tosa et al. (2013). The nodes are the individuals that alternate through a range of behaviour "states," such as grazing, moving between habitat patches and sleeping or resting at one location. The edges indicate time units in which the pair of

Objects

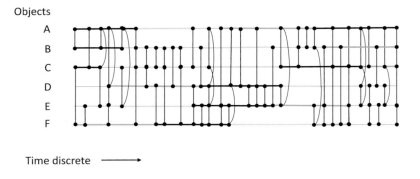

Time discrete ⟶

4 states: black, dark grey, light grey, dotted.

Figure 8.18 Temporal graph of six objects with four states. Pairwise contacts (topology) are affected by states. State transitions are affected by contacts. (A black-and-white version of this figure will appear in some formats. For the colour version, please refer to the plate section.)

individuals registers as being close to each other in the proximity data. There is one node state (yellow in the colour version of the figure) that is obvious for having few proximity records or few changes in proximity, the resting or sleeping state with limited movement.

To pursue the concept of the coevolution of network topology and network function in a system of species interactions with state-and-transition node properties, consider six species of zooplankton that can all prey upon each other depending on their relative sizes at the time of encounter, which in turn depends on age, life-history stage, and nutritional history (see Chapter 4). The "states" used could be these features of individuals or summaries of the whole population for example "all mature adults" or "mostly small juveniles" or "bimodal in size and age." The categories of states need not be identical for all six species. The states could also include division by vertical position in the water column or geographical location. (Yes, the edges could have directions for greater clarity of the nature of the interaction.) One obvious way in which function can affect topology would be for predation rates to switch among potential prey in response to state (e.g. copepods can adjust the prey size selected in response to abundance; Levinton 1982). This suggested example may seem a bit fanciful, but the complexity of some ecological systems is such that this approach might be highly useful, even if abstracted.

As a simplified artificial example, Figure 8.19a illustrates the state and function changes in three species of zooplankton. Species A and B are found in three size classes and prey on the smaller sizes of the other species, with the smallest being preferred. Species C is an alternate prey, but less preferred. All seven nodes occur in three states: absent, rare and abundant. The states of the nodes affect the predation that occurs, the positions of edges, and the function (predation) affects the states of the nodes as increases or decreases in abundance. At time 1, the small and large classes of both A and B are abundant and the large individuals prey preferentially on the small. At time 2, the smallest class is absent, either eaten or grown into the next age class, and the

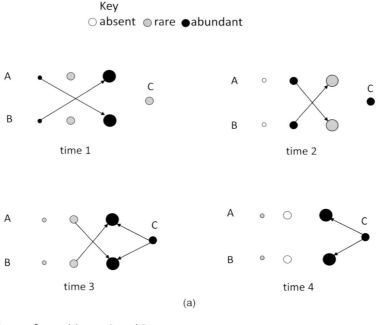

Times of transitions : A and B

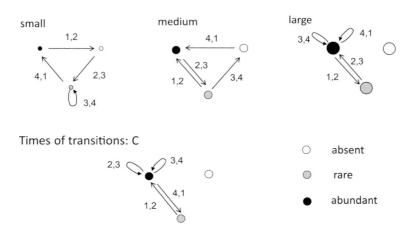

Examples: medium sized A changes from absent to abundant between times 1 & 4;
C changes from abundant to rare between times 4 & 1, and back between 1 & 2.

(b)

Figure 8.19 (a) Species A and B exist in three size classes, each of which can be in any of three states: absent, rare or abundant. Species C is an alternate prey but less preferred. Arrows go from prey to predator. (b) Transitions for species A and B which are different for the different size classes, and transitions for species C, without size classes.

large individuals, now somewhat reduced in number, prey on the less preferred medium sizes, now common. The same sort of pattern occurs in time 3, with the medium classes reduced by growth or predation. The largest classes have been replenished by growth, but they now rely on the alternate prey, species C. The smallest class begins to re-appear as reproduction occurs. At time 4, the middle size classes are absent due to mortality by predation or growth into the large size class, which continues to depend on alternate prey. Time 5 is the same as time 1, with the small classes restored to abundance, and now forming the major prey base of the large sizes.

In the whole cycle, each node has its own sequence of state transitions and their causes, and these are not all the same (Figure 8.19b). While artificial, this example mimics real ecological systems in a simplified form, but it is genuinely time-only, with the nodes and their states located in time, here imitating a seasonal cycle. The function of the network, the transitions of the states of the nodes, and the topology of the network all interact and co-evolve through time. This coevolution of network form and function (or structure and dynamics) will be discussed further in a later chapter (Chapter 11).

While the state transition models are initially non-spatial, another obvious modification is to create a map of the parts of the landscape that are occupied by patches of each identified vegetation category. The purpose of a study of the whole landscape might then be to determine whether there are any spatial neighbour effects on the transitions as well as effects of the spatial location's history of states. This then leads to the use of spatio-temporal graphs to study the history and future of such patches, which will be addressed in a later chapter.

While there are not yet many ecological examples of temporal graphs, there are several models of the analysis of other kinds of data available for us to learn from. Obviously not all temporal graphs are derived from the same form of data, and so the techniques may not translate directly, but the lessons from the literature can be helpful, especially in the suggested use of a hierarchy of restricted randomizations to test hypotheses and suggest answers to questions. There are obviously many phenomena in ecology generally, and in behavioural ecology more specifically where the use of these time-only networks or temporal dynamic graphs, and the theory that goes with them, promises to provide important and valuable insights. We can look forward to seeing more of such studies in the next few years.

9   Spatial Graphs

Introduction

Ecological phenomena and processes occur in a spatial context, whether or not the spatial location is explicit in the data or the analysis. The spatial structure of ecological systems is a critical factor in determining the relationships among objects or species and processes, and important also because there are reciprocal effects of spatial structure on system dynamics, and of processes in time on spatial structure. This reciprocal dependence can be most obvious in graphs which include both space and time (see Chapter 10), but there are many examples where the spatial context is the first priority (think of the phrase that events "take place"). This is especially true for ecological processes related to habitat fragmentation, environmental degradation, land use, climate change and the threat of extinction. In such situations, spatial graphs and the theory that goes with them provide the tools to present, characterize, analyze, test and model spatial systems of ecological interest. This is true, also, of the ecological interactions of predation, facilitation, competition, mutualism, parasitism and so on, that occur in space as well as in time. There are, therefore, many possible applications of spatial graphs in ecological studies (Fall et al. 2007; Dale & Fortin 2010), but the emphasis will be on their use to portray habitat patches in a landscape (nodes) with connections or dispersal between them (edges), with implications for metapopulation and metacommunity structure related to diversity and conservation (Urban & Keitt 2001; Urban et al. 2009).

Spatial graphs are defined by having nodes with spatial locations, usually given by coordinates in one, two or three dimensions. This small modification to aspatial graphs has profound effects on how these graphs are used and interpreted. There may be greater intuitive appeal because the graph is now like a familiar map of point events determined by spatial processes or of objects in a landscape, rather than structure in the abstract, but now there are the complications of the constraints of space.

The first set of questions for any spatial graph is about the locations of the nodes: where are they, what are their relative positions, and what processes determine them? This leads into the realm of spatial analysis and spatial point processes, with the nodes being identified with the dimensionless events of a spatial point pattern (Figure 9.1; see Dale & Fortin 2014; Illian et al. 2008, among many others). Questions about locations do not usually apply to the edges; any edge has its *end-point* positions fixed by the nodes it joins, but the line depicting an edge may not reflect a real trajectory or

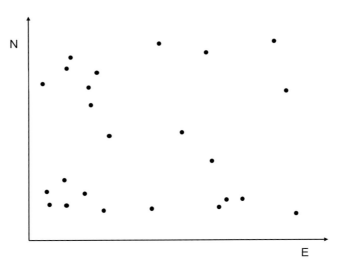

Figure 9.1 Spatial point pattern in two dimensions, x and y, or N and E. The points have no extent.

physical structure. With some exceptions, such as a corridor or bridge that has physical extent, the length of any edge is defined by the distance between the two nodes it joins.

The second set of questions is about edges, concerning which pairs of nodes are joined by edges and the process or rule that determines them. This may be about defining "neighbours" in a spatial context, about which much is already known (Dale & Fortin 2014, Chapter 3) and which will be summarized below. The questions become more complicated when the edges are determined by something other than just proximity: processes such as transport, or spatial objects such as rivers and streams or corridors of hedgerows and cut-lines. It may also be complicated when the edges have clear directionality.

There are many smart things to be done with spatial graphs and the related theory, but the focus will be examples related to diversity and conservation such as how spatially determined processes can affect population and community properties. Much research in landscape ecology begins with patches of habitat and the connections between them, and their effects on organisms; this seems like an ideal system to explore the use of spatial graphs.

Studies that take advantage of spatial graphs will include some of the following:

- Find distinguishing characteristics of the system and its spatial structure.
- Determine key features of the graph for the characteristic of interest, especially those related to connectivity, however defined.
- Use a hierarchy of edge rules and compare the changes in graph characteristics through the hierarchy as edge density and edge length varies, OR compare the results of such topologically defined edges with functionally determined edges when this is possible.

- Use a range of restricted randomizations to determine the "significance" of the observed properties.

The rest of this chapter will provide the background, details, commentary and some examples of this list.

9.1 Properties of Spatial Graphs

9.1.1 Connectivity

In ecological studies, several key properties of spatial graphs for analysis and modelling are related to connectivity. The first property is whether the graph is *connected*, which means there is a path from any node to any other (Figure 9.2a). Then, measures of *connectivity* evaluate the strength or robustness of the connectedness. If the only path between two nodes contains a cut-node or a cut-edge, the path is vulnerable to disconnection, and the connectedness is not very strong (Rayfield et al. 2011). The connectivity of a pair of nodes can be measured by the number of independent paths between them (i.e. sharing no nodes and no edges; Newman 2010) (see Figure 9.2a). The concept can be refined by distinguishing between the number of paths sharing no nodes, giving *node connectivity*, and the number of paths sharing no edges, giving *edge-connectivity*. It can also be modified to assess the graph's vulnerability to the removal of two or more nodes that will disconnect the graph, a *node cut-set* of size 2, 3, 4, . . . ; or to the removal of two or more edges, an *edge cut-set* of size 2, 3, 4, . . . , as shown in Figure 9.2b. Connectivity increases with the size of the minimum cut sets, those that will disconnect the graph with the loss of the fewest nodes or edges. Connectivity, as a refinement of "connected or not," can be extended and adapted to situations where the edges have weights indicating capacity, and while the term is often used informally or imprecisely, it has intuitive appeal (see McRae et al 2008; Minor & Urban 2008; Saura et al. 2014).

9.1.2 Locations, Distances, Proximity

The characteristics of spatial graphs for ecological applications include properties described for aspatial graphs, such as paths and path length, connectedness and components, centrality measures, motifs and so on, but the defining characteristics of spatial graphs are node locations and edge inclusion rules.

There are n nodes and thus potentially $n(n-1)/2$ edges between them (if all are occupied, it is a *complete* graph). The nodes have spatial positions, and so there are measured distances between nodes based on those positions in the reference space, usually Euclidean space. Those distances, and circles of sizes determined by inter-node distances, have an important role in defining which pairs of nodes are joined according to a hierarchy of "topological" neighbour rules. Table 9.1 summarizes that hierarchy of neighbour-rule graphs; in which the edges in each one are a subset of those in the succeeding, more highly connected, networks. For any of these "topological" rules for graph construction, the result is a network of the nodes that are (somehow) neighbours,

Table 9.1 Hierarchy of Neighbour Network Rules for Edges in a Spatial Graph Based on "Topology" Illustrated Previously in Figures 1.19a, 1.19b and 1.19c (with Acronym and Approximate Average Degree for Randomly Arranged Nodes)

---

(1) Mutually nearest neighbour pairs (MNN, 0.62)
(2) All first nearest neighbours (NN, 1.4)
(3) Minimum Spanning Tree (MST, 2.0)
(4) Relative neighbourhood graph (RNG, 2.4)
(5) Gabriel graph (GG, 4.0)
(6) Delaunay triangulation (DT, 6.0)

Note: See Fortin and Dale (2014, Table 3.3) for a somewhat expanded version.

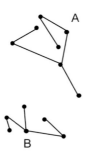

Graph not connected

Graph connected:
A and B connected by only
1 independent path with
2 cut-nodes and 3 cut-edges

(a)

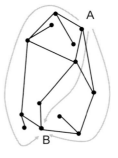

Graph connected:
A and B connected by
3 independent paths

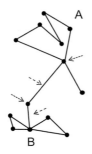

Graph connected;
disconnected by loss of
a cut-node (2 indicated)
or a cut-edge
(2 indicated)

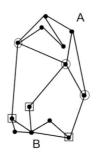

Graph connected;
disconnected by loss of
3-node cut sets
(2 sets indicated)

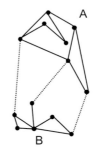

Graph connected;
disconnected by loss of
3-edge cut sets
(1 set indicated)

(b)

Figure 9.2 Connectivity. (a) Graph not connected; graph connected but with cut-points and cut-edges; graph connected with several independent paths between nodes A and B. (b) Graph connected but with cut-points and cut-edges; graph connected with three-node cut-set; graph connected with three edge cut-set.

and may be referred to as "proximity graphs" (see Cardinal et al. 2009). Sparse graphs are formed when each node is joined to the node nearest to it (nearest neighbour rule) or the join is made only if the relationship is reciprocal (mutually nearest neighbours). The Minimum Spanning Tree is a tree that connects all nodes using the smallest possible total length of edges. More edges result if nodes A and B are joined if and only if the intersection of circles centred on A and B with radius AB contains no other nodes (relative neighbourhood graph rule; Toussaint 1980). If the rule is that nodes A and B are joined if and only if the circle on diameter AB is empty yields the Gabriel graph with average degree about 4.0. The last one, the Delaunay triangulation, is found in many applications. It can be created by the rule that the three edges of any triangle of nodes are all included if and only if the circumcircle of the triangle contains no other nodes. The resulting structure is directly related to a partitioning of the plane into polygons, one for each node, being the portion of the plane closer to its own node than to any other. There are many applications of these polygons (called Dirichlet domains or Voronoi or Theissen polygons) in spatial analysis in two or more dimensions (see Okabe et al. 2000).

Several of these neighbour networks in Table 9.1 are members of other well-defined hierarchies of networks. An obvious example is the graph with edges joining each node to its closest neighbour (entry 2 in Table 9.1 nearest neighbours); this is easily extended to more highly connected graphs with edges joining each node to its first nearest neighbour and to its second nearest neighbour; then first, second and third nearest neighbours; and so on. This sequence also has the property of edges as subsets of those in any of the more highly connected graphs. Less obviously, the Gabriel graph is a member of another sequence of edge rules; in it, nodes A and B are joined if and only if the circle on diameter AB contains no other nodes. The larger series of rules is called the β-skeleton series, based on the criterion of no other nodes within an area defined by not just one, but two circles passing through the two focal nodes (for details, see Kirkpatrick & Radke 1985). The Minimum Spanning Tree (MST) occurs in another series that includes the minimum planar graph, which has also been used in ecological studies (James et al. 2005; Fall et al. 2007); it converts each landscape patch into several nodes, not just one, to accommodate perimeter-to-perimeter links rather than centre-to-centre and minimizes the total length of edges used in this way. Most of these rules for the inclusion of neighbour edges can be typified as "empty region graphs" and Cardinal et al. (2009) have provided an appealing summary of this broad family of neighbour networks, illustrating the intellectual and aesthetic appeal of graph theory.

In addition to the "topological" rules for edges, another easy choice is using distance thresholds that reflect species' potential dispersal ability; all pairs of nodes closer than threshold distance T are joined by an edge. Several values of T produce a hierarchy of graphs with nested edge sets moving up or down the hierarchy. A variation is to have an upper and lower threshold so that the edge lengths fall only within a specified range. The upper distance threshold approach has simplicity to recommend it; but one drawback is that a small threshold value can produce nodes with no neighbours, and thus difficult to include in any analysis, as well as nodes with many neighbours (consider the lower left vs the upper right in Figure 9.1). With more edges at a single node, each additional edge may contribute little or less new information to the analysis. Topological

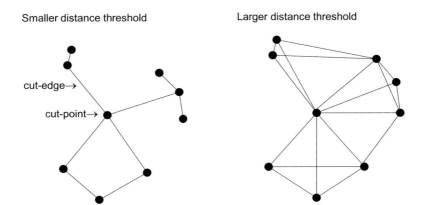

Figure 9.3 Distance threshold edges and connectedness. The graph with the smaller threshold for edge length has several cut-points and cut-edges; the second has none.

rules have the advantage of a more equitable inclusion of nodes, near or far. The other feature of distance threshold rules is that small changes in the threshold can create large changes in the graphs' characteristics, particularly connectedness features such as cut-points and cut-edges (see Figure 9.3). Dale and Fortin (2014) have provided a detailed example using the locations of lakes in a peatland on the Alberta-Saskatchewan border (their Figure 3.22). In that example, a small change in the distance threshold, from 5 km to 4 km, makes dramatic changes to the connectedness and other characteristics of the graph, such as three components becoming nine components. Often, the choice of threshold distance will have sound ecological reasons. For example, in a study of landscape connectivity for conservation purposes, Minor and Urban (2008) joined pairs of landscape patch nodes where they were separated by 1500 m or less, based on the typical dispersal distance for a small songbird.

It is really (really!) important to understand that the edges in these spatial structure graphs based on the positions of nodes are not *data*. They are imposed by the positions of the nodes and the rule chosen, whether as a somewhat arbitrary decision or by design to test specific hypotheses. This means that for the most basic graphs, there is nothing to be learned from randomizations or some of the other techniques we often used to evaluate structure, unless it is the positions of the nodes that are randomized. As soon as there are labels on the nodes or edges, or weights on either, of course, these approaches make sense again.

A smart thing to do with these graphs is to compare the topological rule edges with edges based on function or underlying processes. It may not be easy to determine functional edges for a spatial graph, but it can be worth the effort. For example, different models of the cost or resistance to movement in a network, and known genetic structure or community similarities can be used to evaluate adjacency (neighbour) networks (see e.g. McRae et al. 2008; Gilarranz et al. 2015). While the explanatory power for ecological characteristics, such as species composition, from the nearest neighbour structure of an archipelago may be weak because there are so many factors other than proximity

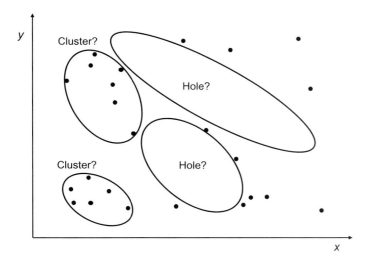

Figure 9.4 Spatial point pattern in two dimensions with possible clusters and possible holes in the pattern.

(wind, currents, shoreline, elevation, habitat, . . .), that of the spatial graph of a river system may be stronger. Stream order and proximity along a watercourse should provide good predictions of similarity of species composition from site to site in an appropriately constructed spatial graph (see Fagan 2002; Grant et al. 2007; Schick & Lindley 2007; Labonne et al. 2008; Peterson et al. 2013; Erös et al. 2012).

There is a gradation of the apparent reliability of the functional edges of a spatial graph and any claims we might want to make of them. The gradation goes from direct observations to convincing deductions, and then to more speculative explanations (e.g. radio-collared animals with positions recorded frequently compared to storm tracks and prevailing winds). The more "iffy" and less convincing the evidence for edges of function, the better it is to rely more on topological or distance rules for the edges of the graph, and the less justifiable the claims for a single "best" path from one habitat patch to another. I think this fact provides a strong argument for considering an approach that uses all possible paths, however weighted, to produce a summary of all routes that might occur; this is the "sum-of-all-paths" method.

9.1.3   Point Pattern Analysis: Clusters, Holes, Modularity, Scale

Given the locations of the nodes, an obvious step is to evaluate any non-randomness, such as clusters of nodes. The simple version is to test whether the positions are consistent with clustering, randomness or overdispersion. That trichotomy is too simplistic because the same pattern can be both clustered and overdispersed, but at different scales (see Dale & Fortin 2014, Figure 4.1). In addition to looking for clusters of nodes, it may be of ecological interest to examine the data for significant holes (see Figure 9.4). In graph theory, the term "modularity" refers to the divisibility of the graph into subgraphs that are internally highly connected, but with few edges between them. A first step, then, is to assess the spatial pattern of the nodes (clusters, holes; apparently random; overdispersion), and the spatial scales of any non-randomness.

The extensive literature of point pattern analysis provides many choices for the detection and characterization of clusters. In general, the analysis of point patterns is based on distances: distances to the first (closest) neighbours; distances from any point (node) to its kth nearest neighbour ($k = 1, 2, 3, \ldots$); the numbers of other nodes within distance t of any node (Ripley's K function); the numbers of other nodes between distance t and $t + \delta t$ of any node (Condit's Ω function); and so on (see Dale & Fortin, 2014, Chapter 4; Illian et al. 2008, among many others). The graph theory equivalent is the detection of "modularity," which is the divisibility of a graph into highly connected subgraphs with few edges between them. This may reflect the community substructure of any spatial graph, and Newman (2006) provided an algorithm for dividing a univariate graph into such subgraphs based on the eigenvectors of a characteristic matrix for the graph.

The complementary task is the detection of "holes" in the point pattern of nodes (Figure 9.4). There are several approaches possible including scan statistics, where a moving template (such as a circle taking a range of diameters) scans over the entire field of the pattern and registers the sizes and locations of areas with strikingly low density (cold spots) or strikingly high density (hot spots) (see Glaz et al. 2001). An alternative to the sliding circle template is to use only circles that are determined pass through triplets of the nodes themselves, the "circumcircles" of the triangles of nodes. Comparison of the observed counts of nodes in any circle with the expected number identifies hot spots and cold spots in the spatial pattern (see Dale & Fortin 2014, Chapter 4). Criteria to narrow the list of cold spots can lead to the identification of holes in the spatial scatter of nodes.

The nodes of a spatial graph can be identified with the point events of spatial pattern analysis, and analyzed by those methods. The relationship between methods of spatial analysis and edge creation rules for spatial graphs is very close, and any one of the standard methods for point pattern analysis can be directly related to one of the spatial graph edge rules, with the graph nodes being the point events that are the subject of the analysis (see Dale & Fortin 2014, Tables 4.2 and 5.1).

Where the edges in a spatial graph have meaning beyond neighbour structure, we may also seek methods that will detect clusters (or "holes") in the pattern of edges (see Figure 9.5). The method chosen will depend on whether the edges represent spatial relationships, functional interactions or physical trajectories or structures. Methods include determining the node degree spatial distribution; conversion to a line graph (edges become nodes; see Chapter 1); analyzing the edges themselves as patterns of linear objects, "fibres" (fibre pattern analysis, see Stoyan et al. 1995; Dale & Fortin 2014, Chapter 3.2); and more to be discovered or developed.

9.1.4   Distance, Path Length, Centrality

Important concepts for these spatial graphs are those of paths, path lengths and distances. As usual, the paths are sequences of nodes and the edges with no elements

Spatial point pattern in two dimensions

Minimum Spanning Tree

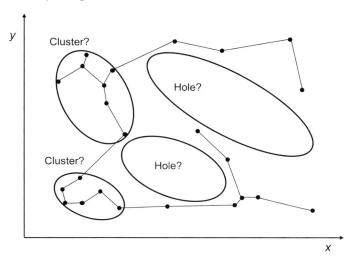

Figure 9.5 Spatial point pattern in two dimensions with possible clusters and possible holes, with Minimum Spanning Tree (MST) as neighbour network.

repeated, and it is possible for a path of fewer links to be longer in its spatial span from first node to last than a path of more links. The features of distances in spatial graphs were described in Chapter 1, and can be summarized as:

- The graph theory distance between nodes, $\delta(u,v)$, is the minimum sum of weights on edges for any path from u and to v.
- In aspatial graphs, that is the minimum number of edges in such a path (geodesic distance) because all the weights are 1. This leads to the following:
  - ○ The *diameter* of the graph is the greatest (geodesic) distance between two nodes, which is also the maximum shortest paths between pairs.
  - ○ The *characteristic path length* is the average of the geodesic distances between all pairs of nodes, which is also the average of the shortest paths between pairs.
  - ○ The *eccentricity* of a node is its greatest distance to any other. The graph diameter is therefore the maximum eccentricity of any node.
  - ○ The *radius* is the minimum eccentricity of any node.
- In a spatial graph, edge e_{uv} has its own spatial length, $d(u,v)$ or $d_s(u,v) = l(e_{uv})$, and so $\delta(u,v)$ is the sum of such lengths for the shortest path between u and v.
- There are two kinds of distance between nodes: the simple spatial distance d_{uv} between their locations, and $\delta(u,v) = $ the sum of the spatial lengths of the edges in the shortest path, $d_p(u,v)$. (Figure 1.10 illustrates these differences.)

A related concept is graph *size*, usually the characteristic path length, which is the average distance of all node pairs. Because the distance between nodes with no paths is

Table 9.2 Centrality Measures for Nodes in Spatial Graphs

Betweenness centrality	The betweenness centrality of node v is the proportion of the shortest paths between any pair of nodes in G that pass through node v.
Closeness centrality	Closeness centrality in spatial graphs measures the average physical distance from node v to all other nodes; nodes with shorter distances have greater centrality.
Eigenvector (spectral) centrality	Includes all possible paths in its measure, not just the shortest paths, but weighting each path by a factor based on its length, λ.
Geographic centrality	For a spatial graph, the betweenness and closeness centralities can be based on geographic distance instead of geodesic distance: $d(u,v)$ instead of $\delta(u,v)$. A simple weighting of a node's geographic centrality in a spatial graph is its distance from the centre of gravity of all N nodes, γ, giving an index between 0 and 1:

$$c_g(v) = \frac{d(v, \gamma)}{\max_u[d(u, \gamma)]}. \tag{9.1}$$

This measure can also be used as a weighting to modify existing measures of centrality into a more spatially responsive form. It can also be the basis for weighting measures of *edge* centrality, rather than the *node* centrality presented in this table.

Note: See Table 3.1 and Figures 3.8a–3.8e.

infinite, it may be preferable to use the average of the distances' inverses, d_{ij}^{-1} so that pairs of nodes with no path contribute zero to the average. Node *centrality* measures a node's importance as a component of the graph's shortest paths; there are many versions, as illustrated in Table 9.2.

Centrality measures can be based on any quantitative characteristic of paths, not only those included here. For example, Hock and Mumby (2015) described a measure of the *reliability* of dispersal paths in connectivity networks, based on the probability that a patch has a "direct effect" on a given neighbour. It is then reasonable to create an index of a node's reliability path centrality: the proportion of all highest reliability paths between any pair of nodes in the network that pass through the focal node. No doubt, other centrality measures can be developed for particular purposes as the need arises.

9.1.5   Connected Components; Cut-Nodes and Cut-Edges

A connected component is a subgraph with at least one path between any pair of nodes. In a spatial digraph (with directed edges), there are several kinds of connected components for any node v: the *out-component* of v is the set of all nodes, u, for which there is a directed path from v to u; the *in-component* of v is the set of all nodes, u, for which there is a directed path from u to v (Nicosia et al. 2012). A *strongly connected* component has directed paths in both directions between any pair of nodes within it, although the paths do not need to be through the same nodes. The connected components of a spatial graph define the subsets of nodes among which movement is possible; and that should be the justification for how the edges are determined. Ecologically, not mathematically, it may be possible to have dispersal between parts of a graph that do not seem connected, even if the probability is low (think of "tunnelling"). On the other hand, dispersal within a connected component of a spatial graph may be rare or vulnerable if it requires paths through cut-nodes or cut-edges, which may represent bottlenecks for movement. Real systems described by spatial graphs tend to have temporal characteristics as well, and so the capacity of nodes or edges may vary through time, or they may actually be intermittent in function. All these variations have implications when the spatial graph refers to a landscape of habitat patches with local extinction by patch and recolonization between patches based on dispersal.

9.1.6   Autocorrelation

Spatial autocorrelation is a key feature of many graphs or networks; it can be positive or negative and often changes sign as well as magnitude with distance. Abundant short-range dispersal can result in positive autocorrelation of population or community properties at short distances, where different environmental conditions produce negative autocorrelation at greater distances. A similar property is *homophily* or the positive assortativeness of neighbour nodes; for spatial graphs this can include the proximity in space of the nodes' edges, as well as similarity in other characteristics such as aggregate degree. The opposite is *heterophily*, indicating dissimilarity of nodes' characteristics, usually when they are close together. For many ecological applications, the way that similarity and dissimilarity change both with physical distance and with the various kinds of connections between sites (nodes) is a key feature to understanding the phenomenon and the processes associated with it.

9.1.7   Planarity

A property of interest for spatial graphs is *planarity*, which simply means that it can be drawn in the plane without any edges intersecting (Harary 1969). Remember that the edges don't have to be straight! For a graph that is not planar, there are several measures of how close to or far from planar it is. The *thickness* of graph G is the minimum number of planar subgraphs the union of which form G. If the graph is planar, thickness = 1. The *crossing number* is the minimum number of pairwise intersections of edges when the graph is drawn in the plane. A planar graph has crossing number = 0. Planarity is a quite intuitive concept of non-crossing edges when drawn in the plane, but is clearly of interest when the edges represent dispersal routes between habitat patches or similar spatial structures in a landscape.

9.2   Techniques for Spatial Graphs: Testing Significance and Other Assessments

9.2.1   Random Assignment and Restricted Randomizations

The simplest significance test for many graph properties is by restricted randomization for the characteristic of interest, based either on the whole graph or on sub-areas or on individual nodes. The characteristics include centrality measures for nodes or for edges, local indices of persistence or autocorrelation (local by node, edge or sub-area), or topological properties such as connectivity or connectedness. The combination of frequency enumeration with the comparison of observed and expected values can also be used, but the restricted randomization approach has much to recommend it. One key technique for this analysis, and one of the strengths of this approach, is to employ more than one randomization procedure (e.g. random edges, randomized edges restricted by number, randomizing edge weights among edges retained in position, . . .). It is an easy step to go from restricted randomization to modelling that includes the same restrictions in the generation of artificial "data" for comparison with the observed results.

9.2.2   Comparison with Models

Although not testing statistical significance, the comparison of graph-theoretical properties with characteristics from other modelling exercises is often used to assess the chosen approach. Spatially explicit population models are often cited as the best way to understand species' distributions in patchy landscapes, but they can be demanding to implement computationally and in the ecological detail required. Minor and Urban (2007) compared spatially explicit modelling for the wood thrush (*Hylocichla mustelina*) in patchy habitat with graph-theoretical analysis that included node degree, betweenness centrality, influx and outflux measures and a quality-weighted area measure for the nodes. They found that the graph theory approach was good at identifying "stepping-stones" in the spatial structure, and its predictions were similar to those of the explicit modelling procedure (Minor & Urban 2007; see also Saura et al. 2014; Rubio et al. 2015).

9.3   Choice and Applications of Techniques

9.3.1   Diversity and Nestedness

The introductory comments for this chapter promised to describe how spatial graphs can be applied to understanding how biological diversity is organized in space, particularly for real or virtual archipelagos of habitat. The first implication of such a physical structure is that there is a natural hierarchy to the organization of diversity in space, for example: diversity among samples within a site on an island; diversity among sites within an island; diversity among islands within the archipelago. Other levels of the same hierarchy are possible, for example if there are island chains or sub-groupings within the archipelago. Of course, the diversity of islands can be partitioned and analyzed differently: by island size, island topographical relief, island distance (to neighbours, to a mainland, . . .), or island age and history if known. The spatial context for island comes into play when their species compositions and diversities are to be correlated with spatial proximity and network connectivity.

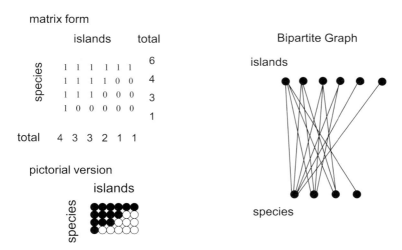

Figure 9.6 Diversity and nestedness: matrix of presence-absence ordered by species frequency and by island richness gives the matrix for nestedness analysis. Also shown in pictorial form and as a bipartite graph.

One characteristic frequently cited in studies of insular communities is nestedness, which is an aspatial characteristic of two-way data such as species on islands, related to asymmetry in the assortativeness of nodes' degrees. In nested data, rare species occur only at the richest sites and species-poor sites have only the most common species (Figure 9.6). Nestedness can also be found in a functional version for two sets of mutualists such as flowering plants and their pollinator insects (see Bascompte & Jordano 2014, Chapter 3) (see also Chapter 7 of this volume). Nestedness in a bipartite graph has nodes of low degree adjacent only to high degree nodes, but high degree nodes joined to nodes with degrees from low to high (Figures 9.6). The degree distribution associated with nestedness is not distinctive, but may be confounded with characteristics associated with different models of network development (e.g. random vs scale free; see Chapter 1).

Nestedness is not itself spatial, but it can be mapped onto the spatial arrangement of the sites, and each site has a nestedness score based on its compositional concordance with all taxa and all sites (see Dale & Fortin 2014, Box 10.1). Those scores then have a spatial structure, which can be visualized as a spatial graph. In addition, each pair of sites has a relative nestedness score, measuring the nesting of their compositions (see Dale & Fortin 2014, Box 10.2), and again these values can be mapped to the pairs of sites, or to the edges that join them. Because the original nestedness graph is bipartite, one set of nodes (the sites) can be constrained to be spatial, and the other nodes (the species) remain non-spatial (Figure 9.7). Spatial neighbours can be determined by any rule (e.g. Delaunay triangulation, Figure 9.7). The original bipartite graph can have edges among the species added to depict any one of many aspatial associations: phytosociological structure, taxonomic relatedness or shared membership in functional groups. Replacing or augmenting the spatially determined neighbour network, inter-site edges

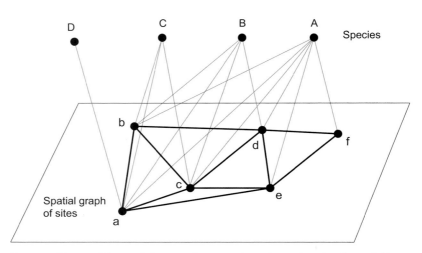

Figure 9.7 The spatial part of the nestedness graph can be analyzed with a neighbour network of the sites in a spatial graph: e.g. Delaunnay neighbours. The species are A, B, C and D; the sites are a, b, c, d, e and f.

can be added to or labelled in the spatial part of the graph, based on one of many criteria and a threshold value for inclusion:

1 Compositional similarity of the communities, measured by any similarity index (many choices, see Legendre & Legendre 2012) or the number of species shared or the level of dendrogram join in a cluster analysis.
2 Similarity of an index of species diversity or of species richness at the sites.
3 Similarity of the site nestedness scores, indicating comparable positions in the nestedness structure.
4 A measure of mutual relative nestedness of the two species complements at the two sites, or a directed edge from the richer site to the poorer indicating the relationship of complete nesting.
5 Physical proximity or ease of dispersal between sites.
6 Similarities in other important site characteristics: island area, range of habitats, geological history, topographic profile and so on.

These characteristics are mainly independent, although not fully so, and combinations can be considered, such as physical proximity weighted by habitat matching, or compositional similarity combined with a high degree of mutual nestedness (this may determine the choice of index).

In addition, two different criteria for edges in a spatial graph can be created and then compared, such as (a) the most favourable dispersal routes between sites and (b) the similarities of species complements of pairs of sites. Clearly, there are insights to be gained from such comparisons. Applying different criteria for placing edges in nestedness graphs allows the evaluation of several hypotheses on species' spatial distributions, such as differential extinction versus differential colonization as explanatory mechanisms

(Darlington 1957; Lomolino 2006). Again, the graph itself is just a skeleton on which the analysis is based; the edges are created by topological or distance rules, and therefore do not really represent data to be studied further.

Two studies of species composition using spatial graphs were discussed in Dale and Fortin (2014, Section 10.3.3.2, Figures 10.15 and 10.16). The first concerns forest bird species on recently isolated islands in Lago Guri in Venezuela (Feeley et al. 2007), and the second is the biogeography of Tenebrionid beetles on long-existing islands in the Aegean Sea (Fattorini & Fowles 2005; Fattorini 2007). Spatial analysis looked at the autocorrelation of species richness and site nestedness scores based on neighbours defined by the Minimum Spanning Tree rules for edge definition in a spatial graph. The Aegean Sea example can be used as a basis for illustrating some of the features of the further graph theory approach to analysis.

The Tenebrionid beetles data included 165 species on 32 islands, but Crete and Euboea were omitted due to their large size, leaving 160 species and 30 islands. Figure 9.8a shows the spatial graph of the sites with edges determined as a Minimum Spanning Tree. The nodes are coded by their global nestedness score, and the edges were evaluated for the relative nestedness of the pairs they join. The basic spatial and correlational analysis used island location, size and species list to give richness, diversity, and nestedness scores for sites, and relative nestedness scores for pairs of sites. The kinds of questions to be asked included:

Is richness correlated with island size?
What is the autocorrelation of island size among adjacent sites in the graph?
What is the autocorrelation of richness for adjacent (MST) sites?
Are the site nestedness scores spatially clustered or intermingled?
What is the autocorrelation of nestedness scores for adjacent sites?
What is the spatial pattern of the relative nestedness scores of the edges?
. . . and so on.

For the beetles in the Aegean, nestedness was found to be high and clustered in the smaller islands in the south-central area with a trend to lower nestedness on the periphery; the relative nestedness of MST neighbours was generally low, negative in fact, except for the three indicated.

To go beyond this spatial analysis, graph theory concepts can now be included; and it is useful to compare results from the MST neighbour graph with the results from a skeleton with more edges and here the Gabriel graph was chosen (Figure 9.8b).

A revised set of questions could be considered, based on the same data, for example:

Is richness correlated with island centrality?
Which measure of node connectivity best predicts species richness?
Which measure of node connectivity best predicts site nestedness?
What neighbour definition gives the highest autocorrelation of neighbouring island sizes?
Are clusters of most similar nodes distance or topologically defined?
. . . and so on.

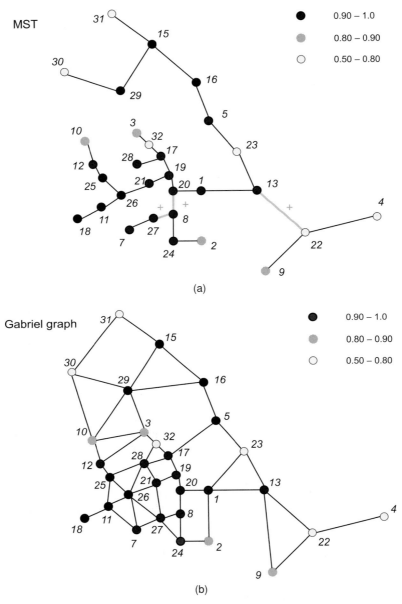

Figure 9.8 Spatial graph of Aegean sites with nestedness codes for nodes. Numbers identify the islands, e.g. 13 = Kos (data from Fattorini 2007). (a) The spatial graph is the MST. All edges negative except three indicated. (b) The spatial graph is the Gabriel graph. (A black-and-white version of this figure will appear in some formats. For the colour version, please refer to the plate section.)

To illustrate, island composition similarity levels (1 to 12), based on the dendrogram of the Dollo parsimony consensus tree given by Fattorini and Fowles (2005), are mapped onto both examples of spatial graphs, MST and Gabriel graph, shown in Figure 9.9a and 9.9b). (The dendrogram itself could be imposed on the spatial graph as in Figure 9.7, but it becomes too complicated to be helpful.) Not only does the proportion of edges increase, but it can cause radical shifts in the apparent roles of particular nodes. For example node 17 in the Aegean (the island of Mikonos) is of relatively low centrality in the MST spatial graph, but it becomes highly central in more than one measure in the Gabriel graph (centrality measures not shown in these figures). In fact, moving up the series of topological graphs with connectivity increasing produces two results: (1) many measures of centrality will converge as nodes that are physically or geographically central achieve higher values of betweenness or closeness centrality; and (2) degree centrality becomes uninformative as nodes' degrees become more uniform, moving toward the average value of 6, as expected in the Delaunay triangulation.

Mapping the compositional similarity results onto the spatial graph also allows the difference between the two neighbour graphs to be clarified. Despite some obvious groupings of neighbouring islands, many adjacent pairs end up with negative relative nestedness scores just because their species compositions are so different, being joined in the Dollo parsimony consensus tree (dendrogram) only at the eighth or ninth (or eleventh) level of joins. Other clustering procedures give different results, of course, but those dissimilarities must be strong to be so obvious in this algorithm.

The difference between analysis from graph theory and other forms of spatial analysis is an interesting one, but the role of structural characteristics of graphs for spatial analysis are illustrated by comparing the MST analysis with Gabriel graph versions for the same data (Figures 9.8 and 9.9). Not all the questions in the list are answered in this discussion, but it should provide some guidance on how to proceed in analyzing spatial data using spatial graphs.

9.3.2 Landscape Patches, Connectivity, Random Walks and Conservation Biology

Along with diversity and nestedness, spatial graphs can be applied to other aspects of conservation ecology in fragmented landscapes, using the analogy of patches as islands. In a network of landscape patches, the patches are the nodes and the edges represent dispersal routes, whether physical like ditches or functional like flyways or merely notional as assumed links. Spatial graphs can quantify the effects eliminating particular elements by modelling the loss of habitat patches or of dispersal corridors (Urban & Keitt 2001). Connectivity is the key feature, and much research has examined measures of landscape connectivity and their ability to predict observed outcomes related to dispersal and conservation (see Pascual-Hortal & Saura 2006; Baranyi et al. 2011). Laita et al. (2011) expressed concern that many connectivity measures may react to landscape characteristics (e.g. patch size vs patch location) in ways that are undesirable for evaluating reserve networks; suggesting there is more work to be done to ensure the correct inferences are derived from graph theory for conservation applications.

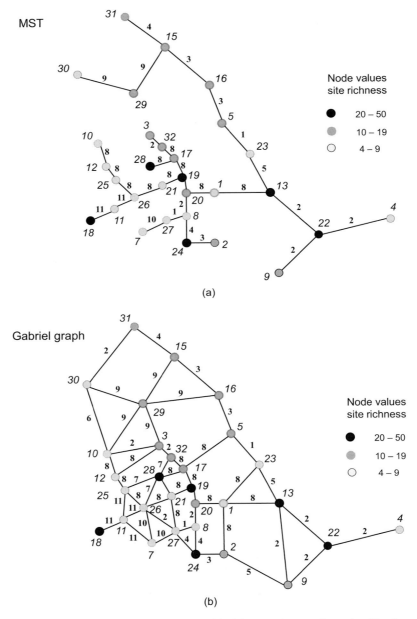

Figure 9.9 Spatial graph of Aegean sites with richness values on the nodes. Numbers identify the islands, e.g. 13 = Kos (data from Fattorini 2007). Edge labels are levels of dendrogram joins; higher values show greater difference. (a) MST as the spatial graph. (b) Gabriel graph. (A black-and-white version of this figure will appear in some formats. For the colour version, please refer to the plate section.)

Keitt et al. (1997) showed how graph theory can characterize connectivity using landscape metrics, such as patch importance, which are computed for different distance thresholds derived from the species' dispersal abilities. Many researchers have used this approach (e.g. Ricotta et al. 2000; O'Brien et al. 2006; Urban et al. 2009) with different edge rules, whether the Minimum Spanning Tree (Urban & Keitt 2001) or the Delaunay triangulation (Fall et al. 2007; Andersson & Bodin 2009). For the landscape and the organisms of interest, the important graph theory features are related to *ecological connectivity*, with implications for spatial integration from the ease and frequency of dispersal, as well as vulnerability versus resilience. The graph theory properties include connectivity (as a formal graph-theoretical measure), connected components, modularity, cut-points and cut-edges, centrality, path lengths, and so on (Fall et al. 2007; Ferrari et al. 2007). The use of two senses of "connectivity" may be confusing; but it reflects actual use in the landscape and conservation literature (see Laita et al. 2011), in which a number of graph-theoretic indices have been proposed and applied for that purpose. This approach has been criticized because of the reliance on habitat quality definitions and thresholds, because it reflects only the emigration-immigration aspects of dynamics, and because it does not work well for large-scale, high-resolution grid data on species distributions in heterogeneous habitats (Moilanen 2011). Despite these stated limitations, the measures can quantify some aspects of landscape spatial structure with a range of indices.

9.3.3   A Long Detour: Random Walks on Graphs

I think that the background of using graphs for patchy landscapes includes not just intuitive ideas about movement and dispersal between patches as a stochastic process (Hock & Mumby 2015), but also ideas captured by the more formal concept of *random walks* from mathematics (e.g. Economo & Keitt 2008). A random walk is a series of random steps, whether in a spatial context or more abstract, but the idea and its formal treatment have applications in physics, economics, chemistry, finance, computer science and so on. Ecologists are most familiar with the random walk model of movement and diffusion in space (Codling et al. 2008) and the correlated random walk which provides more realistic trajectories for animal movement (see Fagan & Calabrese 2014), but a random walk on a graph is different because the walk is constrained to the nodes and edges of its graph. If the landscape is pictured as a spatially organized set of nodes, with the only routes for movement between them being the edges of the graph, it is easy to imagine dispersal processes as the unintentional movement of individual organisms between nodes along any of the edges available. This picture is very similar to a random walk on that landscape graph.

A random walk is created by starting at a chosen node and moving to a randomly chosen neighbour with a given probability, and then this process is repeated (simple!), as illustrated in Figure 9.10. In a *walk* on a graph, elements can be re-used. Obviously, if a graph is not connected, no single random walk can reach all parts of the graph, and so random walks provide information about graph connectivity and other structural properties. This is an area of graph theory that has been very well researched, from the

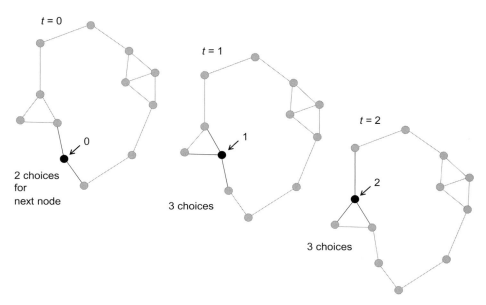

Figure 9.10 Random walk on a graph: random choice at each iteration.

beginning, and there is much information available; Lovász (1993) has provided a good summary.

There are important differences between walks on directed and on non-directed graphs, but here we will focus the latter. The basic properties of random walks are determined by the *spectrum* of the graph (giving us *spectral graph theory*; see Chung 1997), which is the set of eigenvalues of the graph's adjacency or Laplacian matrix (see Chapter 1). Characteristics of the spectrum can be used to evaluate connectivity; for example, the difference between the first and second eigenvalues is called the *spectral gap*, and it can be a measure of the graphs vulnerability to disconnection, with higher values indicating less vulnerability (Figure 9.11; see Donetti et al. 2006). The walk's properties can also be seen through the electrical resistance of the electrical network associated with the graph, for example, where each edge represents a unit of resistance and current enters the graph at one node and leaves at another (Lovász 1993); hence the relationship between spatial graphs in ecology and circuit theory (see McRae & Beier 2007).

The simplest random walk begins at an arbitrarily chosen node, v_0, and at each iteration, or time unit, the walk moves from v_t to any of the node's neighbours, v_{t+1}, with equal probability, so the probability for any neighbour is $1/d(v_t)$. As iteration continues, the frequency of being at any particular node converges to a stationary value; for node i, the long-term frequency (or probability) is proportional to its degree: $p_i = d_i / \Sigma d_i$. This means that the higher a node's degree, the more probable it is to be "occupied" by a random walk, such as a randomly dispersing animal. The result is higher densities are to be predicted at nodes with higher degrees. This provides a simple explanation of why degree can be a measure of connectivity for conservation in a fragmented landscape.

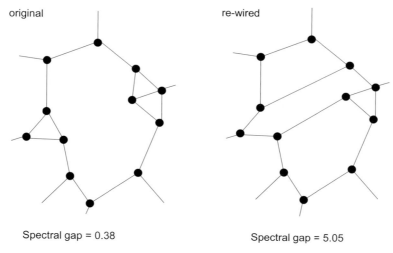

original   re-wired

Spectral gap = 0.38   Spectral gap = 5.05

Figure 9.11 Re-wiring that conserves degree connectivity to find optimal network topologies. Based on Donetti et al. (2006). Spectral gap increases from 0.38 to 5.05.

Each iteration can be treated as a time unit with one "step" in each, but for ecological applications, random walks are not expected to occur that way in real time units; they are more notional or conceptual. However, the expected number of steps or notional time units of iteration to reach a circle of radius r from the starting node is r^2, so that distance can be equated with the square root of time; expressed for a physical system, Brownian motion takes time t to get to distance $\sqrt{t}$ (Lovász 1993). Other properties of interest may be the *access time*, the number steps required to reach node j, starting at node i; the *cover time*, the number of iterations required to reach all nodes; and the *mixing rate*, a measure of how quickly the walk converges to the limiting distribution (Lovász 1993). Among the results that are directly applicable to landscape and conservation ecology include the facts that:

1 The access time from i to j may be different from the access time for j to i (even in a regular graph, where each node has the same degree, not shown). In Figure 9.12, the access time from A to B is much shorter than from B to A, because a random walk starting at A must move initially in the direction of B; from B a random walk can proceed in any of six directions with equal probability, thus starting toward A with probability 1/6.
2 Contrary to intuition, access time does not always increase with the distance between the nodes (Figure 9.12). The access time from A to X, three steps removed, is much less than the access time from X to Y (or Y to X), a shorter distance of two steps. The random walk between X and Y passes through B and therefore has a high probability of diverting to another branch of the graph.
3 Surprisingly (perhaps), adding an edge to a given graph does not necessarily decrease properties related to recolonization such as access time or cover time, but may actually increase them! (Lovász 1993) (Figure 9.13). In Figure 9.13, the addition of edges DG

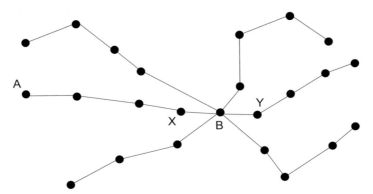

Figure 9.12 Random walks: surprising results. The access time for B to A is much longer than A to B (~6×). The access time from X to A is shorter than from X to Y although Y is closer to X than A.

and EH to the original graph greatly decreases the probability that a random walk will reach node F, thereby greatly increasing the time expected for the walk to reach all nodes at least once (cover time).

Such counter-intuitive results emphasize the importance of understanding the implications of this approach. The results also tell us that:

4 In landscape and conservation applications, the determination of which edges are included in a real or conceptual spatial graph of the system is critical to the predictions we can make about its dynamics. (Yes, we knew this already, really, but the implications of points 2 and 3 above are especially important in this context.)

For ecological applications, there is one more crucial finding (Alon et al. 2011):

5 For some graphs, several simultaneous random walks give a disproportionately faster cover time than only one.

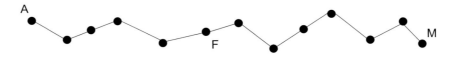

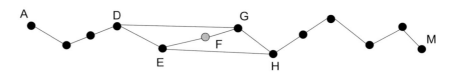

Figure 9.13 Random walks: surprising results. Adding edges can increase access times and cover times: an example. Access time to node F from nodes A to D and H to M is increased and cover time is increased by adding edges DG and EH.

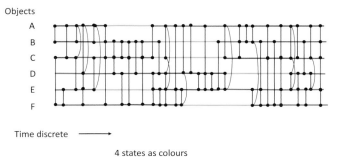

Objects

A
B
C
D
E
F

Time discrete ⟶

4 states as colours

Figure 8.18 Temporal graph of six objects with four states. Pairwise contacts (topology) are affected by states. State transitions are affected by contacts.

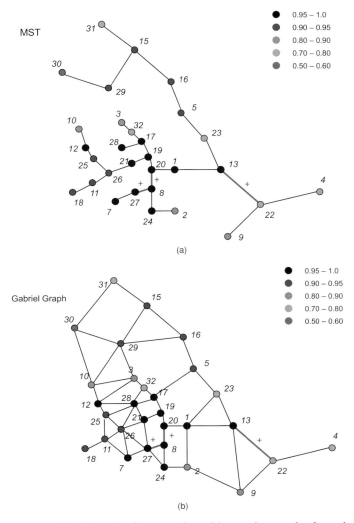

Figure 9.8 Spatial graph of Aegean sites with nestedness codes for nodes. Numbers identify the islands, e.g. 13 = Kos (data from Fattorini 2007). (a) The spatial graph is the MST. All edges negative except three indicated. (b) The spatial graph is the Gabriel graph.

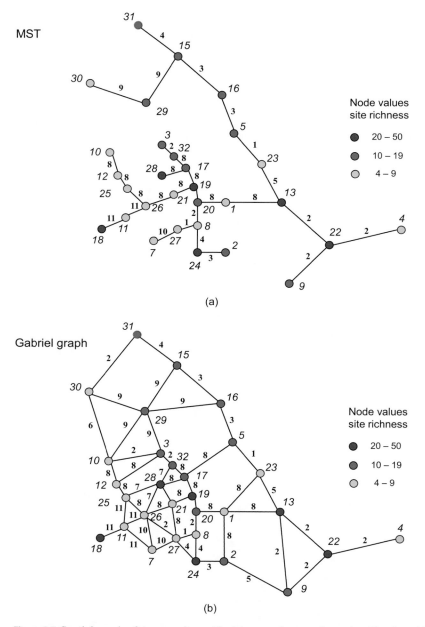

Figure 9.9 Spatial graph of Aegean sites with richness values on the nodes. Numbers identify the islands, e.g. 13 = Kos (data from Fattorini 2007). Edge labels are levels of dendrogram joins; higher values show greater difference. (a) MST as the spatial graph. (b) Gabriel graph.

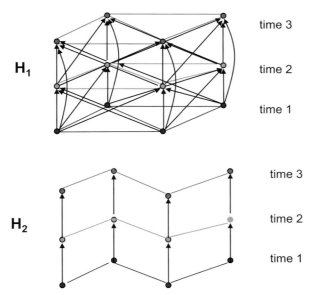

Figure 10.7 Example of spatio-temporal graph with four sites and three times: structure in time and space. H_1: Regional structure in time and space. H_2: Local structure in time and space (nearest neighbours).

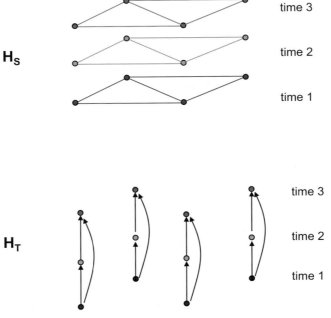

Figure 10.8 Example of spatio-temporal graph with four sites and three times. $\mathbf{H_S}$: Only spatial structure; no history. $\mathbf{H_T}$: Individual history; no neighbour effects; no spatial structure.

Edges of contemporaneity for times 1, 2, 3 & 4.

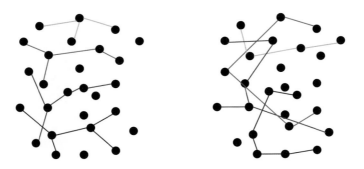

Orderly and close range:
Short edges and few cross-
temporal crossings

Less orderly transmission:
Longer edges and more cross-
temporal crossings

Figure 10.19 Graph of disease spread. Edges of contemporaneity for times 1, 2, 3 and 4. Orderly and close range produces short edges and few cross-temporal crossings. Less orderly transmission produces longer edges and more cross-temporal crossings.

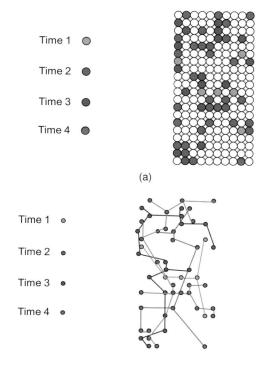

Time 1 ○

Time 2 ●

Time 3 ●

Time 4 ●

(a)

Time 1 ○

Time 2 ●

Time 3 ●

Time 4 ●

(Some points dithered slightly to avoid co-linearity for edges)

(b)

Figure 10.20 *Hevea brasiliensis*: trunk phloem necrosis data (a) colour coded by time of appearance, and (b) edges join locations of contemporaneous disease appearance (MST).

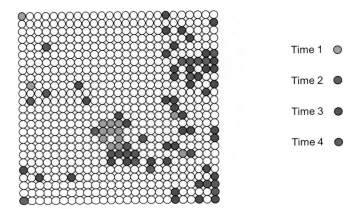

Figure 10.21 Fraser fir mortality (from Benson et al. 2006) with locations coded by time of disease appearance.

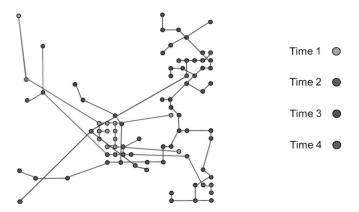

Figure 10.22 Fraser fir mortality (from Benson et al. 2006) with edges joining locations of contemporaneous disease appearance. (Some points dithered slightly to avoid co-linearity for edges.)

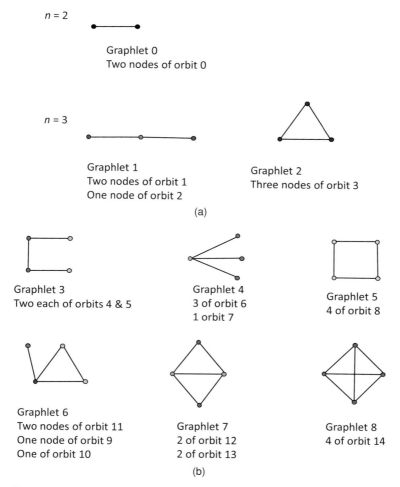

$n = 2$

Graphlet 0
Two nodes of orbit 0

$n = 3$

Graphlet 1
Two nodes of orbit 1
One node of orbit 2

Graphlet 2
Three nodes of orbit 3

(a)

Graphlet 3
Two each of orbits 4 & 5

Graphlet 4
3 of orbit 6
1 orbit 7

Graphlet 5
4 of orbit 8

Graphlet 6
Two nodes of orbit 11
One node of orbit 9
One of orbit 10

Graphlet 7
2 of orbit 12
2 of orbit 13

Graphlet 8
4 of orbit 14

(b)

Figure 11.7 Graphlets and node orbits (a) for $n = 2$ and 3 and (b) for $n = 4$. (c) Graphlets as induced subgraphs. Graph G includes graphlet g6 but not g4. A graphlet is an **induced** subgraph and must include all the sub-graph's edges; g4 is missing one edge of G, as indicated.

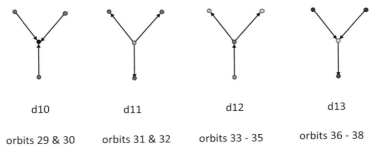

d10   d11   d12   d13

orbits 29 & 30   orbits 31 & 32   orbits 33 - 35   orbits 36 - 38

Figure 11.11 Directed graphlets for digraphs: with directed edges, g4 becomes 4 d-graphlets, d10 to d13 with d-orbits 29 to 38. These clearly distinguish convergence from divergence. Based on Sarajlić et al. (2016).

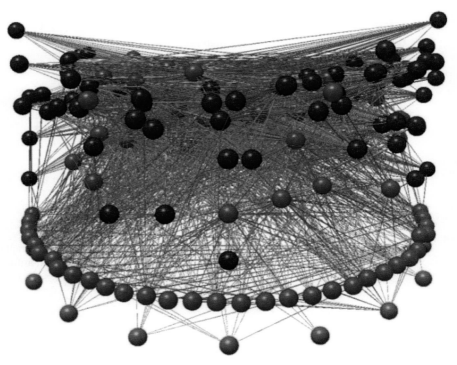

Figure 12.3 Illustration of 3D presentation of complex networks. A network of 4,671 feeding interactions among 68 parasites (in blue) and 117 free-living taxa (green = basal taxa, red = consumers) in the food web of Estero de Punta Banda, Baja California, Mexico. The vertical axis corresponds to trophic level. Credit: Images produced by J. A. Dunne using Network3D software (Dunne et al. 2013).

Running several independent random walks, perhaps even starting from the same node and not from random nodes, can speed up the cover time in number of steps (the expected time for all nodes to be included at least once) for many "interesting" graphs (Alon et al. 2011). In Figure 9.12, a single random walk can get trapped in one of the arms; more starting nodes increase the probability that each arm is covered relatively quickly, without having to pass twice through the bottleneck at node B. Even a random walk starting at B will have difficulty covering the entire graph, and it is easy to see that having many walks will cover the whole graph faster. The implications are that more dispersers from a single source or dispersal from several source patches can decrease the total time to covering sites of recent local extinction, particularly in a complex spatial structure. This is one example where adding edges could greatly reduce (rather than increase) cover time, if the edges were bridges between the arms.

The simplest random walk model provides some helpful insights, but clearly it may not be the best model in every situation. Where wind or water currents produce a directional bias, random walks on digraphs will be a better approximation, but these are not as well behaved as the non-directional versions. For example, there is the difficult question of how to deal with nodes that have 0 in-degree, or nodes with 0 out-degree; one solution is to use randomly chosen nodes to restart the random walk at a randomly chosen node at designated intervals. (This may seem biologically unreasonable, but think of the upstream re-establishment of water plants by transport by waterfowl.) Furthermore, the adjacency matrix of a digraph is usually asymmetric and so is its Laplacian, which means that the spectrum loses many of its "nice" properties and is less easy to interpret as properties of the graph itself; for example, random walks on digraphs may be very slow to converge to the stable distribution. Even with all these concerns, it is clear that this is an approach worth pursuing to understand spatial digraphs of directional structures.

As an aside, random walks on digraphs are often studied for non-spatial situations, such as search and linkages for Web pages based on the influence of other pages. This process can involve ranking by importance as measured by weighted degree, for example by the "PageRank" algorithm, named for Larry Page of Google (see Brin & Page 1998) which is closely related to degree centrality (cf. Newman 2010). This is also related to the competition digraphs of Chapter 6, with the consistency of hierarchies of competitive rankings and with the potential for reversals.

Another modification of the basic random walk is to allow the walk to remain at its currently occupied node with a given probability (say 0.5) at each iteration. This is referred to as a "lazy random walk" and it has useful properties of its own. Other variations are random walks on evolving graphs or dynamic graphs (Avin et al. 2008) and random walks "with choice" where the choice of the next node to be visited is influenced by the history of visits to the current node and (with weighting) to its neighbours (Avin & Krishnamachari 2008; Alexandris & Karagiorgos 2014). Both these changes to the basic model mimic aspects of realistic ecological circumstances, such as variation in the suitability of links between habitat patches and the effects of past patch occupation on current choices for dispersal.

Studying random walks on graphs provides insight into graph theory's application to landscape ecology. It can inform intuitive appreciation of how structure affects dispersal patterns and potential recolonization, when the movement of organisms is considered to be unintentional (possible?) and unbiased (unlikely?). The implications should affect our interpretation of how landscape structure affects patterns of dispersal and colonization and thus the design of multi-patch reserves. Again, it is to be emphasized that the determination of which pairs of patches are truly joined by the equivalent of the graph's edge will have a large effect on the outcomes described here.

9.3.4   End of Detour: Back to Connectivity

The study of random walks on graphs provides background and advice for choosing a measure of connectivity and to understand its properties. How does it respond to the structural details that affect random walks? It may help to run random walks on the spatial structure of the system being studied. While this is just one approach to evaluating connectivity measures, it is an important one since it permits an assessment in complex spatial structures. Because there are many measures to choose from, prior evaluation is obviously a good idea.

> **To Do**: Choose a measure of the chosen version of connectivity that is well behaved in random walks and understand its properties, even to the extent of running random walks on the spatial structure of your system.

To help inform choice among the spatial indices as indicators of ecological connectivity, a summary is provided in table form (Table 9.3). This attempts a synopsis of many sources including Pascual-Hortal and Saura (2006), Galpern et al. (2011), Baranyi et al. (2011), Rayfield et al. (2011) and Yu et al. (2013). The summary is much more specific than the general discussion of graph-theoretical connectivity for spatial graphs; its focus is on measures for ecological connectivity and it does not include all measures from the publications cited.

In this table, the nodes represent habitat patches and their locations (the patch centroid), usually as (x_i, y_i), with patch area as a possible weight, a_i; and the edges join the patches, usually centroid-to-centroid, with the associated physical distance, d_{AB} (labelled nodes) or d_{ij} (indexed). The edges represent potential dispersal between patches. The edges are symmetric, so not directed, and a node's degree, d_i, is just the number of edges attached to it. Path length between nodes can be measured by the number of edges, the shortest being the geodesic distance δ_{ij} or $\delta(A,B)$, or by the sum of the physical lengths of the edges in the path, $d_p (A,B)$.

Clearly, the measures are not all independent, and not all the overlaps of the measures have been commented on explicitly in Table 9.3. We will want to be able to compare graphs or components of different sizes, and so the most useful indices are those that can be first made relative to the number of nodes, n, and then for the number of edges, m. The most interesting and useful indices may be those that evaluate aspects of the structure of the spatial graphs beyond the density of edges m/n; for example, the properties of the spectral gap, which respond to structural robustness even in sparse graphs, merits further investigation. Donetti et al. (2006) have suggested an iterative "re-wiring" approach to

Table 9.3 Graph Theory Measures Related to Ecological Connectivity in Conservation Studies

Measure	Details	Comments
Connectedness: connected versus not connected	All node pairs have a path between them versus some pairs have none. Digraphs can also be "strongly," "unilaterally," or "weakly" connected.	Connectedness allows inter-patch dispersal and recolonization after extinction; disconnected does not.
Connectivity	# independent paths between A and B or κ: κ_n = minimum # nodes or κ_e = minimum # edges removed to disconnect	Related to robustness of network to loss of patch or inter-patch link.
Cut-nodes and cut-edges	# cut-nodes # cut-edges	Larger numbers indicate greater vulnerability to disconnection and reduced dispersal.
Connectance	Proportion of edge positions actually with an edge: $$c(G) = m/\binom{n}{2}$$	Relative density of edges can be related to ease and probability of movement between patches.
Node degree	d_i: a local measure for node i This is the number of neighbours at $\delta(u,v) = 1$	Higher node degree gives more links for possible dispersal; random walk suggests more organisms.
Average node degree	$d.(G) = m/2$: a global measure	Higher value suggests more dispersal possible.
Variance of node degrees	$s^2(d_i)$: inequitable versus uniform degree distribution	High variance indicates "hub and spoke" configuration: rapid dispersal; low value indicates low differentiation: slower dispersal, higher stability (?)
Buffered neighbour counts	The proportion of nodes as neighbours at $\delta(u,v) = 1, 2, 3, \dots$ Local or global measures. Both mean and variance can be used (see Labonne et al. 2008).	Higher means at shorter distances reflect more close source nodes; Variance reflects spatial heterogeneity
Components	K components: $X_1, \dots, X_K$ $K = 1$ is a connected graph; $K > 1$ is disconnected. Closely related to *algebraic connectivity*; K is also the number of 0 eigenvalues of the Laplacian matrix.	More components mean more and smaller isolated subgroups of patches.
Component "size"	# nodes ("order"): X_k has n_k nodes # edges: X_k has m_k nodes Total of patch area: $A_k = \sum_{i \in X_k} \alpha_i$	Related to pool of organisms for inter-patch dispersal and to ease of dispersal. Related to number of organisms available for dispersal.
Graph diameter	Max(δ_{ij}): geodesic path length Max($d_p(v_i,v_j)$); sum of physical edge lengths	Smaller diameter may allow faster dispersal throughout landscape.
Component diameter, X_K	Max(δ_{ij} | both nodes in X_K): geodesic path length Max($d_p(v_i,v_j)$ | both nodes in X_K): sum of physical edge lengths	Smaller diameter may allow faster dispersal throughout component.
Algebraic connectivity	This is the second smallest eigenvalue of the Laplacian matrix (the number of 0 eigenvalues is the number of components).	Larger values indicate greater robustness and fault tolerance; also the ease of synchronization in a dynamic network (Chung 1997).

Table 9.3 (*cont.*)

Measure	Details	Comments
Spectral gap	Like algebraic the gap between the first and second eigenvalues of the adjacency matrix, Δ, indicates when nodes have robust connections to other nodes, even with few edges.	Larger values suggest robust structure even for sparse graphs (Yazdani & Jeffrey 2010); in random walks, it gives faster convergence to limiting distribution.
Harary Index (see Plavšić et al. 1993)	$H = \frac{1}{2} \sum\limits_{i \in X_k}^{n_k} \sum\limits_{j \in X_k}^{n_k} 1/\delta_{ij}$ $1/\delta_{ij} = 0$ if $e_{ij} = 0$. If $K = 1$, then X_k is G the whole graph. Physical path length, $d_p(v_i, v_j)$ can replace δ_{ij}.	Sensitive to the length of dispersal routes; low values indicate more steps and possibly lower rates.
Normalized Harary Index	$H_N = \frac{H - H_{\min}}{H_{\max} - H_{\min}}$. Takes values 0 to 1; allows comparison of graphs or components of different sizes.	Sensitive to the length of dispersal routes relative to the numbers of nodes in the graph or component.
Characteristic path length	$C_g = \frac{1}{n_k(n_k-1)} \sum\limits_{i \in X_k}^{n_k} \sum\limits_{j \in X_k}^{n_k} \delta_{ij}$ $C_p = \frac{1}{n_k(n_k-1)} \sum\limits_{i \in X_k}^{n_k} \sum\limits_{j \in X_k}^{n_k} d_p(v_i, v_j)$ Geodesic and physical distance versions. If $K = 1$, then X_k is G the whole graph.	Shorter average path lengths suggest better dispersal between any pairs of habitat patches.
Path directness	$D = \frac{1}{n_k(n_k-1)} \sum\limits_{i \in X_k}^{n_k} \sum\limits_{j \in X_k}^{n_k} d_{ij} \div d_p(v_i, v_j)$ Average of straight-line distance over path physical length. X_k is the whole graph if $K = 1$.	Values near 1 show that the dispersal routes are spatially efficient; low values indicate indirect routes with many detours, which may increase risk and reduce dispersal success.
Betweenness centrality (node)	Local measure: proportion of shortest paths that go through v_i.	High centrality nodes are more important for dispersal routes and thus for conservation design.
Variance of node betweenness centrality	Global measure of differentiation among nodes for this property.	Low variance: all nodes of equivalent importance. High variance: some nodes are in key locations and highly important (probably "hubs").
Closeness centrality	Local measure: mean geodesic distance of v_i from other nodes. Its variance is another global measure, as above.	High closeness centrality nodes are more important because they are closer to others; high variance indicates greater differentiation for this property.
Eccentricity	Local measure: maximum distance of v_i from any other.	Indicates the node's isolation for potential recolonization.
Meshedness	The number of cycles in G compared to the number in maximal planar graph. Value 0 for trees, and 1.0 for planar graphs. $\mu = \frac{m-n+1}{2n-5}$. Closely related to average degree $= m/2n$.	Higher values indicate greater path redundancy which may make dispersal less risky or easier.
Clustering coefficient	Frequency of ($e_{ij} = 1 \mid e_{kj} = 1$ and $e_{ik} = 1$). Also called transitivity or triad completion.	Another measure of (edge-localized) redundancy for dispersal paths.

finding optimal network topologies (see Figure 9.11), such as avoiding the vulnerability of network structures based on highly connected central hubs; this too merits further investigation for ecological applications.

Table 9.3 is based only on topology or distances in symmetric graphs. Once the edges have other weights attached to them such as cost or resistance or directional bias, a second set of measures related to connectivity come into play. These include measures related to flow capacity and the probability of movement, least cost paths, and circuit theory's "sum of all paths" alluded to in the discussion of random walks. The description of random walks explained why a node's degree could be a reasonable measure of connectivity; the same reasoning works for the "buffered node neighbour counts" (Labonne et al. 2008), the numbers of nodes that have path lengths of $\delta(u,v) = 1, 2,$ $3, \ldots$; more neighbours can act as more proximate sources for random walks or dispersal to the focus node, provided they themselves do not have too many neighbours. (Both the mean and the variance of these counts have properties related to connectivity, as indicated in Table 9.3.) The same reasoning about node degrees applies with modifications when the edges have weights associated with them, provided the variance of those weights is not extreme.

Much of the work on landscape "archipelagos" has focussed on the metapopulation concept of individual species of interest and the effects of landscape structure, as reflected in its spatial graph, on local extinction and recolonization probabilities and rates (Hanski 2009; Fall et al. 2007). Other studies have looked more broadly at the effects of landscape characteristics on the interacting species in the metacommunity, such as plants and their pollinators and their community diversity (Spiesman & Inouye 2013).

The graph-theoretical toolbox typically looks at the vulnerability of dispersal to landscape fragmentation or to path depletion through cut-points and cut-edges, or the requirement for longer (or thus more costly) paths to maintain connectivity. In all of these, the graph nodes are abstracts of the real patches in the landscape, which have shape, area, topography, composition and so on, and the graph edges from which dispersal paths are composed are not necessarily real dispersal routes that might be followed (Figure 9.14). Connections through paths that are shorter or safer, or less costly in energy or other "currency" are often the focus of studies; and those edges are the ones preferred for graph construction, on the criterion of a smaller "effective distance" between habitat patches (see Chardon et al. 2003; Urban et al. 2009; Rayfield et al. 2011). This may include a determination of the single "best" path between nodes, based on least cost, least risk or highest rate of success. The lack of barriers and the centrality of nodes are other factors to be compared with the observed movement or inferred dispersal of the organisms of interest (Garroway et al. 2008; Wang et al. 2008). For example, in a study of the landscape genetics of fisher (*Martes pennanti*) populations in Ontario, node centrality was correlated with the proportion of immigrants, suggesting that the central nodes were high-quality habitat sources of emigrants to other lower quality sites (Garroway et al. 2008). Hock and Mumby (2015) suggested the use of reliability weights for the stochastic links between patches, based on the probability that one patch has a "direct effect" on the other; the most reliable path between non-adjacent

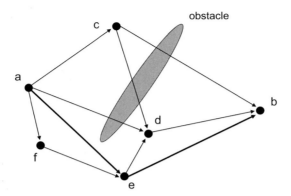

Figure 9.14 Sum of all paths. Because of the obstacle, the least costly path from a to b is a → e → b, but many other paths are possible, and all could contribute to flow:

a → c → b
a → d → b
a → c → d → b
a → e → d → b
a → f → e → b
and so on . . .

patches can then be determined using Dijkstra's algorithm on the log-transformed reliability weights (Hock & Mumby 2015).

Extending the concepts of connectivity and dispersal beyond the "best" path, McRae et al. (2008) used circuit theory, which integrates the effectiveness of many paths for dispersal, to evaluate and predict genetic dispersal in several species. This method looks at the sum of all possible paths, rather than trying to determine which one is best. In two different organisms, mahogany trees and wolverines, the "resistance distance," which incorporates multiple paths, gave much better predictions of observed gene flow than geographic distances or least cost (McRae & Beier 2007). This is a promising development in the application of graph theory in ecology, and of course, the study of electrical circuits is frequently cited as an early inspiration and application of network theory (Kirchhoff 1847; West 2001).

9.3.5   Dendritic Connectivity and Diversity

As familiar as the archipelago context or metaphor may be, and despite the usefulness of spatial graph theory for metacommunities in these insular systems (with parallels for landscape patches), spatial graphs can also be very informative about dendritic systems such as drainage basins or the rivers within them. The dendritic systems we study in ecology can be characterized as follows:

- Usually aquatic, but not always
- Almost always connected, but not always
- Almost all directional
- As abstracted graphs, almost all the same form: rooted trees
- As spatial graphs, almost all two-dimensional, planar, and the same shape (sort of)

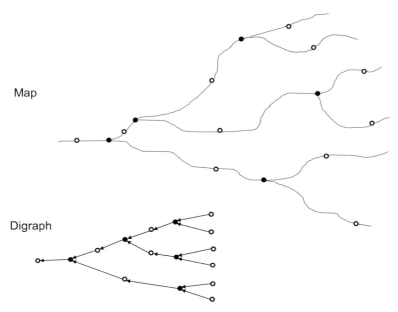

Map

Digraph

Figure 9.15 Map of river system and one version of its digraph: filled nodes are junctions; hollow nodes are reaches.

These systems represent a special case of the archipelago model for conservation ecology, and are special in two ways. First, movement within the network is highly directional for most organisms; that is, downstream. Second, the structure is highly constrained, and there are choices as to how the physical system is translated into a graph (see Grant et al. 2007). An obvious version is to identify the nodes as the junctions of streams with the edges being identified with the stream reaches that link them. Here, both nodes and edges represent habitat, possibly of different characteristics, so that the edges are now "real" objects, not just abstracted or potential connections. This convention produces nodes that have an in-degree of 2 and an out-degree of 1 (Figure 9.15, solid nodes). Another choice is to include the stream reaches as a separate set of nodes having in-degree 1 and out-degree 1 (Figure 9.15, open nodes), with the advantage of showing explicitly that the river reaches are to be considered as habitat locations with the same status as confluences (cf. Grant et al. 2007). Other possibilities include sample locations as nodes (Figure 9.16), possibly many per stream unit, each with their own constraints on the graph's characteristics. Of course, these constraints are determined by the physical structure of the systems as well as choices for the graph elements, but the constraints can make interpretation more straightforward.

The directional nature of these systems and the bias it introduces to movement is expected to affect metapopulation dynamics and community similarity. To complement that intuition, the digraphs that represent these systems produce asymmetric matrices and the random walk results for understanding connectivity become less easy to derive. However, random walks on these directed graphs still provide understanding of some of their properties. The directionality has strong effects on the overall connectivity and dynamics on the system network, with particular problems related to nodes

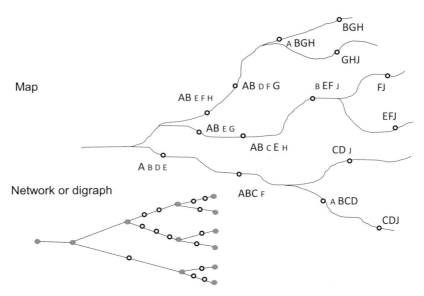

Map

Network or digraph

Figure 9.16 Map of river system with species composition for each site (major and minor components indicated by font size): sample locations are the nodes. In the digraph of the system, hollow nodes are sample sites and solid nodes are stream junctions.

that have zero in-degree or zero out-degree. Multiple random walks can speed up the total cover time in most graphs, as described in Section 9.3.3, but that is essential for many digraphs. All this suggests that, as suspected, the asymmetry of these digraphs has important implications for ecological applications.

In fact, modelling exercises demonstrate that asymmetric connectivity can have a detrimental effect on metapopulation persistence (Bode et al. 2008). In most dendritic aquatic networks, the directionality is strong and directed graphs can depict and quantify the connections and distances between node pairs (Fagan 2002; Grant et al. 2007; Schick & Lindley 2007, Figure 2c). In these dendritic digraphs, Cote et al. (2009) proposed a new dendritic connectivity index, based on the number of barriers and the probability that each one can be passed upstream or downstream; this provides a measure of stream connectivity as appropriate for the directional structure. A more familiar concept is the "buffered node neighbour counts" suggested by Labonne et al. (2008) for dendritic structure graphs; these are the numbers of nodes that have path lengths of $\delta(u,v) = 1$, 2, 3, ... Both the mean and the variance can be useful measures of properties related to connectivity (listed in Table 9.3), and Labonne et al. (2008) using distances up to 5, found similar behaviour for all ten metrics (mean and variance each at of five distances) for metapopulation persistence in individual-based models of demography in dendritic networks. However connectivity is measured or evaluated using node removal analysis (looking for "stepping-stone sites" or cut-nodes), the dendritic structure and directional asymmetry affect rates of extinction and genetic isolation, metapopulation size and persistence, and local variation in species diversity (Treml et al. 2008; Schick & Lindley 2007; Labonne et al. 2008; Bode et al. 2008; Carrara et al. 2012), with at least some of these being affected by the interaction between connectivity and sizes of the patches thus connected (Carrara et al. 2014). Sophisticated randomization tests may not be needed to detect the basic characteristics of some of these data sets, but more research on this application of graph theory to ecological systems can form the foundation of more general conclusions; that seems like a very worthwhile field of endeavour.

For applications of these techniques in ecological studies, as in many other areas of data analysis, in spatial networks there is an important and sometimes difficult relationship between the scale of the process being studied, the scale of the data recorded, and the scale at which the analysis is performed (Caceres & Berger-Wolf 2013; see also Dale & Fortin 2014, Figure 1.8). There is clearly much more to be done in the use of spatial graphs and the theory that goes with them to help understand the effects of spatial structure on ecological function, especially when the structure is asymmetrical. Looking at random walks on graphs can help to formalize or to correct our intuitions about the consequences of connectivity and its different forms. More formal investigations of connectivity, both in graph theory and in ecology, are called for to provide a better understanding.

You can do this too.

9.4 Concluding Comments

When the outline of this book was originally developed, spatial and spatio-temporal graphs dominated, and in the context of the work on spatial graphs, so did applications related to diversity and conservation. The final allocation is more even among the kinds of graphs and the applications described, but the area of spatial and spatio-temporal graphs in conservation ecology remains one of the most active areas for graph theory in ecology. The reconciliation of ecological connectivity and graph theory measures is unresolved, but certainly worth more investigation and discussion. An important distinction is the difference between analysis based on a graph like the Minimum Spanning Tree imposed on the data and used only as a skeleton to investigate properties like autocorrelation, and analysis of the same spatial data using a graph based on other information and more thoroughly based on graph-theoretical concepts. One example of the latter would be evidence for functional connectivity, which is a key factor in conservation ecology.

Spatial graphs, as abstract maps, have intuitive appeal for ecologists, but many applications of interest involve temporal processes on the graphs (such as extinction or dispersal) or dynamics of the graphs themselves (such as loss of a node or the formation of a new edge). These considerations lead naturally to investigations of a spatial-temporal context for graphs and graph theory. That's what's next.

10   Spatio-temporal Graphs

Introduction

Ecological processes occur both in space and in time. Although in some circumstances it is useful to generalize by abstracting structure and function from these dimensions, in other cases, it is important to retain the information of spatial and temporal location. Having described spatial graphs, in which the nodes have spatial locations, and temporal networks, in which persistent nodes have locations in time, an obvious approach that retains information on both spatial and temporal locations is to use spatio-temporal graphs. Spatio-temporal data are simply data that have labels telling when and where they were collected, which is a requirement of good science (Cressie & Wikle 2011, Chapter 1). Such data can be used to form a graph by adding edges between data locations, with the edges determined by any one of a large set of criteria. Following Cressie and Wikle (2011), the treatment of space and time is expected to remain in the scales where Newtonian physical laws can be assumed, which gives the option of treating both space and time as continuous variables to which continuous models, both formal and informal, can be applied. For either space or time, discrete-space and discrete-time models are also options, either arising from continuous versions then discretized, or from the data as originally collected, such as observations on a spatial grid or at regular time intervals (see Cressie & Wikle 2011, Chapter 6).

Lightning strikes are discrete events, but they can provide data located in continuous time and continuous space. Those locations in continuous dimensions can be converted into discrete format. For example, the US National Lightning Detection Network distinguishes and records cloud-to-ground lightning events and their polarity with excellent location accuracy (200 m) and time precision (0.5 microsecond RMS), so that the data are in continuous time and continuous spatial dimensions (see www.vaisala.com/en/products/thunderstormandlightningdetectionsystems/Pages/NLDN.aspx).

Lightning strikes are usually treated as if they have no duration and a single location in space. These data can then be "binned" into discrete time and space, for example by 1 minute or 24 hour periods and by square kilometre or US county. Similarly, Blitzortung is a citizens' lightning detection network, which allows you to hear and to see, on a map, lightning strikes in real time as they occur and you can track them as the storm that generates them moves across the country. (Very cool! Check out http://en.blitzortung.org/live_lightning_maps.php?map=30.) Another example that also gives data in continuous time is the old-fashioned hygrothermograph, which produces continuous records

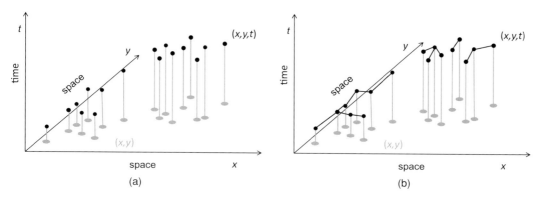

Figure 10.1 Spatio-temporal graphs: nodes have locations in time (t) and space (x, y). Spatio-temporal events are the nodes, e.g. lightning strikes. Edges, if any, may be constructs (e.g. showing clusters). (a) No edges. (b) Edges between events that are nearest spatial neighbours.

of temperature and humidity drawn on a paper-covered cylinder revolving at a constant speed. Modern digital versions produce discrete-time data by recording at regular intervals. Obviously, either version gives data from one location, and so an array of a number of such machines produces data that are in a single spatial arrangement.

In a spatio-temporal graph, the nodes have locations in time and in space; Figure 10.1 shows the locations of cloud-to-ground lightning strikes with the spatial location being the centre of the oval in the x-y plane, and the temporal location being the distance above that plane. The edges have end-points with locations (the nodes) but they may not be truly or fully located in those dimensions along their length, representing abstracted connections between nodes. The edges can represent trajectories, however, where appropriate (Figure 10.2). The simplest would be the almost straight paths such as those of "trapline" foraging bees (think of the term "a bee line"!), which have been the subject of much research (see e.g. Osborne et al. 1999; Lihoreau et al. 2013), but curvilinear is also a possibility where the data allow or physical structures constrain (fish migrating up a mountain stream). There is no need for the dimensions of time and space to be fully Euclidean and literal; three spatial dimensions can be reduced to two or even one, as in the Feynman diagram of particle physics (see also Figures 7.3–7.6 in Cressie & Wikle 2011). Compared to strictly spatial graphs, or to time-only graphs, having both space and time greatly increases the range of ecological phenomena that can be covered, but also the number of ways that the data can be treated, analyzed and interpreted. Whatever dimensions and data are used, spatio-temporal graphs provide a flexible treatment to depict, analyze and model complicated ecological phenomena with spatially and temporally explicit structure and dynamics.

Spatio-temporal graphs can be constructed or portrayed in many ways, based on whether time or space are continuous or discrete, and on the characteristics of the nodes and edges (e.g. transient, persistent, labelled or not and so on). For example, continuous time is often split up for practical reasons into time slices, with potential changes in edges between them, and the option of identity edges if required (Figure 10.3). This

Edges as joins

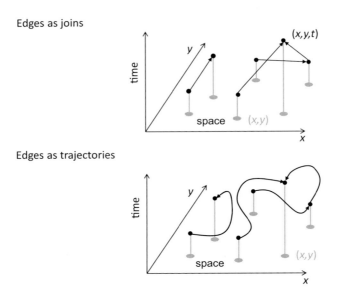

Edges as trajectories

Figure 10.2 Spatio-temporal graphs: nodes have locations in time (*t*) and space (*x*, *y*). Edges as joins, and edges as trajectories.

approach allows the possibility of a simple all-times summary of the edges by labelling with the time slices in which they were present (Figure 10.4); it also permits keeping track of individuals (nodes) that move (Figure 10.5).

All the possibilities cannot be covered here, nor can all the variations that can be usefully applied to ecological studies. Events in time make it possible to determine rates. If data on the locations of occurrences are available, the data will provide information on distances (sometimes functional distances as well as geographic or physical distances). Compared to temporal graphs or to spatial graphs, the spatio-temporal ones have emergent properties; in this case, speed or velocity, which requires both intervals in time and distances in space. Because distance can be measured in more than one way (geographic or physical, path length or cost and so on), there is more than one kind of speed that can be derived for any pair of nodes and time span.

The second emergent property of ecological systems available in spatio-temporal graphs, but not in time-only or space-only structures, is *dynamic spatial (neighbour) interactions*. This broad category includes phenomena like the spread of disease and *ecological memory* in community succession, which there is persistence of characteristics or lasting effects of the neighbourhood's past conditions on successional changes. These effects are closely tied to both temporal and spatial autocorrelation in the phenomenon studied, and either can be positive or negative, depending on the phenomenon and spatial and temporal scales. By combining rates with locations, spatio-temporal graphs also enable us to investigate location-specific or habitat-specific rates, for example, in studying the seasonal sequence of flower anthesis and of pollinator activity.

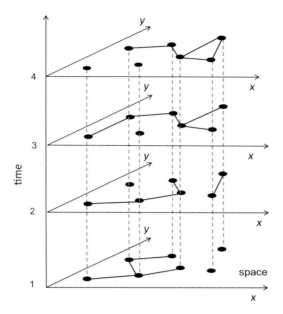

Figure 10.3 Spatio-temporal graphs: time slices show a series of edges through time. Identity edges join instances of the same node in different times, shown by dashed lines.

Temporal graphs, as described in Chapter 8, permit a very useful hierarchy of restricted randomizations for hypothesis testing, and adding spatial information to the graphs extends this facility and permits a sophisticated approach to the study of how space and time affect the ecological systems we study. Furthermore with spatio-temporal networks, theoretical models can be simulated to determine potential processes that could have produced the observed network.

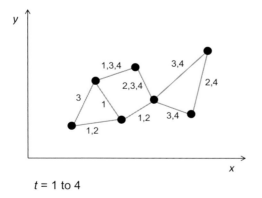

t = 1 to 4

Figure 10.4 Spatio-temporal graphs: all-times summary of edges labelled by time slice in which each occur, in Figure 10.3, for $t = 1$ to 4.

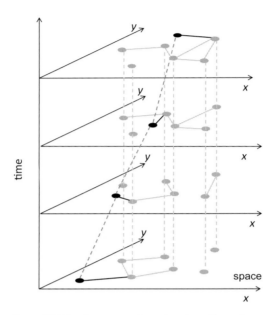

Figure 10.5 Spatio-temporal graphs: time slices show a series of edges through time identity edges join instances of the same node in different times, shown by dashed lines. This permits tracking of nodes even when they move in space.

10.1   Characteristics

Because there are so many different applications of spatio-temporal graphs in ecology, these can be placed in broad categories based on what kind of data the nodes and edges represent and whether time and space are continuous or discrete. Very broadly: are the nodes persistent at locations or do they represent objects that are short-lived or objects that move? Do the edges contain information beyond the structure of connections they represent? Consider a list of ecological examples (very incomplete!) and the nature of their data:

> **Lightning strikes that reach the ground**.
> Nodes are the spatio-temporal locations of the strikes. Processes are storm evolution and movement and the production of cloud-to-ground lightning.
> **Forest stand permanent plots**: effects of neighbours and history on tree stems.
> Nodes are the stems with their spatial locations, and conditions observed at different time periods. Processes are dispersal, germination, response to abiotic conditions, competition, growth, senescence and death.
> **Successional sequences of patches in a landscape** (ecological memory).
> Nodes are the patches with spatial locations and their states observed at time intervals. Processes are dispersal, response to abiotic conditions, facilitation, competition, predation and local extinction.

Animal movement through landscapes (foraging). Nodes are the animals with spatial locations for each, recorded at time intervals, possibly in the context of the landscape patches where they occur. Processes include local movements within a patch, dispersal between patches and migration.

Plant clonal growth by rhizomes or stolons.

Nodes are the plant stems with spatial locations, and recorded times of process responses: shoot appearance, growth, flowering and senescence.

Disease spread through populations (mobile or sessile): orderly or unpredictable.

Nodes are individuals located in space with their states (susceptible, diseased, removed) recorded at time intervals. Processes include transmission, infection, recovery and death.

Metacommunities: Community diversity in real and virtual archipelagos.

Nodes are the "islands" which have locations in space and compositional data recorded at time intervals. Processes include dispersal, establishment, migration and local extinction.

The range of data types is clearly large: from sporadic lightning strikes which are discrete events of little duration but with locations in continuous time and space, to the slow continuous processes of growth, ageing and replacement observed in permanent forest plots at intervals of years, with associated measures of tree stem species, size and status. One way to appreciate this diversity is to classify the spatio-temporal data and their treatments by creating a table of the combinations of characteristics. The details of the original objects or events of interest will not always match those of the data that records them and that then form the basis for the graph. Table 10.1 is one version of such a table (modified from Dale & Fortin 2014, Table 11.2).

Clearly, there are too many possibilities and combinations for all to be described in detail, far less worked through, but the list does provide an impression of the flexibility available. The "taxonomy" of these graphs is important because the same graph-theoretical property (e.g. connectivity) can mean different things depending on context (one time observation vs a series of many times). They also can have different implications if the graph is constructed as a scaffolding or framework on which to base analysis or if it is a real product of the system and its dynamics. That fact leads to some important questions:

Where are the data to be analyzed?
Is the information in the locations of the nodes?
The labels of the nodes? The locations of the edges? The sequence of the edges?
Their labels? How is graph theory to be applied to be most helpful?

The answers to all these questions depend on the systems and processes being studied and the nature of the data that have been collected. Because of the broad range of possibilities, it is impossible or unhelpful to generalize or to attempt general principles, but examining several examples with such questions in mind will help. Before those examples, however, there are two properties of spatio-temporal graphs or networks that are general features to note.

Table 10.1 Characteristics of Spatio-temporal Graphs

Time	The original events or objects may be long-lasting or of very short duration; their records may be in continuous form, or in discrete intervals (e.g. equal steps or order of occurrence; time "slices")
	Continuous-time data can be converted to the discrete form by "binning"
	Explicit time course records can be converted to an integrative summary of the whole time course
	Explicit time values or temporal labels (e.g. time period)
Space	The original events or objects may be point events or they may have length, area or volume; their records may be as continuous data (e.g. real number x,y coordinates) or in discrete format, such as raster, mosaic/polygon or object-referenced data
	Continuous data can be converted to the discrete form by "binning"
	Number of spatial dimensions: 1D, 2D, 3D, as dictated by the system
Nodes	Time: instantaneous (duration close to 0), ephemeral (short duration), transient or intermittent, persistent/permanent
	If persistent: constant or variable in characteristic of interest (e.g. size, state, quality)
	Temporal characteristics: one time snapshot (of contemporaneous nodes) versus integrative summary of many time periods versus sequential time course (nodes as "ancestors" and "descendants")
	Space: fixed or stationary versus moving
	Representing: locations, objects, events
	Properties: categorical, qualitative or quantitative labels; associated functions
Edges	Time: instantaneous (duration close to 0), ephemeral (short duration), transient or intermittent, persistent/permanent
	If persistent: constant or variable in characteristic of interest (e.g. flow rate)
	Temporal characteristics: a single time period versus summary graphs of many time periods indicating contemporaneity versus sequential time course (e.g. edges linking "ancestors and descendants" or "identity" edges linking instances of the same node)
	Space: symmetric versus asymmetric or directional
	Representing: connections, processes, relationships, objects
	Properties: categorical, qualitative or quantitative labels (including signs); associated functions; implicit directionality from any temporal extension
Comment	Kisilevich et al. (2010) have provided a different framework for their taxonomy based on *spatial extension* (points, lines or areas), *spatial location* (fixed or dynamic) and *temporal extension* (single snapshot, updated snapshot or time series).

10.2   Two Spatio-temporal Properties

To start, the focus is on the application of spatio-temporal graphs for investigating issues most directly related to conservation ecology, including landscape dynamics, diversity, succession and ecological memory, but also topics related to the movement of organisms, including animal movement, clonal growth and the spread of disease.

10.2.1   Spatio-temporal Distance and Path Length

In adapting many familiar graph measures for spatio-temporal graphs, the tricky part is defining distance or path length within the graph that combines spatial and temporal

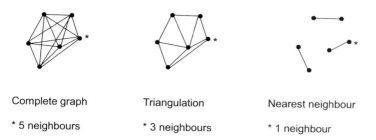

Complete graph   Triangulation   Nearest neighbour

* 5 neighbours   * 3 neighbours   * 1 neighbour

Figure 10.6 One hierarchy of neighbours in a spatial graph: complete graph, triangulation, nearest neighbour. The marked node has 5, 3 and 1 neighbours.

distances in a sensible and useful manner. Then, the rest should easy! The problem is that time and space are not usually commensurable, so there is no easy equivalence to allow a combined measure of multidimensional distance, and thus no obvious way to find the shortest paths between any two nodes, or the nodes that are closest together in space and time (Jacquez 1996). The problem of lack of commensurability in searching for spatio-temporal clusters is easily resolved by using "cylinders" as templates for scan statistics that are equal in their spatial dimensions, but of set length in time (Iyengar 2005; see also Takahashi et al. 2008). This is the equivalent of setting two independent threshold values, one for space and one for time. Two easy fixes are as follows:

1 For cases with fixed permanent nodes, spatially defined distance may be all that is needed for useful measures such as centrality; in a reduced-to-space-only graph, the distance between nodes is what is important.
2 If time occurs as discrete steps, there are many pairs of nodes throughout the time layers that are the same temporal distance apart, and so finding the least spatial distance among those pairs with equal temporal distances may be the solution.

Under special situations, there may be a natural choice for time and distance commensurability, based on the concepts described for random walks on undirected graphs (Chapter 9). If the system is a landscape of habitat patches and dispersal between them is linked to a seasonal or annual cycle, it may be reasonable to consider a rule of "one step per cycle," adjusting the definition of neighbouring patches to capture the usual physical distance of dispersal. This then allows the use of random walks as conceptual or simulation models for the processes of dispersal in this system.

10.2.2 Hierarchical Tests with Spatio-temporal Neighbours

In spatial graphs (space only), for any set of nodes, there are many different rules for determining edges, permitting a range of connectivity from dense and highly connected (e.g. the complete graph with edges for all possible pairs), to very sparse (e.g. single nearest neighbours) (see Figure 10.6). This range of rules allows precise hierarchical hypothesis evaluation: combining contrasting edge rules with conventional statistics to measure dependence, predictions about the characteristics of individual nodes can be made and compared. The complete graph is the equivalent of the null hypothesis that all other nodes are equally good predictors of a node's condition, whereas a more restricted set of neighbours examines the possibility that only (for example) the nearest nodes have related values. This approach compares the results for a null hypothesis condition (with some limitations for nodes and edges) with those of the alternate-hypothesis condition with more restrictions. For example, to test the effects of various kinds of neighbours, the null hypothesis is provided by the complete graph, equivalent to having all the other nodes exerting equal influence on the characteristics of the focal node. The alternative hypothesis is determined by the graph of first-order neighbours in a Delaunay triangulation, equivalent to the claim that those neighbours provide the best explanatory factors, or by only the first nearest neighbour for each node (Figure 10.6).

This concept can be summarized as:

{H0 = complete graph} ≡ "All nodes influence the focal node equally."
{H1 = Delaunay graph} ≡ "Only those first-order neighbours influence the focal node."
{H2 = nearest neighbour graph} ≡ "Only the single closest node affects the focal node."

Spatio-temporal graphs allow the same hierarchical testing with yet more flexibility. Consider a widespread population of plants for which the phenological sequences of the appearance of leaves and flowers have been recorded for many years. The timing of events for any plant can then be evaluated based on a hierarchy of neighbours in space and time:

H₀ No structure: Use all possible edges in time and space (the complete spatio-temporal graph). This is the hypothesis that similarity is independent of time lags and geographic distances.

H₁ "Regional" structure: All edges between first-order neighbours in space and time using one of several edge rules that can give different edge densities (MST, Gabriel, Delaunay, . . .): the hypothesis is that similarity is broadly dependent on time lag and geographic distance (Figure 10.7, top).

H₂ "Local" structure: Only edges between closest neighbours in space and time (Figure 10.7, bottom).

This is equivalent to the hypothesis that similarity depends only on the shortest time differences and shortest spatial distances.

This is in a spatio-temporal context and so there are other alternatives to be tested.

H₀ No structure: independence, as above.

Hₛ Only space matters: Edges occur between spatial neighbours, but not between instances of the same individual at different times. If the control of variation in phenology is based on location, regional or neighbourhood effect, there are no individual effects, and no history (Figure 10.8, top).

H_T Individual control: Only temporal edges between instances of the same plant at different times are used, possibly with several time lags $(t - 1, t - 2, \ldots)$. The

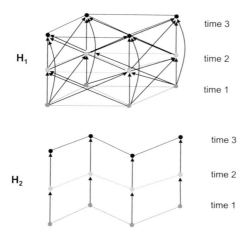

Figure 10.7 Example of spatio-temporal graph with four sites and three times: structure in time and space. **H₁**: Regional structure in time and space. **H₂**: Local structure in time and space (nearest neighbours). (A black-and-white version of this figure will appear in some formats. For the colour version, please refer to the plate section.)

variation among individuals has no spatial component, no neighbour or locality effects, but persists from year to year (Figure 10.8, bottom).

These details give an idea of the precision and flexibility that this hierarchical approach can offer the researcher. An added advantage is that there can be a simple visual

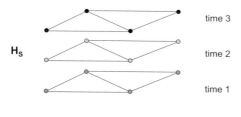

Figure 10.8 Example of spatio-temporal graph with four sites and three times. **H_S**: Only spatial structure; no history. **H_T**: Individual history; no neighbour effects; no spatial structure. (A black-and-white version of this figure will appear in some formats. For the colour version, please refer to the plate section.)

representation of the hierarchy and the relationships within it. Admittedly, however, the graphs used to depict the relationships are created by the hierarchical structure for testing, and so there is very little that real graph theory can tell us about our data. However, if there are quantitative measures associated with the edges, or even with the nodes, then there is much more that we can do in comparing measures of centrality or the resistance of causal paths, and so on.

10.3 Examples of Ecological Applications

The range of applications for spatio-temporal graphs in ecological studies is so diverse that it is difficult to provide general advice or to abstract from that range a list of common measures that may be useful. Instead, it is probably most useful to go through a list of examples that cover much of that range, and learning case-by-case, measures and techniques to use.

10.3.1 Lightning Strikes

Here a database may consist of the spatial coordinates of cloud-to-ground lightning strikes for a particular geographic area (continuous space) and the times at which they occur (continuous time), see Figure 10.1a. The permanent records of those strikes are the nodes. For most purposes, a summary graph that covers an extended block of time would probably be sufficient, given adequate labels, rather than requiring separate graphs for individual days. Obvious choices for the edges of a graph (of course, it could be empty), are edges joining nodes into (a) spatial clusters, (b) temporal clusters and (c) spatio-temporal clusters as in Figure 10.9 (Tango 2010; see Kisilevich et al. 2010). The three clustering results can then be compared to look for trends and orderliness in time and in space. The nodes can be classified according to the characteristics of the lightning strike itself, such as multiplicity and polarity, and edges assigned then between nodes based on those categories. The goal is, of course, prediction, and so cluster detection is not sufficient by itself, but the sequencing of locations is important. This is one example in which the time-only version of the graph that gives temporal clustering and spacing and the spatial network that can be derived both have useful information for the researcher.

Alternatives include drawing edges between nodes that are strikes of the same polarity, energy level, or strike multiplicity, in an effort to detect lightning signatures of other phenomena. There appears to be a spatial correlation of total rainfall with total electrical activity and with positive cloud-to-ground strikes (Soula & Chauzy 2001). More specifically, a study in Texas showed that tornado touchdown was preceded by an increased rate of lightning strikes, an increased proportion of positive polarity strikes, and a spatial concentration of strikes along the tornado path (Snow et al. 2007).

Summary
- Dimensionless point events, recorded in continuous time, continuous space

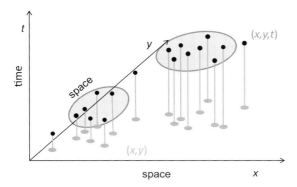

Figure 10.9 Spatio-temporal graph. Possible spatial-temporal clusters are indicated by ovals; edges can be added that create modules for the clusters.

- Single all-times graph with times explicit (or labelled or coded on spatial graph)
- Nodes permanent, recording strike locations
- Edges based on temporal, spatial and spatio-temporal clustering
- Measures: temporal burstiness, spatio-temporal clusters, spatio-temporal sequencing (partial orders), tests of spatio-temporal randomness; node classification by strike category (multiplicity, polarity) as function of neighbour spatial and temporal distance; edge classification by time of day, or time of year
- Comparisons: correlation with elevation, historical record of strikes
- Edges are constructs, not data (unlike "similar" data from fireflies, which could be traced to an individual and its movement)

10.3.2   Permanent Forest Sample Plots

Permanent plots are established in forest stands with all large individual tree stems mapped and measured, along with recorded comments on condition, such as disease or mortality (see Figure 10.3). The plots are then monitored at intervals to determine the effects of neighbouring stems and past conditions on the fates of individual stems, giving one graph per observation time period. The spatial locations of the stems and the dates of the observation are important facts giving the context for any analysis. The graphs to be used are the neighbour networks described in Chapter 1 of this book, within any time period, with edges defining spatio-temporal neighbours in addition to identity edges between time intervals (Figure 10.4).

The goal is to predict the fate of individual stems based on the data from preceding observation periods, and so the recommended approach is to use an iterative process of evaluating the ability of the data from spatial and temporal "neighbours" including the focal tree itself to predict changes in its status (vigorous, living, suppressed, diseased, moribund, dead ...). The hierarchy of neighbours from all stems at all times through reductions in the numbers of spatial neighbours and in the length of history considered

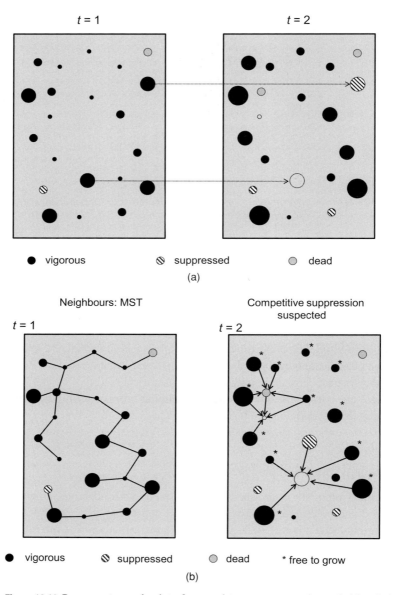

Figure 10.10 Permanent sample plot of mapped tree stems: tree size coded by circle diameter (edges of identity may not be needed). (a) Showing transition of states (e.g. vigorous to suppressed or suppressed to dead). (b) Edges included as spatial neighbour structure (e.g. neighbour network); or indicating functional effect (e.g. competitive suppression).

to perhaps only the three nearest neighbours and only time $t - 1$, allows an evaluation of what is truly important in determining the stem's fate.

The analysis is closely related to spatial point pattern analyses, especially mark correlation analysis, which looks at the spatial scales of positive and negative correlation of quantitative characteristics (see Dale & Fortin 2014, Chapter 4.2). The nodes can appear or disappear between observation times. The edges of the graph form a scaffolding for the analysis; but they are determined by the researcher, and so are not themselves data for analysis. The graph structure is the context, and the information for analysis is in the time-indexed measures and conditions ("marks") associated with each stem (Figure 10.10a). The result here is one graph per time period, and these can certainly be combined into a single graph consisting of many layers or tiers, one for each time slice. It is not clear that there are any real advantages to doing this if the only edges running between time slices are "identity edges" joining instances of the same individual.

Another way to look at such data is to see them as a set of temporal series, each with a spatial location. The question is then that of the relationship among the temporal series, based on their spatial locations, such as the effects of first-order, second-order and third-order neighbours; the characteristics that are most important in those relationships; the quantification of those effects; and so on. Directional edges in space and time could illustrate speculation about sources of competition and suppression among trees (Figure 10.10b).

Summary

- Stems are observed at discrete time intervals, but mapped in continuous space
- One graph or time slice per observation period
- Nodes for locations and conditions of tree stems, but not permanent or in all graphs
- Key data are node states and transitions
- Edges join neighbours within a single time, or may be speculative on causality of change
- Measures: stem transitions as correlated with characteristics of neighbours, stem history and neighbour histories; effect of neighbour graph definitions, path lengths and inter-neighbour distances, both by geodesic distance (spatial order) and time lag
- Comparisons: geodesic distances versus physical distances; possible effects of site differences (e.g. slope) and weather (drought)
- Closely related to marked point pattern analysis

10.3.3   Ecological Memory in Landscape Patch Dynamics

Very simply, "ecological memory" is the set of processes that determine the degree to which an ecological system is affected by its past, together with some evaluation of that effect (Peterson 2002). Ecological memory is partly derived from the interaction of plants and propagules, mobile links such as seed dispersers, and biological legacies, such as remnant trees and vegetation patches in a disturbed landscape (see Garcia et al. 2011). In one example, seed dispersal resilience emerged from the ecological memory conferred by the inter-annual variability in fruit production and the ability of thrushes to track fruit resources across the fragmented landscape (Garcia et al. 2011). Ecological memory also results from the network of species in a system, their interactions with each other and with the environment, and the set of structures that allow recovery after disturbance, thus being directly related to ecological resilience, which is the capacity of the system to survive disturbance (Bengtsson et al. 2003).

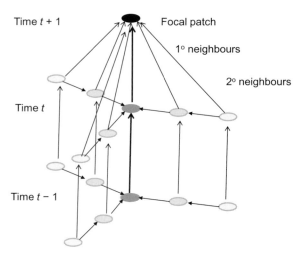

Figure 10.11 Ecological memory: patch status depends on its history and on its neighbours' characteristics (and probably more than just first-order neighbours). Those neighbour characteristics depend on their own histories.

A very simple model of landscape patch dynamics is based on classifying the patches into a small number of categories or states, with transitions between any two states either determined by history and environmental factors with thresholds and feedback loops ("state and transition" models; Phillips 2011) or by simple probability as with Markov models. Depending on the transition probabilities, this can lead to an orderly temporal structure consisting of a cycle of states for each patch, particularly when the transitions are governed by a first-order Markov model with the probability depending only on the current state of the patch, not on its history and not on the states of its neighbours. A more realistic model that includes both some of the patch's own history (states in previous time periods) and characteristics of (at least) first-order neighbouring patches, leads to a much less orderly dynamic structure, which may be more realistic.

As with the analysis of tree stems in permanent plots, the use of a range of graphs with many-to-few neighbours considered for each patch, both in space and in time, combined with similarity measures allow a determination of the spatial and temporal effects on the directions of change in the landscape patches. Tanner et al. (1996) modelled the effects of history (1 to 27 years) on the species composition of intertidal coral reefs and found that although history was important in determining state transition probabilities, it really had only little effect on the dynamics and structure of the system.

Here the data are descriptions of the "state" of each of a number of contiguous forest stands or landscape patches as observed through a number of time periods. Most often, the states are points or steps along a continuum, with demarcated transitions between states. Each patch is represented by a node which has the spatial location of the patch centroid, but the result is a rigid lattice of such nodes (discrete space). Time is also discrete, with the system being observed, and the states recorded, periodically. There are three kinds of edges that can describe which versions of which patches are neighbours. Temporal edges join each patch to one or more previous versions of itself. Spatial edges join patches to current neighbours within the same time period, potentially defined in a number of different ways (topological or distance threshold rules, first-, second-, and third-order neighbours and so on). Spatio-temporal edges join a patch to a selection of historical versions of its current spatial neighbours. This is usually set up as a multi-layered or tiered graph, with one layer representing the spatial layout of each of several time periods, with time-dependent edges running between layers (Figure 10.11). This is one example where the multi-time graph is necessary because more than just identity edges run between time slices.

Summary
- Observations at discrete time intervals, discrete space of landscape polygons
- One layer per time period in a many-layered graph
- Nodes permanent, recording stand or patch locations, but with state that may change from time to time
- Edges based on temporal, spatial, and spatio-temporal "neighbours" include past self
- Measures: rates and conditions for each state-to-state transition; effect of graph definition of neighbours
- Comparisons: similar to Markov model analysis of transitions; non-stationarity is a serious concern, especially under climate change

10.3.4 Animal Movement

Ecological studies of animal movement may be aimed at evaluating territoriality and home range, for which the expectation is no net displacement over time; or at assessing wide-ranging foraging without returning to a home base, dispersal or migration, for which net displacement is expected. Part of either assessment may be to relate the patterns of movement to characteristics of the landscape, such as vegetation type or resource availability, or to time itself in the form of annual, seasonal or daily cycles. It is usually assumed that the actual trajectory between observations is close enough to the straight-line edge used as an approximation, but the danger of that assumption will change with the tine elapsed between observations; one observation per 24 hours will miss any diurnal cycles, apart from any other inaccuracies; but one observation every 3 minutes may not be an efficient expenditure of effort.

It is more obvious for the context of no "home base," perhaps, but one general characteristic of graphs depicting animal movement is how direct or convoluted the paths are, and there are a number of measures of path compactness or tortuosity available (see summary of Dale & Fortin 2014, Chapter 11.6). From a graph theory approach, a measure of interest would be the number of crossings of edges that occur, perhaps expressed as a proportion of edges that cross others. For example, in Figure 10.12a, steps 1 to 9 have fairly constant net movement in the same direction and have no edge crossings. Steps 10 to 20, on the other hand, cover a more compact space, have little net movement overall, and have a high proportion of crossings per edge, although the

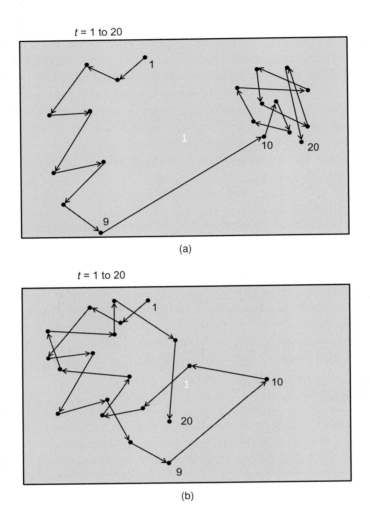

t = 1 to 20

(a)

t = 1 to 20

(b)

Figure 10.12 Animal foraging movement: two examples (a) and (b). The nodes are known locations, and the edges join them in sequence.

crossings are between edges that are nearby in time. Figure 10.12b also has many edge crossings, but they tend to involve edges that are farther apart in time. Indices of those characteristics will clearly differentiate between the two parts of the graph, which are intuitively distinct.

Typically, the data are a simple sequence of observed timed locations with movement between them reasonably understood, perhaps with associated information on behaviour or environment. Usually the time intervals are equally spaced, but even if not, the times of observations are known, and a single graph is used for a number of observation times. If the edges are not actual trajectories (or even if they are?), the sequence of spatio-temporal locations of the graph nodes are the data, and distances and rates and other measures, such as path tortuosity, can be calculated from them (Figure 10.12).

The moving animal creates sequentially appearing permanent nodes of location, with a sequence of edges joining them, providing a pseudo-trajectory that provides an approximation of the actual path followed.

Summary

- Observations in discrete time, continuous space as geographic coordinates
- Single summary graph
- Nodes' permanent records of animal locations at different times
- Edges join sequential nodes providing an approximate trajectory
- Measures: turnings and angles, crossings, tortuosity, speeds, displacements; potential effects of environment and temporal cycles on all of these
- Comparisons: By individual; site to site; season to season; year to year. Many potential sources of non-stationarity or heterogeneity in all characteristics
- The graph could be used, as for the permanent plots, as the "skeleton" for analysis of the associated data for selectivity, autocorrelation as a function of distances, or rates of change (see Dale & Fortin 2014, Chapter 11.6)

10.3.5   Clonal Plants

Many of the characteristics of clonal plant growth are similar to those of interest for animal foraging paths, but of course, as the plants "forage" they also reproduce, resulting in a branching path rather than a single exploration route (Figure 10.13, a sketch based on *Medeola virginiana*; see Bell 1974; Cook 1988). For spatio-temporal graphs of some kinds of clonal growth, more than one kind of node may be required, for example branching points in the clonal structure may or may not also be aerial shoots (Figure 10.13). Similarly, aerial shoots may have different behaviours depending on whether they are flowering shoots or vegetative. The number of node categories required will depend on the biology of the plant and the mechanism of its spread, but it can always be asked how efficiently do the various plant structures use the available space.

$t = 1$ to 3

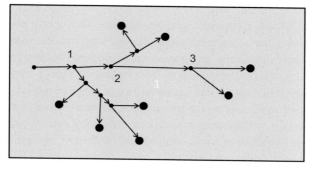

Figure 10.13 Clonal plant growth and foraging. Loosely based on *Medeola virginiana* (see Bell 1974; Cook 1988). There are two kinds of nodes: branch points and aerial shoots.

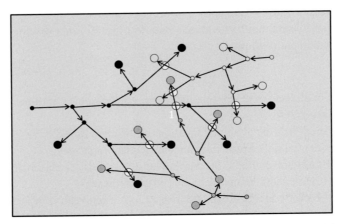

Figure 10.14 Clonal plant network of three clones with root grafts (circled), loosely based on *Populus tremuloides*. This graph uses three kinds of nodes: branch points and stems, coded by different shading for different clones, and root grafts (circled).

Del Mondo et al. (2010) used spatial, spatio-temporal and temporal graphs and neighbour, descendant and ancestor relationships to model spatio-temporal evolution of a clonal network, which they illustrated with the propagation of bramble plants by basal shoots, layering, grafts and from seed.

Initial growth in this example combines features of animal movement and of the spread of disease. The plant stems or their equivalents, the ramets, are the graph's nodes, each with a persistent spatial location, even if the ramets are themselves transient through time. Each node has at least one point in time associated with it: the time or time period that it appeared. The times of other events associated with each ramet may also be included (e.g. flowering, fruiting, senescence, death), similar to records of states and transitions in permanent sample plots. In addition to edges depicting neighbour network structure, clonal proliferation has real trajectories, the rhizomes or other structures by which clonal spread occurs. These structures link "ancestors" to "descendants" and there should be graph edges that approximate them as closely as possible. This is easy with above-ground runners (like strawberry) but less so with roots or rhizomes underground. As with most our examples, there are other sets of edges possible, and comparisons among the sets should prove fruitful: edges of the usual neighbour networks, edges of contemporaneity, and edges of phenological (or other) similarity.

When clonal systems are well established, they frequently form a multi-individual and multi-genet network by root grafts (Figure 10.14), so that they no longer resemble simple animal foraging paths, but more closely resemble transportation networks like rail systems or highways, transporting material of different kinds in different directions. This is true of clonal trees like aspen, single stem trees like pines that form similar networks by root grafts, and also of fungi with rhizomorphs like *Armillaria* (see Lamour et al. 2007) but also of multi-genera networks of vascular plants and mycorrhizae (see Simard et al. 2012). The spatio-temporal graph that represents these spatio-temporal networks then has characteristics of interest like those of transportation networks, including reachability, centrality, and vulnerability or robustness to the loss of network elements (cf. Williams & Musolesi 2016).

Summary

- Observations in discrete time, continuous space for mapped ramets
- Time-labelled summary graph
- Nodes for locations of ramets (persistent), and dates of events or state transitions
- Edges join nodes that are parents and offspring (trajectories)
- Also, edges of neighbour networks; edges of contemporaneity; edges of similarity
- Measures: for growing clone: rates and speeds, node degree and neighbour node degree, neighbour node categories, connectivity, branching angles, space-filling, environmental effects including neighbours and parents ... then once established: spatio-temporal centrality, vulnerability, etc.
- Comparisons: during clonal expansion, similar to animal movement or the spread of disease; compare with spatial models and with models of graph (network) evolution. Established networks resemble those of transportation; compare with those.

10.3.6   Disease Spread: Stationary Organisms

This application for spatio-temporal graphs was introduced by the model of a stand of plants, which is monitored at intervals for the locations of a particular disease (or equivalently an insect pest). The data are the locations of newly diseased plants and of all others (Figure 10.15). More detailed labelling of the nodes can include (previously diseased) recovered and (previously diseased) dead plants at each time of observation. Even better would be information on resistant versus susceptible plants, but that may not be known. The actual paths of infection may not be known, also, although there are some rare cases in which this can be determined (*Armillaria* fungus with its rhizomorphs?) (see Mihail & Bruhn 2005). The choice of nodes and their labels is straightforward, but there are many different possibilities of the edges that we might use, either within individual time "slices," between or among time periods, or in a time-aggregated summary graph (see Chapter 8). It would be most useful to have edges between all possible pairs, or between all neighbour pairs however defined, that could be labelled "transmission possible," "transmission occurred," and "transmission impossible," but usually that information is not available. Of the many choices for edge definitions, here are four choices, all of which use planar graphs from the topological hierarchy that includes the Minimum Spanning Tree, Gabriel graph, and Delaunay triangulation (see Chapters 1 and 9): (1) edges indicating contemporaneity of infection, one graph for each time period (or a time-aggregated version with appropriate labelling); (2) most likely routes from nearest infected neighbours (Figure 10.16), one per time slice or aggregated and labelled; (3) Minimum Spanning Tree in a time-aggregated graph that is constrained to using edges joining nodes that were infected one time unit apart (Figure 10.17, left); or (4) a topological time-aggregated graph connecting all nodes ever infected (Figure 10.18, right; this same list is given in Dale & Fortin 2014, Section 11.8.3, Figure 11.24).

New disease records at times 1 to 4 = ○

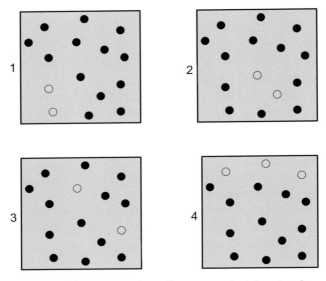

Figure 10.15 Epidemiology: maps of new disease records at time 1 to 4.

One way of looking at the time-aggregated graphs is that these are just spatial graphs with temporal labels (i.e. not truly spatio-temporal), and of course that is true; but they can be easily deconstructed, if necessary, into a more authentic spatio-temporal format.

For the study of how disease spreads, Figure 10.19 illustrates the reasoning behind the choice of edges determined by contemporaneity. If the spread of disease is orderly and progressive, there will be few edge crossings and any edge crossings will involve edges that are close in time. Less orderly transmission will result in more crossings and crossings between edges widely separated in time. Subsequent figures illustrate

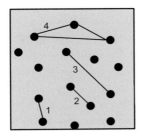

Edges of contemporaneity,
for times 1, 2, 3 & 4.

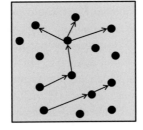

Probable routes of spread
for time steps 1, 2 & 3;
based on nearest neighbours

Figure 10.16 Epidemiology: two kinds of edges, contemporaneity and possible routes of disease spread based on nearest neighbours.

Minimum Spanning Tree,
edges between nodes infected
one time unit apart

Minimum Spanning Tree
of all nodes ever infected

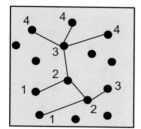 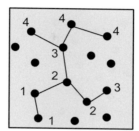

Label is time of infection

Figure 10.17 Epidemiology: MST of new infections one time unit apart, and MST of all nodes ever infected.

two examples of this approach. The first records the incidence of phloem necrosis in *Hevea brasiliensis* (rubber tree) in four time slices (Figures 10.18 and 10.20) (Peyrard et al. 2006), and the second shows mortality in four time periods in a plantation of Fraser fir (Figure 10.21) (Benson et al. 2006). Whichever definition for edges we use, the two examples look very different (Figures 10.19 and 10.20 compared with Figures 10.21 and 10.22). In the *Hevea* contemporaneous appearance graph, there is nothing that looks like orderly spatial spread; there are many crossings and many crossings between edges of more distant times. In the Fraser fir example, while it does not look like the orderly "textbook" diagram, there are fewer edge crossings and more of them

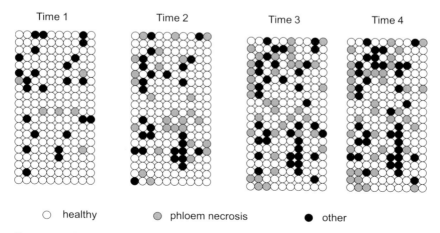

Figure 10.18 *Hevea brasiliensis*: trunk phloem necrosis data for four time periods (from Peyrard et al. 2006).

Edges of contemporaneity for times 1 (black), 2 (dark grey), 3 (light grey) & 4 (dotted).

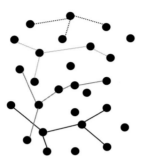 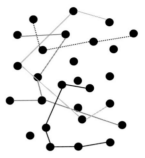

Orderly and close range: Short edges and few cross-temporal crossings

Less orderly transmission: Longer edges and more cross-temporal crossings

Figure 10.19 Graph of disease spread. Edges of contemporaneity for times 1, 2, 3 and 4. Orderly and close range produces short edges and few cross-temporal crossings. Less orderly transmission produces longer edges and more cross-temporal crossings. (A black-and-white version of this figure will appear in some formats. For the colour version, please refer to the plate section.)

are between adjacent time periods; and there is clear spread from the central cluster of disease at time 1, to more cases east and north of the centre as time proceeds. Comparing the two, it is no surprise that while the Fraser fir mortality is caused by a pathogen that is infective, *Phytophthora*, the *Hevea* necrosis does not seem to be an infectious disease (Peyrard et al. 2006).

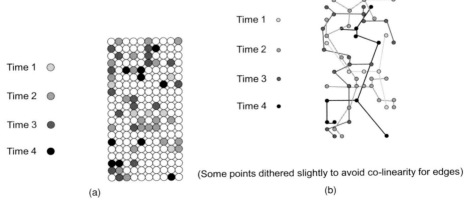

Time 1 ○

Time 2 ○

Time 3 ●

Time 4 ●

Time 1 ○

Time 2 ◉

Time 3 ●

Time 4 •

(Some points dithered slightly to avoid co-linearity for edges)

(a)   (b)

Figure 10.20 *Hevea brasiliensis*: trunk phloem necrosis data (a) colour coded by time of appearance, and (b) edges join locations of contemporaneous disease appearance (MST). (A black-and-white version of this figure will appear in some formats. For the colour version, please refer to the plate section.)

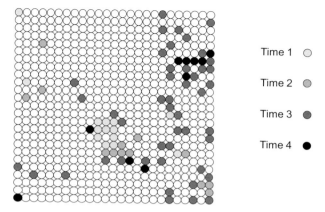

Figure 10.21 Fraser fir mortality (from Benson et al. 2006) with locations coded by time of disease appearance. (A black-and-white version of this figure will appear in some formats. For the colour version, please refer to the plate section.)

Spatio-temporal graphs of diseased and uninfected individuals can also be used to detect spatio-temporal clusters in the data, as described in many works, but the issues related to the non-commensurability of space and time remain, and it is not clear how graph theory itself can contribute to this endeavour. The definition of the edges would have to be carefully chosen to be helpful (see Figure 10.6).

This research topic has been presented as for a stand or plantation of mapped trees monitored for disease, but a common alternative is records of disease appearance for spatial cells at larger scales (e.g. fields or counties or states). The analysis of such data using spatio-temporal graphs is similar to that for individual stems, with some modifications necessary to account for the contiguity of adjacent spatial cells in a regular grid or irregular mosaic.

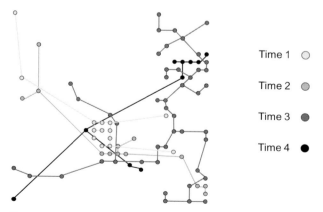

Figure 10.22 Fraser fir mortality (from Benson et al. 2006) with edges joining locations of contemporaneous disease appearance. (Some points dithered slightly to avoid co-linearity for edges.) (A black-and-white version of this figure will appear in some formats. For the colour version, please refer to the plate section.)

Summary

- Observations in discrete time, nodes in continuous space for mapped locations of individuals; or discrete space for plantations (grid) or for areal units (e.g. counties as polygons)
- One graph per observation period, or time-labelled summary graph
- Nodes for locations and conditions of stems or units, permanent for time course
- Key data are node states and transitions: susceptible, diseased, recovered, dead
- Edges join nodes with synchronous changes, neighbours within a single time, or show putative paths of infection ("ancestors" and "descendants")
- Measures: node degree (and by neighbour category), edge lengths, edge crossings, node transition rates, categories of neighbours by geodesic distances (spatial order) and temporal lag; effects on disease flow by spatial structure (cut-nodes, bridges, connectivity, highly connected blocks)
- Comparisons: orderly versus disorderly models; contagion versus random appearance, and so on

10.3.7   Disease Spread: Mobile Organisms

This gets complicated, and a simple summary spatio-temporal graph may not be adequate. If the organisms are territorial animals, the territories may be treated as the stationary objects like sessile organisms and the usual analysis proceeds with only minor adjustments; Craft et al. (2010) have described the case of Serengeti lions, showing how the spatial network of territories can provide a simulated contact network, and then a simulated disease transmission network. The more general answer is that what started as a spatial graph as the basis for the analysis, must then become a contact history graph. One application of the time-only graphs described in Chapter 8 was the recording and analysis of inter-individual contacts, and proximity detectors can be used to track these through time. In their work on modelling disease spread in cattle, Duncan et al. (2012) compared empirical (observed) contact networks with simulations based on mass-action mixing. The recorded networks had more repeated contacts, lower closeness and clustering scores, and greater average path lengths; these graph-theoretical characteristics predict fewer infected animals and lower risk of disease spread.

The topology of (contact) networks affects disease spread, as would be predicted, and Shirley and Rushton (2005) found in a modelling exercise that disease spread was fastest in scale-free graphs and slowest in regular lattices, with random (Erdös-Rényi) graphs and rewired lattices giving intermediate rates. In general, it is found that node degree and connectance (triangle completion) have the strongest effects on disease spread (Keeling 1999; Franc 2003, among many others) but "community structure" or modularity also is important (Salathé & Jones 2010).

Some of the work on disease networks has been focussed on aspatial (or abstracted) time-only contact networks (see Newman 2010, Chapter 17), but sometimes the spatial context of those contact networks is of great importance to the dynamics that result (see Figure 10.23), and including that important spatial context then requires the spatio-temporal graphs. One challenge is to derive static graphs for the epidemiology network

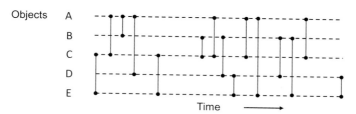

Objects

Temporal order (numbered) of contacts in spatial locations show a clear trend

Figure 10.23 Temporal graph of pairwise contacts with spatial locations, and temporal order (numbered) of contacts in spatial locations.

from the dynamic time-only networks of contacts (Holme 2013). In transferring the results from aspatial models to spatial ones, an important main effect is through the degree of a particular node in the graph. One of the best examples of a study of disease transmission in networks is of lions in the Serengeti, which are territorial and therefore possibly buffered from disease spread. Craft et al. (2010) compared the territory network (a spatial graph) with the contact network (behavioural graph) and then a transmission network (outcome graph), by several measures to determine how "small world" the networks are. One of the key measures was "efficiency," which is the average of the reciprocals of all node-to-node distances. It was suspected that nomadic individuals that move through more than one territory might be important disease vectors. The main finding was that the networks were sufficiently small world, with short paths and high efficiencies for potential disease transmission, that territoriality did not protect against disease, and that the epidemiological impact of nomads was slight.

Contacts between mobile individuals are usually key for disease transmission, and these can be recorded in a temporal aspatial graph. A truly spatio-temporal approach may seem confusing, but it offers the opportunity to look for spatio-temporal trends or hot spots of contacts (Figure 10.23) that may result in the spread of the disease. This is an obvious application for spatio-temporal scan statistics as well as the characteristics of the associated spatio-temporal graphs.

Summary

- Most observation requires discrete time intervals, continuous space for individuals' movements if tracked, otherwise discrete areal units
- One graph per observation period, or time-labelled summary graph; possibly complemented by an aspatial temporal contact graph

- Nodes for locations and conditions of individuals, nodes persist for the full time course
- Key data are node states and transitions: susceptible, diseased, recovered, dead
- Edges join nodes with synchronous changes or contacts in time, or show putative paths of infection
- Measures: node degrees; movement rates; contacts; rates of transmission
- Comparisons: movements versus spatial network versus contact network versus disease transmission network; compare any of the data networks with various random or randomized networks

10.3.8 Metacommunity Dynamics in Real and Virtual Archipelagos

This application may be the most familiar to community ecologists, since it is a temporal or dynamic extension of many discussions based on well-founded theories of island biogeography, the concept of metapopulations in fragmented landscapes, and practical considerations for species and community conservation (Mouquet & Loreau 2002; Leibold 2009; Cerdeira et al. 2010; Ai et al. 2013, among many others).

A simple model begins with the kind of island system described in Chapter 9, with a spatial graph related to the ease or probability of dispersal between the nodes that represent the islands. The islands are habitat patches, too, and the edges between nodes represent potential dispersal of organisms from one patch to another. As with many such examples, there is a range of spatial graphs that can be used to give the spatial structure, with a range of spatial neighbour edge densities, and thus average physical distances and node degrees. The spatial edges may be determined by one of the topological rules (Chapter 1), by physical structures (such as streams and rivers between lakes as islands), by functional factors (storm tracks, vector migration routes), or by similarity measures (e.g. compositional or physiographic similarity). For community considerations, the effectiveness of any edge between nodes will vary with the species as well as with time and environmental conditions. The temporal data are catalogues of species densities associated with each node and their changes through time, based for example, on periodic censuses. Time is therefore discrete. One goal for creating a spatio-temporal graph is to evaluate how well species densities can be predicted from the species on spatial and temporal "neighbours" as well as island size, age and isolation. As with the landscape patch transition example, the density of species s on island i at time t can be modelled by dependence on the current density of s on neighbouring islands (usually first-order neighbours in the spatial graph, but possibly second or third order too); on the density of s on i at times $t - 1$, $t - 2$, $\ldots$; and on past densities on the same neighbouring nodes. Temporal edges join each island to one or more previous instances of itself and to preceding instances of some of its spatial neighbours (as in Figure 10.11). The main exercise is to determine which spatial and temporal neighbours give the best predictions of species composition and turnover, and species densities and their changes through time. Spatio-temporal graphs seem to be an ideal method for this investigation of metacommunities and how spatial structure contributes to their dynamics because they allow a partitioning of the effects of neighbour nodes and their characteristics by time and by space. This approach will complement the time-only studies of trends using long-term data sets such as bird community composition (e.g. Kampichler et al. 2014), single comparisons based on two observation times (Azeria 2004), stand age-for-time substitution (e.g. Zhao et al. 2013b), or spatial studies based on patch size and neighbours (e.g. Husté & Boulinier 2011; and references in Chapter 9). One concern is that important effects may result from factors that act over greater distance or over longer time periods (further back history) than those available or included in the analysis (see Layeghifard et al. 2015).

Summary
- Observations at discrete time intervals, discrete space created by the islands as habitat polygons in a background matrix, or continuous space with mapped coordinates
- One layer per time period in a many-layered graph
- Nodes permanent: island or patch locations, but with time-varying species densities
- Edges based on temporal, spatial, and spatio-temporal "neighbours" include past self; edges may also be physical or functional, or determined by similarity
- Measures: rates and conditions for each density transition; effect of graph definition of spatio-temporal neighbours, topological or functional
- Comparisons: Similar to spatial and temporal regression analysis of densities; finding the best spatio-temporal network for species density predictions; comparing edges based on function with edges based on similarity. Non-stationarity is a serious concern, especially under climate change

10.3.9   Other Applications

Without as much detail, it is worth describing a few other applications where spatio-temporal graphs and networks can be helpful in ecology. One such application of spatio-temporal graphs would be a variant of the last example, the analysis of communities that are periodically extinguished and then re-establish from nothing. Examples for such studies of spatio-temporal patterns of metacommunity structure are the pitcher plant inquiline community (see Kneitel & Miller 2003; Harvey & Miller 1996, among many others), annually temporary ponds (Wilbur 1997), and the annual intertidal communities where ice-scour cleans the surface every winter (Keats et al. 1985; Scrosati & Heaven 2007). The appropriate analysis would provide insights on spatial aspects of community structure and assembly, as immigration and establishment change the graphs of community structure. This is very much a case of the evolution of the graph as the community develops through time. Spatio-temporal graphs are a good approach to understanding metacommunities in general, and how spatial structure affects their dynamics; the difference here is that these are communities that start from "zero," with no opportunity for ecological memory, so that only the most immediate history can have an effect.

In discussing time-only graphs (Chapter 8) and in the treatment of proximity and contact as it affects the spread of disease (this chapter), the use of time-only graphs to track inter-individual proximity or inter-individual contact was described and illustrated. One form of a spatio-temporal graph is to combine the temporal graph of theses contacts with a spatial map of where the contacts took place, to produce a spatio-temporal graph that best suits the needs of the application.

Another application of spatio-temporal graphs is in studies of variation in phenological sequences: the seasonal timing of events such as the first leaf or the first flower on a particular species at a particular location. The topic is of great interest in the current context of global climate change and its effects on seasonal events of importance to conservation efforts. The data consist of several recognizable events that are located accurately in time, and for individual plants or populations located in space. The events may or may not have a prescribed order; for example, a second leaf emergence always occurs after a first leaf emergence, but the first flower anthesis may occur either before or after the emergence of the seventh leaf. The questions of interest concern the relationships among the records at different locations, and trends within and among records. The sites are permanent or persistent nodes with locations. Spatial edges can be based on any rule for a neighbour network, but other inter-site edges are possible. For example, similar dates for equivalent events (first leaf, first flower, second flower and so on) may determine an edge between two sites or common features of the records at two sites. This application to phenology is similar to spatio-temporal graph analysis of time-point events over an array of sites, such as fire scars on trees, or of continuous records over a spatial array of sites, for example meteorological records, pollen sequences, or meteorological records reconstructed (postdicted) from pollen sequences.

There are more ecological examples of studies of the development or evolution of structural spatial graphs such as the developing structure of foraging trails created by ants (see Buhl et al. 2009). Kost et al. (2005) have reported on the foraging trails of leaf cutter ants (*Atta* sp.) in the New World (Brazil, French Guiana and Panama); these trail systems evolve through time in the short term, with ephemeral foraging trails being established and abandoned as branches of longer-lasting trunk trails, but with the characteristics of the systems changing as colonies mature with larger and more complex trail systems that exploit a broader range of leaf sources. The authors used a combination of fractal analysis and circular and conventional statistics, but the trails are *rooted trees* (the ant nest is the root from which the sub-trees emerge), and graph-theoretic measures such as graph diameter and branch order would help evaluate the dynamics of these trail networks.

Also in the domain of physical structures is a recent example that uses spatio-temporal graphs to model marine dunes under the English Channel (Thibaud et al. 2013). The representation of the physical structure and its movement with time illustrates an approach to spatio-temporal analysis that should have many applications in the general field of environmental science.

The last example is not from the mainstream of ecological literature, but it serves as a good model of studies that could be carried out on populations in the ecological context. This is a study of spatio-temporal patterns of human migration worldwide (Davis et al. 2013) based on five observation periods (by decade 1960 to 2000). The network nodes are countries and the edges are directed and weighted, being the number of migrants from country i living in country j (there is no edge if the number is 0). They examined a number of network measures: node degree, nearest neighbour degree, connectance, transitivity (clustering coefficient), and average path length (geodesic). Connectance and transitivity increased linearly with year as average path length declined, and the degree distribution shifted upward. All these are consistent with the "small world" characteristic for this migration network. The authors go on to discuss some of the details of the patterns in the network, such as groups of countries that preferentially interact, forming migration communities (modularity considered informally) related to historical, cultural, and economic factors (Davis et al. 2013).

10.4   Concluding Comments

Compared to the time-only graphs of Chapter 8 and the spatial graphs of Chapter 9, networks with both time and space have greatly increased range for the ecological phenomena that can be included for the range of treatments that can be accommodated.

Ecologists are very familiar with spatio-temporal data sets and have large numbers of them at their disposal for summary, analysis and interpretation. Depending on the purpose or need, one or other of the dimensions may be dropped from subsequent treatment, and often both are ignored. This is despite the fact that determining causation is seen as the "holy grail" of science and that goal requires keeping track of "when," and keeping track of "where" for that context ("no History without Geography"; Cressie & Wikle 2011, Chapter 1). The use of spatio-temporal graphs in ecological applications has, so far, been relatively rare. One reason is that, while we like graphs for depicting and analyzing data in part because they are easy to comprehend, once they include the dimensions of space and time they can quickly become complicated, and more so as the size of the data set increases. The difficulty lies not in handling, drawing or analyzing the data, it seems to be at the interpretation stage (i.e. the human, not hardware or software) when it comes to large data sets (Compieta et al. 2007). One could argue that adding lines (the graph's edges) to a visualization of the data, when correctly chosen, can clarify the structure by "telling a story" about its contents. On the other hand, some examples that might be treated as spatio-temporal graphs may be more easily summarized as change in spatial characteristics, particularly if there are only two or three observation times (e.g. before and after some event). The other reason that these data sets may not be portrayed and analyzed explicitly as spatio-temporal graphs or networks is that some of the big environmental data sets are derived from observations on a spatial grid taken at regular time intervals, so that the spatio-temporal lattice can be understood rather than being made explicit; the edges are not really necessary to understand the relationships among the observations (see e.g. Figure 5.1, 5.23, 7.3, or 9.23 in Cressie & Wikle 2011). Last, however, is the fact that these techniques are relatively new and relatively unfamiliar, and it may take some time, as well as a growing body of good examples, for these methods to become comfortable or obvious choices for ecological research.

11 Graph Structure and System Function: Graphlet Methods

Introduction

Ecological networks are dynamic. Not only do the nodes change their characteristics and existing edges change in strength or capacity, but elements can appear or disappear. In predation, if one prey species becomes rare, the predator may respond by switching to another prey species, removing one edge from the food web graph and adding one. There is interplay between the states of nodes and edges and the topology of the network; networks with such reciprocal interactions are called *adaptive networks* (Do & Gross 2012). For dynamic interactions among structural units, the behaviour of the whole system will depend both on its global structure and on very local topology of functional connections (edges) between structural units (nodes). In adaptive networks, synchronization of cycles is an emergent property of interest (think of population outbreaks in insects or small mammals; e.g. Bjørnstadt et al. 1999, among many others), and it is affected by both global topological measures and aspects of very local configuration (Do & Gross 2012). Graph theory measures that are importance to synchronization include clustering coefficients, graph diameters, the distributions of the node degrees, and edge weights or capacities. The structural characteristics reflect how the whole might have been generated, and they determine how the entire system functions. There is a difference between changes to the topology, through the loss or gain of nodes and edges, and dynamic changes to the characteristics and weights of the nodes and edges while they persist. One critical effect is how these characteristics affect the system's resilience or robustness (Estrada 2006; Alenazi & Sterbenz 2015; see Newman 2010, Chapter 18).

Ecological interactions between species vary in space and time (Poisot et al. 2015). There is temporal turnover even when the species are continuously present, for example in pollination interactions (Petanidou et al. 2008), and the interaction strength varies with season and time of day, as measured by the proportion of events (Bascompte & Jordano 2014). Similar variations are found in trophic, competition and other interaction networks. In food webs, the same set of species can have variable network structure with different factors across space and time (McCann 2012). The regional list of species together with all possible interactions can be thought of as a *meta-web* (parallel to terms such as metapopulation and metacommunity; see Dunne 2006), as if all taxa co-occurred at one site. Then, any observed food web can be considered as one realization of the possibilities in the meta-web. If there are several sites with different realizations,

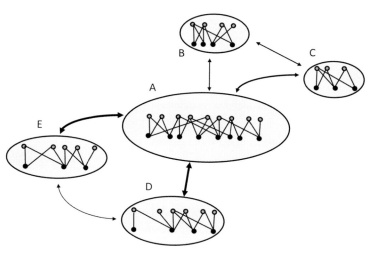

Figure 11.1 Graph-of-bipartite-graphs: pollination mutualisms in patches. The graph with patches as nodes is a spatial graph. The oval's size represents patch area; the thickness of the spatial edges indicates species movement rates. The graphs of plants and pollinators are ecological graphs with edges representing species' mutualistic interactions. Based on Hagen et al. (2012, Figure 20).

the networks at the sites and the spatial graph of the sites' locations form a graph-of-graphs (see Hagen et al. 2012, Figures 16–18). In many applications of the meta-web concept, the interactions that are counted as "possible" for its construction may be limited by mismatches in habitat, water depth, season and so on, which create "forbidden links" (cf. Bascompte & Jordano 2014). For any kind of interaction network, therefore, specific local instances are realizations of a *meta-network* which includes all possibilities, removing forbidden links, even as they change through time and space. Changes can take the form of the gain or loss of species (the nodes) due to local extinctions and recolonization from linked patches (see Hagen et al. 2012, Figure 20; a graph-of-graphs simplified in Figure 11.1), or the gain or loss of edges that represent their interactions. Both need to be included in evaluating changes or the similarities between realizations (Poisot et al. 2012; Carstensen et al. 2014). Changes in network structure or function can be caused by forces internal to the system as its elements interact or by external factors. For example, in networks of species replacements in successional vegetation, we can ask how much of the change can be attributed to the species associations within the vegetation, and how much to external forces (cf. Alacántra & Rey 2014). In their useful commentary on meta-networks and the interplay of spatial graphs (physical structure) and ecological graphs (species interactions as function), Hagen et al. (2012) focus on fragmentation (mainly anthropogenic), but their comments can apply to any system of stable fragments (patches) of different sizes and isolation.

It is a truism that "Form follows function," but also that "Function follows form"; in ecological networks, the question is how both aspects affect each other and what can be learned about each from knowledge of the other. The purpose in using graph theory to

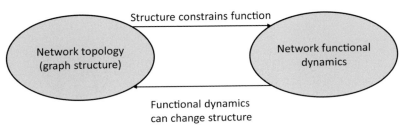

Figure 11.2 The reciprocal effects of network topology (graph-theoretical characteristics) and its functional dynamics.

study dynamic ecological networks is to determine the relationship between form and function, pattern and process or structure and dynamics. The focus is not the technical field of dynamic network analysis, which is a whole book on its own (see Carley 2003; Kocarev & Vattay 2010), but it is more closely related to adaptive network models (see Do & Gross 2012). As suggested, the interplay between the two aspects of the network, topology and states, can be driven by the system itself, which is then essentially self-organization (Figure 11.2), or it is affected by external factors and their trends, such as climate change (Figure 11.3; see Woodward et al. 2010), or by other interaction networks (Figure 11.4). The challenge for ecologists is to determine how much and under what circumstances an understanding of function (network dynamics) can be derived from observed form (network topology). The question is "How can methods based on graph theory help ecologists understand the dynamic functioning of ecological systems from knowledge of their structure?"

As an example, the elements of a mycorrhizal network develop in response to its functional needs and the environment it encounters, but the functions can be modified or rebalanced according to the circumstances (Simard et al. 2012). One can distinguish between the **dynamics of networks**, which are the changes in network topology and

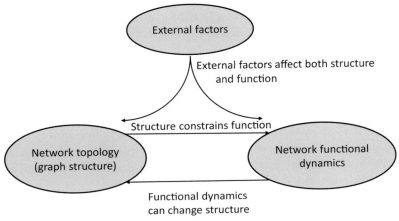

Figure 11.3 The interplay of network structure and function is affected by external factors.

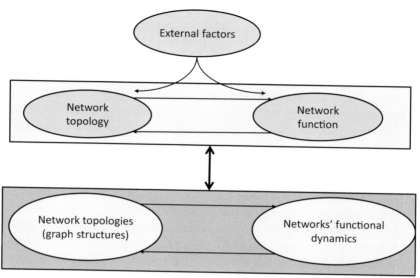

Figure 11.4 The interplay of structure and function in one interaction network is affected by networks of a range of other interactions.

any rules that govern those changes, and the **dynamics on networks**, which are the changes in the properties of the network nodes within constant network topology (see Ganguly et al. 2009). The study of adaptive networks looks at both aspects together and their mutual feedback (Gross & Blasius 2008, their Figure 1 redrawn as Figure 11.5). Many of the important structural characteristics of a network may be maintained, even as the nodes or the edges between nodes turn over or change (see state transition commentary in Chapter 8). Bryden et al. (2011) studied community structure in

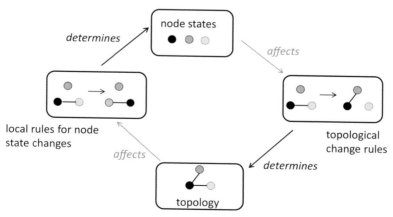

Figure 11.5 The reciprocal effects of network topology (graph-theoretical characteristics) and network functional dynamics indicated by node states. Redrawn from Gross and Blasius (2008, Figure 1).

co-evolving networks (states and topology) and described how they can achieve consistent structure of modules as a dynamic equilibrium in which the identity and composition of the modules change.

To introduce a dangerous analogy, consider a railway. (The similarity between the adaptive networks of biological systems and those of railways or roads has been noted elsewhere; see Gross & Blasius 2008; Tero et al. 2010.) A railway is a network that can be represented by a graph with the tracks being the edges, and nodes representing junctions, switches, stations, waypoints or any other stationary fixed features. The first function of the network is to support the movement of machines and cargo along the tracks, and those dynamics can be quantified by the rates and amounts of materials moved by the trains over each section of track and in each direction (that's the dynamics *on* the network). The state of the network is defined by the states of the nodes and edges: most simply "what is where" on the tracks. The second function of machines on the railway is the upkeep or modification of the rail system itself. The locations of tracks at any point in time have been determined by the history of opportunity and need, and by the energetics and cost of the system. However, the functions of the train system itself ("what needs to be where") will lead to changes in the tracks, and the railway's machines can modify, rebuild, reroute, or otherwise change the network (new lines, new switches, new grades, . . .). Therefore, while the tracks (structure) determine or constrain the function of the machines that use them (the dynamics *on* the network); the functioning machines can also change the structure, and accumulated changes over time are the dynamics *of* (not *on*) the network. External forces and the changes they cause may also lead to the need for changes in the system. A more ecological analogy would be a meandering river, in which stream flow modifies the spatial characteristics of the river, in turn affecting stream flow.

One last thought from this railway example, and here the analogy becomes dangerous (but why I chose it), is that sometimes the function of network components can be inferred from their structure. You don't need to see the round-house turntable in action to know what it does, based on its structure. Similarly, the difference between asymmetric switches with tapered moving rails and rectilinear rail crossing points, and between how those track elements affect train movement, are also obvious from their shape and structure . . . but, you do need to know something about trains before this understanding of function from form will work. We might make the same argument for ecological phenomena, particularly for spatial graphs, where the functional difference for dispersal between a string of "stepping-stone" patches and compact and isolated clusters may be obvious (see Saura et al. 2014). McIntire and Fajardo (2009), for example, have argued that in some cases process can be deduced given a defined a priori hypothesis, ecological knowledge, and precise spatial (or possibly temporal) analysis. One of the six examples they cite concerns the invasion of exotic trees (*Acer platanoides*) based on the work by Fang (2005) in which a comparison of the tree-size versus distance from invasion origin graphs for exotic versus native permits a distinction between active invasion and native suppression. This is similar to a comparison of the spatial patterns of invasion from an advancing edge for "frontal advance" versus "saltation" (cf. Little & Dale 1999). Ecologists are usually more comfortable in drawing conclusions about network topology from observed functional dynamics, most often in a spatial context (see Gilarranz et al. 2015), although not always (see Albert et al. 2013). The analogy is that there is something to be learned about the constraints on functional dynamics from the topology of the network at a local scale. Again, understanding function from observing form requires additional knowledge.

Inferring process from pattern is difficult, but as one success in a very different endeavour, consider the work of Mnih et al. (2013, 2015) on "deep reinforcement learning," which looks at the ability of machine learning to "reverse engineer" a computer game and determine its underlying rules from observing it being played. This work produced the first model to learn "control policies" from "high-dimensional sensory input"; in essence, this was a test of artificial intelligence learning the rules of old Atari games based only on the pixels of the screen and the score generated by the game. The "agent" was able to achieve the same level of performance as professional human games testers across a range of 49 different games. Whether or not this achievement is true artificial intelligence, it demonstrates the algorithmic ability to extract the rules of process from observed patterns, which is clearly important to this discussion.

Ecologists are wary of deducing function from form, and the worry applies also to interaction networks where the correlations between network metrics and ecological system processes may be sampling effects (Ulrich 2009). There is, however, much to be learned by looking at network structure carefully and in detail to help understand network dynamics. A realistic parallel to predicting dynamics from topology and structure in ecology is the current research on protein interaction networks. In that work, combining knowledge of the topology and physical shape of a protein with knowledge of its place and neighbours in the interaction network, together with the topology of that network itself, seems to allow good predictions of the protein's function and its role in the network (see Pržulj et al. 2004; Winterbach et al. 2013; Peterson et al. 2012; Pržulj 2010). The search for understanding ecological function based on combined knowledge of the system structure and of the organisms themselves does not seem so far-fetched, given the successes in the parallel molecular biology endeavour. Those studies provide suggestions on how ecologists can proceed, and they use methods based on small subgraphs called *graphlets*, which are the subject of this chapter.

11.1   Graphs for Structure and Dynamics in Ecological Systems

The "structure" here is the graph and its topology, the nodes and node pairs joined by edges, that determine the dynamics of the interaction network in its current configuration. Network functions include the flow of energy, the cycling of elements, effects on population densities (whether they grow or decline, and thus affecting selection and evolution), and effects on community composition. In animal populations, these effects may also be found through the functioning of social networks of affinities (Chapter 5) in unexpected ways (Kurvers et al. 2014). In plant populations, it has been shown that the production of offspring in the short-lived monocarpic herb *Erysimum mediohispanicum* (Brassicaceae) could be related to characteristics of the mutualistic pollination network: nestedness, connectivity and clustering (Gómez et al. 2011). The network changes to be considered include local extinction (of a node); the loss of an interaction (an edge), perhaps due to behavioural switching, seasonal cycles and phenology; or life-history stage differences. For example, in a host-parasite network of small mammals and their ectoparasites, large temporal variation in persistent host species can change their functional roles, and the function of parasites with strong negative effects on hosts can facilitate the general spread of parasites (Pilosof et al. 2013). In any system, some of these changes are brought about or inhibited or enhanced by interactions with other elements in a broader network, including competitors, predators, parasites and so forth. Real understanding of all-species interaction networks should include the full range of inter-specific links (Montoya et al. 2006). If the sum-of-all-paths approach to complex networks is required when we are not so inclusive, we need to know the "cost" of what is left out when only one kind of interaction is considered. If the goal is to integrate structure and dynamics through their reciprocal effects, we should endeavour to include parts of the structure of which the importance is not yet known, until we know what parts can be safely left out.

Studying the network topology, just nodes and edges, at one moment in time is "easy" in comparison with quantifying all the pairwise interactions to be included in a large (*n* select 2) array of differential equations to describe the dynamics of each pair. Species interaction networks are expected to be dynamic themselves, changing through time in response to the forces of their own internal functional dynamics or in response to forces that are truly external, such as climate change. What is needed is a "common language" of analysis that will work for a range of interactions considered together and in systems that are influenced by environmental cycles and long-term trends.

Whichever set of these complications we include or exclude, the central puzzle is the relationship between graph structure (topology) and network dynamics (function and change through time). The challenge is to use the accessible knowledge of local structure (think of the distribution of nodes' degrees) to make inferences about the global characteristics of the network (think of small world vs scale free) and thus about its function and its evolution through time, past and future. Studies of adaptive networks suggest that they are capable of robust self-organization of their topology based on local rules and feedback to local dynamics of the topology (Gross and Blasius 2008). If this can be pursued for important ecological networks, this is obviously something ecologists should DO in applying graph theory approaches to ecological questions. The rest of this chapter provides an introduction to a method that does exactly that, and then a discussion of the implications for research on ecological systems.

Studies of synchronization of cyclic phenomena (technically "phase oscillators"), which occur in many natural phenomena including population cycles of small mammals, insects and birds (Bjørnstadt et al. 1999; Liebhold et al. 2004; Mortelliti et al. 2015, among many others), provide insights into the relationship between structure and function in dynamic networks. In particular, work by Do and colleagues (see Do & Gross 2012) demonstrated that the propensity to synchronization in such networks is related to the topology of small multi-node subgraphs within them. They used a new graph-based notation by which the algebraic stability conditions can be mapped onto topological stability criteria. As in most ecological examples, the focus of the discussion of synchronization is on stability, whereby small perturbations are not magnified and trajectories that are close to the system's steady state remain close. Their work points to an approach based on graphlets, which are small but multi-node subgraphs, to be described next.

11.2   Graph Characteristics and Methods Based on Graphlets

In ecological studies using graphs or networks, the most familiar measures of structure are related either to the whole graph (e.g. connectance or diameter) or to individual nodes (e.g. degree or centrality), but characteristics based on small subgraphs should also be considered, particularly if these can indicate the relationship between structure and function and the likely local roles of individual nodes. Graphlets are small connected subgraphs, of two, three, four or five nodes, which can be enumerated as local structures of a larger interaction graph. These are good candidates as the basis for studying the relationship between network topology and dynamics, aided by a focus on the frequency of different graphlets and on the frequency of nodes at particular locations in the graphlets.

Remember that the *degree* of a network node is an indicator of the network's robustness to its loss or removal, based in part on the discussion of inference based on random walks on the graph (the argument for degree centrality, see Chapter 9). The loss of random nodes usually has little impact, but the loss of the most highly connected nodes leads to instability (Montoya et al. 2006; Solé & Montoya 2001). These observations lead to questions such as: Do the degrees of first neighbours affect robustness and vulnerability? How does nestedness or other forms of asymmetry affect robustness? Are these responses the same for different interactions or opposite for mutualisms versus antagonisms?

The key to investigating such questions lies in methods based on graphlets, which both generalize the concept of a node's degree and extend the identification of common *motifs* in networks. Motifs are identifiable small subgraphs of networks, and networks from different systems have different characteristically common motifs (Milo et al. 2002). For example, networks of genetic transcription have large numbers of the motifs called "feed-forward loop" and "bi-fan," whereas ecological trophic networks commonly have those called "3-chain" and "bi-parallel" (Figure 11.6), with the feed-forward loop being unexpectedly rare. Graphlets can go beyond identifying subgraph shapes by looking also at the positions of nodes within the subgraphs, as will be described, but with the understanding that the node's position in the system network can indicate something about its functional role in the system.

The material that follows is based on the work of Pržulj and co-workers described in a series of papers (Pržulj 2007; Milenkovic & Pržulj 2008; Yaveroglu et al. 2014), and it is the last paper of that series that promises most for ecological networks and the dynamic interplay between structure and function. This is somewhat complicated, however, and it will take some background to build up to the most interesting result.

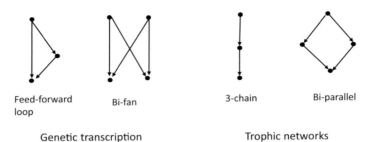

Feed-forward
loop

Bi-fan

3-chain

Bi-parallel

Genetic transcription

Trophic networks

Figure 11.6 Common motifs in network digraphs: two from genetic transcription and two from trophic networks.

A graphlet is an induced connected subgraph of an undirected graph with three, four or five nodes. *Induced* just means that all edges of the nodes' subset that are in the original graph must be included in the graphlet; a motif, on the other hand, can be a partial subgraph. Graphlets can be used as indicators of local structure and by counting the different graphlets to determine their frequencies. These frequencies often provide significant information about local network structure (Ahmed et al. 2015) and the fine structure of two networks can be compared using their graphlet relative frequencies. Ahmed et al. used this approach to evaluate the Facebook social network of California universities, and found that Caltech was considerably different from all the others (their Figure 6) probably because of their unique housing arrangements for undergraduate students (Ahmed et al. 2015). This analysis treats graphlets as motifs, but there is more that can be done with them.

Another method is to classify every node according to the graphlets in which it occurs (often many) and its positions in those graphlets where distinguishable, because position may suggest functional role. Nodes that are distinguishable by position within a single graphlet belong to different automorphism "orbits"; nodes that are topologically indistinguishable within a single graphlet belong to the same orbit. Starting with two nodes and a single edge joining them as a "level 0" graphlet, the nodes are equivalent and both are labelled as "orbit 0," as in Figure 11.7a. For any node in any graph, the number of such graphlets in which the node occurs is its degree. For $n = 3$, there are two graphlets; the first is graphlet 1, a two-edge chain with two indistinguishable end-nodes (orbit 1) and a central node between them (orbit 2). The second three-node graphlet is a triangle with all nodes equivalent (orbit 3, see Figure 11.7a). For $n = 4$, there are six graphlets, giving orbits 4 to 14 (Figure 11.7b); $n = 5$ provides another 21 graphlets with orbits 15 to 72 (see Pržulj 2007). This gives, in total, for $n = 2, 3, 4$, and 5, graphlets 0 to 29 and distinguishable orbits 0, 1, 2, ..., 72. Any graph can then be characterized by counts of the graphlets and by counts of the nodes' orbits that it contains as induced subgraphs, as illustrated in Figure 11.7c.

The local topology of any node can be summarized by the graphlets in which it occurs and its positions within them, as indicated by its orbits. For example, the end node in graphlet 9, which defines orbit 15, is also in orbits 0, 1 and 4 because of its end position

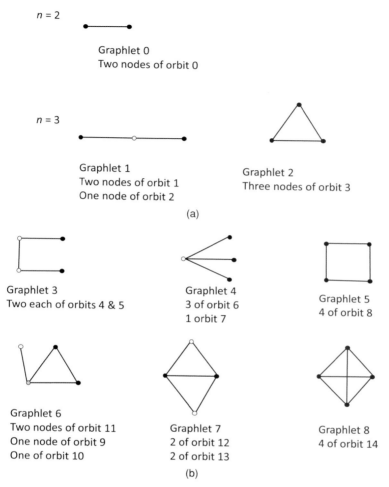

$n = 2$

Graphlet 0
Two nodes of orbit 0

$n = 3$

Graphlet 1
Two nodes of orbit 1
One node of orbit 2

Graphlet 2
Three nodes of orbit 3

(a)

Graphlet 3
Two each of orbits 4 & 5

Graphlet 4
3 of orbit 6
1 orbit 7

Graphlet 5
4 of orbit 8

Graphlet 6
Two nodes of orbit 11
One node of orbit 9
One of orbit 10

Graphlet 7
2 of orbit 12
2 of orbit 13

Graphlet 8
4 of orbit 14

(b)

Figure 11.7 Graphlets and node orbits (a) for $n = 2$ and 3 and (b) for $n = 4$. (c) Graphlets as induced subgraphs. Graph G includes graphlet g6 but not g4. A graphlet is an **induced** subgraph and must include all the sub-graph's edges; g4 is missing one edge of G, as indicated. (A black-and-white version of this figure will appear in some formats. For the colour version, please refer to the plate section.)

in graphlets 0, 1 and 3 (see Figure 11.8). Any node can therefore be characterized by a list of its orbits, or by a 73-place vector of 1s and 0s indicating its orbits, known as the node's "signature." This is the graphlet degree signature (GDS) or graphlet degree vector. The signatures of any two nodes can be compared and clusters of nodes created based on node similarities (Milenkovic & Pržulj 2008). It is also possible to look at the combined signatures of all nodes belonging to the same orbit: the number of nodes of each orbit attached to nodes of any given orbit, giving 73 separate 73-place signatures.

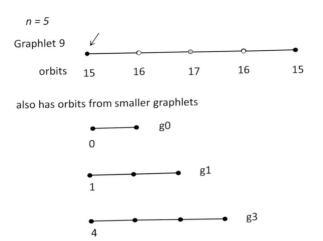

Figure 11.8 Non-independence among graphlets. Graphlet 9 and its node in orbit 15 counts also as touching orbits 0, 1 and 4.

To characterize the structure of an entire graph, the graphlet signatures of all its nodes can be combined in a plot of the orbits' relative frequencies. Figure 11.9 illustrates this approach plotting the frequencies of the orbits for the smaller graphlets (up to $n = 4$, so orbits 0 to 14) for two very similar networks (based loosely on Milenkovic & Pržulj 2008, Figure 2, the yeast proteins SMD1 and SMD2). The orbits, especially when the larger graphlets ($n = 5$) are included, are not independent, as Figure 11.8 illustrates, showing that a node of orbit 15 necessarily includes orbits 0, 1 and 4 as well. This redundancy in the information provided by the orbit frequencies is something to be accounted for. The original suggestion by Milenkovic and Pržulj (2008) was to assign each orbit a score that is the number of orbits it includes and then to derive a weight from these scores to be used to account for the lack of independence in the relative frequencies of node orbits in an entire graph. This weighting allows a direct orbit-by-orbit comparison of the graphlet signatures of two graphs, or an overall measure of difference or similarity, as illustrated in the work cited. These degree vectors and signature similarities can be used to tie topological or structural similarity to predictions about function in systems such as protein-protein interactions (Milenkovic & Pržulj 2008). A straightforward variant of this approach is to use the distributions of the graphlet degrees (GDD) to measure the similarity or *agreement* of two networks (Pržulj 2007).

More recent work (Yaveroglu et al. 2014) provides an appealing refinement. Given the lack of independence among the graphlet orbits, linear equations were used to reduce the 73 orbits of the 2-to-5-node graphlets to 56 that were non-redundant, and to reduce the 15 orbits of the 2-to-4 node graphlets to 11. Any correlations that remain among the reduced list of orbits reflect the structure of the network itself. It turns out that the 11 based on the smaller graphlets provide real advantages, and these are used for any graph to derive an 11×11 graphlet correlation matrix (GCM) from the correlations between the elements of the graphlet degree vector. These correlations can be interpreted to

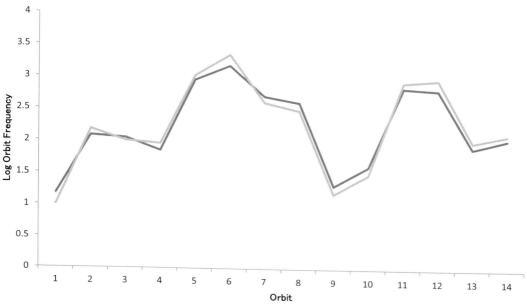

Figure 11.9 Graphlet degree distribution: comparison of similar networks using frequencies of nodes in graphlet orbits. Loosely based on small graphlet orbits in Milenkovic and Pržulj (2008, Figure 2, yeast proteins SMD1 and SMD2).

reveal the structural characteristics of any network graph of any size. For any two graphs, the Euclidean distance between the corresponding entries of the two matrices gives the graphlet correlation distance (GCD-11). This GCD-11 was found to be a very good measure for comparing the structure of graphs, based on extensive testing by Yaveroglu et al. (2014); it is fast to compute, responsive the graphs' characteristics, and robust to noise in the data or random losses.

Why am I telling you all this? ... and in such detail? The reason lies in one example used in the Yaveroglu paper, which describes the changing structure of the world trading network from 1962 to 2010. The nodes of the network are countries, and the edges represent the volume of trade between pairs of countries in any given year. Clearly, this is an adaptive network, and somewhat self-organizing, in which topology and flow interact and "co-evolve" with time. The authors describe some of the richness of detail that can be determined by the graphlet-based method about the structure and function of this network, and how those have changed through the 48 years. Furthermore, the relationship between a nodes orbit signature and its other characteristics (here for example, population, GDP, and employment level) can be determined from the correlations in a Canonical Correspondence Analysis (CCA), allowing interpretation of the node's structural role with those measured characteristics. The overall process of analysis is a complex series of steps, and the determination of those correlations is a crucial step. For example, the product of population and GDP is positively associated with the hubs of cross-shaped graphlets, whereas measures related to transactions in goods, services and income are negatively correlated with orbits that are leaf nodes in graphlets ("BCA" in Figure 4b of Yaveroglu et al. 2014). Such correlations allow generalizations about the roles of nodes in the network: which are in tight trading clusters, which act as brokers between less connected pairs, and which are peripheral in the network. Similar categories, of clusters, connecting nodes and peripheral elements, are to be expected in applications of this analysis to other systems such as trophic networks. Repeated observation allows an assessment of how the different roles change through time and, perhaps, what drives those changes.

One feature of the world trade network example is that the orbits fall into two groups: 4, 6 and 9, reflecting peripheral structures and the rest (0, 2, 5, 7, 8, 10, 11) representing nodes in mediator or "broker" positions. Therefore, the authors used the bigger set of orbits to calculate "peripheral" versus "broker" scores for individual nodes, here representing trading countries, which can be followed through time as their roles in world trade changed through time, with higher broker scores being indicative of increasing economic success and influence. For example, there is a marked increase in China's "broker" score starting about the year 2000, and a steady decline in Britain's throughout the time period; another detail is the obvious increases in the peripheral scores of countries that joined the EU around the time of its formation. In addition, the authors show the correlation between landmark changes in crude oil prices and changes in the structure of the trade network, and correlations between countries' economic attributes and the graphlet degrees derived by this approach. This is rich stuff indeed!

Reading the material, I kept thinking how revealing this method could be for investigating the changing structure and function of complex ecological systems, and the relationship between the two aspects of these systems. Noting changes to the network graph is not enough; we could get lost in the detail of one node replacing another that is essentially equivalent, or an edge forming or disappearing or substituting for a similar edge, without affecting the important features of the graph structure or the fundamental characteristics of the network function. We need to be able to distinguish between trivial modifications and those that are more substantial. That's what the graphlet counts do; they show which changes in the structure are the major ones, those that will be correlated with the evolution of the network's dynamics. This feature can be especially useful where we want to include many kinds of ecological interactions, as perhaps we must, to get as full an understanding as possible of the interplay of topology and function. Often, we will need to also include network responses (form and function) to external forces such as climate change (see Woodward et al. 2010). After all, the world trade network, the subject of that rich example, includes and aggregates interactions that are the same as competition, predation, and various forms of mutualism, and it responds to long-term trends as well as cycles. Here the graph theory approach to network analysis of ecological systems will really pay off … and, yes, this method is implemented in R (Yaveroglu et al. 2015).

Further advances in graphlets for dynamic networks are based on directed graphlets for digraphs (Sarajlić et al. 2016; Trpevski et al. 2016). Where only one edge is allowed per pair of nodes (i.e. no reciprocal pairs of edges), $n = 2$, 3 and 4, provide 39 directed graphlets and 128 directed orbits (Figure 11.10). This seems to be especially important

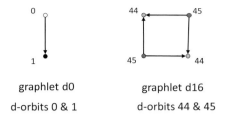

graphlet d0   graphlet d16

d-orbits 0 & 1   d-orbits 44 & 45

Figure 11.10 Graphlets for digraphs: for $n = 2, 3, 4$ and only one edge per pair of nodes, there are 39 directed graphlets and 128 directed orbits. Here are two examples: d0 with d-orbits 0 and 1, and graphlet d16 with d-orbits 44 and 45. Based on Sarajlić et al. (2016).

because the graphlets can then distinguish between, for example, divergent and convergent processes (e.g. graphlets d11 and d12 compared to d10 and d13 in Figure 11.11). Trpevski et al. (2016) used a modified approach for brain effective connectivity networks in which edges could be either unidirectional or reciprocal, and directional edges have a sign indicating inhibitory or excitatory. (In the Sarajlić approach reciprocal edges are treated by counting two graphlets, one for each direction, as in their Figure 1c.) They also focussed on the graphlets with $n = 3$: with two edges forming a "wedge" or with three edges forming a triangle. They found that the signature vectors were dominant the excitatory effective brain networks, and that the excitatory networks shoed strong causal patterns than the inhibitory ones.

For either set of digraph graphlets, the most profitable applications seem to be correlational: the graphlet correlation matrix (Trpevski et al. 2016), and the correlation of graphlet degrees with other node attributes determined by Canonical Correspondence Analysis (CCA; Yaveroglu et al. 2014; Sarajlić et al. 2016). Applications to ecological networks seem promising; Sarajlić et al. (2016) have suggested that these methods allow sophisticated analysis and interpretation of topology for directed networks from any area of science. The potential for analyzing ecological networks using correlation measures for directed graphlets seems to be both obvious and enormous.

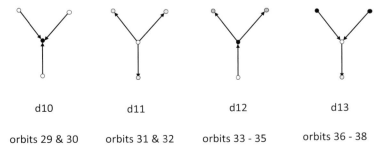

| d10 | d11 | d12 | d13 |

orbits 29 & 30   orbits 31 & 32   orbits 33 - 35   orbits 36 - 38

Figure 11.11 Directed graphlets for digraphs: with directed edges, g4 becomes 4 d-graphlets, d10 to d13 with d-orbits 29 to 38. These clearly distinguish convergence from divergence. Based on Sarajlić et al. (2016). (A black-and-white version of this figure will appear in some formats. For the colour version, please refer to the plate section.)

Table 11.1 A Checklist of Methods Based on Graphlets

Graphlet frequencies	Counts of the 29 $n = 3, 4, 5$ graphlets (show local structure)
	Compare networks by simple similarity or distance measure
Graphlet degree signature	73 orbits in $n = 2, 3, 4, 5$ graphlets give each node 73 coordinates
	Measure node local similarity by comparing signatures
Graphlet degree distribution	Counts of nodes from each orbit
	Measure network agreement by comparing normalized GDDs
Graphlet correlation matrix	Matrix of correlations based on reduced list of orbits (11)
	Correlations of orbits provide clear structural profile
Graphlet correlation distance	Euclidean distance between corresponding GCM values
	Compares structural characteristics of two graphs
CCA correlations	Canonical Correspondence Analysis
	Compares nodes' graphlet degrees with other node attributes
Directed graphlet measures	Any of the above can be modified for directed graphlets

This is certainly one smart thing ecologists can do in applying graph theory to the systems we study. Because there is such a range of ways to use graphlets, and more certain to follow, Table 11.1 provides a summary of current graphlets-based methods.

The graphlet approaches look very promising for understanding ecological networks, given the clear parallel with the protein interaction networks that are intensively studied. Those networks seem to have been the inspiration for the graphlet research, because the doctoral theses of both Dr Pržulj and Dr Milenkovic were based on them (Pržulj 2005; Milenkovic 2008), and if the parallel between the two kinds of networks is substantial, the method should transfer to good effect. The exploration of graphlet methodology and application is, however, far from over. There are already specific applications for temporal networks (Hulovatyy et al. 2015), and the promise for spatial networks seems great; think of working out structure and function relationships in mycorrhizal systems (see Simard et al. 2012; Southworth et al. 2005).

Other characteristics of these networks may be informative on the relationship between structure and function. The existence of *modular* structure seems to affect function and stability (see Melián et al. 2009). Does the size of the modules or their position in the network affect their effectiveness as stabilizers or destabilizers? What is the interaction between modular structure and other characteristics? Does modularity "fall out" from a graphlet analysis? Probably yes, based on GDS node clustering in Milenkovic and Pržulj (2008) and the world trade example in Yaveroglu et al. (2014).

Strongly connected components seem to be important structural elements for the functioning of marine trophic networks. Do they have a general and predictable effect on persistence and robustness? What is the effect of compartments on stability or robustness in these networks? In particular, do strongly connected components work in the graphlet context to tell us something important about stability of the system? In general, how can we use the graphlets, which indicate function based on topology to provide definitive evaluation of overall stability?

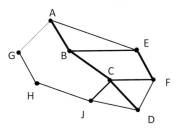

Figure 11.12 Sum of all paths in a physical context (like circuit theory). Thicker lines indicate less resistance or more capacity. The flow from A to D may have the least resistance along path A, B, C, D, but the total flow includes all possible paths, e.g. A, E, F, C, J, D ... and perhaps even all possible walks.

This endeavour is the equivalent of the complete trophic impact approach to food webs, or of the sum-of-all-paths view of spatial graphs describing genetic or information flow. Figure 11.12 gives an artificial example, but illustrates that the total flow between two nodes in a graph of function is due not just to the path of least resistance (A, B, C, D), but to all possible paths, including those that are less direct. Similarly, the interactions of a plant and its pollinator are not an isolated relationship; they take place in the context of the competitors of both plant and pollinator, the pollinator's parasitoids and predators, the plant's herbivores and their predators, omnivores, and so on (Figure 11.13). Therefore, in addition to integrating structure and dynamics and the interplay of

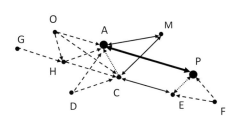

Edge symbols:

Solid = mutualistic
Dotted = competition
Dashed = predation etc.

A and P are single species; the other nodes are sets of species.
Plant A and pollinator P have competitor sets C and E.
M are the mycorrhizal fungi of A and C; D are their pathogens.
F are predators and parasitoids of P and E.
H are the herbivores of A and C.
G are predators of H.
O are omnivores.

Figure 11.13 Sum of all paths for species interaction networks. Understanding the interaction of plant species A and pollinator P fully needs to include paths involving other sets of species: competitors of A, {C}, and of B, {E}; {M}, the mycorrhizal fungi of plants A and C, and their pathogens {D}; predators and parasitoids of P and E, {F}; the herbivores of A and C, {H}; the predators of H, {G}; the omnivores that eat both plants and herbivores, {O}, and so on.

those two for some defined set of species and their interactions (e.g. nectar-producing plants and their pollinators), there is also a need to integrate the various kinds of inter-actions that can be found within the broader ecological network. This is an ambitious assignment, and one that may end up with many questions and few firm answers, and a greater reliance on answers based on models rather than experimental data, but that's a start.

The dynamics of these networks are two-fold: first, the function of the network as it exists; second, the changes in the network itself as it develops or evolves. The graph-theoretical properties of the network, its topology, determine the former and affect the latter; but equally, function and ongoing development affect changes in structural characteristics (Figure 11.3). For ecologists, the primary concern in studying these networks is to predict their stability or persistence in the context of change, whether the change is essentially internal to the network perhaps driven by (co-)evolution, or whether it is driven by external forces such as anthropogenic fragmentation or climate change (Figure 11.4; see cite Woodward et al. 2010). The most direct topological change to consider is the loss or addition of a node in the network (usually a species) or the loss or addition of a single edge (one pairwise interaction). Less obvious changes, such as variation in rates of predation, pollen transfer or frugivory, may be equally important for network modifi-cation (particularly for "keystone species" or "keystone links," as discussed in Chapter 4), although perhaps more difficult to assess. This basic argument for this chapter how-ever, is that any attempt to understand the interplay between network structure and its functional dynamics (and how those change each other through time) cannot be limited only to a single kind of inter-specific interaction.

There is good reason to be optimistic that graphlet approaches can help with under-standing function based on topology, and the world trade example provides a good almost-ecological example of how that can work. The difficulty is that in an inclu-sive ecological system, the edges represent interactions that are fundamentally differ-ent from each other (Figure 11.13), whereas the world trade network has edges that are essentially the same. The same graphlet spectrum summarizing the intimate topology of the system for our interpretation will have different functional implications depend-ing on the interactions encoded by the edges. This will be true whether the edges all represent the same relationship (Figure 11.14, first three panels), or several different relationships, as in our "all interactions" version (Figure 11.13) or the last panel of Figure 11.14. The complexity is similar to the challenges experienced at the molecular level with genes, proteins, metabolites and pharmaceuticals all interacting in differ-ent ways both within and between categories. To return to our dangerous analogy of a railway, true ecological systems move and transform information and energy, and are like having nodes of stations, yards and waypoints interlinked not just by a single rail carrier, but by competing railway companies, by canals and by trucks on roads; com-plemented by telephone, radio and Internet; and complicated by weather, disasters and saboteurs. There is no doubt that all interactions are important, but being all-inclusive will make the interpretation of ecological structure and function more difficult to work out.

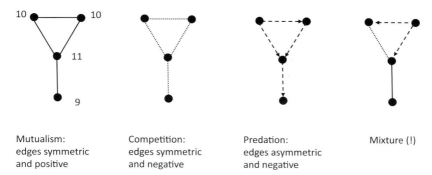

Figure 11.14 Graphlet 6 and its three-node orbits (9, 10, 11) contribute to the structural spectrum of a larger network. The same spectrum of structures will have different functional implications depending on the interactions coded by the edges.

On the other hand, I may be exaggerating the complexity of ecological systems compared to the world trade network model, and one could suggest that in that example, interactions among subunits that are similar to competition, predation, sabotage and collaboration are all actually present in the data, but summarized by the aggregated measures that are used. Similarly, because local topology and the positions of nodes in commonly occurring small subgraphs, have already provided insight into how structure affects functional dynamics, including more kinds of interactions in the networks analyzed should give more insight into this interaction. This area of research is obviously very complex, with hard problems to be solved, but recent progress provides an indication of how this may proceed.

11.3   Concluding Comments

The networks studied in ecology change in time and in space, with changes in both the nodes (often their states) and the edges (where they occur and their functional weights). The changes may be caused by external forces, interactions with other kinds of ecological networks, or by the reciprocal changes internal to the network under scrutiny; that is the relationship between graph structure and system dynamics.

The main theme is the "co-evolutionary" relationship between form and function, topology and dynamics or pattern and process, using graph theory to characterize the form of the ecological network and determining how that topology affects the dynamics and how the functioning of the network in turn affects its structure. The analogies of a railway, road, meandering river, or molecular interaction networks (like protein-protein) indicate what we already know: that system topology alone is probably not enough to teach us about the relationship with dynamics, but it is required, and can be combined with other information (about railways, rivers, or biological molecules) to provide that insight. With sufficient understanding of the system, the positions of network nodes in the whole graph or in its characteristic graphlets can indicate their roles in system function, which is the goal of this form of analysis. Graphlet-based methods are a promising approach to this, based on graphs and graph theory. There is much here left to explore and learn from (e.g. PPI network studies as models for ecological ones). It is a difficult endeavour, but there are examples of how it can be done, and there will be more in the near future, including examples of graph structure and system dynamics in ecological applications.

12   Synthesis and Future Directions

Introduction

To complete the presentation of relevant material, it remains to provide a synthesis of the themes and their associated techniques developed in previous chapters, augmented by some guidance on understanding the relationship between ecological characteristics and properties or procedures in graph theory. This includes reviewing the applicability of some major results from graph theory in an ecological context and indicating extensions of methods to other areas for application. As usual for a book's final chapter, it can also offer some indications or predictions on developments yet to be made and directions for researchers to pursue.

There is too much detail to review it all, but the original interest in graph theory as applied to ecological studies came from its usefulness in quantifying and testing hypotheses about ecological structure. In addition, it is known that network characteristics, even as vague as small world versus scale free, can provide some information on the processes that generated the structure and on its current dynamics. The intention to demonstrate the relationship between structure and dynamics has been pursued throughout, but especially in Chapter 11 on graphlets and their interpretation.

12.1   Comparisons and Matching

First is a review some of the critical steps in the application of graph theory to ecological studies. The most important step is probably the evaluation of what is observed. That evaluation can take the form of traditional or numerical assessment of statistical significance, the improbability of the observed outcome, or it can take the form of measurements of inconsistencies or change. Table 12.1 summarizes, in very short form, the range of approaches to evaluation covered in this book, with the matching examples and home chapter(s).

Overall, the material covered shows clearly some unifying themes that emerge again and again from the details and the discussion: orderliness, predictability, stability, hierarchies and sub-groupings and asymmetry of several kinds. Of that list, which is certainly incomplete, "orderliness" is an umbrella term for a large subset of the list, which pairs in interesting ways with "stability" or "resilience," and "asymmetry" applies both to the ecological phenomenon and to the graph theory properties that may go with it. These

Table 12.1 Approaches to Evaluation

Approach	Examples (Chapter Where Described)
Random edge addition	General graph characteristics (3)
	Numbers of cyclic or transitive sub-digraphs (tournaments) (6)
	Bipartite graph characteristics (7)
Randomization	Labels in join counts for segregation versus aggregation (9)
Restricted randomization	Shuffling edges but node degrees fixed (3, 5)
	Random spanning trees (3)
Random walks	Subgraph composition (9)
Internal hierarchies	Order of neighbour = path length (colonization steps) (10)
	Trophic levels (4)
Hierarchies of graphs	MNN, NN, MST . . . (9)
	Distance thresholds . . . (9)
Hierarchical testing	Time not space; space not time; neither; both (10)
Partial ordering, nodes	Degree; in-degree, out-degree, or difference (digraphs) (1, 6)
	Weights e.g. inertia, patch area, species abundance (9, 10)
Partial ordering, edges	Degree in line graph = degrees of end-nodes − 2 (1)
	Weights e.g. distance, flow rate (9,10,11)
Autocorrelation, nodes	Site nestedness scores; island areas; plant growth rates (9, 10)
Autocorrelation, edges	Distances, travel times, flow rates, index values (9, 10)
Join counts	Segregation or aggregation of disease classes (10)
Regression	Effects of neighbours by order on growth rates (10)
Logistic regression	Effects of neighbours by order on state transitions (10)
Edge crossings (spatial)	Orderliness of disease spread, animal foraging paths (10)
Subgraphs	
Strongly connected	Ecosystem trophic network subsets (4)
Blocks	Population subsets (5)
Modules	Organizational or functional "themes" or subgraphs (4)
Motifs	Small identifiable substructures for comparison (6, 7)
Graphlets	Relationship to neighbours indicates functional role (11)
Digraph triplets	Transitivity of dominance (competition; tournaments) (6)
Signed graphs	Balance, based on positive and negative edges (5)
Sub-tournaments	Competitive outcomes with pairwise "winners" (6)
Cluster detection (nodes)	Population or species subsets (3, 5, 8, 9)
Cluster detection (edges)	"Link communities" (1, 3, 9)
Partitioning	Community structure and graphs-of-graphs (5)
Finding inconsistencies	Competitive reversals, tournament paradoxes, nestedness anomalies, trophic level jumps or multi-level feeding, spatial saltation (3, 6, 9)
Measuring network flow	Energy in trophic networks; gene flow circuit theory; transport; asymmetric connectivity; reciprocal evolution (4, 7, 10)
	Form and function or structure and dynamics (11).
Recording network change	Interaction networks (mutualism, parasitism) changing with time (season, climate) (3, 7)
	Aspatial temporal graphs (8)
	Structure determines function, but functional dynamics affect structure (11)

are not really the same as the concepts of focus in the standard network analysis, but they are closely related. The current version of network analysis that is well covered elsewhere has not been ignored, but we need to look beyond that paradigm to take full advantage of what graph theory has to offer ecologists. Some of the material in this volume leads in that direction, but there is a long way yet to go. A start has been made.

Many of the characteristics of ecological systems that can be treated by graph theory are related somehow to the orderliness of the system, its consistency or predictability or non-randomness. For simplicity, we can contrast orderliness with randomness and independence, because it is only some sort of lack of independence that makes prediction possible (see Dale & Fortin 2014: "The irony is that the lack of independence is what makes prediction and hypothesis generation possible, but its very existence causes problems for the testing of hypotheses . . . "). Therefore, groupings of species, for example, would be interpreted as being somehow more orderly than a system in which the species seemed to respond individually and independently. (Interesting discussions can develop in a graduate seminar by exploring the evidence for comments like this.) For many of the structures examined in applications of graph theory to ecological phenomena, there are one or two such characteristics that are key to evaluating and understanding the phenomenon, and mostly, these match very well to equivalent graph theory properties. For example, one critical characteristic of multi-species competition is the consistency of the outcomes that indicates a hierarchy of competitive ability. This ecological property matches well with the graph-theoretical property of transitivity, both qualitative and quantitative, in the digraph representing competition. The matches between ecological orderliness and graph theory properties are not perfect, but Table 12.2 provides an indication of the matches that are most convincing. It is not always entirely obvious what the directions of the match may be even if it is clear that we have the right match of characteristics.

It should be evident in the material and the examples presented that the graph theory methods and understanding do not need to be super-sophisticated to be useful, or even powerful; some of the simplest concepts are the most helpful. On the other hand, it is fair to say that much of the sophisticated work in graph theory has not found its application in ecology (yet) and promises insights that would be impossible otherwise.

The important ecological characteristics can also be discussed in the context of how they can be related to the stability, persistence or resilience of their system. The list for stability is shorter because it includes only those with an explicit temporal component, and again, the matches between ecology and graph theory may be imperfect, and may at times seem contradictory when compared with the "orderliness" discussion above. For example, one critical characteristic of multi-species competition is the consistency that allows a hierarchy of competitive ability. This ecological property matches transitivity in the digraph representing competition, but inconsistency may be what allows the persistence of "weak" competitors, and thus sustained coexistence (see Ulrich et al. 2014; Soliveres et al. 2015; Permogorskiy 2015).

In general, stochastic effects will reduce predictability, although if the "degrees of freedom" are limited, for example in the possible stages of ecological succession for which only some transitions are possible, the predictability may still be high (consider

Table 12.2 Matching Ecological Orderliness and Graph Theory Properties

Ecological Orderliness or Structure	Graph Theory Property
Competition: outcome consistency	Transitivity, strict hierarchies with no reversals
Key nodes in spatial or S-T paths	Centrality of several kinds
Classification sub-groupings	More k-leaf-node subtrees formed in dendrograms, m_k, and few terminal singles
Trophic network layer orderliness	Strictness of levels/parts; partial orderings
Trophic network complexity	Direct path lengths, path "choice"/diversity
Trophic network dependence structure	Modularity, intervality; modularity; degree distribution
Keystone species	Centrality, sum of all paths
Spatial neighbour structure	Join counts, distance, autocorrelation
Social network orderliness	Balance, transitivity
Social network subgroups	Modularity, connectance, cut-points
S-T point pattern sequences	Neighbour distance and order; path crossings
Temporal sequence organization	Reachability, burstiness, transitivity
Mutualism strictness	Bipartite modularity, homophily/heterophily
Nestedness of pairings	Node degree relationships
Transmission or cause	Reachability in time-only graphs; reversibility
Ecological memory	Temporal edge persistence; "history" effect in S-T graphs

Note: More non-randomness and more predictability of structure can be matched with graph theory characteristics that reflect that orderliness.

a Markov models for these, Figure 12.1). Allowing more transitions may make the sequence of system states seem less orderly (Figure 12.1), but stochastic transitions may maintain diversity by preventing a single state from becoming fixed (Figure 12.2). The example shown is based on a graph of state transitions, but the same sort of argument applies to trophic networks in which predators have a choice of resources and their use of these can vary through time, to probabilistic colonization events of habitat islands, or to the outcomes of competitive interactions whenever there is a stochastic element to the outcomes.

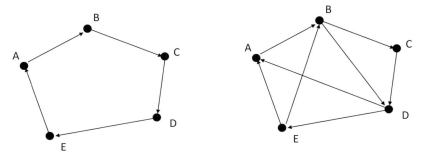

Figure 12.1 Stochastic effects reduce predictability. Five patch classes or stages: fewer possible transitions can make the stochastic system more orderly. For the left graph, one possible sequence is ABBCCDEAAABCDDDEABCDDD... For the right graph, one is ABBDAAABCDEEBBCDDABCDDD...

Table 12.3 Matching Ecological Stability and Graph Theory Properties

For Stability or Coexistence	Graph Theory Property
Competition hierarchy reversals	Intransitivity, hierarchies with reversals
Social network dynamics	Dynamic balance and intransitivity, may prevent extinctions
Trophic network hierarchy	Blurred levels (e.g. omnivory) may aid persistence
Trophic network dimensionality	Graph intervality
Keystones species	Degree and neighbour degree distributions; centrality
Composition nestedness	Node degree relationships

Note: Ecological characteristics that enhance stability or coexistence or resilience can be matched to some graph theory characteristics. In some cases, greater orderliness (Table 12.2) can increase stability (e.g. modularity in trophic networks), in other cases the opposite may be true (e.g. strict competition hierarchies may enhance extinctions rather than coexistence). In other examples, the relationship between stability and orderliness may be both positive and negative, depending on context and focus. For example, highly connected and highly important nodes (hubs) can provide a stabilizing influence under normal conditions, but also represent vulnerability for the network under rare circumstances (Solé & Montoya 2001).

These relationships are certainly fascinating, and potentially controversial. Without straying too far into the realm of theoretical and mathematical ecology, developing Table 12.3 brings into focus questions such as: Does greater modularity in a trophic network or in a mutualistic system increase stability or persistence? Does reachability in time-only or spatio-temporal graphs, related to disease spread, increase or decrease stability. How does nestedness of species compositions in a real or virtual archipelago affect extinction and colonization dynamics? Nested mutualistic interactions reduce effective competition and increase coexistence and biodiversity (Bascompte & Jordano 2014) but trophic networks are more likely to be more stable if they have compartmentalized and weakly connected structures (Thébault & Fontaine 2010). As in the discussion on orderliness

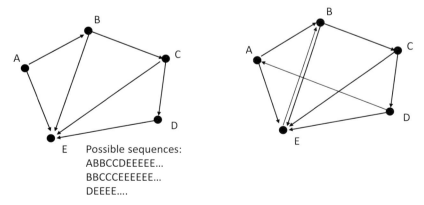

Possible sequences:
ABBCCDEEEEE...
BBCCCEEEEEE...
DEEEE....

Figure 12.2 Stochastic graph transitions may preserve diversity. Five patch stages converging to E. Adding stochastic transition edges can preserve diversity and coexistence. Added transitions for stochastic change diversifies sequences, and prevents state E from becoming fixed.

related to Table 12.1, we may agree which graph-theoretical characteristics are most closely related to the ecological stability, and thus which are the ones to evaluate, but it may not be clear whether the effect is to increase or to decrease the stability.

12.2   What Next?

Some insights into the current state of applications of graph theory in ecology have been provided here, trying (without too much formal theory) to convey some of the excitement of what has already been accomplished, and to portray accurately how ecologists can use this knowledge in their own work. Although much has been done already, it should be clear that there is much more that we can do with existing known techniques as well as with new and exciting methods yet to be developed. As always, for ecologists, the main goal is to elucidate and understand the relationship between two complementary aspects of ecological systems, which can be expressed as "pattern and process" or "form and function" or "structure and dynamics," whatever tools are available to help with this project. I can enumerate just some of the possibilities ahead, but what seems in order is more of the same, more that is different, more that is new, and more that we cannot yet imagine.

12.2.1   More of the Same: More Data

There is much to be gained by using existing methods that have already been applied in ecology to more and perhaps more broadly based data. In many cases, our understanding of the ecological systems of interest is based on few studies, for example fewer than ten trophic networks (e.g. Figure 12.3, and see Melián & Bascompte 2004, who used five). Given the difficulty of collecting high-quality data, that poverty may continue. More data and data from novel systems will enable us to generalize the understanding gained with greater confidence. There is also much to be learned from the more familiar methods when they can be applied to "big data," data from large spans of space or time or data that is finely detailed. A single critical example is the study of climate and weather and the effects of climate change on biological systems, which generates huge amounts of data, both meteorological and biological (see Woodward et al. 2010). Fortunately, techniques and software have already been produced for the analysis of big graphs and big networks for many applications including those of interest in ecology (see Sakr 2013; Kepner et al. 2013). In fact, graph theory seems to be the essential key to the analysis of big data (Marsten 2014; Eifrem 2014) because of its use in evaluating how the data are structured. Some of the value in the network format for ecological data is in the power to visualize and explore that structure and the relationships within it (Raymond & Hosie 2009), after all, we often tell students that the first step in analysis is to plot the data; but it can also be useful in suggesting or evaluating plausible causal structures (Pearl 1988). In some cases of big data, networks are both the data and the mechanism of analysis (see Cui et al. 2016); just as in computing graphs, trees may be both the objects of interest and the data structure in which they are stored (Newman 2010, 291).

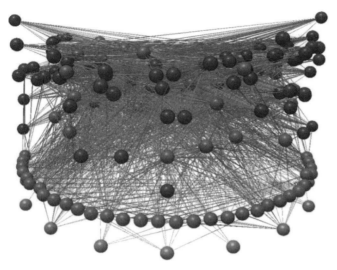

Figure 12.3 Illustration of 3D presentation of complex networks. A network of 4,671 feeding interactions among 68 parasites (in blue) and 117 free-living taxa (green = basal taxa, red = consumers) in the food web of Estero de Punta Banda, Baja California, Mexico. The vertical axis corresponds to trophic level. Credit: Images produced by J. A. Dunne using Network3D software (Dunne et al. 2013). (A black-and-white version of this figure will appear in some formats. For the colour version, please refer to the plate section.)

In addition, graphs are an essential part of many of the recent developments in modern statistics more generally, including structures like trees, random forests, neural networks and undirected graphical models for continuous and discrete variables, with known or unknown structure (see Hastie et al. 2009), although those applications are well outside the focus of this book.

In some cases, combining methods or approaches that have already been used separately will be very helpful, gaining insights from combined analysis. For example, looking at the network of interactions among plants, pollinators, and mycorrhizae (Cahill et al. 2008) can tell us much more than just the bipartite approaches of plant and pollinator or plant and fungus. In the spatial context (Chapter 9), the phrase "sum of all paths" referred to all possible routes between locations (and paths between nodes); the multipartite approach could be termed "the sum of all sorts" to include all the kinds of interactions, whether direct or indirect. Another promising combination is to look at network function in the context of spatial structure; Baskerville et al. (2011) used a Bayesian group model on Serengeti trophic network data to identify modular structure that combines trophic guild structure with spatial pattern. This latter example reflects the organization of this book: first by ecological function (predation, social interactions, mutualism and so on) and then by location or dimension (time only, space only, space and time); that paper presents a good application of what is essentially a function × location analysis. Similar combined analyses for other systems should prove to be worthwhile.

12.2.2   More That Is Different: Applying Existing Techniques That Have Not Been Used

Second, there are many existing techniques that have not been applied to ecological systems, but clearly should be. One obvious example is the graphlets spectrum approach described in Chapter 11. Such approaches may assist with what I see as an important development from the ecological view, the integration of different categories of interactions into a synthesis of ecological network studies. This includes the fascinating interplay of system structure and system dynamics discussed in Chapter 11. There is also a role for developments in general systems theory beyond but including ecology, such as the integration or reconciliation of network and hierarchy structures, one having units treated as equals and one with units ranked in a partially ordered set. Perhaps these could be treated as "heterarchical" structures that combine features of both, allowing the structural elements to be unranked or ranked in several different ways (see Cumming 2016). Many ecological networks that have already been described do have at least one partial order inherent in their structure (e.g. food web trophic structure) and sometimes more than one (e.g. trophic structure and body size). A general understanding of the relationships among partial orders in such systems could help in understanding the properties of the graphs that depict them for analysis.

In Chapter 3, the ongoing work on kernel approaches to structural comparisons was mentioned, and the topic deserves further discussion with a view to future use and further development. The general approach of kernel functions is popular in machine learning and the graph kernels in that application can be based on (random) walks, paths, small subgraphs of limited size (like motifs or the graphlet subgraphs), or subtree patterns (Shervashidze et al. 2011). Two graphs can be compared by measuring their similarity using "graph kernels" (Vishwanathan et al. 2010; Shervashidze et al. 2011). Kernel-based approaches are available for pattern analysis particularly as related to machine learning (Shawe-Taylor & Cristianini 2004) and their use for the comparison of "large" graphs has become important in applications in molecular biology and chemo-informatics, as well as telecommunications and social networks (Borgwardt et al. 2007; Vishwanathan et al. 2010; see also Schölkopf et al. 2004 and Gärtner 2008). In addition, to follow up on the discussion of using graphlet methods to infer function from structure, Borgwardt et al. (2005) described the use of graph kernels to predict protein function based on similarity in sequence, structure, amino acid motifs and so on.

The basic advantage of the kernel approach is based on the concept of mapping an object of interest, x, from its own data space into a "feature space" in which analysis is simplified by some mapping function, $\varphi(x)$. In order to compare two such objects of interest, x and x', it may not be ' ecessary to convert each one explicitly using function φ (which may be computationally demanding), but rather we can define a kernel function based on the cross product or equivalent for which $k\,(x,\,x') = \,<\varphi(x),\,\varphi(x')>$. This more direct step for comparison is called the "kernel trick" and the kernel function is some measure of the similarity of x and x', because it takes higher values with the more features shared.

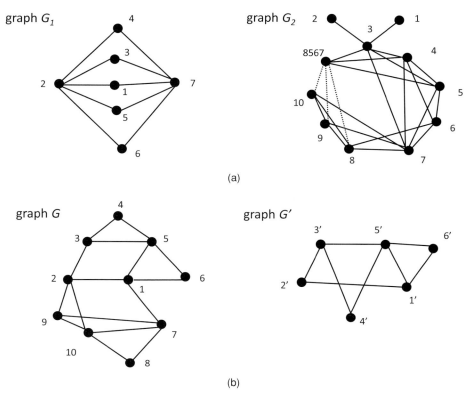

Figure 12.4 Comparing nodes in a graph using graph kernels based on random walks. (a) In G_1, random walks from nodes 2 or node 7 will be very similar. They also belong to the same graphlet orbits. In G_2, random walks from nodes 1 or node 2 will be very similar and they belong to the same orbits . . . but random walks can become trapped in long cycles in the large multi-ring subgraph. (b) Within G, random walks from nodes 8 and 9 will be similar although their graphlet orbits are different. Independent random walks on G and G' from nodes 4 and 4' will have certain similarities based on structure (based on Vishwanathan et al. 2010).

The kernel approach can be used to evaluate the similarity of two nodes in the same graph. (These comments are based loosely on Kondor & Lafferty [2002] and presentations by Vishwanathen that are available on the Web, e.g. www.stat.purdue.edu/~vishy/talks/Graphs.pdf and https://archive.org/details/Microsoft_Research_Video_103902.) Random walks on graphs are useful in evaluating important characteristics of graph structure (Chapter 9), and for example, in Figure 12.4a, nodes 2 and 7 "look the same" (and have the same graphlet orbits) and the random walks that start from either node will be very similar (identical, really). A simple suggestion for the basis of comparison would be counts of the number and lengths of random walks between the two nodes i and j. This suggestion does not work as hoped because the random walk can get "lost" in repeated cycles, as mentioned in Chapter 9, and illustrated in Figure 12.4a. A quick fix is to down-weight long walks (in case they represent these cycles) and a simple weighting for walks of length k is $\lambda^k/k!$, where λ is an appropriately chosen weight parameter between 0 and 1. Where $\mathbf{A}$ is the adjacency matrix of the graph (with 1s in positions corresponding to edges and 0s elsewhere), $\mathbf{A}^k$ enumerates the walks of length k between nodes i and j. Therefore the kernel that measures the similarity of the two nodes is

$$K(i, j) = \left[\sum_{k=1} \frac{\lambda^k}{k!} A^k\right]_{ij} = [e^{\lambda A}]_{ij}. \tag{12.1}$$

The Laplacian matrix can be substituted for the adjacency matrix, and similar results are available based on "lazy" random walks in which each iteration may stay on the current node with a constant probability, rather than always moving to an adjacent node. In addition, the same analysis applies well, with appropriate changes, when the edges of the graph have weights associated with them. Overall, this seems like an elegant solution for nodes within a graph, but will the same approach work for comparing whole graphs?

For comparing whole graphs, the kernel is a function of the two graphs, G and G', that measures their similarity and so comparing graphs requires the construction of a kernel between the graphs that "captures the semantics inherent in the graph structure" (Vishwanathan et al. 2010). This is not a guidebook of graph theory algorithms, but there is one that deserves inclusion because it ties together some themes very well (and it is so cool!): random walk graph kernels (following Vishwanathan et al. 2010).

Random walks are a good basis for evaluating structural characteristics of graphs and these kernels are based on the idea of having random walks on the two graphs to be compared and determining the number of walks that match. Vishwanathan et al. (2010) explained the concept and its application using *direct product graphs*. $G_\times$ is the direct product graph of G and G'; it has nodes corresponding to all pairs of nodes, one from each of G and G', and edges in $G_\times$ joining nodes if and only if both pairs are joined in G and G'. Figure 12.5a gives an example (it's almost like a graph-of-graphs). If $\mathbf{A}$ and $\mathbf{A}'$ are the adjacency matrices of the original graphs, then the adjacency matrix of the direct product graph is the Kronecker product of the two; each "1" in $\mathbf{A}$ is replaced by a full copy of $\mathbf{A}'$, producing what is essentially a "matrix-of-matrices" (see Figure 12.6a and 12.6b). The adjacency matrix is $\mathbf{A}_\times = \mathbf{A} \otimes \mathbf{A}'$. The same holds for the normalized adjacency matrices: $A_\times = A \otimes A'$.

The direct product used here is also called the *tensor product*; it is not the Cartesian product that may be more intuitive, and illustrated for contrast in the last panels of Figure 12.5b, with the matrix version in Figure 12.6c.

Running a random walk on $G_\times$ is equivalent to running independent random walks on the original graphs (Gärtner et al. 2003). To create the kernel, a weight matrix, $\mathbf{W}_\times$ is associated with $G_\times$, and with appropriate definitions, $\mathbf{W}_\times = \mathbf{A}_\times$, or with normalization, $W_\times = A_\times$. The kth power of the adjacency matrix gives walks of length k. The kernel is then based on the probability of simultaneous random walks on G and G', both of length k. It is essentially a sum over all walk lengths (the "sum of all walks") but with a length-dependent coefficient, $\mu(k)$, to eliminate repeated cycles by down-weighting very long walks (Vishwanathan et al. 2010).

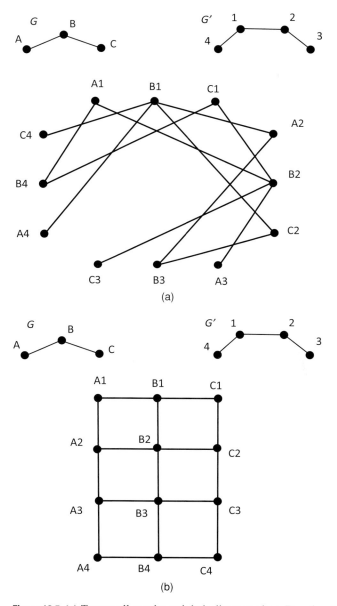

Figure 12.5 (a) Two small graphs and their direct product. Based on Vishwanathan et al. (2010). (b) Two small graphs and their Cartesian product.

This definition compares the two graphs but allows much flexibility in the actual measure, particularly in using different versions of $\mu(k)$ to emphasize or down-weight walks of different lengths. The full details can be found in Vishwanathan et al. (2010), but it looks like a promising method for applications in ecological studies. The joking comment above was that this method is the "sum of all walks," to parallel the phrase

	A	B	C
A	0	1	0
B	1	0	1
C	0	1	0

	1	2	3	4
1	0	1	0	1
2	1	0	1	0
3	0	1	0	0
4	1	0	0	0

(a)

	A1	B1	C1	A2	B2	C2	A3	B3	C3	D1	D2	D3
A1	0	.	.	.	1	.				.	1	.
B1	.	0		1		1				1		1
C1	.		0		1						1	.
A2	.	1		0				1				.
B2	1	1			0		1	1				.
C2	.	1				0		1				.
A3	.				1		0					.
B3	.			1		1		0				.
C3	.				1				0			.
A4	.	1								0		.
B4	1	1									0	.
C4	.	1	.	.	.	.	.	.	.	.	.	0

(b)

	A1	B1	C1	A2	B2	C2	A3	B3	C3	D1	D2	D3
A1	0	1	0	1	.	.				.	.	.
B1	1	0	1	0	1							.
C1	0	1	0	0	0	1						.
A2	1	0	0	0	1	0	1					.
B2	.	1	0	1	0	1	0	1				.
C2	.		1	0	1	0	0	0	1			.
A3	.			1	0	0	0	1	0	1		.
B3	.				1	0	1	0	1	0	1	.
C3	.					1	0	1	0	0	0	1
A4	.						1	0	0	0	1	0
B4	.							1	0	1	0	1
C4	.	.	.	.	.	.	.	.	1	0	1	0

(c)

Figure 12.6 (a) Adjacency matrices of graphs G and G′. (b) Adjacency matrix of the direct product of graphs G and G′ (off-diagonal zeros omitted for clarity). The Kronecker product of the original matrices. (c) Adjacency matrix of the Cartesian product of graphs G and G′ (most off-diagonal zeros omitted for clarity).

about the "sum of all paths" used elsewhere (e.g. Chapter 9); there is actually a "sum-of-all-paths" version of this approach, using paths instead of walks, or a "sum of all shortest paths" (see Borgwardt & Kriegel 2005).

As suggested in Chapter 3, combining this method with tree-based kernels is an obvious approach to comparing the dendrograms or classification structures, such as those discussed in Chapter 2. Comparing trees requires a determination of all possible subtrees (tree motifs of all sizes) and a count of these for each tree: $h_i(T)$ occurrences of the ith subtree in tree T. For trees T and T', the basic kernel is then

$$K(T, T') = \sum_{i=1} h_i(T)h_i(T').$$ (12.2)

(Gärtner 2008). Tree-based kernels have been used in the analysis of natural languages (see Moschitti 2006; Sun et al. 2011) and Poon et al. (2013) provide a good example of this approach in studying the shapes of phylogenetic trees. In a complementary application of the technique, Oh et al. (2006) used kernel-based comparisons of metabolic networks to construct phylogenetic trees for a broad range of organisms, which confirmed the scheme of three domains (Archaea, Eukaryota, Eubacteria) rather than just two.

A final example of kernel-based analysis returns to the structure and dynamics theme of Chapter 11. Noting that the shapes of phylogenetic trees of viruses (structure) are determined by host adaptation and virus transmission among hosts (dynamics), phylogenetic inference attempts to estimate parameters of these processes from phylogeny shape, Poon (2015) describes an inspiring study. The study uses subset tree kernel functions to compare phylogenetic tree shapes generated under different phylogenetic situations; the distance measures thus derived are then combined with an ABC (approximate Bayesian computation) framework to estimate parameters from the simulated data (the "kernel-ABC" method). The combined approach was applied to data from an outbreak of recombinant HIV in China, and proved to provide a versatile approach for phylogenetic inference.

Looking ahead to further development and refinement of these kernel-based methods, we can ask what level of detail might they be used to achieve. Given the overall measure of similarity between two (large) graphs or trees, can the method identify parts of the graphs that are most or least similar; characteristics of the graphs that are most or least similar; or how similarity changes with scale, such as the number of nodes in a walk, path or sub-tree? The localized graphlet-based kernel approach seems to be the likely way to proceed, although this is yet to be done explicitly (see Shervashidze et al. 2009; Lugo-Martinez & Radivojac 2014). Clearly this is a promising approach that can offer ecologists more help in future versions.

12.2.3 More That Is New: Developing Novel Methods

Third, it is obvious that more and valuable methods based on graph theory are yet to be developed for ecological applications, and those may await the work of theoreticians and application ecologists alike, both for systems studies and conservation projects. Given recent history of this field, there are going to be lots of exciting approaches that have not even been thought of yet, far less developed and applied. My greatest familiarity with graphs and graph theory may be mainly from applications for spatial or spatially derived data, and so I am not in the best position to provide well-founded predictions for the whole field. There seems to be more to be discovered in all the areas described in these chapters, but it is my guess that the areas that will benefit ecologists most with surprising results from further research are time-only graphs (think of proximity or encounter data), other uses for graph fragments, motifs or graphlets (remember "It's all about subgraphs."), and random walks on graphs (perhaps scales of similarity or dissimilarity in comparing graphs with kernel functions). The last two are closely related, and random walk–type kernels can be based on graphlets as well as graphs or trees (Shervashidze et al. 2009; Lugo-Martinez & Radivojac 2014; software available!). (As an aside, in Figure 12.4a nodes 2 and 7 give "identical" random walks and have the same graphlet orbit vectors; in Figure 12.4b, nodes 8 and 9 have different graphlet vectors, but still produce highly similar random walks.)

Building on what is known is an obvious way to proceed in all areas of applying graph theory; that's the call for "more that is new"; but unexpected and valuable ideas will arise both from theoretical studies and from or inspired by applications well outside ecology. That's the call for the fourth sort of "more": "more that we cannot yet imagine."

12.2.4   More That We Cannot Imagine: What We Need to Learn

The last area of need is not really within the scope of this book, but it recurred throughout its development. We need to know more (a lot more) about the basic ecology of the systems we study. Perhaps this may seem to be a depressing thought, but however well studied some systems are, for example the boreal ecosystem at Kluane discussed in Chapter 4, and however much effort and expense has provided insight into some of the components, there is still so much yet to begin. Consider all the invertebrates and all the below-ground interactions that are certainly important (Lankau et al. 2010) in that "relatively simple" ecosystem, and then consider the complexities that must exist in the speciose communities of warm forests, wetlands, coral reefs or productive savannahs. There is also the need to include both the many direct inter-specific interactions, trophic and non-trophic (Abrams et al. 1996; Bukovinszky et al. 2008; Ings et al. 2008; Ohgushi 2008; Sotomayor & Lortie 2015; Kéfi et al. 2015), and also the indirect interactions of various importance and strengths, such as those described and illustrated in Chapter 4 (Figure 4.16). As stated previously, including a range of different ecological interactions will require a revised system to code edges by category and some modifications of the measures of graph structure.

In Chapter 11, a parallel was drawn between the study of ecological interactions and molecular level research on proteins and protein-protein interactions. In order to make good predictions about a protein's function, two kinds of information are needed: the molecule's chemical topology and three-dimensional configuration, and its place in the protein-protein interaction network (Pržulj et al. 2004; Pržulj 2010; Peterson et al. 2012; Winterbach et al. 2013; Yugandhar & Gromiha 2016). In the field of ecological networks, the "program" is not as clearly laid out but it seems implicit in much of the research described here. In order to make predictions about ecological function and dynamics, two kinds of information are required: (1) the basic biology of the organisms and (2) their places in the multi-process interaction networks of competition, predation, mutualism and so on. Once again, graph theory is the obvious and perhaps only approach to this complex topic which requires and deserves greater effort.

12.3 Concluding Comments

Preparing this book has been both an exciting adventure and a humbling review of the gaps in my knowledge, an exploration of what is to be learned and an alluring opening to future exploration. I might wish that I had attempted the task sooner, but the accumulating wealth of this field is very current and moving forward very quickly. It has been fascinating to watch the organization of this book itself change as it developed (structure and dynamics, indeed!), and to accept the new perspectives as they occurred.

The case for the exceptional usefulness and general under-use of graph theory and its concepts for ecological studies was both strong and convincing a decade ago, but the recent advances and exemplars of applications in other fields make the case overwhelming. As stated in the opening chapter, not all the promising approaches or applications currently have ecological examples or even real examples from other fields, but there are many rich possibilities to be explored. In applying networks and graph theory to developing ecological hypotheses and to answering ecological questions, there are just so many smart things that can be done! Future developments and new applications will be exciting indeed and I am looking forward to watching and participating in that progress. On applications of graph theory in ecology, there is much fascinating work to be done and there will obviously be much more to be said in the future.

Glossary

Introduction

This glossary does not include every term used in the book, but it provides only the basics of graph theory. The intention is not to be too formal in the presentation, keeping mathematical notation and equations to a minimum.

A ***graph*** is a mathematical object made up of two sets:

1 {nodes}. These are points or dots in a diagram representing the graph; they are also called vertices (often denoted by v), and;
2 {edges} = {pairs of nodes}. These are lines in a graph diagram, also called arcs or links. In a diagram, they can be straight or curved without meaning, because they represent relationships. Edges may cross with no node at the intersection; the crossings are not structural (see Figure G1).

Figure G1. A graph with 6 labelled nodes (•) and 9 edges (—)

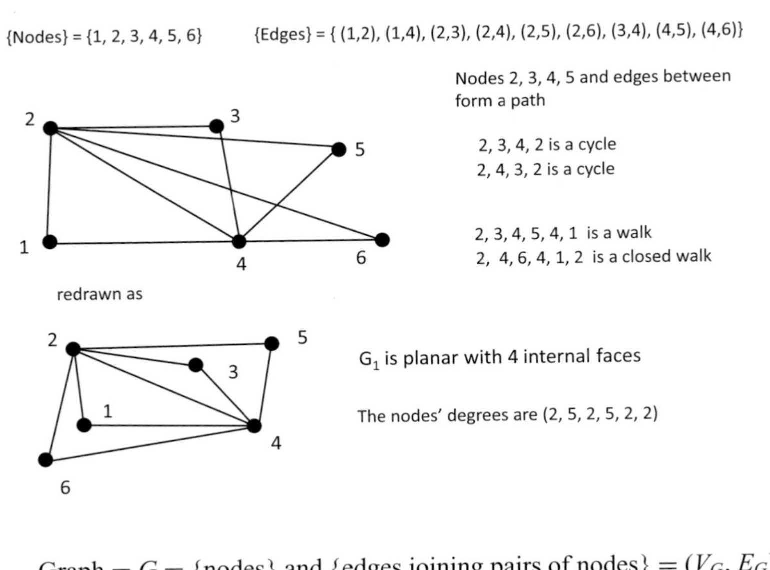

{Nodes} = {1, 2, 3, 4, 5, 6}   {Edges} = { (1,2), (1,4), (2,3), (2,4), (2,5), (2,6), (3,4), (4,5), (4,6)}

Nodes 2, 3, 4, 5 and edges between form a path

2, 3, 4, 2 is a cycle
2, 4, 3, 2 is a cycle

2, 3, 4, 5, 4, 1 is a walk
2, 4, 6, 4, 1, 2 is a closed walk

redrawn as

G_1 is planar with 4 internal faces

The nodes' degrees are (2, 5, 2, 5, 2, 2)

Graph $= G = $ {nodes} and {edges joining pairs of nodes} $= (V_G, E_G) = $ sets $\{v_i | i = 1 \text{ to } n\}$ and $\{e(i, j)\}$.

The edge designation $e(i, j)$ can be abbreviated to e_{ij}. The number of edges is m.

In a basic graph, the pairs are unordered, with e_{ij} equivalent to e_{ji}, and the maximum number of edges is $n(n-1)/2$. In a directed graph, or ***digraph***, the edges have directions; e_{ij} is not equivalent to e_{ji} and the maximum number of edges is $n(n-1)$, and it is possible to have both e_{ij} and e_{ji} (Figure G2). The nodes can have labels or weights, and the edges can have weights (including signs, $+$ or $-$) as well as directions.

Figure G2. Graph and digraph on 4 nodes

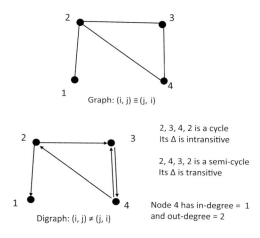

Graph: (i, j) ≡ (j, i)

2, 3, 4, 2 is a cycle
Its Δ is intransitive

2, 4, 3, 2 is a semi-cycle
Its Δ is transitive

Digraph: (i, j) ≠ (j, i)

Node 4 has in-degree = 1
and out-degree = 2

A ***network*** is a graph that includes quantitative information: the nodes usually represent *things* (e.g. people, species, islands . . .) with weights indicating size, abundance, potential etc. The edges typically represent *connections* (e.g. interactions like cooperation, relationships such as similarity, physical links like contiguity or migration routes . . .) with weights indicating their characteristics, such as intensity, rates and capacity (Figure G3).

However, the term "network" and the term "graph" are now often treated as synonymous, but despite this apparent synonymy, *graph theory* still seems to be more about structure and *network theory* seems to be more about flow or transmission. In addition, "network" may be the structure depicted and "graph" its depiction, as in "the graph of the transportation network."

Terms in Alphabetical Order

***Adjacency matrix*, A:** a square matrix with elements $a_{ij} = 1$ when nodes i and j are joined by an edge, and 0 otherwise.

***Algebraic connectivity*:** the second eigenvalue of the *Laplacian matrix*; it has predictive properties for graph connectivity and robustness to deletions.

Figure G3. Network of co-authorship

Nodes (authors) weighted by publication totals

Edges weighted by publications co-authored by the pair indicated

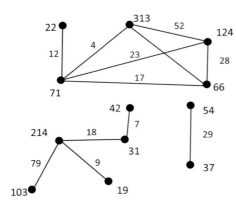

Digraph: Edges could be split
by seniority in author lists, e.g.

Arborescence: a directed rooted tree; it is a digraph with no semicycles. There is exactly one directed path from the root to any other node, and at most one between any two nodes (Figure G6). There is at most one directed path between any two nodes.

Aspatial graph: the positions of the elements, in particular the nodes, are not interpreted as spatial locations, even if the structure originally had a spatial context or source; space is ignored in the graph itself. The network in Figure G3 is aspatial; the positions of the nodes are related to the locations of the authors.

Assortative versus *disassortative*: general terms describing higher versus lower frequencies of like-to-like edges applying to any characteristics associated with nodes, not just node degree. In social networks, the term *homophily* is also used for having stronger and more frequent associations between nodes of greater similarity; its opposite is *heterophily*.

Assortativity coefficient: a correlation measure, r, with values between -1 and $+1$, based on the bivariate frequencies of the degrees of neighbour nodes, that distinguishes between assortative networks with $r > 0$ indicating positive autocorrelation and disassortative networks with $r < 0$ indicating negative autocorrelation of neighbouring node degrees. This concept is very similarity to *modularity*, which measures the relative frequency of "like-to-like" joins, as in a join-count statistic.

Balance (in signed graphs or signed digraphs): the proportion of cycles that are positive, having an even number of negative edges (Figure G8).

Betweenness: measures the frequency with which a node occurs in the shortest paths between other pairs of nodes.

***Bipartite graph*:** the nodes fall into two subsets with edges only between the subsets, not within (Figure G9c).

***Block*:** a maximal connected subgraph lacking cutpoints. In Figure G5, BCDE is a block.

***Centrality*:** a measure of the importance of a node's position in the shortest paths between other pairs of nodes.

***Characteristic path length*:** of G, the median of the means of path distances from node i to all other nodes j in G.

***Closed walk*:** a walk that begins and ends at the same node.

***Clustering coefficient*:** a measure of the probability that two neighbours of a given node (say, j and k as neighbours of node i, with edges e_{ji} and e_{ik}) are themselves neighbours (joined by e_{jk}). The matrix version is, given the adjacency matrix entries $a_{ij} = 1$ and $a_{ik} = 1$, the clustering coefficient is the probability that $a_{jk} = 1$. This is sometimes referred to as *triad completion* or *triadic closure*.

Complement of graph G is G': it has the same nodes as G, $V_G = V_{G'}$, and edges between all and only those pairs of nodes not joined by an edge in G (see Figure G4). The edges of graph G and G' together account for all possible edges, the complete graph.

Figure G4. Complement of graph G_1

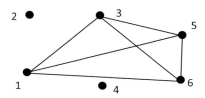

{Nodes} = {1, 2, 3, 4, 5, 6}

{Edges} =
{ (1,3), (1,5), (1,6), (3,5), (3,6), (5,6)}

Nodes' degrees are (3, 1, 3, 0, 4, 3)

Subgraph of G_1:
a Tree (no cycles)

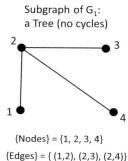

{Nodes} = {1, 2, 3, 4}
{Edges} = { (1,2), (2,3), (2,4)}

Induced subgraph of G_1
(all possible edges from G_1)

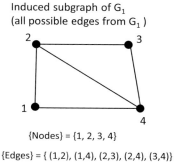

{Nodes} = {1, 2, 3, 4}
{Edges} = { (1,2), (1,4), (2,3), (2,4), (3,4)}

***Complete graph*:** there is an edge between every pair of nodes (also called a *clique*).

***Component*.** A graph that is not connected consists of a number of maximally connected subgraphs called components.

Connectance*:** while ***connectedness and ***connectivity*** are closely related, connectance is different; it is the proportion of the positions for edges that actually have an edge.

For a simple graph, it is $m/[n(n-1)/2]$. Connectance tells little about graph topology; two graphs with the same connectance can be structurally very different.

Connected graph: there is a path between any two nodes; otherwise the graph is disconnected (Figure G5).

Figure G5. Connected graph

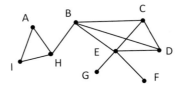

Nodes HBEF with edges between form a path. Nodes AIH with 3 edges form a cycle. Nodes BCDE with their 6 edges, form a subgraph and a complete graph and a block.

Graph is disconnected by removal of cut-point (B) or cut-edge (B-H).

AHI and (B)CDEFG are the components of the disconnected graph.

Connectedness: *edge connectedness* is the smallest number of edges that can be removed that will disconnect the graph. *Node connectedness* is the smallest number of nodes that can be removed that will disconnect the graph.

Connectivity: A graph is said to have high *connectivity* if either the edge connectedness or node connectedness is large.

Crossing number: of a graph is the smallest number of pairwise intersections of edges when the graph to be drawn in the plane.

Cut-edge (or **bridge**): an edge in a connected graph the removal of which disconnects the graph (Figure G5).

Cut-point: a node in a connected graph the removal of which disconnects the graph (Figure G5).

Cut-set: a set of edges the removal of which disconnects the graph; the *cut size* is the number of edges between the two clusters of a partitioned graph whose removal will disconnect them.

Cycle: a path that begins and ends at the same node, with no node or edge used more than once (sometimes called a *loop*). A cycle is a path that is a closed walk. In a digraph, a cycle must follow the directions of the edges; a polygon of edges in a digraph that do not form a cycle is a *semi-cycle* (Figure G2).

Degree: the number of edges attached to a node. In a digraph, each node has both an in-degree, the number of edges of which it is the sink, and an out-degree, the number of edges of which it is the source (Figures G1 and G2).

Degree matrix, **D**: a square matrix that has 0s everywhere but on the main diagonal, which lists the degrees of the nodes. (For a digraph, this can be either the in-degree or the out-degree.)

Diameter: a graph's diameter is the maximum distance between any two nodes, where distance is the length of the shortest path between the two (Figure G7).

Digraph: A ***directed graph*** consists of a set of nodes with a set of edges that have direction, so that the edge from A to B is different from the edge from B to A. In a ***digraph***, $e(i, j)$ is not equivalent to $e(j, i)$, meaning that A → B ≠ B → A (Figure G1). It is possible that a particular pair of nodes is joined by two edges, one in each direction, i.e. both A → B and B → A (Figure G2).

Directed acyclic graph: a graph with directed edges that contains no directed cycles but may have semi-cycles; i.e. its underlying graph may not be a tree and may have non-directed cycles. Figure G6 shows a directed tree and a directional acyclic graph. In the directed tree, there is at most one directed path between any two nodes; in the acyclic digraph, there can be several. Every aborescence is a directed acyclic graph but not every acyclic graph is an aborescence.

Figure G6. Directional graphs: directed tree and directed acyclic graph

Directed rooted tree or arborescence
(underlying graph has no cycles)

Directed acyclic graph
(underlying graph has cycles)

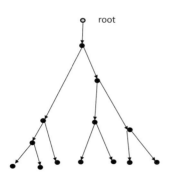
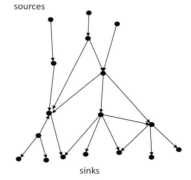

Distance: (between nodes) can be measured in several ways, number of edges in the shortest path, physical distance in a spatial graph, or costs in a transportation network (Figure G7).

Distance graph: a kind of spatial graph, in which the nodes occur at locations in a Euclidean metric space and the edges between them take the values of the Euclidean distances between the points in that space (e.g. spatial graph; Figure G7).

Figure G7. Distance and path length

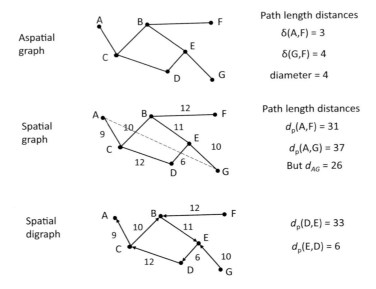

Aspatial graph

Path length distances

$\delta(A,F) = 3$

$\delta(G,F) = 4$

diameter = 4

Spatial graph

Path length distances

$d_p(A,F) = 31$

$d_p(A,G) = 37$

But $d_{AG} = 26$

Spatial digraph

$d_p(D,E) = 33$

$d_p(E,D) = 6$

Empty graph: has nodes but no edges. In Figure G4, upper panel, nodes 1, 2 and 4 form an empty subgraph.

Forest: acyclic graph that is not connected; it consists of components that are trees.

Geodesic path: the shortest or minimum weight path between two nodes.

Geometric graph: a spatial graph in *d*-dimensional space, which uses a measure of distance within the space, possibly Euclidean. Edges are determined by an upper threshold on internode distance.

Graph: a mathematical object made up of two sets: (1) {nodes}, the points in a graph diagram, and (2) {edges} = {pairs of nodes}, represented by the lines joining nodes in pairs (Figure G1).

Graphlet: a subgraph of up to five nodes. What is counted is not the graphlets themselves but the frequency of nodes at each distinct location in all graphlets. In general, a *motif* is counted even if it is not an *induced subgraph* of the graph being analyzed; in graphlet analysis, only induced subgraphs are considered (see Figure G4).

Graph-of-graphs: a structure in which each node of a graph at one level consists of, or has associated with it, a graph of its own.

Incidence matrix, B: a rectangular matrix in which the rows are the nodes and the columns are the edges; for an undirected graph, the elements $b_{ik} = 1$ when edge *k* is attached to node *i*, and 0 otherwise. For a digraph, $b_{ik} = 1$ when node *i* is the source of edge *k*, $b_{ik} = -1$ when it is the sink, and 0 otherwise.

Joint degree distribution: tabulates the bivariate distribution of the degrees of nodes joined by an edge, $f(d_i, d_j)$, where $e_{ij} \neq 0$, in order to determine whether the degrees of neighbouring nodes are positively or negatively autocorrelated. The frequency can be converted into the *assortativity coefficient*, which distinguishes between positive autocorrelation and negative autocorrelation of neighbouring node degrees. These measures can be calculated from the adjacency matrix, **A**.

***Laplacian matrix*, L:** a square matrix derived by subtracting the *adjacency matrix* from the *degree matrix*: $\mathbf{L} = \mathbf{D} - \mathbf{A}$.

***Lattice graph*:** can be drawn as a regular lattice in two dimensions; the edges form a regular tiling of the plane. The lattice is usually square, as for spatial raster data, but possibly triangular or hexagonal. All nodes except those on the boundaries have the same degree.

***Length*:** a path's length is the sum of the weights of the edges in the path; in simple cases, the number of edges. The graph theory *distance* between any two nodes in a graph is just the shortest path between them (Figure G7). In some applications, the shortest or minimum weight path is called a *geodesic* path. In a spatial graph or spatial digraph, paths also have physical distance lengths or lengths determined by transport costs (Figure G7).

***Line graph*:** G' derived from G; nodes in G' are the edges of G, edges in G' join edges from G that share a node in G.

***Module*:** a subgraph with a high relative frequency of joins between nodes within it and few outside; it can also refer to a high frequency of edges between nodes with similar characteristics (e.g. labels). *Modules* of nodes are also called "clusters" or "communities." In a graph or digraph with signed edges, well-defined modules have only positive edges within them and negative edges external to them (Figure G8).

Figure G8. Modules

(**a**) Graph: nodes (•) and signed edges: (solid = plus; dotted = minus). Three complete subgraph modules: {G,F}, {A,H,I} & {B,C,D,E}.

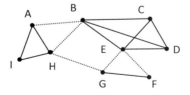

(**b**) Digraph of directional edges (digraph) with signs (solid = plus; dotted = minus). Two modules.

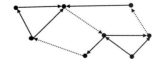

Both have a high degree of balance.

Modularity: the tendency of network neighbours to have similar characteristics, or index of the relative frequency of "like-to-like" joins in the network graph (similar to a join-count statistic). It can also refer to how easily the graph can be *partitioned* into distinct modules with high internal but low external *connectivity*.

Motif: a small subgraph of defined structure that recurs in the graph(s) being studied. Motifs have three or four nodes, and the frequency of each is used to make inferences about structure.

Network: a graph that includes quantitative information, usually representing aspects of a real system (Figure G2): the nodes represent *things* (e.g. species, islands) with weights indicating size, abundance, potential etc.; the edges represent *connections* (e.g. interactions like predation, relationships such as similarity, physical links like contiguity or migration routes) with weights indicating their characteristics such as intensity, rates, capacity etc. In many biological applications, "network" and "graph" are treated as synonyms.

Partitioning: the process or problem of dividing a graph into smaller components based on specific characteristics or criteria. For example, to divide a graph into modules or node clusters maximizing edges within clusters and minimizing edges between.

Path: an alternating sequence of nodes and edges in which each node is attached to the next node in the sequence by an edge; and each edge in the path is joined to the subsequent edge at a node to which they are both attached (Figure G1). No node or edge may be used more than once in the same path.

Path graph: an unbranched tree; for *n* nodes, the 2 end nodes have degree 1, and all the other $n - 2$ nodes have degree 2. Adding an edge between the two end nodes converts a path graph to a ring graph, and removing any edge from a ring graph creates a path graph.

Phylogenetic tree: this tree depicts evolutionary history with nodes of degree 1 (*leaves*) representing the taxa, a *root* of degree 1, representing the common ancestor, and *branch nodes* of degree 3, indicating points of evolutionary divergence.

Planar graph: can be drawn in a two-dimensional plane with no edges crossing. (Remember that the edges do have to be drawn as straight lines; they can curve around the outside. G_1 in Figure G1 is planar as is the full graph in Figure G5.) A *minimum planar graph* is a spatial planar graph (no edges crossing) that uses the smallest total length of edges.

Random walk: a walk from node to node in which, at each iteration, the next edge to be included is chosen at random according to some rule, such as equal probability for all edges attached to the current node.

Reciprocity of a digraph: the proportion of all edges that are members of reciprocal pairs of edges between the same two nodes (in opposite directions). The digraph in Figure G2 has two edges out of five that form a reciprocal pair; one of six node pairs has both reciprocal edges.

Reciprocity index of a digraph: measures the frequency of bidirectional edges, the proportion of edges that occur in pairs between the same two nodes. For an unsigned digraph and its adjacency matrix, the reciprocity index is $R = \Sigma\Sigma\ [a_{ij} \times a_{ji}] \div \Sigma\Sigma\ a_{ij}$. For the digraph in Figure G2, that is 0.25.

Regular graph: all nodes have the same degree. A *complete graph*, which has all possible edges (each node has degree $n - 1$) is a regular graph; so is a *ring graph* where the nodes all have degree 2 (e.g. Figure G9c).

Ring graph: each node has two adjacent neighbours (degree 2), and there is only one cycle: the whole graph; this must be a connected graph, most clearly drawn as a simple ring (Figure G9c).

Semi-cycle: In a digraph, walks, paths and cycles must follow the directions of the edges they include; similar-looking subgraphs that do not follow the edge directions are called semi-walks, semi-paths and semi-cycles; therefore a *semi-cycle* is a closed polygon of nodes and edges without repetition that does not follow all the directions of the edges it includes (see Figure G2).

Signed digraph: the edges have both signs and directions. In the adjacency matrix, each element, a_{ij}, takes one of three values, $+1$, 0 or -1; for any pair of nodes, there are nine edge combinations possible. Edge signs are indicated by solid for positive and broken for negative (Figure G8b).

Signed graph: the edges have signs, $+$ or $-$ (essentially a binary weight), indicating the nature of the relationship portrayed, such as reinforcing versus antagonistic interactions. Edge signs are usually indicated by solid for positive and broken or dashed for negative (Figure G8a).

Spanning tree: a connected subgraph of G that is a tree and includes all nodes of G; a *minimum spanning tree* does so with the smallest total edge length. In Figure G4, the subgraph with three edges (bottom left) is a spanning tree of the induced subgraph with five edges.

Spatial graph and digraph: the nodes have spatial locations; this means that edges, and thus paths, have weights that are physical distances or weights related to transport or communication (Figure G7).

Spatio-temporal graph and digraph: the nodes of these graphs have locations in both time and space, which means the edges, and thus paths, have physical and temporal distances.

Spectral properties: a graph's **spectrum** is the set of eigenvalues of the adjacency or Laplacian matrix. The **spectral gap** is the difference between the first and second eigenvalues of the adjacency matrix. The **algebraic connectivity** is the second eigenvalue of the Laplacian matrix. Both have predictive properties for connectivity and robustness to deletions.

Subgraph: J is a subgraph of graph G, if it includes only nodes that are a subset of the nodes of G, and edges that are a subset of the graph's edges that join pairs of nodes in J. More formally, V_J is a subset of V_G and E_J is a subset of $E_G \cap V_J \times V_J$. A subgraph is *induced* if it contains all the edges of G it possibly can, so that $E_J = E_G \cap V_J \times V_J$. The difference is illustrated in Figure G4, lower panels.

Temporal or **"time-only" graph**: the nodes have locations in time, which means that there is directionality inherent in the whole structure and "distance" is measured in time.

Tournament: an unsigned digraph with exactly one directed edge between each pair of nodes. A property of interest for tournaments is *transitivity*. The triangle is transitive if edges A → B and B → C are accompanied by A → C; it is intransitive if it has the form A → B, B → C and then C → A (see Figure G1, lower panel). The transitivity of the entire tournament is measured by the proportion of triangles that are transitive.

Transitivity of a triangle in a digraph: based on the directional interactions among three nodes: if A → B and B → C, then A → C, the triangle of edges is transitive (see Figure G2).

Tree: a connected graph that contains no cycles; see Figure G9a. A *rooted tree* has a single node designated as the root; all other nodes can be characterised by their distance (path length) from the root, creating an intrinsic ordering for the tree; see Figure G9b.

Figure G9. Trees and a regular ring graph

(*a*) A tree has no cycles and is connected.

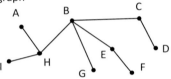

diameter = 4

(*b*) A rooted tree.

B is the root node
A, I, G, F & D are leaf nodes.
H, C & E are branch nodes.

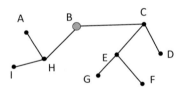

diameter = 5

(*c*) The nodes in a regular graph all have the same degree (here 2).
This is a ring graph.
It is also bipartite (ABCD | EFGH).

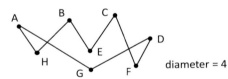

diameter = 4

Triangulation: a planar graph in which the edges create a plane tiling of cntiguous triangles, not necessarily identical. Spatial graphs based on geographic regions or political boundaries are often represented as Delaunay or other triangulations.

Walk: any alternating sequence of nodes and edges in which each node is attached to the next node in the sequence by an edge; unlike a path, a walk can use the same elements more than once (Figure G1).

Weighted graph: nodes can have weights, such as counts, and edges can have numerical weights, such as relationship intensity or measures of similarity or "distance" (Figure G3 and spatial graphs in Figure G7).

References

Abarca-Arenas, L.G. & Ulanowicz, R.E. (2002). The effects of taxonomic aggregation on network analysis. *Ecological Modelling*, **149**, 285–296.

Abdi, R.H. (2007). RV coefficient and congruence coefficient. In N. Salkind (ed.), *Encyclopedia of Measurement and Statistics*, pp. 849–853. Thousand Oaks, CA: Sage.

Abrams, P.A., Menge, B.A., Mittelbach, G.G., Spiller, D.A. & Yodzis, P. (1996). The role of indirect effects in food webs. In G. Polis & K.O. Winemuller (eds), *Food Webs: Integration of Patterns and Dynamics*, pp. 371–395. New York: Chapman & Hall.

Agresti, S., De Meo, P., Ferrara, E., Piccolo, S. & Provetti, A. (2015). Trust networks: Topology, dynamics, and measurements. *IEEE Internet Computing*, **19**, 26–35.

Ahmed, N.K., Neville, J. & Kompella, R. (2014). Network sampling: From static to streaming graphs. *ACM Transactions on Knowledge Discovery from Data*, **8**, 1–56.

Ahmed, N., Neville, J., Rossi, R.A. & Duffield, N. (2015). Efficient graphlet counting for large networks. *Proceedings of the IEEE International Conference on Data Mining*, 1–10.

Ahn, Y.-Y., Bagrow, J.P. & Lehman, S. (2010). Link communities reveal multiscale complexity in networks. *Nature*, **466**, 761–764.

Ai, D., Gravel, D., Chu, C. & Wang, G. (2013). Spatial structures of the environment and of dispersal impact species distribution in competitive metacommunities. *PLoS ONE*, **8**, e68927.

Airola, A., Pyysalo, S., Björne, J., Pahikkala, T., Ginter, F. & Salakoski, T. (2008). All-paths graph kernel for protein-protein interaction extraction with evaluation of cross-corpus learning. *BioMed Central Bioinformatics*, **9** (Suppl. 11): S2; doi:10.1186/1471-2105-9-S11-S2.

Albert, E.M., Fortuna, M.A., Godoy, J.A. & Bascompte, J. (2013). Assessing the robustness of networks of spatial genetic variations. *Ecology Letters*, **16**, 86–93.

Albert, R. & Barabási, A.-L. (2002). Statistical mechanics of complex networks. *Reviews of Modern Physics*, **74**, 47–97.

Alcántara, J.M. & Rey, P.J. (2012). Linking topological structure and dynamics in ecological networks. *The American Naturalist*, **180**, 186–199.

(2014). Community dynamics: lessons from a skeleton. In M. Benítez, O. Miramontes & A. Valiente-Banuet (eds), *Frontiers in Ecology, Evolution and Complexity*, pp. 1–8 Mexico City: CopIt-arXives.

Alcántara, J.M., Rey, P.J. & Manzaneda, A.J. (2015). A model of plant community dynamics based on replacement networks. *Journal of Vegetation Science*, **26**, 524–537.

Alenazi, M.J.F. & Sterbenz, J.P.G. (2015). Comprehensive comparison and accuracy of graph metrics in predicting network resilience. Paper presented at the International Conference of Reliable Communication Networks, Kansas City, MO.

Alexandris, J. & Karagiorgos, G. (2014). Enhanced random walk with choice: an empirical study. *International Journal on Applications of Graph Theory in Wireless ad hoc Networks and Sensor Networks*, **6**, doi:10.5121/jgraphoc.2014.6101.

Allesina, S., Bodini, A. & Bondavalli, C. (2005). Ecological subsystems via graph theory: the role of strongly connected components. *Oikos*, **110**, 164–176.

Allesina, S. & Levine, J.M. (2011). A competitive network theory of species diversity. *Proceedings of the National Academy of Science*, **108**, 5638–5642. doi:10.1073/pnas.101442818.

Almeida-Neto, M., Guimarães, P.R. & Lewinsohn, T.M. (2007). On nestedness analysis: rethinking matrix temperature and anti-nestedness. *Oikos*, **116**, 716–722.

Almeida-Neto, M., Guimarães, P.R., Loyola, R.D. & Ulrich, W. (2008). A consistent metric for nestedness analysis in ecological systems: reconciling concept and measurement. *Oikos*, **117**, 1227–1239.

Alon, N., Avin, C., Koucky, M., Kozma, G., Lotker, Z. & Tuttle, M.R. (2011). Many random walks are faster than one. *Combinatorics, Probability and Computing*, **20**, 481–502.

Altermatt, F., Seymour, M. & Martinez, N. (2013). River network properties shape α-diversity and community similarity patterns of aquatic insect communities across major drainage basins. *Journal of Biogeography*, **40**, 2249–2260.

Amarasekare, P. (2009). Competition and coexistence in animal communities. In S.A. Levin (ed.), *The Princeton Guide to Ecology*, pp. 196–201. Princeton, NJ: Princeton University Press.

Anderson, T.K. & Sukhdeo, M.V.K. (2011). Host centrality in food web networks determines parasite diversity. *PLoS ONE*, **6** (10), e26798.

Andersson, E. & Bodin, Ö. (2009). Practical tool for landscape planning? An empirical investigation of network based models of habitat fragmentation. *Ecography*, **32**, 123–132.

Angelini, R., Aloísio, G.R. & Carvalho, A.R. (2010). Mixed food web control and stability in a Cerrado river (Brazil). *Pan-American Journal of Aquatic Sciences*, **10**, 421–431.

Arditi, R. & Michalski, J. (1996). Nonlinear food web models and their responses to increased basal productivity. In G. Polis & K.O. Winemuller (eds), *Food Webs: Integration of Patterns and Dynamics*, pp. 122–133. New York: Chapman & Hall.

Atmar, W. & Patterson, B.D. (1993). The measure of order and disorder in the distribution of species in fragmented habitat. *Oecologia*, **96**, 373–382.

Avin, C., Koucký, M. & Lotker, Z. (2008). How to explore a fast-changing world (Cover time of a simple random walk on evolving graphs). In L. Aceto, I. Damgard, L.A. Goldberg, M.M. Halldórsson, A. Ingólfsdóttir & I. Walukiewicz (eds), *Automata, Languages and Programming*, pp. 121–132 Berlin: Springer.

Avin, C. & Krishnamachari, B. (2008). The power of choice in random walks: an empirical study. *Computer Networks*, **52**, 44–60.

Azeria, E.T. (2004). *Community Dynamics of Insular Biotas in Space and Time*. PhD thesis, Swedish University of Agricultural Sciences, Uppsala.

Banašek-Richter, C., et al. (2009). Complexity in quantitative food webs. *Ecology*, **90**, 1470–1477.

Baranyi, G., Saura, S., Podani, J. & Jordán, F. (2011). Contribution of habitat patches to network connectivity: redundancy and uniqueness of topological indices. *Ecological Indicators*, **11**, 1301–1310.

Barbosa, P., Hines, J., Kaplan, I., Martinson, H., Szczepaniec, A. & Szendrei, Z. (2009). Associational resistance and associational susceptibility: having right or wrong neighbours. *Annual Review of Ecology, Evolution and Systematics*, **40**, 1–20.

Barbour, A.D., Karonski, M. & Rucinski, A. (1989). A central limit theorem for decomposable random variables with applications to random graphs. *Journal of Combinatorial Theory*, Series B, **47**, 125–145.

Barcelo, H. & Laubenbacher, R. (2006). Graph-theoretic tools for dynamic network analysis. http://math.la.asu.edu/~helene/papers/blsocialjan06.pdf.

Bang-Jensen, J. & Gutin G. (2009). *Digraphs: Theory, Algorithms and Applications*. 2nd ed. London: Springer.

Bascompte, J. (2007). Networks in ecology. *Basic and Applied Ecology*, **8**, 485–490.

(2009). Disentangling the web of life. *Science*, **325**, 416–419.

Bascompte, J. & Jordano, P. (2007). Plant-animal mutualistics networks: the architecture of biodiversity. *Annual Review of Ecology, Evolution and Systematics*, **38**, 567–593.

(2014). *Mutualistic Networks*. Princeton, NJ: Princeton University Press.

Bascompte, J., Jordano, P., Melián, C.J. & Olesen, J.M. (2003). The nested assembly of plant-animal mutualistic networks. *Proceedings of the National Academy of Sciences*, **100**, 93Sep-8338.

Bascompte, J. & Stouffer, D.B. (2009). The assembly and disassembly of ecological networks. *Philosophical Transactions of the Royal Society, Series B*, **364**, 1781–1787.

Baskerville, E.B., Dobson, A.P., Bedford, T., Allesina, S., Anderson, T.M. & Pascual, M. (2011). Spatial guilds in the Serengeti food web revealed by a Bayesian group model. *PLoS Computational Biology*, **7**, e1002321; doi:10.1371/journalpcbi.1002321.

Bassett, D.S., Wymbs, N.F., Porter, M.A., Mucha, P.J., Carlson, J.M. & Grafton, S.T. (2011). Dynamic reconfiguration of human brain networks during learning. *PNAS*, **108**, 7641–7646 doi:10.1073/pnas0.1018985108.

Bastolla, U., Fortuna, M.A., Pascual-Garcia, A., Ferrera, A., Luque, B. & Bascompte, J. (2009). The architecture of mutualistic networks minimizes competition and increases biodiversity. *Nature*, **458**, 1018–1021; doi:10.1038/nature07950.

Beiler, K.J., Durall, D.M., Simard, S.W., Maxwell, S.A. & Kretzer, A.M. (2009). Architecture of the wood-wide web: *Rhizopogon* spp. genets link multiple Douglas-fir cohorts. *New Phytologist*, **185**, 543–553.

Belgrano, A., Scharler, U.M., Dunne, J. & Ulanowicz, R.E. (2005). *Aquatic Food Webs: An Ecosystem Approach*. Oxford: Oxford University Press.

Bell, A.D. (1974). Rhizome organization in relation to vegetative spread in Medeola virginiana. *Journal of the Arnold Arboretum*, **55**, 458–468.

Bellay, S., Lima, D.P., Takemoto, R.M. & Luque, J.L. (2011). A host-endoparasite network of neotropical marine fish: are there organizational patterns? *Parasitology*, **138**, 1945–1952.

Benedek, Z., Jordán, F. & Báldi, A. (2007). Topological keystone species complexes in ecological interaction networks. *Community Ecology*, **8**, 1–7.

Bengtsson, J., Angelstam, P., Elmqvist, T., Emanuelsson, U., Folke, C., Ihse, M., Moberg, F. & Nyström, M. (2003). Reserves, resilience, and dynamic landscapes. *AMBIO*, **32**, 389–396.

Benson, D.M., Grand, L.F., Vernia, C.S. & Gottwald, T.R. (2006). Temporal and spatial epidemiology of Phytophthora root rot in Fraser fir plantations. *Plant Disease*, **90**, 1171–1180.

Beth, T., Borcherding, M. & Klein, B. (1994). Valuation of trust in open networks. Paper presented at the 3rd European Symposium on Research in Computer Security, Brighton, UK.

Bienert, A., Queck, R., Schmidt, A., Bernhofer, Ch. & Maas, H.-G. (2010). Voxel space analysis of terrestrial laser scans in forests for wind field modeling. *International Archive for Photogrammetry, Remote Sensing, and Spatial Information Science*, **38**, 92–97.

Biggs, N.L., Lloyd, E.K. & Wilson, R.J. (1976). *Graph Theory 1736–1936*. Oxford: Oxford University Press.

Bille, P. (2005). A survey on tree edit distance and related problems. *Theoretical Computer Science*, **337**, 22–34; doi:10.1016/j.tcs.2004.12.030.

Bjørnstadt, O.N., Stenseth, N.C. & Saitoh, T. (1999). Synchrony and scaling in dynamics of voles and mice in northern Japan. *Ecology*, **80**, 622–637.

Blanchet, F.G., Legendre, P. & Borcard, D. (2008). Modelling directional spatial processes in ecological data. *Ecological Modelling*, **215**, 325–336.

Blanchet, F.G., Legendre, P., Maranger, R., Monti, D. & Pepin, P. (2011). Modelling the effect of directional spatial ecological processes at different scales. *Oecologia*, **166**, 357–368.

Blick, R. & Burns, K.C. (2009). Network properties of arboreal plants: are epiphytes, mistletoes and lianas structured similarly? *Perspectives in Plant Ecology, Evolution and Systematics*, **11**, 41–52; doi:10.1016/j.ppees.2008.10.002.

Blonder, B. & Dornhaus, A. (2011). Time-ordered networks reveal limitations to information flow in ant colonies. *PLoS ONE*, **6** (5), e20298.

Blonder, B., Wey, T.W., Dornhaus, A., James, R. & Sih, A. (2012). Temporal dynamics and network analysis. *Methods in Ecology and Evolution*, **3**, 958–972; doi:10.1111/j.2041-210X.2012.00236.x.

Blüthgen, N., Fründ, J., Vazquez, D.P. & Menzel, F. (2008). What do interaction network metrics tell us about specialization and biological traits? *Ecology*, **89**, 3387–3399.

Blüthgen, N., Menzel, F. & Blüthgen, N. (2006). Measuring specialization in species interaction networks. *BMC Ecology*, **6**. doi:0.86/472-6785-6-9.

Bode, M., Burrage, K. & Possingham, H.P. (2008). Using complex network metrics to predict the persistence of metapopulations with asymmetric connectivity patterns. *Ecological Modelling*, **214**, 201–209.

Bonacich, P.F. (1972). Power and centrality: a family of measures. *American Journal of Sociology*, **92**, 1170–1182.

Borcard, D., Gillet, F. & Legendre, P. (2011). *Numerical ecology with R*. New York: Springer Science.

Borcard, D., Legendre, P., Avois-Jacquet, C. & Tuomisto, H. (2004). Dissecting the spatial structure of ecological data at multiple scales. *Ecology*, **85**, 1826–1832.

Borgatti, S.P. (2005). Centrality and network flow. *Social Networks*, **27**, 55–71.

Borgwardt, K.M. & Kriegel, H.-P. (2005). Shortest-path kernels on graphs. Paper presented at the International Conference on Data Mining, Houston, TX.

Borgwardt, K.M., Ong, C.S., Schönauer, S., Vishwanathan, S.V.N., Smola, A.J. & Kriegel, H.-P. (2005). Protein function prediction via graph kernels. *Bioinformatics*, **21** (s1), 1–10; doi:10.1093/bioinformatics/bti1007.

Borgwardt, K.M., Petri, T., Vishwanathan, S.V.N. & Kriegel, H.-P. (2007). An efficient sampling scheme for comparison of large graphs. Paper presented at the Conference on Mining and Learning with Graphs, Firence, Italy.

Boyland, N.K., James, R., Mlynski, D.T., Madden, J.R. & Croft, D.P. (2013). Spatial proximity loggers for recording animal social networks: consequences of inter-logger variation in performance. *Behavioural and Ecological Sociobiology*, **67**, 1877–1890.

Brandes, U. & Fleischer, D. (2005). Centrality measures based on current flow. In V. Diekert & B. Durand (eds), *Proceedings of the 22nd Annual Symposium on Theoretical Aspects of Computer Science*, pp. 533–544. Berlin: Springer.

Brin, S. & Page, L. (1998). The anatomy of a large-scale hypertextual Web search engine. *Computer Networks & ISDN Systems*, **30**, 107–117.

Brooks, C.P., Antonovics, J. & Keitt, T.H. (2008). Spatial and temporal heterogeneity explain disease dynamics in a spatially explicit network model. *American Naturalist*, **172**, 1415-Sep9.

Brüggemann, R. & Carlsen, L. (2006). *Partial Order in Environmental Sciences and Chemistry.* Berlin: Springer.

Bryden, J., Funk, S., Geard, N., Bullock, S. & Jansen, V.A.A. (2011). Stability in flux: community structure in dynamic networks. *Journal of the Royal Society Interface*, **8**, 1031–1040.

Buhl, J., Hicks, K., Miller, E.R., Persey, S., Alinvi, O. & Sumpter, D.J.T. (2009). Shape and efficiency of wood ant foraging networks. *Behavioural Ecology & Sociobiology*, **63**, 451–460.

Bukovinszky, T., van Veen, F.J.F., Jongema, Y. & Dicke, M. (2008). Direct and indirect effects of resource quality on food web structure. *Science*, **319**, 804–807.

Bunescu, R. & Mooney, R. (2005). A shortest path dependency kernel for relation extraction. In *Proceedings of Human Language Technology Conference and Conference on Empirical Methods in Natural Language Processing*, pp. 724–731. Vancouver, Canada: Association for Computational Linguistics.

Bunn, A.G., Urban, D.L. & Keitt, T.H. (2000). Landscape connectivity: a conservation application of graph theory. *Journal of Environmental Management*, **59**, 265–278.

Burkle, L. & Irwin, R. (2009). The importance of interannual variation and bottom-up nitrogen enrichment for plant-pollinator networks. *Oikos*, **118**. doi:10.1111/j.1600-0706.2009.17740.x.

Buss, L.W. & Jackson, J.B.C. (1979). Competitive networks: nontransitive competitive relationships in cryptic coral reef environments. *American Naturalist*, **113**, 223–234.

Butts, C.T. (2009). Revisiting the foundations of network analysis. *Science*, **325**, 414–416.

Caceres, R.S. & Berger-Wolf, T. (2013). Temporal scale of dynamic networks. In P. Holme & J. Saramäki (eds), *Temporal Networks*, pp. 65–94. Berlin: Springer.

Cahill, J.F., Jr, Elle, E., Smith, G.R. & Shore, B.H. (2008). Disruption of a belowground mutualism alters interactions between plants and their floral visitors. *Ecology*, **89**, 1791–1801.

Cahill, J.F., Kembel, S.W. & Gustafson, D.J. (2005). Differential genetic differences on competitive effect and response in Arabidopsis thaliana. *Journal of Ecology*, **93**, 958–967.

Canard, E.F., Mouquet, N., Mouillot, D., Stank, M., Miklisova, D. & Gravel, D. (2014). Empirical evaluation of neutral interactions in host-parasite networks. *The American Naturalist*, **183**, 468–479.

Cantor, M., Shoemaker, L.G., Cabral, R.B., Flores, C.O., Varga, M. & Whitehead, H. (2015). Multilevel animal societies can emerge from cultural transmission. *Nature Communications*, **6**. doi:10.1038/ncomms9091.

Capitán, J.A., Arenas, A. & Guimerà, R. (2013). Degree of intervality of food webs: from body-size to models. *Journal of Theoretical Biology*, **334**, 35–44.

Cardinal, J., Collete, S. & Langerman, S. (2009). Empty region graphs. *Computational Geometry: Theory and Applications*, **42**, 183–195.

Careddu, G., Costantini, M.L., Calizza, E., Carlino, P., Bentivoglio, F., Orlandi, L. & Rossi, L. (2015). Effects of terrestrial input on macrobenthic food webs of a coastal sea are detected by stable isotope analysis in Gaeta Gulf. *Estuarine, Coastal and Shelf Science*, **154**, 158–168.

Carley, K.M. (2003). Dynamic network analysis. In R. Breiger, K.M. Carley & P. Pattison (eds), *Dynamic Social Network Modeling and Analysis: Workshop Summary and Papers*, pp. 133–145. Washington, DC: Committee on Human Factors, National Research Council.

Carrara, F., Altermatt, F., Rodriguez-Iturbe, I. & Rinaldo, A. (2012). Dendritic connectivity controls biodiversity patterns in experimental metacommunities. *Proceedings of the National Academy of Sciences*, **15**, 5761–5766.

Carrara, F., Rinaldo, A., Giometto, A. & Altermatt, F. (2014). Complex interaction of dendritic connectivity and hierarchical patch size on biodiversity in river-like landscapes. *The American Naturalist*, **183**, 13–25.

Carstensen, D.W., Sabatino, M., Trøjelsgaard, K. & Morellato, L.P.C. (2014). Beta diversity of plant-pollinator networks and the spatial turnover of pairwise interactions. *PLoS ONE*, **9** (11), e112903.

Cartozo, C.C., Garlaschelli, D. & Caldarelli, G. (2006). Graph theory and food webs. In M. Pascual & J.A. Dunne (eds), *Ecological Networks: Linking Structure to Dynamics in Food Webs*, pp. 93–117. Oxford: Oxford University Press.

Cartwright, D. & Harary, F. (1956). Structural balance: a generalization of Heider's theory. *Psychology Review*, **63**, 277–293.

Casteigts, A., Flocchini, P., Quattrociocchi, W. & Santoro, N. (2011). Time-varying graphs and dynamic networks. arXiv:1012.0009v3 [cs.DC].

Cayley, A. (1857). On the theory of analytical forms called trees. *Philosophical Magazine*, **13**, 19–30.

Cerdeira, J.O., Pinto, L.S., Cabeza, M. & Gaston, K.J. (2010). Species specific connectivity in reserve-network design using graphs. *Biological Conservation*, **143**, 408–415.

Céréghino, R., Giraudel, J.L. & Compin, A. (2001). Spatial analysis of stream invertebrates distribution in the Adour-Garonne drainage basin (France), using Kohonen self-organization maps. *Ecological Modelling*, **146**, 167–180.

Chan, J., Bailey, J. & Leckie, C. (2008). Discovering correlated spatio-temporal changes in evolving graphs. *Knowledge & Information Systems*, **16**, 53–96.

Charbonneau, D., Blonder, B. & Dornhaus, A. (2013). Social insects: a model system for network dynamics. In X.P. Holme & X.J. Saramäki (eds), *Temporal Networks*, pp. 217–244. Berlin: Springer.

Chardon, J.P., Adriaensen, F. & Matthysen, E. (2003). Incorporating landscape elements into a connectivity measure: a case study for the Speckled Wood Butterfly (*Pararge aegeria* L.). *Landscape Ecology*, **18**, 561–573.

Chartrand, G. & Lesniak, L. (2005). *Graphs and Digraphs*. 4th ed. Boca Raton, FL: Chapman & Hall/CRC.

Chave, J. (2009). Competition, neutrality, and community organization. In S.A. Levin (ed.), *The Princeton Guide to Ecology*, pp. 264–273. Princeton, NJ: Princeton University Press.

Chen, H.-W., Liu, W.-C., Davis, A.J., Jordán, F., Hwang, M.-J. & Shao, K.-T. (2008). Network position of hosts in food webs and their parasite diversity. *Oikos*, **117**, 1847–1855.

Chetkiewicz, C.-L., St. Clair, C. & Boyce, M. (2006). Corridors for conservation: integrating pattern and process. *Annual Review of Ecology, Evolution and Systematics*, **37**, 317–342.

Chung, F.R.K. (1997). *Spectral Graph Theory*. Providence, RI: American Mathematical Society.

Clay, K. (1990). The impact of parasitic and mutualistic fungi on competitive interactions among plants. In J.B. Grace & D. Tilman (eds), *Perspectives on Plant Competition*, pp. 391–412. San Diego, CA: Academic Press.

Codling, E.A., Plank, M.J. & Benhamou, S. (2008). Random walk models in biology. *Journal of the Royal Society Interface*, **5**, 813–834.

Cohen, J.E. & Palka, Z.J. (1990). A stochastic theory of community food webs. V. Intervality and triangulation in the trophic-niche overlap graph. *The American Naturalist*, **135**, 435–463.

Cohn, R.D. (1999). Comparisons of multivariate relational structures in serially correlated data. *Journal of Agricultural, Biological & Environmental Statistics*, **4**, 238–257.

Colinvaux, P.A. (1979). *Why Big Fierce Animals Are Rare: An Ecologist's Perspective*. Princeton, NJ: Princeton University Press.

Compieta, P., Di Martino, S., Bertolotto, M., Ferrucci, F. & Kechadi, T. (2007). Exploratory spatio-temporal data mining and visualization. *Journal of Visual Languages & Computing*, **18**, 255–279; doi:10.1016/j.jvc.2007.02.006.

Cook, R.E. (1988). Growth in *Medeola virginiana* clones. I. Field observations. *American Journal of Botany*, **75**, 725–731.

Cormen, T.H., Leiserson, C.E., Rivest, R.L. & Stein, C. (2009). *Introduction to Algorithms*. 3rd ed. Cambridge, MA: MIT Press.

Corson, F. (2010). Fluctuations and redundancy in optimal transport networks. *Physical Review Letters*, **104**, 048703.

Cote, D., Kehler, D.G., Bourne, C. & Wiersma, Y.F. (2009). A new measure of longitudinal connectivity for stream networks. *Landscape Ecology*, **24**, 101–113.

Craft, M.E. & Caillaud, D. (2011). Network models: an underutilized tool in wildlife epidemiology. *Interdisciplinary Perspectives on Infectious Diseases*, **2011**. doi:10.1155/2011/676949.

Craft, M.E., Volz, E., Packer, C. & Meyers, L.A. (2010). Disease transmission in territorial populations: the small-world network of Serengeti lions. *Journal of the Royal Society Interface*, **8**. doi:10.1098/rsif.2010.0511.

Cressie, N.A.C. (1993) *Statistics for Spatial Data*. 2nd ed. New York: John Wiley.

Cressie, N. & Wikle, C.K. (2011). *Statistics for Spatio-Temporal Data*. Hoboken, NJ: John Wiley.

Croft, D.P., Madden, J.R., Franks, D.W. & James, R. (2011). Hypothesis testing in animal social networks. *Trends in Ecology and Evolution*, **26**, 502–507.

Cui, S., Hero, A.O., Luo, Z.-Q. & Moura, J.M.F. (2016). *Big Data over Networks*. Cambridge: Cambridge University Press.

Cumming, G.S. (2016). Heterarchies: Reconciling networks and hierarchies. *Trends in Ecology and Evolution*, **XX31**. doi.org/10.1016/j.tree.2016.04.009.

Dale, M.R.T. (1977a). Graph theoretical analysis of the phytosociological structure of plant communities: the theoretical basis. *Vegetatio*, **34**, 137–154.

(1977b). Graph theoretical analysis of the phytosociological structure of plant communities: an application to mixed forest. *Vegetatio*, **35**, 35–46.

(1982). Phytosociological structure of seaweed communities and the invasion of *Fucus serratus* in Nova Scotia. *Canadian Journal of Botany*, **60**, 2652–2658.

(1984). The contiguity of upslope and downslope boundaries of species in a zoned community. *Oikos*, **42**, 92–96.

(1986). Overlap and spacing of species' ranges on an environmental gradient. *Oikos*, **47**, 303–308.

(1999). *Spatial Pattern Analysis in Plant Ecology*. Cambridge: Cambridge University Press.

Dale, M.R.T. & Fortin, M.-J. (2009). Spatial autocorrelation and statistical tests: some solutions. *Journal of Agricultural, Biological, and Environmental Statistics*, **14**, 188–206.

(2010). From graphs to spatial graphs. *Annual Review of Ecology, Evolution, and Systematics*, **41**, 21–38.

(2014). *Spatial Analysis*. 2nd ed. Cambridge: Cambridge University Press.

Dale, M.R.T., John, E.A. & Blundon, D.J. (1991). Contact sampling for the detection of interspecific association: a comparison in two vegetation types. *Journal of Ecology*, **79**, 781–792.

Dale, M.R.T. & Moon, J. (1988). Statistical tests on two characteristics of the shapes of cluster diagrams. *Journal of Classification*, **5**, 21–38.

Dale, M.R.T. & Thomas, A.G. (1987). The structure of weed communities in Saskatchewan fields. *Weed Science*, **35**, 348–355.

Danon, L., Ford, A.P., House, T., Jewell, C.P., Keeling, M.J., Roberts, G.O., Ross, J.V. & Vernon, M.C. (2011). Networks and the epidemiology of infectious disease. *Interdisciplinary Perspectives on Infectious Diseases*, **2011**. doi:10.1155/2011/284909.

Darlington, P.J. (1957). *Zoogeography: The Geographical Distribution of Animals*. New York: John Wiley.

Darwin, C. (1862). *On the Various Contrivances by Which British and Foreign Orchids Are Fertilized by Insects and on the Good Effects of Intercrossing*. London: John Murray.

David, F.N., Kendall, M.G. & Barton, D.E. (1966). *Symmetric Functions and Allied Tables*. Cambridge: Cambridge University Press.

Davis, J.A. (1967). Clustering and structural balance in graphs. *Human Relations*, **29**, 181–187.

Davis, K.F., D'Odorico, P., Laio, F. & Ridolfi, L. (2013). Global spatio-temporal patterns in human migration: a complex network perspective. *PLoS ONE*, **8**, e53723; doi:10.1371/journal.pone.0053723.

Decout, S., Manel, S., Miaud, C. & Luque, S. (2012). Integrative approach for landscape based graph connectivity analysis: a case study with the common frog (*Rana temporaria*), in human dominated landscapes. *Landscape Ecology*, **27**, 267–279.

de Jong, P., Aarssen, L.W. & Turkington, R. (1983). The analysis of contact sampling data. *Journal of Ecology*, **71**, 545–559.

Del Mondo, G., Stell, J.G., Claramunt, C. & Thibaud, R. (2010). A graph model for spatio-temporal evolution. *Journal of Universal Computer Science*, **16**, 1452–1477.

Demattei, C. & Cucala, L. (2009). Multiple spatio-temporal cluster detection for case event data: an ordering-based approach. *Communications in Statistics: Theory & Methods*, **40**, 3 Mar-5872.

den Boer, P.J. (1968). Spreading of risk and stabilization of animal numbers. *Acta Biotheoretica*, **18**, 165–194.

Deshpande, M., Kuramochi, M., Wale, N. & Karypis, G. (2005). Frequent substructure-based approaches for classifying chemical compounds. *IEEE Transactions on Knowledge and Data Engineering*, **17**, 1036–1050.

de Vries, H., Stevens, J.M.G. & Vervaecke, H. (2006). Measuring and testing the steepness of dominance hierarchies. *Animal Behaviour*, **71**, 585–592.

Di Battista, G., Eades, P., Tamassia, R. & Tollis, I.G. (1994). Algorithms for drawing graphs. *Computational Geometry*, **4**, 235–282.

Ding, C., He, X., Xiong, H., Peng, H. & Holbrook, S.R. (2006). Transitive closure and metric inequality of weighted graphs: detecting protein interaction modules using cliques. *International Journal of Data Mining and Informatics*, **1**, 162–177.

Do, A.-L.J. & Gross, T. (2012). *Self-Organization in Continuous Adaptive Networks*. Aalborg, Denmark: River.

Donetti, L., Neri, F. & Munoz, M.A. (2006). Optimal network topologies: expanders, cages, Ramanujan graphs, entangled networks and all that. *Journal of Statistical Mechanics*, **8**, P 8007; arXiv:cond-mat/0605565v2.

Doreian, P. & Mrvar, A. (1996). A partitioning approach to structural balance. *Social Networks*, **18**, 149–168.

Dormann, C.F. (2006). Competition hierarchy, transitivity and additivity: investigating the effect of fertilization on plant-plant interactions using three common bryophytes. *Plant Ecology*, **191**, 171–184.

(2011). How to be a specialist? Quantifying specialization in pollination networks. *Network Biology*, **1**, 1–20.

Dormann, C.F., Fründ, J., Blüthgen, N. & Gruber, B. (2009). Indices, graphs, and null models: analyzing bipartite ecological networks. *The Open Ecological Journal*, **2**, 7–24.

Dorogovtsev, S.N. & Mendes, J.F.F. (2002). Evolution of networks. *Advances in Physics*, **51**, 1079–1187.

Dos Santos, D.A., Fernandez, H.R., Cuezzo, M.G. & Dominguez, E. (2008). Sympatry inference and network analysis in biogeography. *Systematic Biology*, **57**, 432–448.

Doyle, F.I. & Smith, J.N.M. (2001). Raptors and scavengers. In C.J. Krebs, S. Boutin & R. Boonstra (eds), *Ecosystem Dynamics of the Boreal Forest: The Kluane Project*, pp. 377–404 Oxford: Oxford University Press.

Dray, S., Chessel, D. & Thioulouse, J. (2003). Co-inertia analysis and the linking of the ecological data tables. *Ecology*, **84**, 3078–3089.

Dray, S., Legendre, P. & Peres-Neto, P.R. (2006). Spatial modelling: a comprehensive framework for principal coordinate analysis of neighbour matrices (PCNM). *Ecological Modelling*, **196**, 483–493.

Dray, S., Pélissier, R., Couteron, P., Fortin, M.-J., Legendre, P., Peres-Neto, P.R., Bellier, E., et al. (2012). Community ecology in the age of multivariate multiscale spatial analysis. *Ecological Monographs*, **82**, 257–275.

Drewe, J.A., Weber, N., Carter, S.P., Bearhop, S., Harrison, X.A., Dall, S.R.X., McDonald, R.A. & Delahay, R.J. (2012). Performance of proximity loggers in recording intra- and inter-species interactions: a laboratory and field-based validation study. *PLoS ONE*, **7**, e39068.

Duboscq, J., Romano, V., Sueur, C. & MacIntosh, A.J.J. (2015). Network centrality and seasonality interact to predict lice load in a social primate. *Scientific Reports*, **6**, 22095; doi:10.1038/srep22095.

Duncan, A.J., Gunn, G.J., Lewis, F.I., Umstatter, C. & Humphry, R.W. (2012). The influence of empirical contact networks on modelling diseases in cattle. *Epidemics*, **4**, 117–123.

Dunne, J.A. (2006). The network structure of food webs. In M. Pascual & J.A. Dunne (eds), *Ecological Networks: Linking Structure to Dynamics in Food Webs*, pp. 27–86. Oxford: Oxford University Press.

Dunne, J.A., Lafferty, K.D., Dobson, A.P., Hechinger, R.F. & Kuris, A.M. (2013). Parasites affect food web structure primarily through increased diversity and complexity. *PLoSBiol*, **11** (6): e1001579; doi:10.1371/journal.pbio.1001579.

Dunne, J.A., Williams, R.J. & Martinez, N.D. (2002a). Network structure and biodiversity loss in food-webs: robustness increases with connectance. *Ecology Letters*, **5**, 558–567.

(2002b). Food-web structure and network theory: the role of connectance and size. *Proceedings of the National Academy of Science*, **99**, 12917–12922.

Durrett, R. (2007). *Random Graph Dynamics*. Cambridge: Cambridge University Press.

Dyer, R.J., Chan, D.M., Gardiakos, V.A. & Meadows, C.A. (2012). Pollination graphs: quantifying pollen pool covariance networks and the influence of intervening landscape on genetic connectivity in the North American understory tree, *Cornus florida* L. *Landscape Ecology*, **27**, 239–251.

Dyer, R.J. & Nason, J.D. (2004). Population graphs: the graph theoretic shape of genetic structure. *Molecular Ecology*, **13**, 1713–1727.

Economo, E.P. & Keitt, T.H. (2008). Species diversity in neutral metacommunities: a network approach. *Ecology Letters*, **11**, 52–62.

Edgington, E.S. (1995). *Randomization Tests*. 3rd ed. New York: Marcel Dekker.

Efron, B. & Tibshirani, R.J. (1993). *An Introduction to the Bootstrap*. New York: Chapman & Hall.

Eifrem, E. (2014). Graph theory: key to understanding big data. *Wired*, May 5.

Eiler, A. (2006). Evidence for the ubiquity of mixotrophic bacteria in the upper ocean: implications and consequences. *Applied and Environmental Microbiology*, **72** (12), 7431–7437; doi:10.1128/AEM.01559-06.

Erdös, P. (1963). On a problem in graph theory. *Mathematical Gazette*, **47**, 220–223.

Erdös, P., Harary, F. & Tutte, W.T. (1965). On the dimension of a graph. *Mathematika*, **12**, 118–122.

Erdös, P. & Moon, J.W. (1964). On subgraphs of the complete bipartite graph. *Canadian Mathematical Bulletin*, **7**, 35–39.

Erdös, P. & Rényi, A. (1960). On the evolution of random graphs. *Publications of the Mathematical Institute of the Hungarian Academy of Sciences*, **5**, 17–61.

Erös, T., Olden, J.D., Schick, R.S., Schmera, D. & Fortin, M.-J. (2012). Characterizing connectivity relationships in freshwaters using patch-based graphs. *Landscape Ecology*, **27**, 303–317.

Escoufier, Y. (1973). Le traitement des variables vectorielles. *Biometrics*, **29**, 751–760.

Escudero, A., Pajarón, S. & Gavilán, R. (1994). Saxicolous communities in the Sierra del Moncayo (Spain): a classificatory study. *Coenoses*, **9**, 15–24.

Estrada, E. (2006). Network robustness to targeted attacks: the interplay of expansibility and robustness. *The European Physical Journal B*, **52**, 563–574.

(2007). Characterization of topological keystone species: local, global and "meso-scale" centralities in food webs. *Ecological Complexity*, **4**, 46–57.

(2012). *The Structure of Complex Networks: Theory and Applications*. Oxford: Oxford University Press.

Estrada, E. & Bodin, Ö. (2008). Using network centrality measures to manage landscape connectivity. *Ecological Applications*, **18**, 1810–1825.

Facchetti, G., Iacono, G. & Altafini, C. (2011). Computing global structural balance in large-scale signed social networks. *Proceedings of the National Academy of Sciences*, **108**, 20953–20958.

Fagan, W.F. (2002). Connectivity, fragmentation, and extinction risk in dendritic metapopulations. *Ecology*, **83**, 3243–3249.

Fagan, W.F. & Calabrese, J.M. (2014). The correlated random walk and the rise of movement ecology. *Bulletin of the Ecological Society of America*, **95**, 204–206.

Fall, A., Fortin, M.-J., Manseau, M. & O'Brien, D. (2007). Spatial graphs: principles and applications for habitat connectivity. *Ecosystems*, **10**, 448–461.

Fang, W. (2005). Spatial analysis of an invasion front of *Acer platanoides*: dynamic inferences from static data. *Ecography*, **28**, 283–294.

Farine, D.R. & Whitehead, H. (2015). Constructing, conducting and interpreting animal social network analysis. *Journal of Animal Ecology*, **84**, 1144–1163.

Fattorini, S. (2007). Non-randomness in the species-area relationship: testing the underlying mechanisms. *Oikos*, **116**, 678–689.

Fattorini, S. & Fowles, A.P. (2005). A biogeographical analysis of the tenebrionid beetles (Coleoptera, Tenebrionidae) of the island of Thasos in the context of the Aegean Islands (Greece). *Journal of Natural History*, **39**, 3919–3949.

Fedor, A. & Vasas, V. (2009). The robustness of keystone indices in food webs. *Journal of Theoretical Biology*, **260**, 372–378.

Feeley, K.J., Gillespie, T.W., Lebbin, D.J. & Walter, H.S. (2007). Species characteristics associated with extinction vulnerability and nestedness rankings of birds in tropical forest fragments. *Animal Conservation*, **10**, 493–501.

Ferrari, J.R., Lookingbill, T.R. & Neel, M.C. (2007). Two measures of landscape graph connectivity: assessments across gradients in area and configuration. *Landscape Ecology*, **22**, 1315; doi:10.1007/s10980-007-9121-7.

Flitcroft, R.L., Burnett, K.M., Reeves, G.H. & Ganio, L.M. (2012). Do network relationships matter? Comparing network and instream habitat variables to explain densities of juvenile coho salmon (*Oncorhynchus kisutch*) in mid-coastal Oregon, USA. *Aquatic Conservation: Marine and Freshwater Ecosystems*, **22**, 288–302.

Fodor, E. (2013). Linking biodiversity to mutualistic networks: woody species and ectomycorrhizal fungi. *Annals of Forest Research*, **56**, 53–78.

Fortin, M.-J. & Payette, S. (2002). How to test the significance of the relation between spatially autocorrelated data at the landscape scale: a case study using fire and forest maps. *Ecoscience*, **9**, 213–218.

Fortuna, M.A. & Bascompte, J. (2008). The network approach in ecology. In F. Valladares, A. Camacho, A. Elosegui, M. Estrada & C. Garcia (eds), *Unity in Diversity: Reflections on Ecology after the Legacy of Ramon Margalef*, pp. 371–93. Madrid: Fundación BBVA.

Fortuna, M.A., Garcia, C., Guimarães, P.R. & Bascompte, J. (2008). Spatial mating networks in insect-pollinated plants. *Ecology Letters*, **11**, 490–498.

Fortuna, M.A., Gómez-Rodriguez, C. & Bascompte, J. (2006). Spatial network structure and amphibian persistence in stochastic environments. *Proceedings of the Royal Society B: Biological Sciences*, **273**, 1429–1434.

Fortuna, M.A., Popa-Lisseanu, A.G., Ibañaz, C. & Bascompte, J. (2009). The roosting spatial network of a bird-predator bat. *Ecology*, **90**, 934–944.

Fortunato, S. (2010). Community detection in graphs. arXiv:0906.0612v2 [physics.soc-ph].

Fowler, N.L. (1990). Disorderliness in plant communities: comparisons, causes, and consequences. In J.B. Grace & D. Tilman (eds), *Perspectives on Plant Competition*, pp. 291–306. San Diego, CA: Academic Press.

Franc, A. (2003). Metapopulation dynamics as a contact process on a graph. *Ecological Complexity*, **1**, 49–63; doi:10.1016/jecocom.2003.10.02.

Frank, K. (1995). Identifying cohesive subgroups. *Social Networks*, **17**, 27–56.

Frean, M. & Abraham, E.R. (2001). Rock-scissors-paper and the survival of the weakest. *Proceedings of the Royal Society of London B*, **268**, 1323–1327.

Freckleton, R.P. & Watkinson, A.R. (2001). Predicting competition coefficients for plant mixtures: reciprocity, transitivity and correlations with life-history traits. *Ecology Letters*, **4**, 348–357.

Freeman, L.C., Borgatti, S.P. & White, D.R. (1991). Centrality in valued graphs: a measure of betweenness based on network flow. *Social Networks*, **13**, 141–154.

Fuller, M.M., Wagner, A. & Enquist, B.J. (2008). Using network analysis to characterize forest structure. *Natural Resource Modelling*, **21**, 225–247.

Galpern, P., Manseau, M. & Fall, A. (2011). Patch-based graphs of landscape connectivity: a guide to construction, analysis and application for conservation. *Biological Conservation*, **144**, 44–55.

Ganguly, N., Deutsch, A. & Mukherjee, A. (2009). *Dynamics on and of Complex Networks*. Boston: Birkhäuser.

Ganio, L.M., Torgersen, C.E. & Gresswell, R.E. (2005). A geostatistical approach for describing spatial pattern in stream networks. *Frontiers in Ecology and Environment*, **3**, 138–144.

Gao, X., Xiao, B., Tao, D. & Li, X. (2010). A survey of graph edit distance. *Pattern Analysis and Applications*, **13**, 113–129; doi:10.1007/s10044-008-0141-y.

Garcia, D., Zamora, R. & Amico, G.C. (2011). The spatial scale of plant-animal interactions: effects of resource availability and habitat structure. *Ecological Monographs*, **81**, 103–121.

Garroway, C.J., Bowman, J., Carr, D. & Wilson, P.J. (2008). Applications of graph theory to landscape genetics. *Evolutionary Applications*, **1**, 620–630.

Gärtner, T. (2003). A survey of kernels for structured data. *ACM SIGKDD Explorations Newsletter*, **5** (1), 49–58.

(2008). *Kernels for Structured Data*. Singapore: World Scientific.

Gärtner, T., Flach, P.A. & Wrobel, S. (2003). On graph kernels: hardness results and efficient alternatives. In *Proceedings of the Sixteenth Annual Conference on Learning Theory and Seventh Annual Workshop on Kernel Machines, Lecture Notes in Artificial Intelligence*, pp. 129–143. New York: Springer.

Gasalla, M.A., Rodrigues, A.R. & Postuma, F.A. (2010). The trophic role of the squid Loligo plei as a keystone species in the South Brazil Bight ecosystem. *ICES Journal of Marine Science*, **67**, 1413–1424.

Gehring, C.A., Mueller, R.C., Haskins, K.E., Rubow, T.K. & Whitham, T.G. (2014). Convergence in mycorrhizal fungal communities to drought, plant competition, parasitism, and susceptibility to herbivory: consequences for fungi and host plants. *Frontiers in Microbiology*, **5**, 306; doi:10.3389/micb.2014.00306.

Gilarranz, L.J. & Bascompte, J. (2012). Spatial network structure and metapopulation persistence. *Journal of Theoretical Biology*, **297**, 11–16.

Gilarranz, L.J., Hastings, A. & Bascompte, J. (2015). Inferring topology from dynamics in spatial networks. *Theoretical Ecology*, **8** doi:10.1007/s12080-014-0231-y.

Girvan, M. & Newman, M.E.J. (2002). Community structure in social and biological networks. *Proceedings of the National Academy of Sciences*, **99**, 7821–7826.

Glaz, J., Naus, J. & Wallenstein, S. (2001). *Scan Statistics*. New York: Springer.

Gleick, J. (1987). *Chaos: The Making of a New Science*. New York: Viking.

Godfrey, S.S. (2013). Networks and the ecology of parasite transmission: a framework for wildlife parasitology. *International Journal for Parasitology: Parasites and Wildlife*, **2**, 235–245.

Godfrey, S.S., Moore, J.A., Nelson, N.J. & Bull, C.M. (2010). Social network structure and parasite infection patterns in a territorial reptile, the Tuatara (*Sphenodon punctatus*). *International Journal of Parasitology*, **40**, 1575–1585.

Gollo, L.L. & Breakspear, M. (2014). The frustrated brain: from dynamics on motifs to communities and networks. *Philosophical Transactions of the Royal Society, Series B*, **369**; doi:10.1098/rstb.2013.0532.

Gómez, J.M., Perfectii, F. & Jordano, P. (2011). The functional consequences of mutualistic network architecture. *PLoS ONE*, **6**, e16143; doi.10.1371/journal.pone.0016143.

Gómez, S., Montiel, J., Torres, D. & Fernández, A. (2012). MultiDendrograms: variable-group agglomerative hierarchical clusterings. arXiv:1201.1623v2.

Goodall, D.W. (1966). The nature of the mixed community. *Proceedings of the Ecological Society of Australia*, **1**, 84–96.

Gordon, A.D. & Birks, H.J.B. (1972). Numerical methods in Quaternary paleoecology. I. Zonation of pollen diagrams. *New Phytologist*, **71**, 961–979.

(1974). Numerical methods in Quaternary paleoecology. II. Comparison of pollen diagrams. *New Phytologist*, **73**, 221–249.

Grace, J.B., Guntespurgen, G.R. & Keough, J. (1993). The examination of a competition matrix for transitivity and intransitive loops. *Oikos*, **68**, 91–98.

Graham, S.P., Hassan, H.K., Burkett-Cadena, N.D., Guyer, C. & Unnasch, T.R. (2009). Nestedness of ectoparasite-vertebrate host networks. *PLoS ONE*, **4**, e7873; doi:10.1371/journal.pone.0007873.

Grant, E.H.C., Lowe, W.H. & Fagan, W.F. (2007). Living in the branches: population dynamics and ecological processes in dendritic networks. *Ecology Letters*, **10**, 165–175.

Greenland, S., Pearl, J. & Robins, J.M. (1999). Causal diagrams for epidemiological research. *Epidemiology*, **10**, 37–48.

Grime, J.P. (1979). *Plant Strategies and Vegetation Processes*. New York: John Wiley.

Grindrod, P., Parsons, M.C., Higham, D.J. & Estrada, E. (2011). Communicability across evolving networks. *Physical Review E*, **83**, 046120; doi:10.1103/PhysRevE.83.046120.

Gross, T. & Blasius, B. (2008). Adaptive coevolutionary networks: a review. *Journal of the Royal Society Interface*, **5**, 259–271.

Guerrero, C., Milenkovic, T., Pržulj, N., Kaiser, P. & Huang, L. (2008). Characterization of the proteasome interaction network using a qtax-based tag-team strategy and protein interaction network analysis. *Proceedings of the National Academy of Sciences*, **105**, 13333–13338.

Guha, R., Kumar, K., Raghavan, P. & Tomkins, A. (2004). Propagation of trust and distrust. Paper ACM 1-58113-844-X/04/0005 presented at ACM WWW, New York.

Guillaume, J.-L. & Latapy, M. (2006). Bipartite graphs as models of complex networks. *Physica A*, **371**, 795–813.

Guimerà, R. & Sales-Pardo, M. (2006). Form follows function: the architecture of complex networks. *Molecular Systems Biology*, **2** Article 42. doi:10.1038/msb4100082.

(2009). Missing and spurious interactions and the reconstruction of complex networks. *Proceeding of the National Academy of Sciences*, **52**, 22073–22078.

Hagen, M., et al. (2012). Biodiversity, species interactions and ecological networks in a fragmented world. *Advances in Ecological Research*, **46**, 89–185.

Hamede, R.K., Bashford, J., McCallum, H. & Jones, M. (2009). Contact networks in a wild Tasmanian devil (*Sarcophilus harrisii*) population: using social network analysis to reveal seasonal variability in social behavior and its implications for transmission of devil facial tumour disease. *Ecology Letters*, **12**, 1–11.

Hammer, A.C. & Pitchford, J.W. (2005). The role of mixotrophy in plankton bloom dynamics and the consequences for productivity. *ICES Journal of Marine Science*, **62**, 833–840.

Hampton, S.E., Strasser, C.A., Tewksbury, J.J., Gram, W.K., Budden, A.E., Batcheller, A.L., Duke, C.S. & Porter, J.H. (2013). Big data and the future of ecology. *Frontiers of Ecology and Environment*, **11**, 156–162; doi:10.1890/120103.

Hanski, I. (2009). Metapopulations and spatial population processes. In S.A. Levin (ed.), *The Princeton Guide to Ecology*, pp. 177–185. Princeton, NJ: Princeton University Press.

Harary, F. (1953). On the notion of balance of a signed graph. *Michigan Mathematical Journal*, **2**, 143–146.

(1959). On the measurement of structural balance. *Behavioral Science*, **4**, 316–323.

(1969). *Graph Theory*. Reading MA: Addison-Wesley.

Harary, F. & Gupta, G. (1997). Dynamic graph models. *Mathematical & Computer Modelling*, **25**, 79–87.

Harper, J.L. (1977). *Population Biology of Plants*. London: Academic Press.

Harvey, E. & Miller, T.E. (1996). Variance in composition of inquiline communities in leaves of *Sarracenia purpurea* L. on multiple spatial scales. *Oecologia*, **108**, 562–566.

Hastie, T., Tibshirani, R. & Friedman, J. (2009). *The Elements of Statistical Learning: Data Mining, Inference, and Prediction*. 2nd ed. New York: Springer.

Hobaiter, C., Poisot, T., Zuberbühler, K., Hoppitt, W. & Gruber, T. (2014). Social network analysis shows direct evidence for social transmission of tool use in wild chimpanzees. *PLOS Biology*, **12**, e1001960.

Hock, K. & Mumby, P.J. (2015). Quantifying the reliability of dispersal paths in connectivity networks. *Journal of the Royal Society Interface*, **12**, 20150013; doi:10.1098/rsif.2015.0013.

Hodges, K.E., Krebs, C.J., Hik, D.S., Stefan, C.I., Gillis, E.A. & Doyle, C.E. (2001). Snowshoe hare demography. In C.J. Krebs, S. Boutin & R. Boonstra (eds), *Ecosystem Dynamics of the Boreal Forest: The Kluane Project*, pp. 141–178 Oxford: Oxford University Press.

Hofmann, T., Schölkopf, B. & Smola, A.J. (2008). Kernel methods in machine learning. *The Annals of Statistics*, **36**, 1171–1220; doi:10.1214/009053607000000677.

Hollén, L.I. & Radford, A.N. (2009). The development of alarm call behavior in mammals and birds. *Animal Behaviour*, **78**, 791–800.

Holme, P. (2013). Epidemiologically optimal static networks from temporal network data. *PLoS Computational Biology*, **9**, e1003142.

Holme, P. & Saramäki, J. (2011). Temporal networks. *Physics Reports*, **519**, 97–125.

(2013). *Temporal Networks*. Berlin: Springer.

Holt, R.D. (2002). Food webs in space: on the interplay of dynamic in stability and spatial processes. *Ecological Research*, **17**, 261–273.

(2009). Predation and community organization. In S.A. Levin (ed.), *The Princeton Guide to Ecology*, pp. 274–281. Princeton, NJ: Princeton University Press.

Holt, R.D. & Hoopes, M.F. (2005). Food web dynamics in a metacommunity context: modules and beyond. In P. Holyoak, M.A. Leibold & R.D. Holt (eds), *Metacommunities: Spatial Dynamics and Ecological Communities*, pp. 68–93. Chicago: Chicago University Press.

Holyoak, M. (2000). Habitat subdivision causes changes in food web structure. *Ecology Letters*, **3**, 509–515.

Horn, H.S. (1975). Markovian processes of forest succession. In M.L. Cody & J.M. Diamond (eds), *Ecology and Evolution of Communities*, pp. 196–211. Cambridge, MA: Belknap Press.

(1976). Succession. In R.M. May (ed.), *Theoretical Ecology: Principles and Applications*, pp. 187–204. Philadelphia: Saunders.

Horváth, D.X. & Kertész, J. (2014). Spreading dynamics on networks: the role of burstiness, topology and non-stationarity. *New Journal of Physics*, **16**. doi:10.1088/1367-2630/16/7/73037.

Howard, T.G. (2001). The relationship of total and per-gram rankings in competitive effect to the natural abundance of herbaceous perennials. *Journal of Ecology*, **89**, 110–117.

Huffaker, C.B. (1958). Experimental studies on predation: dispersion factors and predator-prey oscillations. *Hilgardia*, **27**, 343–383.

Hulovatyy, Y., Chen, H. & Milenkovic, T. (2015). Exploring the structure and function of temporal networks with dynamic graphlets. *Bioinformatics*, **31**, 1171–1180.

Husté, A. & Boulinier, T. (2011). Determinants of bird community composition on patches in suburbs of Paris, France. *Biological Conservation*, **144**, 243–252.

Ilany, A., Barocas, A., Koren, L., Kam, M. & Geffen, E. (2013). Structural balance in the social networks of a wild mammal. *Animal Behaviour*, **85**, 1397–1405.

Illian, J.B., Penttinen A., Stoyan H. & Stoyan, D. (2008). *Statistical Analysis and Modelling of Spatial Point Patterns*. New York: John Wiley.

Ings, T.C., et al. (2008). Ecological networks – beyond food webs. *Journal of Animal Ecology*, **78**. doi:10.1111/j.1365-2656.2008.01460.x.

Itzhaki, Z., Akiva, E. & Margalit, H. (2010). Preferential use of protein domain pairs as interaction mediators: order and transitivity. *Bioinformatics*, **26**, 2564–2570.

Ives, A.R. & Godfray, H.C.J. (2006). Phylogenetic analysis of trophic associations. *The American Naturalist*, **168**, E1–E14; www.jstor.org/stable/10.1086/505157.

Iyengar, V.S. (2005). Space-time clusters with flexible shapes. *Morbidity and Mortality Weekly Report*, **54**, 71–76.

Jacquez, G.M. (1996). A *k* nearest neighbour test for space–time interaction. *Statistical Medicine*, **15**, 1935–1949.

James, A., Pitchford, J.W. & Plank, M.J. (2012). Disentangling nestedness from models of ecological complexity. *Nature*, **487**, 227–230.

James, P., Rayfield, B., Fortin, M.-J., Fall, A. & Farley, G. (2005). Reserve network design combining spatial graph theory and species' spatial requirements. *Geomatica*, **59**, 323–333.

James, P.M.A., Fleming, R.A. & Fortin, M.-J. (2010). Identifying significant scale-specific spatial boundaries using wavelets and null models: spruce budworm defoliation in Ontario, Canada, as a case study. *Landscape Ecology*, **25**, 873–887.

James, P.M.A., Fortin, M.-J., Fall, A., Kneeshaw, D. & Messier, C. (2007). The effects of spatial legacies following shifting management practices and fire on boreal forest age structure. *Ecosystems*, **10**, 1261–1277.

James, R., Croft, D.P. & Krause, J. (2009). Potential banana skins in animal social network analysis. *Behavioural Ecology and Sociobiology*, **63**, 989–997.

Jelínková, H., Tremblay, F. & DesRochers, A. (2009). Molecular and dendrochronological analyses of natural root grafting in *Populus tremuloides* (Salicaceae). *American Journal of Botany*, **96**, 1500–1505; doi:10.3732/ajb.0800177.

Jiang, L.Q. & Zhang, W.J. (2015). Determination of keystone species in CSM food web: A topological analysis of network structure. *Network Biology*, **5**, 13–33.

Johnson, S., Domínguez-García, V. & Muñoz, M.A. (2013). Factors determining nestedness in complex networks. *PLoS ONE*, **8** doi:10.1371/journal.pone.0074025.

Jones, D.A. (1966). On the polymorphism of cyanogenesis in *Lotus corniculatus*: Selection by animals. *Canadian Journal of Genetics and Cytology*, **8**, 556–567.

Joppa, L.N., Bascompte, J., Montoya, J.M., Solé, R.V., Sanderson, J. & Pimm, S.L. (2009). Reciprocal specialization in ecological networks. *Ecology Letters*, **12**, 961–969; doi:101111/j.1461-0248.2009.01341.x.

Jordán, F. (2009). Keystone species and food webs. *Philosophical Transactions of the Royal Society, Series B*, **364**, 1733–1741.

Jordán, F., Liu, W.-C. & Davis, A.J. (2006). Topological keystone species: measures of positional importance in food webs. *Oikos*, **112**, 535–546.

Jordán, F., Takács-Sánta, A. & Molnár, I. (1999). A reliability theoretical quest for keystones. *Oikos*, **86**, 453–462.

Jordano, P. (1987). Patterns of mutualistic interactions in pollination and seed dispersal: connectance, dependence asymmetries, and coevolution. *American Naturalist*, **129**, 657–677.

  (2010). Coevolution in multispecific interactions among free-living species. *Evolution, Education, and Outreach*, **3**, 40–46.

Jordano, P., Bascompte, J. & Olesen, J.M. (2003). Invariant properties in coevolutionary networks of plant-animal interactions. *Ecology Letters*, **6**, 69–81.

  (2006). The ecological consequences of complex topology and nested structure in pollination webs. In N.M. Waser & J. Olleton (eds), *Plant-Pollinator Interactions*, pp. 173–199. Chicago: Chicago University Press.

Juenger, M. & Mutzel, P. (2003). *Graph Drawing Software*. Berlin: Springer.

Kampichler, C., Angeler, D.G., Holmes, R.T., Leito, A., Svensson, S., van der Jeungd, H.P. & Wesolowski, T. (2014). Temporal dynamics of bird community composition: an analysis of baseline conditions from long-term data. *Oecologia*, **175**, 1301–1313; doi:10.1007/s00442-014-2979-6.

Karsai, M., Kivelä, M., Pan, R.K., Kaski, K., Kertész, J., Barabási, A.L. & Saramäki, J. (2011). Small but slow world: how network topology and burstiness slow down spreading. *Physical Review E*, **83**, 025102. arXiv:1006.2125v3.

Katz, L. (1953). A new status index derived from sociometric analysis. *Psychometrica*, **18**, 39–43.

Keats, D.W., South, G.R. & Steele, D.H. (1985). Algal biomass and diversity in the upper subtidal at a pack-ice disturbed site in eastern Newfoundland. *Marine Ecology Progress Series*, **25**, 151–163.

Keddy, P.A. & Shipley, B. (1989). Competitive hierarchies in herbaceous plant communities. *Oikos*, **54**, 234–241.

Keeling, M.J. (1999). The effects of local spatial structure on epidemiological invasions. *Proceedings of the Royal Society of London, Series B*, **266**, 859–867.

(2005). The implications of network structure for epidemic dynamics. *Theoretical Population Biology*, **67**, 1–8.

Keeling, M.J. & Eames, K.T.D. (2005). Networks and epidemic models. *Journal of the Royal Society Interface*, **2**, 295–307; doi:10.1098/rsif.2005.0051.

Kéfi, S., Berlow, E.L., Wieters, E.A., Joppa, L.N., Wood, S.A., Brose, U. & Navarrete, S.A. (2015). Network structure beyond food webs: mapping non-trophic and trophic interactions on Chilean rocky shores. *Ecology*, **96**, 291–303.

Keitt, T.H., Urban, D.L. & Milne, B.T. (1997). Detecting critical scales in fragmented landscapes. *Conservation Ecology*, **1**, 4. www.consecol.org/vol1/iss1/art4/.

Kempe, D., Kleinberg, J. & Kumar, A. (2002). Connectivity and inference problems for temporal networks. *Journal of Computer Systems Science*, **64**, 820–842.

Kent, M. & Coker, P. (1992). *Vegetation Description and Analysis*. Boca Raton, FL: CRC Press.

Kepner, J., Ricke, D.O. & Hutchison, D. (2013). Taming biological big data with D4M. *Lincoln Laboratory Journal*, **20**, 82–91.

Kernighan, B.W. & Lin, S. (1970). An efficient heuristic procedure for partitioning graphs. *Bell System Technical Journal*, **49**, 291–307.

Kim, H. & Anderson, R. (2012). Temporal node centrality in complex networks. *Physical Review E*, **85**, 026107.

Kirchhoff, G. (1847). Über die Auflösung der Gleichungen. *Annals of Physical Chemistry*, **72**, 497–508.

Kirkpatrick, D.G. & Radke, J.D. (1985). A framework for computational morphology. *Computational Geometry, Machine Intelligence and Pattern Recognition*, **2**, 217–248.

Kisilevich, S., Mansmann, F., Nanni, M. & Rinzivillo, S. (2010). Spatio-temporal clustering: a survey. In O. Maimon & L. Rokach (eds), *Data Mining and Knowledge Discovery Handbook*, pp. 855–874. New York: Springer.

Kitching, R.L. (2000). *Food Webs and Container Habitats*. Cambridge: Cambridge University Press.

Klovdahl, A.S. (1985). Social networks and the spread of infectious diseases: the AIDS example. *Social Science and Medicine*, **21**, 1203–1218.

Kneitel, J.M. & Miller, T.E. (2003). Dispersal rates affect species composition in metacommunities of *Sarracenia purpurea* L. inquilines. *American Naturalist*, **162**, 165–171.

Kocarev, L. & Vattay, G. (2010). *Complex Dynamics in Communication Networks*. Berlin: Springer.

Kolaczyk, E.D. (2009). *Statistical Analysis of Network Data*. New York: Springer.

Kolaczyk, E.D. & Csárdi, G. (2014). *Statistical Analysis of Network Data with R*. New York: Springer.

Kondoh, M., Kato, S. & Sakato, Y. (2010). Food webs are built up with nested subwebs. *Ecology*, **91**, 3123–3130.

Kondor, R.I. & Lafferty, J. (2002). Diffusion kernels on graphs and other discrete input spaces. *Proceedings of the International Conference on Machine Learning* (ICML).

Kondor, R., Shervashidze, N. & Borgwardt, K.M. (2009). The graphlet spectrum. Paper presented at the 26th International Conference on Machine Learning, Montreal.

Kost, C., de Oliveira, E.G., Knoch, T.A. & Wirth, R. (2005). Spatio-temporal permanence and plasticity of foraging trails in young and mature leaf-cutting ant colonies (*Atta* sp.). *Journal of Tropical Ecology*, **21**, 677–688.

Kostakos, V. (2009). Temporal graphs. *Physica A*, **388**, 1007–1023.

Kovanen, L., Karsai, M., Kaski, K., Kertész, J. & Saramäki, J. (2011). Temporal motifs in time-dependent networks. *Journal of Statistical Mechanics*, **11**, P11005; arXiv:1107.5646v2.

(2013a). Temporal motifs. In P. Holme & J. Saramäki (eds), *Temporal Networks*, pp. 119–134. Berlin: Springer.

Kovanen, L., Kaski, K., Kertesz, J. & Saramäki, J. (2013b). Temporal motifs reveal homophily, gender-specific patterns, and group talk in call sequences. *Proceedings of the National Academy of Sciences*, **110**, 18070–18075.

Krause, A.E., Frank, K.A., Mason, D.M., Ulanowicz, R.E. & Taylor, W.W. (2003). Compartments revealed in food-web structure. *Nature*, **426**, 282–285.

Krause, J., Croft, D.P. & James, R. (2007). Social network theory in the behavioural sciences. *Behavioural Ecology and Sociobiology*, **62**, 15–27.

Krebs, C.J. (2010). Of lemmings and snowshoe hares: the ecology of northern Canada. *Proceedings of the Royal Society, Series B*, **278** doi:10.1098/rspb.2010.1992.

Krebs, C.J., Boutin, S. & Boonstra, R. (2001). *Ecosystem dynamics of the boreal forest: the Kluane project*. Oxford: Oxford University Press.

Krishna, A., Guimarães, P.R., Jordano, P. & Bascompte, J. (2008). A neutral-niche theory of nestedness in mutualistic networks. *Oikos*, **117**, 1609–1618; doi:10.1111/j.2008.0030-1299.16540.x.

Kunegis, J. (2014). Applications of structural balance in signed social networks. arXiv:1402.6865v1 [cs.S1].

Kunegis, J., Schmidt, S., Lommatzsch, A., Lerner, J., De Luca, E.W. & Albayrak, S. (2010). Spectral analysis of signed graphs for clustering, prediction, and visualization. In *Proceedings of the 10th SIAM International Conference on Data Mining*, pp. 559–570. SIAM: Columbus, Ohio.

Kurvers, R.H.J.M., Krause, J., Croft, D.P., Wilson, A.D.M. & Wolf, M. (2014). The evolutionary and ecological consequences of animal social networks: emerging issues. *Trends in Ecology and Evolution*, **29**, 326–335

Labonne, J., Ravigné, V., Parisi, B. & Gaucherel, C. (2008). Linking dendritic network structures to population demogenetics: the downside of connectivity. *Oikos*, **117**, 1479–1490.

Laird, R.A. & Schamp, B.S. (2006). Competitive intransitivity promotes species coexistence. *American Naturalist*, **168**, 182–193.

(2008). Does local competition increase the coexistence of species in intransitive networks? *Ecology*, **89**, 237–247.

Laita, A., Kotiaho, J.S. & Mönkkönen, M. (2011). Graph-theoretic connectivity measures: what do they tell us about connectivity? *Landscape Ecology*, **26**, 951–967.

Lamour, A., Termorshuizen, A.J., Volker, D. & Jeger, M.J. (2007). Network formation by rhizomorphs of *Armillaria lutea* in natural soil: their description and ecological significance. *FEMS Microbial Ecology*, **62**, 222–232.

Landau, H.G. (1951). On dominance relations and the structure of animal societies: I. Effects of inherent characteristics. *Bulletin of Mathematica Biophysics*, **13**, 1–19.

Lankau, R.A., Wheeler, E., Bennett, A.E. & Strauss, S.Y. (2010). Plant-soil feedbacks contribute to an intransitive competitive network that promotes genetic and species diversity. *Journal of Ecology*, **99** doi 10.1111/j.1365-2745.2010.01736.x.

Lapointe, F.-J. & Legendre, P. (1990). A statistical framework to test the consensus of two nested classifications. *Systematic Zoology*, **39**, 1–13.

(1995). Comparison tests for dendrograms: a comparative evaluation. *Journal of Classification*, **12**, 265–282.

Lawson, A.B. (2013). *Bayesian Disease Mapping: Hierarchical Modeling in Spatial Epidemiology*. Boca Raton, FL: CRC Press.

Layeghifard, M., Makarenkov, V. & Peres-Neto, P.R. (2015). Spatial and species compositional networks for inferring connectivity patterns in ecological communities. *Global Ecology and Biogeography*, **24**, 718–727.

Leal, W., Llanos, E.J., Retrepo, G., Suarez, C.F. & Patarrayo, M.E. (2016). How frequently do clusters occur in hierarchical clustering analysis? A graph theoretical approach to studying ties in proximity. *Journal of Cheminformatics*, **8** doi:10.1186/s13321-016-0114-x.

Lee, S.H., Kim, P.-J. & Jeong, H. (2006). Statistical properties of sampled networks. *Physical Review E*, **73** 016102.

Legendre, P. (1993). Spatial autocorrelation: trouble or new paradigm? *Ecology*, **74**, 1659–1673.

Legendre, P. & Fortin, M.-J. (1989). Spatial pattern and ecological analysis. *Vegetatio*, **80**, 107–138.

Legendre, P. & Legendre, L. (2012). *Numerical Ecology*. 3rd ed. Amsterdam: Elsevier.

Leibold, M.A. (2009). Spatial and metacommunity dynamics in biodiversity. In S.A. Levin (ed.), *The Princeton Guide to Ecology*, pp. 312–319. Princeton, NJ: Princeton University Press.

Leskovec, J. & Faloutsos, C. (2006). Sampling from large graphs. In *Proceedings of the 12th ACM SIGKDD International Conference on Knowledge Discovery and Data Mining*, pp. 631–636. ACM: New York, USA

Leskovec, J., Huttenlocher, D. & Kleinberg, J. (2010). Signed networks in social media. Paper ACM 978-1-60558-929-9/10/04 presented at ACM CHI, Atlanta, GA, USA.

Lesne, A. (2006). Complex networks: from graph theory to biology. *Letters in Mathematical Physics*, **78**, 235–262.

Levine, J.M. (1999). Indirect facilitation: evidence and predictions from a riparian community. *Ecology*, **80**, 1762–1769.

Levinton, J.S. (1982). *Marine Ecology*. Engelwood Cliffs, NJ: Prentice Hall.

Libralato, S., Christensen, V. & Pauly, D. (2006). A method for identifying keystone species in food web models. *Ecological Modelling*, **195**, 153–171.

Liebhold, A., Koenig, W.D. & Bjørnstadt, O.N. (2004). Spatial synchrony in population dynamics. *Annual Review of Ecology, Evolution & Systematics*, **35**, 467–490.

Lihoreau, M., Raine, N.E., Reynolds, A.M., Stelzer, R.J., Lim, K.S., Smith, A.D., Osborne, J.L. & Chittka, L. (2013). Unravelling the mechanisms of trapline foraging in bees. *Communicative & Integrative Biology*, **6**, e22701.

Little, L.R. & Dale, M.R.T. (1999). A method for analyzing spatio-temporal pattern in plant establishment, tested on a *Populus balsamifera* clone. *Journal of Ecology*, **87**, 620–627.

Liu, W., Li, D., Wang, J., Xie, H., Zhu, Y. & He, F. (2009). Proteome-wide prediction of signal flow direction in protein interaction networks based on interacting domains. *Molecular and Cellular Proteomics*, **8**, 2063–2070.

Loewe, K., Grueschow, M., Stoppel, C.M., Kruse, R. & Borgelt, C. (2014). Fast construction of voxel-level functional connectivity graphs. *BMC Neuroscience*, **15**, 78; doi:10.1186/1471-2202-15-78.

Lomolino, M.V. (2006). Investigating causality of nestedness in insular communities: selective immigrations or extinctions. *Journal of Biogeography*, **23**, 699–703.

Loreau, M. (2010). *From Populations to Ecosystems*. Princeton, NJ: Princeton University Press.

Lorenz, K. (1991). *Here Am I – Where Are You?* New York: Harcourt.

Lovász, L. (1993). Random walks on graphs: a survey. In *Combinatorics: Paul Erdös Is Eighty*, pp. 1–46 Bolyai Mathematical Studies, vol. 2. Budapest: Keszthely.

Lugo-Martinez, J. & Radivojac, P. (2014). Generalized graphlet kernels for probabilistic inference in sparse graphs. *Network Science*, **2**, 254–276.

Lundberg, J. & Moberg, F. (2003). Mobile link organisms and ecosystem functioning: implications for ecosystem resilience and management. *Ecosystems*, **6**, 87–98.

Lundgren, J.R. & Maybee, J.S. (1984). Food webs with interval competition graphs. In *Graphs and Applications: Proceedings of the First Colorado Symposium on Graph Theory*, pp. 231–244. New York: John Wiley.

Luque, S., Saura, S. & Fortin, M.-J. (2012). Landscape connectivity analysis for conservation: insights from combining new methods with ecological and genetic data. *Landscape Ecology*, **27**, 153–157.

Maiya, A.S. (2011). *Sampling and Inference in Complex Networks*. PhD thesis, Department of Computer Science, University of Illinois at Chicago.

Malliaros, F.D. & Vazirgiannis, M. (2013). Clustering and community detection in directed networks: a survey. *Physics Reports*, **533**, 95–142; arXiv:1308.0971v1 [cs.SI].

Manly, B.F.J. (2006). *Randomization, Bootstrap, and Monte Carlo Methods in Biology*. 3rd ed. Boca Raton, FL: Chapman & Hall/CRC.

Mantzaris, A.V. & Higham, D.J. (2013). Dynamic communicability predicts infectiousness. In P. Holme & J. Saramäki (eds), *Temporal Networks*, pp. 283–294. Berlin: Springer.

Marsh, M.K., McLeod, S.R., Hutchings, M.R. & White, P.C.L. (2011). Use of proximity loggers and network analysis to quantify social interactions in free-ranging wild rabbit populations. *Wildlife Research*, **38**, 1–12.

Marsten, R. (2014). Is graph theory key to understanding big data? *Wired*, March.

Martinez, N.D. (1991). Artifacts or attributes? Effects of resolution on the Little Rock Lake food web. *Ecological Monographs*, **61**, 367–392.

(1992). Constant connectance in community foodwebs. *American Naturalist*, **139**, 1208–1218.

Mason, O. & Verwoerd, M. (2007). Graph theory and networks in biology. *IET Systems Biology*, **1**, 89–119.

May, R.M. (2006). Network structure and the biology of populations. *Trends in Ecology and Evolution*, **21**. doi:10.1016/tree.2006.03.013.

Maynard-Smith, J. (1982). *Evolution and the Theory of Games*. Cambridge: Cambridge University Press.

McCann, K. (2009). The structure and stability of food webs. In S.A. Levin (ed.), *The Princeton Guide to Ecology*, pp. 305–311. Princeton, NJ: Princeton University Press.

(2012). *Food Webs*. Princeton, NJ: Princeton University Press.

McIntire, E.J.B. & Fajardo, A. (2009). Beyond description: the active and effective way to infer processes from spatial patterns. *Ecology*, **90**, 46–56.

McQuaid, C.F. & Britton, N.F. (2013). Network dynamics contribute to structure: nestedness in mutualistic networks. *Bulletin of Mathematical Biology*, **75**, 2372–2388.

McRae, B.H. & Beier, P. (2007). Circuit theory predicts gene flow in plant and animal populations. *Proceedings of the National Academy of Sciences*, **10**, 19885–19890.

McRae, B.H., Dickson, B.G., Keitt, T.H. & Shah, V.B. (2008). Using circuit theory to model connectivity in ecology, evolution, and conservation. *Ecology*, **89**, 2712–2724.

Medan, D., Perazzo, R.P.J., Devoto, M., Burgos, E., Zimmermann, M.G., Ceva, H. & Delbue, A.M. (2007). Analysis and assembling of network structure in mutualistic systems. *Journal of Theoretical Biology*, **246**, 510–521.

Melián, C.J. & Bascompte, J. (2004). Food web cohesion. *Ecology*, **85**, 352–358.

Melián, C.J., Bascompte, J., Jordano, P. & Křivan, V. (2009). Diversity in a complex ecological network with two interaction types. *Oikos*, **118**, 122–130.

Menge, B.A. (1995). Indirect effects in a marine rocky intertidal interaction webs: patterns and importance. *Ecological Monographs*, **65**, 21–74.

Meyers, L.A. (2006). Predicting epidemics on directed contact networks. *Journal of Theoretical Biology*, **240**, 400–418.

    (2007). Contact network epidemiology: bond percolation applied to infectious disease prediction and control. *Bulletin of the American Mathematical Society*, **44**, 63–86.

Miele, V., Picard, F. & Dray, S. (2014). Spatially constrained clustering of ecological networks. *Methods in Ecology and Evolution*, **5**, 771–779.

Mihail, J.D. & Bruhn, J.N. (2005). Foraging behavior of *Armillaria* rhizomorph systems. *Mycological Research*, **109**, 1195–1207.

Milenkovic, T. (2008). *Graph-Theoretical Approaches for Studying Biological Networks*. PhD thesis, Department of Computer Science, University of California, Irvine.

Milenkovic, T. & Pržulj, N. (2008). Uncovering biological network function via graphlet degree signatures. *Cancer Informatics*, **6**, 257–273.

Milo, R., Shen-Orr, S., Itzkovitz, S., Kashtan, N., Chklovskii, D. & Alon, U. (2002). Network motifs: simple building blocks of complex networks. *Science*, **298**, 824–827.

Min, B. & Goh, K.I. (2013). Burstiness: measures, models, and dynamic consequences. In P. Holme & J. Saramäki (eds), *Temporal Networks*, pp. 41–64. Berlin: Springer.

Minor, E.S. & Urban, D.L. (2007). Graph theory as a proxy for spatially explicit population models in conservation planning. *Ecological Applications*, **17**, 1771–1782.

    (2008). A graph-theory framework for evaluating landscape connectivity and conservation planning. *Conservation Biology*, **22**, 297–307.

Mitchell, R.J. (1992). Testing evolutionary and ecological hypotheses using path analysis and structural equation modelling. *Functional Ecology*, **6**, 123–129.

Mladenoff, D. (1999). *Spatial Modeling of Forest Landscape Change*. Cambridge: Cambridge University Press.

Mnih, V., et al. (2015). Human-level control through deep reinforcement learning. *Nature*, **518**, 529–533; doi:10.1038/nature14236.

Mnih, V., Kavukcuoglu, K., Silver, D., Graves, A., Antonoglu, I., Wierstra, D. & Riedmiller, M. (2013). Playing Atari with deep reinforcement learning. ArXiv 1312.5602.

Moilanen, A. (2011). On the limitations of graph-theoretic connectivity in spatial ecology and conservation. *Journal of Applied Ecology*, **48**, 1543–1547; doi:10.1111/j.1365-2664.2011.02062.x.

Montoya, J.M., Pimm, S.L. & Solé, R.V. (2006). Ecological networks and their fragility. *Nature*, **442**, 259–264.

Moody, J. (2008). *Static Representations of Dynamic Networks*. Durham, NC: Duke Population Research Institute.

Moon, J.W. (1968). *Topics on Tournaments*. New York: Holt, Rinehart, Winston.

Morin, P.J. & Lawler, S.P. (1996). Effects of food chain length and omnivory on population dynamics in experimental food webs. In G. Polis & K.O. Winemuller (eds), *Food Webs: Integration of Patterns and Dynamics*, pp. 122–133. New York: Chapman & Hall.

Morris, R.J., Gripenberg, S., Lewis, O.T. & Roslin, T. (2014). Antagonistic interaction networks are structured independently of latitude and host guild. *Ecology Letters*, **17**, 340–349.

Mortelliti, A., Westgate, M., Stein, J., Wood, J., & Lindenmayer, D.B. (2015). Ecological and spatial drivers of population synchrony in bird assemblages. *Basic & Applied Ecology*, **16**, 269–278.

Moschitti, A. (2006). Making tree kernels practical for natural language processing. Paper presented at the Conference of the European Chapter of the Association for Computational Linguistics, Trento, Italy.

Mouillot, D., Krasnov, B.R. & Poulin, R. (2008). High intervality explained by phylogenetic constraints in host-parasite webs. *Ecology*, **89**, 2043–2051.

Mouquet, N. & Loreau, M. (2002). Coexistence in metacommunities: the regional similarity hypothesis. *American Naturalist*, **159**, 420–426.

Mouritsen, K.N., Poulin, R., McLaughlin, J.P. & Thieltges, D.W. (2011). Food web including metazoan parasites for an intertidal ecosystem in New Zealand. *Ecology Archives*, **92**, 92–173; doi:10.1890/11-0371.1.

Mucha, H.-J., Bartel, H.-G. & Dolata, J. (2005). Techniques of rearrangements in binary trees (dendrograms) and applications. *MATCH (Communications in Mathematical and Computer Chemistry)*, **54**, 561–582.

Mucha, P.J., Richardson, T., Macon, K., Porter, M.A. & Onnela, J.-P. (2010). Community structure in time-dependent, multiscale, and multiplex networks. *Science*, **328**, 876–878; doi:10.1126/science.1184819.

Murphy, M.A., Dezzani, R.D.S., Pilliod, D.S. & Storfer, A. (2010). Landscape genetics of high mountain frog metapopulations. *Molecular Ecology*, **19**, 3634–3649.

Murtagh, F. (1984). Counting dendrograms: a survey. *Discrete Applied Mathematics*, **17**, 191–199.

Nacher, J.C., Ueda, N., Yamada, T., Kanehisa, M. & Akutsu, T. (2004). Clustering under the line graph transformation: application to reaction network. *BioMed Central Bioinformatics*, **5**, 207; doi:10.1186/1471-2105-5-207.

Naujokaitis-Lewis, I.R., Rico, Y., Lovell, J., Fortin, M.-J. & Murphy, M.A. (2013). Implications of incomplete networks on estimation of landscape genetic connectivity. *Conservation Genetics*, **14**, 287–298.

Neutel, A.M., Heesterneek, J.A.P. & de Ruiter, P.C. (2002). Stability in real food webs: weak links in long loops. *Science*, **296**, 1120–1123.

Newman, M.E.J. (2002). Assortative mixing in networks. *Physics Review Letters*, **89**, 208701.
(2006). Modularity and community structure in networks. *Proceedings of the National Academy of Sciences*, **103**, 8577–8582.
(2010). *Networks: An Introduction*. Oxford: Oxford University Press.

Newman, M.E.J., Barabási, A.-L. & Watts, D., eds (2006). *The Structure and Dynamics of Networks*. Princeton, NJ: Princeton University Press.

Newman, M.E.J. & Girvan, M. (2004). Finding and evaluating community structure in networks. *Physics Review E*, **69**, 026113; arXiv: cond-mat/0308217v1.

Newman, M.E.J. & Park, J. (2003). Why social networks are different from other types of networks. *Physics Review E*, **68**, 036122; arXiv:cond-mat/0305612v1.

Newman, M.E., Watts, D.J. & Strogatz, S.H. (2002). Random graph models of social networks. *PNAS*, **99**, 2566–2572.

Nguyen-Phuc, B.T. & Dale, M.R.T. (2014). Sub-graphs in competitive hierarchies. Unpublished discussion manuscript, University of Alberta.

Nicosia, V., Tang, J., Mascolo, C., Musolesi, M. & Latora, V. (2013). Graph metrics for temporal networks. In P. Holme & J. Saramäki (eds), *Temporal Networks*, pp. 15–40. Berlin: Springer.

Nicosia, V., Tang, J., Musolesi, M., Mascolo, C., Russo, G. & Latora, V. (2012). Components in time-varying graphs. *Chaos*, **22**, 023101; arXiv: 1106.2134v3.

O'Brien, D., Manseau, M., Fall, A. & Fortin, M.-J. (2006). Testing the importance of spatial configuration of winter habitat for woodland caribou: an application of graph theory. *Biological Conservation*, **130**, 70–83.

Oh, S.J., Joung, J.-G., Chang, J.-H. & Zhang, B.-T. (2006). Construction of phylogenetic trees by kernel-based comparative analysis of metabolic networks. BioMed Central Bioinformatics. doi:10.1186/1471-2105-7-284.

Ohgushi, T. (2008). Herbivore-induced indirect interaction webs in terrestrial plants: the importance of non-trophic, indirect and facilitative interactions. *Entomologia Experimentalis et Applicata*, **128**, 217–229.

Okabe, A., Boots, B., Sugihara, K. & Chiu, S.N. (2000). *Spatial Tessellations: Concepts and Applications of Voronoi Diagrams*. 2nd ed. Chichester: Wiley.

Okabe, A. & Sugihara, K. (2012). *Spatial Analysis along Networks*. New York: John Wiley.

Okey, T.A. & Pauly, D. (1999). Trophic mass-balance model of Alaska's Prince William Sound ecosystem, for the post-spill period 1994–1996. University of British Columbia, Vancouver.

Olesen, J.M., Bascompte, J., Dupont, Y.L., Elberling, H., Rasmussen, C. & Jordano, P. (2011b). Missing and forbidden links in mutualistic networks. *Proceedings of the Royal Society, Series B*, **278**, 725–732.

Olesen, J.M., Bascompte, J., Elberling, H. & Jordano, P. (2008). Temporal dynamics in a pollination network. *Ecology*, **89**, 1573–1582.

Olesen, J.M., Stefanescu, C. & Traveset, A. (2011a). Strong long-term temporal dynamics of an ecological network. *PLoS ONE*, **11**, e26455.

Openshaw, S. (1984). *The Modifiable Area Unit Problem*. Norwich: Geo Books.

Osborne, J.L., Clark, S.J., Morris, R.J., Williams, I.H., Riley, J.R., Smith, A.D., Reynolds, D.R. & Edwards, A.S. (1999). A landscape-scale study of bumble bee foraging range and constancy, using harmonic radar. *Journal of Applied Ecology*, **36**, 519–533.

Paine, R.T. (1969). A note on trophic complexity and community stability. *The American Naturalist*, **103**, 91–93; doi:10.1086/282586.

(1980). Food webs: linkage, interaction strength, and community infrastructure. *Journal of Animal Ecology*, **49**, 667–685.

Palka, Z. (1981). On pendant vertices in random graphs. *Colloquium Mathematicum*, **45**, 159–167.

Panisson, A., Gauvin, L., Barrat, A. & Cattuto, C. (2012). Fingerprinting temporal networks of close-range human proximity. www.sociopatterns.org.

Pascual, M. & Dunne, J.A. (2006). *Ecological Networks: Linking Structure to Dynamics in Food Webs*. New York: Oxford University Press.

Pascual-Hortal, L. & Saura, S. (2006). Comparison and development of new graph-based landscape connectivity indices: towards the prioritization of habitat patches and corridors for conservation. *Landscape Ecology*, **21**, 959–967.

Paulau, P.V., Feenders, C. & Blasius, B. (2015). Motif analysis in directed ordered networks and applications to food webs. *Scientific Reports*, **5**, 11926; doi:10.1038/srep11926.

Pearl, J. (1988). *Probabilistic Reasoning in Intelligent Systems: Networks of Plausible Inference.* 2nd ed. San Mateo, CA: Morgan Kaufman.

 (2009). *Causality: Models, Reasoning and Inference.* 2nd ed. Cambridge. Cambridge University Press.

Penny, D. & Hendy, M.D. (1985). The use of tree comparison metrics. *Systematic Zoology*, **34**, 75–82.

Perkins, S.A., Cagnacci, F., Stradiotto, A., Arnoldi, D. & Hudson, P.J. (2009). Comparison of social networks derived from ecological data: implications of inferring infectious disease dynamics. *Journal of Animal Ecology*, **78**, 1015–1022.

Permogorskiy, M.S. (2015). Competitive intransitivity among species in biotic communities. *Biology Bulletin Reviews*, **3**, 226–233.

Petanidou, T., Kallimanis, A.S., Tzanopoulos, J., Sgardelis, S.P. & Pantis, J.D. (2008). Long-term observation of a pollinator network: fluctuation in species and interactions, relative invariance of network structure and implications for estimates of specialization. *Ecological Letters*, **11**, 564–575.

Petchey, O.L. & Gaston, K.J. (2002). Functional diversity (FD), species richness, and community composition. *Ecology Letters*, **5**, 402–411.

 (2007). Dendrograms and measuring functional diversity. *Oikos*, **116**, 1422–1426.

Peterson, E.E., Ver Hoef, J.M., Isaak, D.J., Falke, J.A., Fortin, M.-J., Jordan, C., McNyset, K., et al. (2013). Modeling dendritic ecological networks in space: an integrated network perspective. *Ecology Letters*, **16**, 707–719.

Peterson, G.D. (2002). Contagious disturbance, ecological memory, and the emergence of landscape pattern. *Ecosystems*, **5**, 329–338.

Peterson, G.J., Pressé, S., Peterson, K.S. & Dill, K.A. (2012). Simulated evolution of protein-protein interaction networks with realistic topology. *PLoS ONE*, **7**, e39052; doi:100.1371/journal.pone.0039052.

Petraitis, P.S. (1979). Competitive networks and measures of intransitivity. *American Naturalist*, **114**, 921–925.

Peyrard, N., Pellegrin, F., Chadoeuf, J. & Nandris, D. (2006). Statistical analysis of the spatio-temporal dynamics of rubber tree (*Hevea brasiliensis*) trunk phloem necrosis: no evidence of pathogen transmission. *Forest Pathology*, **36**, 360–371.

Phillips, J.D. (2011). The structure of ecological state transitions: amplification, synchronization, and constraints in responses to environmental change. *Ecological Complexity*, **8**, 336–346.

Phillips, S.J., Williams, P., Midgley, G. & Archer, A. (2008). Optimizing dispersal corridors for the Cape Proteaceae using network flow. *Ecological Applications*, **18**, 1200–1211.

Pielou, E.C. (1977). *Mathematical Ecology.* New York: John Wiley.

Pillai, P., Loreau, M. & Gonzalez, A. (2009). A patch-dynamic framework for food web metacommunities. *Theoretical Ecology*, **3** doi:10.1007/sl2080-009-0065-1.

Pilosof, S., Fortuna, M.A., Vinarski, M.V., Korallo-Vinarskaya, N.P. & Krasnov, B.R. (2013). Temporal dynamics of direct reciprocal and indirect effects in a host-parasite network. *Journal of Animal Ecology*, **82**, 987–996.

Pinkerton, M.H. & Bradford-Grieve, J.M. (2014). Characterizing foodweb structure to identify potential ecosystem effects of fishing in the Ross Sea, Antarctica. *ICES Journal of Marine Science*, **71** doi:10.1093/icejms/fst230.

Pinto, N. & Keitt, T.H. (2009). Beyond the least-cost path: evaluating corridor redundancy using a graph-theoretic approach. *Landscape Ecology*, **24**, 253–266.

Piraveenan, M., Prokopenko, M. & Zomaya, A.Y. (2008). Local assortativeness in scale-free networks. *Europhysics Letters*, **84**, 28002.

(2012). Assortative mixing in directed biological networks. *IEEE/ACM Transactions on Computational Biology and Bioinformatics*, **9**. doi:101109/TCBB.2010.80.

Plavšić, D., Nikolić, S., Trinajstić, N. & Mihalić, Z. (1993). On the Harary Index for the characterization of chemical graphs. *Journal of Mathematical Chemistry*, **12**, 235–250.

Podani, J. & Dickinson, T.A. (1984). Comparison of dendrograms: a multivariate approach. *Canadian Journal of Botany*, **62**, 2765–2778.

Poisot, T., Canard, E., Mouillot, D., Mouquet, N. & Gravel, D. (2012). The dissimilarity of species interaction networks. *Ecology Letters*, **15**, 1353–1361.

Poisot, T. & Gravel, D. (2014). When is an ecological network complex? Connectance drives degree distribution and emerging network properties. *PeerJ*, **2**, e251; doi 10.7717/peerj.251.

Poisot, T., Stanko, M., Miklisova, D. & Morand, S. (2013). Facultative and obligate parasite communities exhibit different network properties. *Parasitology*, **140** doi:10.1017/S003118201300851.

Poisot, T., Stouffer, D.B. & Gravel, D. (2015). Beyond species: why ecological interaction networks vary through space and time. *Oikos*, **124**, 243–251.

Polis, G.A. & Winemiller, K.O., eds (1996). *Food Webs: Integration of Patterns and Dynamics*. New York: Chapman & Hall.

Poon, A.F.Y. (2015). Phylodynamic inference with kernel ABC and its application to HIV epidemiology. *Molecular Biology and Evolution*, **32** doi:10.1093/molbev/msv123.

Poon, A.F.Y., Walker, L.W., Murray, H., McCloskey, R.M., Harrihan, P.R. & Liang, R.H. (2013). Mapping the shapes of phylogenetic trees from human and zoonotic RNA viruses. *PLoS ONE*, **8**, e78122; doi:10.1371/journal.pone.0078122.

Poos, M., Walker, S.C. & Jackson, D.A. (2009). Functional diversity indices can be driven by methodological choices and species richness. *Ecology*, **90**, 341–347.

Porphyre, T., Stevenson, M., Jackson, R. & McKenzie, J. (2008). Influence of contact heterogeneity on TB reproduction ratio Ro in a free-living brushtail possum *Trchosurus vulpecula* population. *Veterinary Research*, **39**, 31.

Poulin, R. (2010). Network analysis shining light on parasite ecology and diversity. *Trends in Parasitology*, **26**, 492–498.

Poulin, R. & Guégan, J.-F. (2000). Nestedness, anti-nestedness, and the relationship between prevalence and intensity in ectoparasites assemblages of marine fish: a spatial model of species coexistence. *International Journal for Parasitology*, **30**, 1147–1152.

Prado, P.I. & Lewinsohn, T.M. (2004). Compartments in insect-plant associations and their consequences for community structure. *Journal of Animal Ecology*, **73**, 1168–1178.

Proulx, S.R., Promislow, D.E.L. & Phillip, P.C. (2005). Network thinking in ecology and evolution. *Trends in Ecology and Evolution*, **20**, 345–352.

Pržulj, K., Wigle, D.A. & Jurisica, I. (2004). Functional topology in a network of protein interactions. *Bioinformatics*, **20**, 340–348.

Pržulj, N. (2005). *Analyzing Large Biological Networks: Protein-Protein Interactions Example*. PhD thesis, Graduate Department of Computer Science, University of Toronto.

(2007). Biological network comparison using graphlet degree distribution. *Bioinformatics*, **23**, e177–e183.

(2010). Protein-protein interactions: making sense of networks via graph-theoretic modelling. *Bioessays*, **33** doi:10.1002/bies.201000044.

Purchase, H.C. (2002). Metrics for graph drawing aesthetics. *Journal of Visual Languages & Computing*, **13**, 501–516.

Raman, K. (2010). Construction and analysis of protein-protein interaction networks. *Automated Experimentation*, **2**, 2; doi:10.1186/1759-4499-2-2.

Raschke, M., Schläpfer, M. & Nibali, R. (2010). Measuring degree-degree association in networks. *Physics Review E*, **82**, 037102.

Rayfield, B., Fortin, M.-J., & Fall, A. (2011). Connectivity for conservation: a framework to classify network measures. *Ecology*, **92**, 847–858.

Raymond, B. & Hosie, G. (2009). Network-based exploration and visualization of ecological data. *Ecological Modelling*, **220**, 673–683.

Restrepo, G., Mesa, H. & Llanos, E.J. (2007). Three dissimilarity measures to contrast dendrograms. *Journal of Chemical Informatics & Modeling*, **47**, 761–770.

Rezende, E.L., Albert, E.M., Fortuna, M.A. & Bascompte, J. (2009). Compartments in a marine food web associated with phylogeny, body mass, and habitat structure. *Ecological Letters*, **12**, 779–788.

Richters, O. & Peixoto, T.P. (2011). Trust transitivity in social networks. *PLoS ONE*, **6**, e18384; doi:10.1371/journal.pone.0018384.

Ricotta, C., Stanisci, A., Avena, G. & Blasi, C. (2000). Quantifying the network connectivity of landscape mosaics: a graph-theoretical approach. *Community Ecology*, **1**, 89–94.

Robinson, V.B. (2009). Fuzzy sets in spatial analysis. In A.S. Fotheringham & P.A. Rogerson (eds), *The Sage Handbook of Spatial Analysis*, pp. 225–241. London: Sage.

Roxburgh, S.H. & Wilson, J.B. (2000). Stability and coexistence in a lawn community: mathematical prediction of stability using a community matrix with parameters derived from competition experiments. *Oikos*, **88**, 395–408.

Rozdilsky, I.D., Stone, L. & Solow, A. (2004). The effects of interaction compartments on stability for competitive systems. *Journal of Theoretical Biology*, **227**, 277–282.

Rozenfeld, A.F., Arnaud-Haond, S., Hernandez-Garcia, E., Eguiluz, V.M., Serrao, E.A. & Duarte, C.M. (2008). Network analysis identifies weak and strong links in a metapopulation system. *Proceedings of the National Academy of Sciences*, **105**, 18824–18829.

Rubinov, M. & Sporns, O. (2010). Complex network measures of brain connectivity: uses and interpretations. *NeuroImage*, **52**, 1059–1069.

Rubio, L., Bodin, O., Brotons, L. & Saura, S. (2015). Connectivity conservation priorities for individual patches evaluated in the present landscape: how durable and effective are they in the long term? *Ecography*, **38**, 782–791.

Ryder, T.B., Horton, B.M., van der Tillaart, M., Morales, J.D.D. & Moore, I.T. (2012). Proximity data-loggers increase the quantity and quality of social network data. *Biology Letters*, **8** doi:10.1098/rsbl.2012.0536.

Sakr, S. (2013). Processing large-scale graph data: a guide to current technology. IBM developerWorks, /library/os-giraph/.

Salathé, M. & Jones, J.H. (2010). Dynamics and control of diseases in networks with community structure. *PLoS Computational Biology*, **6**, e1000736; doi:10.1371/journal.pcbi.1000736.

Sanfeliu, A. & Fu, K.-S. (1983). A distance measure between attributed relational graphs for pattern recognition. *IEEE Transactions on Systems, Man and Cybernetics*, **13**, 353–363; doi:10.1109/TSMC.1983.6313167.

Santos, E. & Young, J.D. (1999). Probabilistic temporal networks: a unified framework for reasoning with time and uncertainty. *International Journal of Approximate Reasoning*, **20**, 263–291.

Sarajlić, A., Malod-Dognin, N., Yaveroglu, O.N. & Pržulj, N. (2016). Graphlet-based characterization of directed networks. *Scientific Reports*, **6**, 35098; doi:10.1038/srep35098.

Särkkä, A. & Renshaw, E. (2006). The analysis of marked point patterns evolving through space and time. *Computational Statistics and Data Analysis*, **51**, 1698–1718.

Satniczenko, P.P.A., Kopp, J.C. & Allesina, S. (2012). The ghost of nestedness in ecological networks. *Nature Communications*, **4** doi:10.1038/ncomms2422.

Saura, S., Bodin, Ö. & Fortin, M.-J. (2014). Stepping stones are crucial for species' long-distance dispersal and range expansion through habitat networks. *Journal of Applied Ecology*, **51**, 171–182.

Savolainen, R. & Vepsäläinen, K. (1988). A competition hierarchy among boreal ants: impact on resource partitioning and community structure. *Oikos*, **51**, 135–155.

Schick, R.S. & Lindley, S.T. (2007). Directed connectivity among fish populations in a riverine network. *Journal of Applied Ecology*, **44**, 1116–1126.

Schjelderup-Ebbe, T. (1975). Contributions to the social psychology of the domestic chicken. In M.W. Schein (ed.), M. Schleidt and W.M. Schleidt (trans.), *Social Hierarchy and Dominance. Benchmark Papers in Animal Behavior*, vol. 3, pp. 35–49. Stroudsburg, PA: Dowden, Hutchinson and Ross. (Reprinted from *Zeitschrift für Psychologie*, 1922, 88, 225–252.)

Schoenly, K. & Cohen, J.E. (1991). Temporal variation in food web structure: 16 empirical cases. *Ecological Monographs*, **61**, 267–298.

Schölkopf, B., Tsuda, K. & Vert, J.-P. (2004). *Kernel Methods on Computational Biology*. Cambridge, MA: MIT Press.

Schreiber, S.J. & Killingback, T.P. (2013). Spatial heterogeneity promotes coexistence of rock-paper-scissor metacommunities. *Theoretical Population Biology*, **86**, 1–11.

Scrosati, R.A. & Heaven, C.S. (2007). Spatial trends in community richness, diversity, and evenness across rocky intertidal environmental stress gradients in Eastern Canada. *Marine Ecology Progress Series*, **342**, 1–14.

Shawe-Taylor, J. & Cristianini, N. (2004). *Kernel Methods for Pattern Analysis*. Cambridge: Cambridge University Press.

Shervashidze, N., Schweitzer, P., van Leeuwen, E.J., Mehlhorn, K. & Borgwardt, K.M. (2011). Weisfeiler-Lehman graph kernels. *Journal of Machine Learning Research*, **12**, 2539–2561.

Shervashidze, N., Vishwanathan, S.V.N., Petri, T., Mehlhorn, K. & Borgwardt, K. (2009). Efficient graphlet kernels for large graph comparison. In *Proceedings of the 12th International Conference on Artificial Intelligence and Statistics (AISTATS) 2009*, pp. 488–495. Clearwater Beach, USA: Society for Artificial Intelligence and Statistics

Shipley, B. (1993). A null model for competitive hierarchies in competition matrices. *Ecology*, **74**, 1693–1699.

  (2000). *Cause and Correlation in Biology*. Oxford: Oxford University Press.

  (2009). Confirmatory path analysis in a generalized multilevel context. *Ecology*, **90**, 363–368.

Shipley, B. & Keddy, P.A. (1994). Evaluating evidence for competitive hierarchies in plant communities. *Oikos*, **69**, 340–345.

Shirley, M.D.F. & Rushton, S.P. (2005). The impacts of network topology on disease spread. *Ecological Complexity*, **2**, 287–299.

Shizuki, D. & McDonald, D.B. (2012). A social network perspective on measurements of dominance hierarchies. Faculty Publications in the Biological Sciences, University of Nebraska. http://digitalcommons.unl.edu/bioscifacpub/234.

Siegel, A.F. & Sugihara, G. (1983). Moments of particle size distributions under sequential breakage with applications to species abundance. *Journal of Applied Probability*, **20**, 1516-Aug 4.

Silvertown, J. & Wilson, J.B. (2000). Spatial interactions among grassland plant populations. In U. Dieckmann, R. Law & J.A.J. Metz (eds), *The Geometry of Ecological Interactions: Simplifying Spatial Complexity*, pp. 28–47. Cambridge: Cambridge University Press.

Simard, S.W., Beiler, K.J., Bingham, M.A., Deslippe, J.R., Philip, L.J. & Teste, F.P. (2012). Mycorrhizal networks: mechanisms, ecology and modelling. *Fungal Biology Reviews*, **26**, 39–60.

Smith, D. (2000). The population dynamics and community ecology of root hemiparasitic plants. *American Naturalist*, **155**, 13–23.

Snow, R., Snow, M. & Kufa, N. (2007). GIS analysis of lightning strikes within a tornadic environment. In *Proceedings of the 3rd IASME/WSEAS International Conference, Agios, Greece*, pp. 466–471. WEAS Press

Sokal, R.R. & Rohlf, F.J. (1962). The comparison of dendrograms by objective methods. *Taxon*, **11**, 33–40.

Solé, R.V. & Montoya, J.M. (2001). Complexity and fragility in ecological networks. *Proceedings of the Royal Society London, Series B*, **268**, 2039–2045.

Soliveres, S., et al. (2015). Intransitive competition is widespread in plant communities and maintains their species richness. *Ecology Letters*, **18**, 790–798; doi:10.1111/ele.12456.

Sotomayor, D.A. & Lortie, C.J. (2015). Indirect interactions in terrestrial plant communities: emerging patterns and research gaps. *Ecosphere*, **6**, 103; doi:10.1890/ES14-00117.1.

Soula, S. & Chauzy, S. (2001). Some aspects of the correlation between lightning and rain activity in thunderstorms. *Atmospheric Research*, **56**, 355–373.

Southworth, D., He, X.-H., Swenson, W., Bledsoe, C.S. & Horwath, W.R. (2005). Application of network theory to potential mycorrhizal networks. *Mycorrhiza*, **15**, 589–595.

Spiesman, B.J. & Inouye, B.D. (2013). Habitat loss alters the architecture of plant-pollinator interaction networks. *Ecology*, **94**, 2688–2696.

Sporns, O., Honey, C.J. & Kötter, R. (2007). Identification and classification of hubs in brain networks. *PLoS ONE*, **2** (10), e1049; doi:01.1371/journal.pone.0001049.

Sporns, O. & Kötter, R. (2004). Motifs in brain networks. *PLoS Biology*, **2**. doi:10.1371/journal.pbio.0020369.

Staniczenko, P.P.A., Kopp, J.C. & Allesina, S. (2012). The ghost of nestedness in ecological networks. *Nature Communications*, **4**, 1391; doi:10.1038/ncomms2422.

Starling, F.L. do R.M. 2000. Comparative study of the zooplankton composition of six lacustrine ecosystems in central Brazil during the dry season. *Review of Brasilian Biology*, **60**, 101–111.

Stouffer, D.B. & Bascompte, J. (2010). Understanding food-web persistence from local to global scales. *Ecology Letters*, **13**, 154–161.

(2011). Compartmentalization increases food web persistence. *Proceedings of the National Academy of Sciences*, **108**, 3648–3652.

Stouffer, D.B., Camacho, J. & Amaral, L.A.N. (2006). A robust measure of food web intervality. *Proceedings of the National Academy of Sciences*, **103**, 19015–19020.

Stouffer, D.B., Camacho, J., Jiang, W. & Amaral, L.A.N. (2007). Evidence for the existence of a robust pattern of prey selection in food webs. *Proceedings of the Royal Society*, **274**, 1931–1940.

Stoyan, D., Kendall, W.S. & Mecke, J. (1995). *Stochastic Geometry and Its Applications*. 2nd ed. Chichester: Wiley.

Strauss, R.E. (1982). Statistical significance of species clusters in association analysis. *Ecology*, **63**, 634–639.

Strickland, C., Dangelmayr, G., Shipman, P.D., Kumar, S. & Stohlgren, T.J. (2015). Network spread of invasive species and infectious diseases. *Ecological Modelling*, **309**–310, 1–9.

Strimmer, K. & Moulton, V. (2000). Likelihood analysis of phylogenetic networks using directed graphical models. *Molecular Biology & Evolution*, **17**, 875–881.

Sugihara, G. (1980). Minimal community structure: an explanation of species abundance patterns. *American Naturalist*, **116**, 770–787.

(1982). *Niche Hierarchy: Structure, Organization, and Assembly in Natural Communities*. PhD dissertation, Princeton University.

(1984). Graph theory, homology and food webs. In S.A. Levin (ed.), *Population Biology: Proceedings of Symposia in Applied Mathematics*, pp. 83–101. Providence, RI: American Mathematical Society.

Sugihara, G., Bersier, L.-F., Southwood, T.R.E., Pimm, S.L. & May, R.M. (2003). Predicted correspondence between species abundances and dendrograms of niche similarities. *Proceedings of the National Academy of Sciences*, **100**, 5246–5251.

Sun, J., Zhang, M. & Tan, C.-L. (2011). Tree sequence kernel for natural language. In *Proceedings of the Twenty-Fifth AAAI Conference on Artificial Intelligence*, pp. 921–926. Menlo Park, USA: AAAI Press

Suweis, S., Simini, F., Banavar, J.R. & Maritan, A. (2013). Emergence of structural and dynamical properties of ecological mutualistic networks. *Nature*, **500**, 449–452.

Takahashi, K., Kulldorff, M., Tango, T. & Yih, K. (2008). A flexibly shaped space-time scan statistic for disease outbreak detection and monitoring. *International Journal of Health Geographics*, **7**, 14; doi:10.1186/1476-072X-7-14.

Tang, J., Leontiadis, I., Scellato, S., Nicosia, V., Mascolo, C., Musolesi, M. & Latora, V. (2013). Applications of temporal graph metrics to real-world networks. In P. Holme & J. Saramäki (eds), *Temporal Networks*, pp. 135–159. Berlin: Springer.

Tang, J., Musolesi, M., Mascolo, C. & Latora, V. (2009). Temporal distance metrics for social network analysis. Paper presented at the 2nd SIGCOMM Workshop on Online Social Networks, Barcelona.

Tango, T. (2010). *Statistical Methods for Disease Clustering*. New York: Springer.

Tanner, J.E., Hughes, T.P. & Connell, J.H. (1996). The role of history in community dynamics: a modeling approach. *Ecology*, **77**, 108–117.

Teng, J. & McCann, K.S. (2004). Dynamics of compartmented and reticulate food webs in relation to energetic flows. *American Naturalist*, **164**, 85–100.

Tero, A., Takagi, S., Saigusa, T., Ito, K., Bebber, D.P., Fricker, M.D., Yumiki, K., Kobayashi, R. & Nakagi, T. (2010). Rules for biologically inspired adaptive network design. *Science*, **327**, 439–442.

Thébault, E. & Fontaine, C. (2010). Stability of ecological communities and the architecture of mutualistic and trophic networks. *Science*, **329**, 853–856; doi:10.1126/science.1188321.

Thedchanamoorthy, G., Piraveenan, M., Kasthuriratne, D. & Senanayake, U. (2014). Node assortativity in complex networks: an alternative approach. *Procedia Computer Science*, **29**, 24 Feb-49461; doi:10.1016/j.procs.2014.05.229.

Theobald, D.M. (2006). Exploring the functional connectivity of landcapes using landscape networks. In K.R. Crooks & M. Sanjayan (eds), *Connectivity Conservation*, pp. 416–444. Cambridge: Cambridge University Press.

Thibaud, R., Del Mondo, G., Garlan, T., Mascret, A. & Carpentier, C. (2013). A spatio-temporal graph model for marine dune dynamics analysis and representation. *Transactions in GIS*, **17**, 742–762.

Thomas, A.G. & Dale, M.R.T. (1991). Weed communities in spring-seeded crops in Manitoba. *Canadian Journal of Plant Science*, **71**, 1069–1080.

Thompson, J.N. (2006). Mutualistic webs of species. *Science*, **312**, 372–373.

Thompson, R.M., Hemberg, M., Starzomski, B.M. & Shurin, J.B. (2007). Trophic levels and trophic tangles: the prevalence of omnivory in real food webs. *Ecology*, **88**, 612–617.

Thornton, B.M., Knowlton, J.L. & Kuntz, W.A. (2015). Interspecific competition and social hierarchies in frugivorous birds of Costa Rica. *Journal of Young Investigators*, **29** (2), 1–5.

Toju, H., Guimarães, P.R., Olesan, J.M. & Thompson, J.N. (2015). Below-ground plant-fungus network topology is not congruent with above-ground plant-animal network topology. *Science Advances*, **1** doi:10.1126/sciadv.1500291.

Tosa, M.I., Schauber, E.M. & Nielsen, C.K. (2013). Familiarity breeds contempt: combining proximity loggers and GPS reveals female white-tailed deer (*Odocoileus virginianus*) avoiding close contact with neighbours. *Journal of Wildlife Diseases*, **51**, 70–88.

Toussaint, G.T. (1980). The relative neighbourhood graph of a finite planar set. *Pattern Recognition*, **12**, 261–268.

Treml, E.A., Halpin, P.N., Urban, D.L. & Pratson, L.F. (2008). Modeling population connectivity by ocean currents, a graph-theoretic approach for marine conservation. *Landscape Ecology*, **23**, 19–36.

Trpevski, I., Dimitrova, T., Boshkovski, T., Stikov, N. & Kocarev, L. (2016). Graphlet characteristics in directed networks. *Scientific Reports*, **6**, 37057; doi:10.1038/srep37057.

Tufte, E.R. (1983). *The Visual Display of Quantitative Information.* Cheshire, CT: Graphics Press.

Tutte, W.T. (1998). *Graph Theory as I Have Known It.* Oxford: Clarendon Press.

Ulanowicz, R.E. & Puccia, C.J. (1990). Mixed trophic impacts in ecosystems. *Coenoses*, **5**, 7–16.

Ulrich, W. (2009). Ecological interaction networks: prospects and pitfalls. *Ecological Questions*, **11**, 17–25.

Ulrich, W., Almeida-Neto, M. & Gotelli, N.J. (2009). A consumer's guide to nestedness analysis. *Oikos*, **118**, 3–17.

Ulrich, W., Soliveres, S., Kryszwski, W., Maestre, F.T. & Gotelli, N.J. (2014). Matrix models for quantifying competitive intransitivity from species abundance data. *Oikos*, **123**, 1057–1070; doi:10.1111/oik.01217.

Urban, D.L. & Keitt, T. (2001). Landscape connectivity: a graph-theoretic perspective. *Ecology*, **82**, 1205–1218.

Urban, D.L., Minor, E.S., Treml, E.A. & Schick, R.S. (2009). Graph models of habitat mosaics. *Ecology Letters*, **12**, 260–273.

Valls, A., Coll, M. & Christensen, V. (2015). Keystone species: toward an operational concept for marine biodiversity conservation. *Ecological Monographs*, **85**, 29–47.

van Langevelde, F., van der Knaap, W.G.M. & Claassen, G.D.H. (1998). Comparing connectivity in landscape networks. *Environment and Planning B: Planning and Design*, **25**, 849–863.

van Veen, F.J.F., Morris, R.J. & Godfray, H.C.J. (2006). Apparent competition, quantitative food webs, and the structure of phytophagous insect communities. *Annual Review of Entomology*, **51**, 187–208.

van Wijk, B.C.M., Stam, C.J. & Daffertshofer, A. (2010). Comparing brain networks of different size and connectivity density using graph theory. *PLoS ONE*, **5** (10), e13701.

Vázquez, A. (2013). Spreading dynamics following bursty activity patterns. In P. Holme & J. Saramäki (eds), *Temporal Networks*, pp. 161–173. Berlin: Springer.

Vázquez, A., Flammini, A., Maritan, A. & Vespignani, A. (2003). Global protein function prediction from protein-protein interaction networks. *Nature Biotechnology*, **21**, 697–700; doi:10/1038/nbt825.

Vázquez, D.P., Chacoff, N.P. & Cagnolo, L. (2009). Evaluating multiple determinants of the structure of plant-animal mutualistic networks. *Ecology*, **90**, 2039–2046.

Vázquez, D.P., Morris, W.F. & Jordano, P. (2005a). Interaction frequency as a surrogate for the total effect of animal mutualists on plants. *Ecology Letters*, **8**, 1088–1094.

Vázquez, D.P., Poulin, R., Krasnov, B.R. & Shenbrot, G.I. (2005b). Species abundance and the distribution of specialization in host-parasite interaction networks. *Journal of Animal Ecology*, **74**, 946–955.

Vehrencamp, S.L. (1983). A model for the evolution of despotic versus egalitarian societies. *Animal Behaviour*, **31**, 667–682.

Vepsäläinen, K. & Czechowski, W. (2014). Against the odds of the ant competition hierarchy: submissive *Myrmica rugulosa* block access of the dominant *Lasius fuliginosus* to its aphids. *Insectes Sociaux*, **61**, 89–93.

Ver Hoef, J., Peterson, E. & Theobald, D. (2006). Spatial statistical models that use flow and stream distance. *Environmental and Ecological Statistics*, **13**, 449–464.

Vinayagam, A., Zirin, J., Roesel, C., Hu, Y., Yilmazel, B., Samsonova, A.A., Neumüller, R., Mohr, S.E. & Perrimon, N. (2014). Integrating protein-protein interaction networks with phenotypes reveals signs of interactions. *Nature Methods*, **11**, 94–99; doi:10.1038/nmeth.2733.

Vishwanathan, S.V.N., Schraudolph, N.N., Kondor, R. & Borgwardt, K.M. (2010). Graph kernels. *Journal of Machine Learning Research*, **11**, 1201–1242.

Wagner, H.H. & Fortin, M.-J. (2013). A conceptual framework for the spatial analysis of landscape genetic data. *Conservation Genetics*, **14**, 253–261.

Walker, R., Arima, E., Messina, J., Soares-Filho, B., Perz, S., Vergara, D., Sales, M., Pereira, R. & Castro, W. (2013). Modeling spatial decisions with graph theory: logging roads and forest fragmentation in the Brazilian Amazon. *Ecological Applications*, **23**, 239–254.

Walker, S.C., Poos, M.S. & Jackson, D.A. (2008). Functional rarefaction: estimating functional diversity from field data. *Oikos*, **117**, 286–296.

Wang, Y.-H., Yang, K.-C., Bridgman, C.L. & Lin, L.-K. (2008). Habitat suitability modeling to correlate gene flow with landscape connectivity. *Landscape Ecology*, **23**, 989–1000.

Wardle, G.M. (1998). A graph theory approach to demographic loop analysis. *Ecology*, **79**, 2539–2549.

Waser, N.M. & Ollerton, J. (2006). *Plant-Pollinator Interactions*. Chicago: University of Chicago Press.

Wasserman, S. & Faust, K. (1994). *Social Network Analysis: Methods and Applications*. Cambridge: Cambridge University Press.

Watts, A.G., Schlichting, P., Billerman, S., Jesmer, B., Micheletti, S., Fortin, M.-J., Funk, W.C., Hapeman, P., Muths, E. & Murphy, M.A. (2015). How spatio-temporal habitat connectivity affects amphibian genetic structure. *Frontiers in Genetics*, **6**, Article 275.

Watts, D.J. (1999). *Small Worlds: The Dynamics of Networks between Order and Randomness*. Princeton, NJ: Princeton University Press.

    (2003). *Six Degrees: The Science of a Connected Age*. New York: W.W. Norton.

Webb, C.O., Ackerly, D.D., McPeek, M.A. & Donaghue, M.J. (2002). Phylogenies and community ecology. *Annual Review of Ecology and Systematics*, **33**, 475–505.

Weigelt, A., Schumacher, J., Walther, T., Bartelheimer, M., Steinlein, T. & Beyschlag, W. (2007). Identifying mechanisms of competition in multi-species communities. *Journal of Ecology*, **95**, 53–64.

West, D.B. (2001). *Introduction to Graph Theory*. 2nd ed. Upper Saddle River, NJ: Prentice Hall.

Wey, T., Blumstein, D.T., Shen, W. & Jordán, F. (2008). Social network analysis of animal behavior: a promising tool for the study of sociality. *Animal Behaviour*, **75**, 333–344.

Wilbur, H.M. (1997). Experimental ecology of foodwebs: complex systems in temporary ponds. *Ecology*, **78**, 2279–2302.

Williams, M.J. & Musolesi, M. (2016). Spatio-temporal networks: reachability, centrality and robustness. *Royal Society Open Science*, **3** doi:10.1098/rsos.160196.

Williams, R.J. & Martinez, N.D. (2004). Limits to trophic levels and omnivory in complex food webs: theory and data. *American Naturalist*, **163**, 458–468.

Williams, R.J., Berlow, E.L., Dunne, J.A. & Martinez, N.D. (2002). Two degrees of separation in complex food webs. *Proceedings of the National Academy of Sciences*, **99**, 12913–12916.

Winemiller, K.O. (1990). Spatial and temporal variation in tropical fish trophic networks. *Ecological Monographs*, **60**, 331–367.

Winterbach, W., Van Mieghem, P., Reinders, M.J.T., Wang, H. & de Ridder, D. (2013). Local topological signatures for network-based prediction of biological function. In *Pattern Recognition in Bioinformatics, Proceedings of the 8th IAPR conference, Nice 2013*, pp. 23–24. Berlin: Springer.

Wolfram, S. (2002). *A New Kind of Science*. Champagne: Wolfram Media.

Woodward, G., Ebenman, B., Emmeson, M., Montoya, J.M., Olesen, J., Valido, A. & Warren, P.H. (2005). Body size in ecological networks. *Trends in Ecology and Evolution*, **20**. doi:10.116/j.tree.2005.04.05.

Woodward, G., et al. (2010). Ecological networks in a changing climate. *Advances in Ecological Research*, **42**, 72–122; doi:10.1016/S0065-2504(10)42002-4.

Wu, H., Cheng, J., Huang, S., Ke, Y. & Xu, Y. (2014). Path problems in temporal graphs. *Proceedings of the VLDB Endowment*, **7**, 721–729.

Yaveroglu, O.N., Fitzhugh, S.M., Kurant, M., Markopoulou, A., Butts, C.T. & Pržulj, N. (2015). ergm.graphlets: a package for ERG modeling based on graphlet statistics. *Journal of Statistical Software*, **65** (12), 1–29

Yaveroglu, O.N., Malod-Dognin, N., Davis, D., Levnajic, Z., Janjic, V., Karapandza, R., Stojmirovic, A. & Pržulj, N. (2014). Revealing the hidden language of complex networks. *Scientific Reports*, **4**, 4547; doi:10.1038/srep04547 (2014).

Yazdani, A. & Jeffrey, P. (2010). A complex network approach to robustness and vulnerability of spatially organized distribution networks. arXiv:1008.1770v2.

Yu, D., Liu, Y., Xun, B. & Shao, H. (2013). Measuring landscape connectivity in an urban area for biological conservation. *Clean – Soil, Air, Water*, **41**, 1–9.

Yugandhar, K. & Gromiha, M.M. (2016). Analysis of protein-protein interaction networks based on binding affinity. *Current Protein and Peptide Science*, **17**, 72–81.

Zhao, K., Karsai, M. & Bianconi, G. (2013a). Models, entropy and information of temporal social networks. In P. Holme & J. Saramäki (eds), *Temporal Networks*, pp. 95–117. Berlin: Springer.

Zhao, Q., Azeria, E.T., Le Blanc, M.-L., Lemaître, J. & Fortin, D. (2013b). Landscape-scale disturbances modified bird community dynamics in successional forest environment. *PLoS ONE*, **8**, e81358; doi:10.1371/journal.pone.0081358.

Index

Appendix

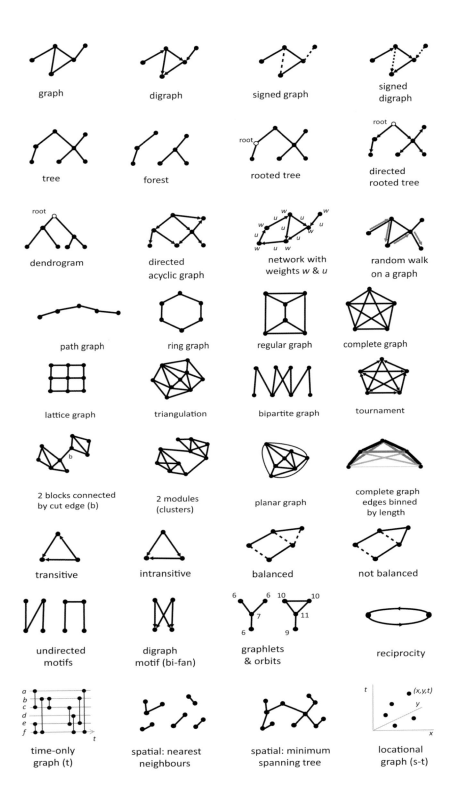

graph

digraph

signed graph

signed digraph

tree

forest

rooted tree

directed rooted tree

dendrogram

directed acyclic graph

network with weights w & u

random walk on a graph

path graph

ring graph

regular graph

complete graph

lattice graph

triangulation

bipartite graph

tournament

2 blocks connected by cut edge (b)

2 modules (clusters)

planar graph

complete graph edges binned by length

transitive

intransitive

balanced

not balanced

undirected motifs

digraph motif (bi-fan)

graphlets & orbits

reciprocity

time-only graph (t)

spatial: nearest neighbours

spatial: minimum spanning tree

locational graph (s-t)